Reflections and Meditations

An Annual Devotional

Dr. Pearl T. Morgan-Bell

World rights reserved. This book or any portion thereof may not be copied or reproduced in any form or manner whatever, except as provided by law, without the written permission of the publisher, except by a reviewer who may quote brief passages in a review.

This book was written to provide truthful information in regard to the subject matter covered. The author assumes full responsibility for the accuracy of all facts and quotations as cited in this book. The opinions expressed in this book are the author's personal views and interpretation of the Bible, Spirit of Prophecy, and/or contemporary authors and do not necessarily reflect those of TEACH Services, Inc.

This book is sold with the understanding that the publisher is not engaged in giving spiritual, legal, medical, or other professional advice. If authoritative advice is needed, the reader should seek the counsel of a competent professional.

Copyright © 2013 TEACH Services, Inc.
ISBN-13: 978-1-57258-171-4 (Paperback)
ISBN-13: 978-1-57258-172-1 (ePub)
ISBN-13: 978-1-57258-173-8 (Mobi)
Library of Congress Control Number: 2013948440

Published by

www.TEACHServices.com • (800) 367-1844

Dedicated To

Christians everywhere who want to meet their Lord at daybreak

Acknowledgement

My profound thanks and praise go to my wonderful God and the ever-present Holy Spirit that guided me as I attempted this mammoth task for the Lord. He instructed me to do this after I had gone through ten days of prayer accompanied by a raw food diet. I submitted myself to be led and guided by the Holy Spirit who has allowed me to prepare this document so that it can help some traveler in his or her journey on the road of life. May your spiritual walk be enhanced as God speaks to you each day. Any day is the right day to read a text. Every new day is the beginning of your new year with the Lord.

I just want to praise the Lord from whom all blessings flow. Be blessed; be transformed into the image of the Son of God, our Brother, companion, and Dayspring. I also acknowledge my caregiver, Constance Matonhodze, whose prayer, support, and encouragement has helped me; to Maryann Dawkins and Monica and Ron Bell, who have been my eyes and ears; and to the rest of the family: three sons, two sisters and nieces who await the release of this volume. To Irone, my devoted friend and support, who is also anxiously awaiting the release. I also thank the publishers, TEACH Services, Lincoln Balfour, author consultant, and Kalie Kelch and the editorial staff for their tireless work in seeing this book to publication. Special thanks also to Pastor Ken Knosp for his pastoral review.

May you all be blessed!

Dr. Pearl

Table Contents

Introduction..7

New Every Morning...9

Abide With Us Today..27

This Is the Day the Lord Has Given....................46

Listen to His Voice..66

God Speaks...85

God's Humors...104

Your Holiest Is My Utmost................................125

Intimacy With Jesus..144

Avoid Careless Chatter......................................163

Fix Your Eyes on the Holy.................................181

The Power of God's Name.................................201

Sent by God..220

Study to Meet God's Approval..........................240

We Are More Than Conquerors........................260

My Own ABC's of Assurance.............................280

The Names of God...281

Bibliography..283

Introduction

The Holy Spirit has inspired me to search in God's Words to find a devotional text for each day drawing from the twenty-six letters of the alphabet. Every twenty-six days a new cycle begins, making fourteen different cycles each year with two extra days to complete the 365/366 days each year.

Each day you will find commentary about God's word. I hope these collected thoughts help you maintain your spiritual, mental, moral, and emotional stability in Christ. "Thou wilt shew me the path of life: in thy presence is fulness of joy; at thy right hand there are pleasures for evermore" (Ps. 16:11). Let the Word of God abide richly in you and give you peace.

These reflections are borne out of my own relationship with the Triune God—the Father, Son, and the ever present Holy Spirit. I aim to grow in my knowledge of God every single day.

"Search the scriptures; for in them ye think ye have eternal life: and they are they which testify of me" (John 5:39). This was Jesus' admonition to his first disciples; this message is also for us—His second disciples.

In the year 2011, someone sent me an e-mail that had one-line sentences using the alphabetical method. Before this correspondence arrived on my screen, I had already written my own alphabetical scriptural guideline titled "ABC's of Assurance." After I had received this, I was inspired to do a much deeper investigation into the Word of God to see what I could extrapolate from it to not only bless me but also millions of readers. You will find my personal ABC's of Assurance at the end of this book. The correspondence from the email was written by Cindy Blackmore and was titled "The Holy Alphabet."

A-lthough things are not perfect

B-ecause of trials or pain

C-ontinue in thanksgiving

D-o not begin to blame.

E-ven when the times are hard

F-ierce winds are bound to blow

G-od is forever able

H-old on to what you know.

I-magine life without His love

J-oy would cease to be

K-eep thanking Him for all the things

L-ove imparts to you.

M-ove out of "camp complaining"

N-o weapon that is known

O-n earth can yield the power

P-raise can do alone.

Q-uit looking at the future

R-edeem the time at hand

S-tart every day with worship

T-o thank is a command.

U-ntil we see His coming

V-ictorious in the sky,

W-e'll run the race with gratitude

X-alting God Most High

Y-es, there'll be good times, and yes, some will be bad ….

Z-ion awaits in glory … where none shall ever be sad!

We must remember that "this is the day which the LORD hath made; we will rejoice and be glad in it" (Ps. 118:24). Every day is a new beginning; every moment is new; every hour is new; every week is new; every month is new; and every year is new. Every day we are born anew not by our own volition, but through the power of God. The words of my elementary school song address the newness of our daily activities and interactions:

New every morning is thy love	New mercies each returning day,
Our waking and uprising prove;	Hover around us while we pray;
Through sleep and darkness safely brought	New perils passed, new sins forgiven,
Restored to life and power and thought.	New thoughts of God, new hopes of heaven.

As we begin each day, let us pray that, through meditation on His word, we can build, develop, cultivate, and nurture our faith in God as we experience a new relationship with Him.

Let us join with the psalmist in this prayer for protection as we begin this *new* journey. "My voice shalt thou hear in the morning, O LORD; in the morning will I direct my prayer unto thee, and will look up" (Ps. 5:3).

May the Holy Spirit fill you as you read, digest, and meditate on what it is that God wants to say to you through His written Word each day.

New Every Morning

Day 1

And *thine ears shall hear a voice behind thee, saying, This is the way, walk ye in it, when ye turn to the right hand, and when ye turn to the left. Isaiah 30:21*

This text invites the reader to be in communion with the Triune God: Father, Son, and the Holy Spirit. It evokes a unique voice amid the discordant sounds seeking to engross the mind. It tweaks our spiritual sensibilities to recognize the distinctive voice of the Holy Spirit as it speaks and gives direction to the seeker of truth.

Because we have a journey to take, the text enjoins us to stop, wait, and listen. When we make room for the Holy Spirit in our lives, we will undoubtedly hear the voice saying, "This is the way." When God is in control of our entire life situations, we can make no mistakes, plan a bad and unfruitful trip, or take detours. If we remain in touch with our Leader, all our actions and activities will be directed by God.

This text also calls for willing obedience. We live in an age where disconnect is rampant; this cannot be so for the child of God. If you have chosen to let him be your Guide, then the inner voice will urge you to yield and lay all your plans before him. The Leader knows the right way, and the voice does not admit any detour.

Let us practice listening for that special voice for it is IT that speaks (or whispers) in the ear. Our ears must be cleaned out; no wax such as fear, doubt, or uncertainty should be allowed to remain and harden in there. We need to have our ears and hearts spiritually irrigated so that the special voice can be clearly heard, detected, and understood.

Amidst the storms of Mount Horeb, Elijah heard the still small voice. Do you want to hear that still small voice directing your life? God speaks: "Be still, and know that I am God" (Ps. 46:10). May we all pray for the gift of an acute, sensitive ear to hear and a mouth to utter "shew me thy ways, O LORD; teach me thy paths" (Ps. 25:4).

Day 2

Behold *the handmaid of the Lord; be it unto me according to thy word. Luke 1:38*

Here is commingled joy and submission. The angel appeared to Mary, the young engaged virgin, and told her that she was highly favored because God had chosen her to be the bearer of his precious Gift to the world—His Son.

On hearing the salutation, "Hail, thou that art highly favoured" (verse 28), Mary was overwhelmed with a holy awe and fear. She pondered over his words and then engaged in an interactive questioning: "How can this be possible since I know not a man? I have no intimacy with my fiancée." The angel saw her fear and consternation and told her how God would perform this "strange act." "The Holy Ghost shall come upon thee, and the power of the Highest shall overshadow thee" (verse 35).

Having heard this account from the heavenly messenger, Mary submitted herself to the divine assignment. She contemplated the salutation and the message, and she concluded, "if God says so, if He ordains it thus, who am I to question God? So here I am a simple handmaid, may His will be done" (author paraphrase). Then in one joyful outburst she exclaimed: "BEHOLD the handmaid of the Lord; be it unto me according to thy word" (verse 38).

Following her submission, she uttered the most wonderful hymn of praise ever came from mortal lips—"The Magnificat." She praised God who had chosen her the least among the maidens, took away her reproach and possible shame, and elevated her to a most coveted position.

Are you willing today to let God use you as He chooses? God made us all for His own purpose. May we willingly say, "Lord, I yield myself to You this moment to be used as You see fit. I am available to You, so please use me today."

Day 3

> **Can** *there any good thing come out of Nazareth? John 1:46*

Nazareth had a bad reputation comparable to any of today's cities with a ghetto: South Bronx of New York City, Watts in California, Chicago's south side, or even Soweto in South Africa. Every major city has an "off limits" area to the more cultured and refined classes. All kinds of devious and unseemly behaviors are practiced there. So it was with Nazareth during the early messianic period.

Jesus was now selecting his followers whom He would teach, train, and later commission to carry forth the "everlasting gospel" to all men. Philip, one of his first disciples, responded to the invitation and unselfishly shared it with his brother, Nathaniel. Philip said to him, "We have found him [the Messiah], of whom Moses in the law, and the prophets, did write; Jesus of Nazareth, the son of Joseph" (verse 45).

Phillip gave a glowing report of this pure, noble, upright, and dignified young man, but Nathaniel, in scornful derision and skepticism, stuck up his nose at the idea. He retorted, "I do not know what has come over you; as far as I know, nothing good has ever or can ever come out of Nazareth; you must be dreaming or you have been fooled" (author paraphrase). Phillip remained unruffled and simply issued the invitation: "Come and see" (verse 46).

Jesus, who saw Nathaniel coming to Him, declared, "Behold an Israelite indeed, in whom is no guile [meaning deceit]" (verse 47). Nathaniel's simplicity, innocence, and devotion to spiritual things had endeared him to Jesus. He asked Jesus how He knew and recognized him. Jesus' response must have triggered a profound depth of spiritual confession for upon learning that Jesus saw him when he was under the fig tree perhaps meditating and praying, he was moved to exclaim, "Rabbi, thou art the Son of God; thou art the King of Israel" (verse 49). Nathaniel's hope was fulfilled, and his prayers had been answered once he was able to meet with the One for whom he had been praying. As a convert of John the Baptist, he was in expectancy of the Messiah as well.

There are many practitioners of the "Nathaniel Syndrome," who categorize people based on their locality, origin, race, status and social standing. The interaction between Jesus, Phillip, and Nathaniel shows very clearly that it is not your country, social standing, wealth or education that matters to Jesus, but it is your heart relationship. People from any station in life, any street, town or ghetto are all the same to Jesus. He came to set all men free; there is no discrimination or partiality in his arena. All men stand before Him as sinners in need of his cleansing and atoning blood. He came to free all men from the curse and bondage of sin.

As Nathaniel, let us maintain and practice that simplicity of faith, looking and expecting to see or find Jesus even though He is not far from any of us. May we be reminded that "the eyes of the LORD are in every place, beholding the evil and the good" (Prov. 15:3), and wherever people are, God is also there.

Day 4

> *As the **deer** pants for streams of water, so my soul pants for you, my God.*
> *Psalm 42:1, NIV*

One definition of the word "pant" is to long for or to crave. With this in mind, I have often wondered about the deer's watering habits. I have never seen them approach any watering spots to drink water. There is no water in their habitation, so they are always thirsting and hankering to get water to slake their thirst. No doubt that is the reason why they will chew on any green, juicy herb within their reach.

King David also found himself in a spiritual desert where he had a thirst for the living God. He needed to feel God's presence near him. He was alone, isolated, parched, destitute, and dehydrated because he could not hear or receive any signals from God. His soul longed to make contact with the Source of infinite power. He needed a refreshing. In his anguish he found solace in poetry and cried out agonizingly, "My soul is parched; I need to hear Your voice; I need to feel Your hand; I am lost without You; I am drowning on dry land; I need You Lord God of Host; I need to feel You near me. Reach out to me and let me feel Your Presence; I NEED You O, My God! Not a word, just a nod will quench my thirsty soul for I know You are there" (author paraphrase).

King David became a deer (metaphorically) languishing for a spiritual connection. Do you feel the need for God as King David did? Do you pant for God and need His presence near you? Do you crave for God because you lack spiritual nourishment and are thirsty for his Word and desire his Power? God is only a prayer away, and He will hear you when you call. He is the very best Friend in the entire world. If that is your need, then pray, "Dear God, quench my thirsty soul."

Some people pant for transient things, but let us pray that we may crave for a lasting relationship with God.

When Christ abides in us, our thirst for *everything* will be quenched. Let us seek God first, for He truly satisfies. King David advises, "O taste and see that the LORD is good: blessed is the man that trusteth in him" (Ps. 34:8). When He satisfies our divine hankering, our parched desires will be slaked and we will be fully refreshed. Jesus said, "But seek ye first the kingdom of God, and his righteousness; and all these things shall be added unto you" (Matt. 6:33). There will be no more thirst. Great news!

Day 5

*The **entrance** of thy word giveth light; it giveth understanding to the simple.*
Psalm 119:130

At all buildings, there are usually two signs: an *entrance* and an *exit*. We enter the building through the entrance, be it a door or a gate. In a similar manner, as we begin our walk with God, we need to find the door or gateway that provides entrance to Him. King David tells us how to enter into this new experience. If we read the Word of God, it will give us light, for it is light.

When we embark on our Christian journey, we do not know what lies ahead, hence the need for light. Thus, the Word—read, studied, and memorized—will shine upon the path. No successful action can be achieved in darkness. In creating the world, the first object the Creator called into being was light. "And the earth was without form, and void; and darkness was upon the face of the deep.... And God said, Let there be light: and there was light." (Gen. 1:2, 3). Referring to God's illuminating truths, David said, "Thy word is a lamp unto my feet, and a light unto my path" (Ps. 119:105). This biblical reference confirms the function of the Word: it gives light so the seekers/adventurers will know where and how to place their steps.

Besides giving light, the Word also gives understanding. The Word then has a dual purpose: giving light and opening the mind to comprehend. It then becomes the *key* to open any door and provide the entrance required. Without direction and understanding, seekers cannot see the path and are sure to stumble for they are unable to find the entrance. May we allow the Word to find entrance into our hearts and minds so that it can guide us into knowledge and the acquisition of wisdom!

Day 6

> **Freely** *ye have received, freely give. Matthew 10:8*

What a charge and a challenge! Everyone likes freebies. All around in different markets and stores are signs and sales urging prospective shoppers to "take one; it is *free*" or "buy one and get the other free."

During harvest time many farmers leave baskets of produce at their gates saying "free, help yourselves." The notion of getting something for nothing is very endearing. Who doesn't want a free meal, a free ride, a free checking account, or a free book? The idea of freeness is ingrained in our psyche.

Even though the gift is free, it has conditions and constraints: Give and you shall receive. One text states, "Good measure, pressed down, and shaken together, and running over, shall men give unto your bosom" (Luke 6:38). Here, the overt message is to give freely so that you will receive freely, with no strings attached.

The core of the message uproots selfishness, covetousness, and greed. God gives all things freely: air, life, breath, mind, heart, soul, and body. All He asks in return is that we freely yield ourselves to him. In this reciprocal activity, God is neither forcing nor coercing anyone into submission. Our response is a free choice. In the Garden of Eden, our first parents had their choice–freedom in obedience or slavery in disobedience. We all know the result of their choice.

God gives the sunshine and the rain freely. He allows the beautiful flowers to freely bedeck the environment at different seasons of the year. He fills our skies with song and chirping birds for our pleasure. He gives His grace, patience, love, care, mercy, and lovingkindness freely without our asking. He does not hold back; both the obedient and the rebellious have the opportunity to receive bountifully of His gracious gifts–especially the gift of life.

Our heavenly Father's final act is the free gift of His most prized possession, His only Son. The Gift of heaven redeems and restores humanity into the unsullied image He first created. May God's example serve to inspire us to share *freely* what we possess with those in need, remembering that all that we possess is a free gift from God.

Day 7

> **Give** *unto the* L*ord* *the glory due unto his name: bring an offering, and come before him.*
> *1 Chronicles 16:29*

God is to be praised and glorified for He is great, and there is none else beside Him. He is the Almighty; He is the Creator; He gives and sustains life; He controls all nature. He commands and all nature responds to His call. He tells the storm, "Peace; be still!" And the sea is made calm (see Matt. 8:23–27).

God is great! There is no other God beside him. He holds up worlds and the starry heavens; the planets and all the hosts of heaven obey His voice. God's name is worthy to be praised. Give Him the glory; His kindness and mercies are new every morning. We are His creatures, and we must never cease to give Him glory, for He is the Creator and Sustainer. When we enter the Tabernacle, the synagogue, or the meeting place, we ought to take an offering of thanksgiving to show our appreciation for all He has given us. God does not need our money, but we *give* in grateful praise for who He is.

God's name is revered among the earth. He is everything to all humanity. He is the Prince of Peace; He is the I AM, the Rabbi, and the King of glory. He is the Lord of hosts, the heavenly Father, the Holy One of Israel, and the everlasting God. He is the most high God. Because Jehovah is all encompassing, the apostle Paul affirms, "In him we live, and move, and have our being" (Acts 17:28). Therefore, man has neither alternative nor recourse but to *give glory* to the name of the Lord.

May we at all times and under all occasions lift up the name of God, for He alone is worthy of our praise, honor, and worship. "Praise waiteth for thee, O God, in Sion [Zion]; and ... unto thee shall all flesh come" (Ps..65:1, 2). Let His name be glorified!

Day 8

> *Behold, I send you forth as sheep in the midst of wolves: be ye therefore wise as serpents, and* **Harmless** *as doves. Matthew 10:16*

Doves are wonderful creatures from the avian family. One looking at them would think that they are silly. They are found in the most inane places: under bridges, the eaves of houses, and anywhere there is human habitation. They are mindless creatures that do not squawk, twitter, and chirp as other birds do. They are non-competitive, and their cooing is seldom heard. They are restive in nature.

Doves have been used to symbolize the purity, wholeness, and innocence of life. After the flood Noah sent a dove to test the readiness of the land to receive his cargo. After two tests the bird returned with an olive branch in its beak signaling that he could disembark.

At Jesus' baptism God's approval was signified by the Holy Spirit resting on Jesus' head in the form of a dove, and the voice was heard saying, "Thou art my beloved Son, in whom I am well pleased" (Mark 1:11). The dove symbolizes the affirmation and the presence of the Holy Spirit in our lives. Consequently, the Word of God counsels us to have a dove-like posture by maintaining a singularity of purpose with our minds focused on the pure and untainted. Doves do not engage in combat or bird fight; they do not pick at each other even when perched side by side. They are calm and demonstrate wisdom; human beings can learn from them.

Jesus was sending out His disciples to face the challenges of ministry; they would face a hard, indifferent, and antagonistic world, so He forewarned them of the cynicism and rejection they would meet. They were to know the Word and be fully armed with truth so that they would not be discouraged or dismayed in the face of criticism and rejection. They were presenting Jesus, the Good News of the gospel, hence opposition was certain. Many of them would be snares for the enemy who would try to eliminate them; it was essential that they stand on the principle of truth—the sure Word of God.

Jesus knew that the disciples would face confrontation and traditional bigotry, so He warned them that "offences will come: but woe unto him, through whom they come!" (Luke 17:1). As practicing Christians we need to heed the Lord's counsel to the first disciples. We must walk in the light given us and be careful to not make others stumble. By so doing, we will be a savoring influence to others rather than causing harm.

Let us take our cue from the doves: generating peace, wholeness and balance, simplicity, and innocence so there can be harmony among all with whom we interact. Let the quiet, loving solitude of the dove permeate within our lives now and throughout all our waking days. May we be as *harmless* (meaning innocent) as the doves but wise enough to shun and avoid evil.

Day 9

> **Incline** *my heart unto thy testimonies, and not to covetousness. Psalm 119:36*

A significant portion of Psalms is filled with prayers: prayers for upright living, for understanding, for protection, for forgiveness, and also for punishment. They constitute the entire gamut of human emotions, from seeking justice and knowledge to asking for deliverance and direction.

In Psalm 119:34 David asks for understanding so he can keep the law with his whole heart. Not satisfied with that request, he seeks a deeper relationship with God and asks Him for help to *incline*—bend, lean, turn—his heart unto God's testimonies. David recognizes his condition. No doubt he has reached one of his "prodigal moments," and so he pleads for purity of heart and mind. He does not want to be inclined to what others have or long for their possessions.

This is every sinner's prayer: to ask God for the outpouring of the Holy Spirit to incline our hearts toward awareness of God's Word, to hide His truths in our minds, and to delight in the testimonies of what God has done, can do, and will do for us. With such a prayer on our lips, we will be restrained from a covetous eye.

Let us pray this prayer, asking God to help us to long for the testimonies of what God has done for His people and learn more of His truths. May our experience be an inheritance forever that will cause our heart to rejoice!

Day 10

Judge *not, that ye be not judged. Matthew 7:1*

We live in a blame-casting society. Humankind hardly ever wants to accept responsibility or accountability for their actions, and they are always looking for someone else on whom to transfer their behavior. Then they will assert, "See, he is not better than I; look what he does; he is just as bad as I."

We are all sinners and do not have the luxury of being judgmental. We should not assess, calculate, or declare right from wrong. That is not our prerogative; it's God's. Scripture goes on to say that "with what measure ye mete, it shall be measured to you again" (verse 2). We are not privy to people's motives and should leave alone those things of which we have no knowledge. God has not abrogated His power and given it to mere humans to pass judgment on any of his fair creation. The faultfinders and the naysayers need to examine themselves— see their own faults and failures before passing judgment on others. Let the wise, faithful, and true Judge do all the judging.

Even if you think you are blameless, you have no legitimacy to evaluate other people's behaviors. Who says that person needs your intervention? The case of Moses' intervention on behalf of his Israelite brother whom he sought to defend was abruptly rejected on the grounds of his wanting to be judge. Having recognized that his previous secret was known among many, Moses fled the scene.

None of us should set ourselves up as the final authority of right living and behavior. We should not assess others by our own standards; neither should we judge their inner motives. God knows all hearts, and He has not asked for assistants. Let us keep our eyes focused on the glory of our God; let kindness prevail among us, and let us not transfer our own inept behaviors unto others or magnify their weaknesses. We should check first to see if we deserve the same criticism. A very Christlike rule to follow is *to judge* ourselves first and then lovingly forgive and help our neighbor. Judgment and justice belong to God. May we adhere to Christ's command.

Day 11

Know *ye that the Lord he is God: it is he that hath made us, and not we ourselves; we are his people, and the sheep of his pasture. Psalm 100:3*

To have knowledge and to want to know something is human inquisitiveness. Everyone wants to have knowledge of how something works or is constructed. Man's curiosity leads him into this never ending quest to know.

In every realm of learning: classical, mediaeval, scientific, ecclesiastical, eschatological, or philosophical, humanity is seeking to know what he does not. People continually pursue this incessant quest into the unknown. This is an important exercise because without knowledge, humankind remains in ignorance, which results in sorrow, misery, woes, and misgivings.

In humankind's quest to know the essence of things, they need to stop and recognize that all knowledge resides in God, the All-knowing and Omniscient One. God, the Creator, is the originator, manufacturer, engineer, and developer of all ideas. He is everything for every existing object that comes from His hand, His mouth, and His workmanship. There is no deficiency in His repertoire of knowledge. He invites us to seek knowledge and to know Him, to become familiar with Him, to spend time with Him, and to develop a forever friendship with Him.

King David, a man "after God's own heart," summons us to know who the Great God is: "It is he that hath made us and not we ourselves"—Creator. Humankind loves to take ownership and believes that they are self-existing and self-maintaining. David wanted all humankind to recognize their impunity and nothingness. He emphasized that without God, they are nothing. We did not make ourselves. Therefore, man needs to give homage and honor to God, the Creator. Where is your understanding? We cannot make or create anything. Whatever we do put together, God had already laid the foundation and provided the seed to engender the new thing. God is the Creator of everything in heaven above and in the earth below. We do not and cannot exist without God. If He stretches out His hand and recalls the very air we breathe, all created beings—humans, beasts, the birds of the air, the fish in the sea, and all things that live and move—would die instantly. We live and breathe by His presence, not without it. Did you *know* that?

The most important question is: how does one get to know God? God is very near to us. All nature speaks of Him: the gentle flowers, the sweet sounding birds, the babbling brooks, the quiet creeks, the roaring rivers, and the mighty seas with their rolling billows as well as the lofty mountain peaks. All these things attest to the greatness of God and His control over His creation. When one spends time reading God's Word, God will help us to get to *know* Him.

We are called to action: to know, to find out, to discover, to be aware, and to be cognizant of God. Humankind must use all their capabilities to know God, to experience Him, and to spend time with Him in order to become intimately involved with Him. It is our solemn obligation and duty to get to know this God: the Jehovah Jireh, the Provider, the Jehovah Uzzi, my Strength, and the El Shaddai. May you seek to *know* Him today, this very moment.

Day 12

> **Let** *not your heat be troubled: ye believe in God, believe also in me. John 14:1*

Assurance and more assurance is the substance of this text. There is much angst in this world and in our daily lives that cause much disease and distress. The ability to eke out a living for the family, education for the children, maintain spousal relationships, paying the bills, interacting with neighbors, etc., can cause endless amounts of distress. It has been so since sin despoiled fair Edenic atmosphere and unleashed myriads of challenges on the human family.

With the disruption came misery, murder, uncertainties, doubts, fear, anxiety, worry, sickness, incurable diseases, wars, distress in society, restlessness among families, and incessant wars. Neighborhoods are not safe anymore; children are being kidnapped and slaughtered; we have rampant spousal disorder and unfaithfulness; the troubles escalate and go on *ad infinitum*. The comforting thought is that Jesus says, "Do not trouble yourselves" (author paraphrase).

When Jesus came, walked, and lived, everyone expected Him to rein in peace and bring stability to the nation. Because He was the Life Giver, the Healer, the Restorer, the people sought to make Him a ruler, which would settle their fears and quell their anxiety. They asked Him, "Lord, wilt thou at this time restore again the kingdom to Israel?" (Acts 1:6). We long for peace and political security. Jesus was a different kind of a man with a different kind of mission in mind.

The time when Jesus and the disciples walked and worked, the social conditions were similar to ours. People lived in fear and terror of being overrun by the political and religious authorities and truly longed for a respite. They wanted rest from the harassment and oppression of their neighbors. Jesus' mission was not a political one; He came to seek and to save those who were lost and dead in trespasses and sin. His mission was that of restoration and healing. He comforted the downtrodden and gave sight to the blind—both physically and spiritually.

Having chosen His special twelve disciples, He trained, equipped, and commissioned them to go into the entire world to replicate His mission. Somehow, they were overwhelmed with the awesomeness of the task and were filled with anxieties, primarily because Jesus was returning to His Father's side in the heavenly courts, and they would be left without a mentor. Jesus calmed their fears and spoke these very reassuring and immortalized words, "Let not your heart be troubled; ... I am in charge and will always be with you; you will never be alone" (author paraphrase). These words were their marching order. Jesus stated, "Believe in Me; I cannot lie; I will come again and receive you so you will be with me always" (author paraphrase).

Those reassuring words are also the Christian's mantra. God does not lie; His words stand fast. May you keep calm and fear not because Heaven has the cure for every disease, disorder, and distress.

Day 13

Do all things without **Murmurings** *and disputings. Philippians 2:14*

God's Word provides direction on how to live according to God's plan: graciously, sublimely, and relationally. The apostle Paul writing to the newly converted saints at Philippi became aware of their un-Christ like behavior, and rather than berating or chastening them, he directed them to the Word and its precepts. In verse 13, he reminded them that God had chosen each of them and that He would work out His will and good pleasure in their lives.

The primary problem seemed hinged on leadership. As their leader, the apostle Paul felt responsible to counsel the administrators regarding their dealing with the new believers. He advised them to continue following God's leading and the Holy Spirit's direction because if they did, they were guaranteed success. With the Holy Spirit's free access in their lives and in the management of the church, there would be no legitimacy for any murmuring or dispute among them. None would seek for the highest position or the right to be called leader or chief. Where the Spirit of God is present, there is freedom, peace, humility, love, common understanding, and an abundance of graciousness.

Rather than disputing for leadership, they were to study and meditate on God's word in preparation for the challenging times the young flock would face. It is a known phenomenon that when a group of people chooses to follow Christ, persecution and opposition from the status quo follows. The enemy does not want to release anyone from his stronghold to join the family of God. That is why, in our small groups, gatherings, and assemblies, there is no place for strife, emulations, pretentiousness, or murmurings as to who should be in charge. All newly organized Christian fellowships are to work harmoniously with brotherly love under the Holy Spirit's guidance so that God's church can experience real Christian growth.

The problems that existed in the young Philippi church are commonly found in all new church plantings. Therefore, members must be watchful and not allow the enemy to come in and steal their joy. Though it was given more than 2,000 years ago, Paul's counsel is just as appropriate for church leaders in the twenty-first century. In today's world of increasing knowledge and education in and among the congregants, it is incumbent for church leaders to heed Paul's counsel and serve the Lord with gladness, dignity, and integrity.

Day 14

> **No** *man hath seen God at any time, the only begotten Son, which is in the bosom of the Father, he hath declared him. John 1:18*

Man in his finite, sinful state cannot dwell in the presence of an infinite, sinless God. He is not able to see God for "God is a Spirit: and they that worship him must worship him in spirit and in truth" (John 4:24). God is divine and self-existent; He is the source and personification of all material and spiritual life. It is through Him that all things consist. God is eternal in relationship to time—that is why He is forever and ever and from everlasting to everlasting. He cannot be compared to anything or to anyone; He is God, the one and only Creator.

Before sin's entry, God spoke to Adam face to face. Adam saw Him and communed openly with his Maker. Paul tells us that in the sin-free new earth, humanity will again commune with God face to face: "But then face to face ... even as also I am known" (1 Cor. 13:12).

Besides Adam, God revealed himself to Moses at the burning bush, to Elijah in the cave through a still small voice, and to Joshua in his sojourn with ancient Israel, but none were able to see His face, for sinful men cannot behold the sinless, holy, and awesome God. Humankind, in their natural state, cannot behold God in his majesty, purity, and sublimity. He is described as a "consuming fire" (Deut. 4:24) to Moses at the bush, hence sinful humans cannot survive in God's presence. Again, the men who bound the three Hebrew youth and threw them into Nebuchadnezzar's furnace were killed by the fury and intensity of God's presence in the fire.

Sinful humanity cannot see God and live. After Adam and Eve sinned, they went into hiding and could no longer face the righteous God. "I heard thy voice, and I was afraid, because I was naked; and I hid myself" (Gen. 3:10). When God invited Moses to meet with Him on Mount Sinai to receive the Decalogue, he had to turn his back because he could not see the face of God.

That was then; this is now. Jesus came veiled in the Father's glory, cleared the way, and opened the gate so that everyone can access eternal life. John said, "Behold, he cometh with clouds; and every eye shall see him" (Rev. 1:7). Jesus, our Elder Brother, is now interceding on our behalf to determine whether we qualify to face Him and the Father and live with them eternally. When this happens humanity will again enjoy the Edenic bliss and the communion they once had with the heavenly throng. We shall see God's face and live in a sin-free environment. That will be insurmountable joy! We shall *see* God in His fullness and wholeness with no fear of His consuming power. Every saved person shall see Him face to face and be with Him forever. May we plan now to meet our Father, the holy angels, and most of all, our Beloved Brother, Jesus.

Day 15

> *After this manner therefore pray ye:* **Our** *Father which art in heaven, Hallowed be thy name. Matthew 6:9*

This is the formal address Jesus told His disciples to use when they approach God through prayer. The "our" carries a very personal and intimate note. He is *our* Father, not anybody else's. Like our earthly Dad, He claims us as His own and loves each of us dearly and equally. There is no room for jealous feelings because He is Father for all His children and treats everyone with favor and equanimity. Everyone can find their place under His arms. He can embrace and hug each of us because He has a place for each of His children. He is the great, great Father of all, and we are all His children. God has no grandchildren, nieces, nephews, or stepchild. Everyone is His child, so everyone has a Father. He is the greatest and grandest Father of all. No wonder He is called the everlasting Father

We can always approach *our* Dad without fear or anxiety. Whenever I approach Him, He says, "Yes, daughter, what do you want now?" His greeting has always touched me greatly because it draws me to Him and reminds me that He will listen to my request. Thus being assured, He and I can engage in one sweet Communion. He is my forever friend, and I keep an unceasing conversation with Him. He is my Papa, Dad, Daddy, and Father. He can be yours, too. Let Him be your Dad today.

Our Father loves and cares for us, so in return, we approach Him reverently and respectfully. It's not the kind of fear or dread that some earthly fathers generate in their children causing them to tremble and shake. God is a loving and caring Father. Can you imagine one father engendering billions of children! Only He in whom eternity, omnipotence, and omniscience resides could make this possible. He is our Father, and He can do anything. He nurtures all the peoples of the world: red and yellow, black and white–all are precious in His sight. He provides for all His created beings. He arranges the cycles of nature so that everyone's needs are bountifully supplied. There is no famine or dearth in this Father's storehouse. This is our Father—yours and mine.

As His children we can walk the busy streets, lanes, and avenues or drive on multi-lane highways, sail on the great waterways in massive ocean liners, and soar the skies in jet planes without fear or tremor because *our* Father is at the helm guiding and directing us. He is always taking care of us. No other father has the capacity or capability of being at every place at the same time. That is the reason why we ascribe praise and honor, glory and reverence to Him for there is no other Father like our Father. He is personal and loving. He is always accessible. He not only provides guidance for us in our time of need but He also does all He can to protect our future inheritance. What a Father! Let us therefore bow down and worship this sensitive, caring, and loving Father of *ours*. He is all things to all humankind. What a great Dad!!

Day 16

> **Prove** *me now herewith, saith the* LORD *of hosts, if I will not ... pour you out a blessing, that there shall not be room enough to receive it. Malachi 3:10*

Jehovah God has put His reputation on the line to all believers. He is giving all humanity the chance to try Him out. It is like duel between two fencers—where you ask yourself which is better and who will be the one to give the deadly life threatening thrust. I imagine that God says to His believing people, "Call on Me; trust Me and see what happens to you."

Everywhere you go, people are always asking for proof. We live in a society that is dedicated to evidence. "Show me; let me see" is their battle cry. "I have to see it to believe it!" They ask for proof of your identity, your capacity, ability, or skill to perform what you portend. God says, "I am dependable; I am not a man that I should prevaricate; I will never fail you nor reject you; I am a never-failing God; I will be with you even to the end of the age" (Num. 23:19, author paraphrase).

God invites us to taste and to try; it is a message artfully penned by David, "O taste and see that the LORD is good: blessed is the man that trusteth in him" (Ps. 34:8). And the senior prophet Malachi recalled the exact challenge the Lord himself gave out. "Prove me now, today; take a chance with me; expend your energy and verve on me and see what I will do for you; you will have an abundant supply-even an over abundance of whatever you need" (Mal. 3:10, author paraphrase).

Since God is the owner, manufacturer, developer, engineer, and Creator of all, there is no lacking in His farmsteads. He gives to all His children freely and according to their needs. He is, has been, and will be the only sustaining power and force in the universe, hence His children will always be abundantly satiated. All that God asks is that we trust and believe His promises. The apostle Paul affirmed God's promise by saying, "But my God shall supply all your need ... by Christ Jesus" (Phil. 4:19).

Therefore, whatever you need, God, your Father, will supply you richly. He says that He will open the windows of heaven and pour out so many unimaginable blessings that you will not have enough storehouses to contain them. He will make you abundantly rich in good health, wisdom, intelligence, physical strength, spiritual stability, and economic resourcefulness. Whatever you need, try God and let Him *prove* Himself to be the God He really is–the *Adon Kol HaAretz*–the Lord of all the earth.

When the widow of Zarephath ministered to the prophet Elijah and made his meal before her family's meal, she believed that was going to be her last meal before they died. The famine decimated everyone, but because of her obedience, faithfulness, and trust, God *proved* Himself to her and gave her sustenance for all the remaining days of the famine. God did it for her, and He will do it again and again for all those who request it of Him.

Day 17

Quench *not the Spirit. 1 Thessalonians 5:19*

Before our Lord Jesus ascended to heaven, He promised His disciples to send them the Comforter, the Holy Spirit, to equip and empower them for ministry. He assured them that through the Holy Spirit, they would do greater works than they could imagine.

On the Day of Pentecost–only forty days after Jesus left them–that promise was realized, and the Holy Spirit came down in copious showers on the 120 gathered in the upper room; they were all filled with the Holy Ghost and onlookers chastised them as early morning drunks.

The gift of the Holy Spirit is to empower as John says, "He shall teach you all things, and bring all things to your remembrance, whatsoever I have said unto you" (John 14:26). Jesus also told them that the Holy Ghost will "guide them into all truth" (John 16:13). This comforting message was not only for His first disciples, but to all who should come after them, believe in His name, and accept Him as their Lord. Peter says, "To all that are afar off, even as many as the Lord our God shall call" (Acts 2:39). That includes us.

Information is available to those who lack knowledge about the Holy Spirit's operation. The Holy Spirit will enlighten and lead you to the discovery of truth. This is the third person of the Godhead, who is an active, vibrant, energizing, life-giving being. We see its active role at the creation of the world, "And the Spirit of God moved upon the face of the waters" (Gen. 1:2).

While Jesus was here among men, the Holy Spirit was not as visibly engaged, but when He returned to His Father, He authorized the Holy Spirit to replace Him and be a constant presence with the disciples. Its presence is Jesus' fulfillment of the promise that He would never leave them alone. Jesus affirmed, "I will not leave you comfortless: I will come to you" (John 14:18). They needed that assurance.

The Holy Spirit is a very active, engaging agent of the Godhead touching men and women's hearts everywhere so that they can respond to God's call of mercy. It is the Holy Spirit that convicts men of their sin. The Holy Spirit has a personality–it can be grieved and feel rejection just as we do. Paul advises Christians, "And grieve not the holy Spirit of God, whereby ye are sealed unto the day of redemption" (Eph. 4:30). It can be lied to such as in the case of Ananias and Sapphira who tried to deceive the apostolic community but the Holy Spirit struck them down and eliminated their hypocrisy from stifling the growth of the young church.

We cannot and should not quench the Holy Spirit's nudging; it is God's presence among humanity. He speaks to all and urges us to yield to its promptings, and when we do not respond, the Holy Spirit will turn away. Paul admonishes all Christians to be on constant alert for the promptings of the Spirit as it convicts us of sins and urges repentance. May we give this Holy Agent free access in all our interactions for it is God's voice to us.

Day 18

Restore *unto me the joy of thy salvation. Psalm 51:12*

This is the core of David's reconciliatory prayer. After he had committed the double sin of adultery and murder, he felt that God had rejected him. In deep anguish he acknowledged his gruesome act and engaged in one long contrite prayer for cleansing.

Recognizing how scrofulous and hideous his act was, he asked God to wash him thoroughly from that iniquity. He wanted God to purge him with hyssop and make him clean and to neither hide His face from him nor remove the Holy Spirit from his life. Then David finally cried out, "Restore unto me the joy of thy salvation" (author paraphrase). He wanted God to give back that which he had lost. He knew he had lost fellowship and communion with God and was overcome with a sense of desperation, isolation, alienation, and loss.

In his despair and seeming separation, a deep sense of loneliness overwhelmed him. In his plea for reconnection, he confessed his wrong, surrendered, and entreated God to let the fellowship and sweet communion he once had with Him be returned; hence the word *restore*. David wanted the assurance that some of God's joy was still available to him.

Our God is a God of restoration. He promises that He will "restore to you the years that the locust hath eaten" (Joel 2:25). God will restore to each of us the loose connection that has separated us from Him. He is waiting to restore in all His children the perfect righteous character of His Son. He is eager to give us His image because ours is so deeply marred and obscured by sin. When His image is perfectly restored in us, we shall rejoice greatly in the Lord because we will be one with Him. David craved reunion with his heavenly Father; he did not want to be a castaway. He genuinely repented and God heard and answered his plea. God will do the same for every sinner who genuinely repents and forsakes their sins.

David's prayer is every sinner's prayer. It is the prayer of contrition, repentance, and surrender. All who have wondered from God's precepts and have confronted their error must seek God's favor for restoration. Confession, genuine repentance, godly sorrow, and surrender must prevail in order for the sinner to be reinstated to their rightful place and again enjoy fellowship with the triune God and the heavenly hosts. Joy and rejoicing will then be restored.

At this very moment, God is waiting to grant you full restoration, so please do not keep Him waiting. Yield to Him now, and let the great compassionate God *restore* His image in you. May you pray this prayer: "Lord, I have sinned. I want to reconnect with You right now; will You please accept me? Amen."

Day 19

Surely *the Lord is in this place; and I knew it not. Genesis 28:16*

Jacob had an encounter with God at Bethel. Moses had one with Him at the burning bush, and Gideon had one with Him when the figure with the drawn sword greeted him with "the Lord is with thee, thou mighty man of valour" (Judges 6:12). Now Jacob, because of his odd and indiscrete behaviors, needed to meet God. Have you had an encounter with God through a dream or a vision? It must be a wonderful experience to have a meeting with God, the Majesty of heaven.

When an individual meets God, several things can happen. They can either be consumed by God's awesomeness, sinlessness, purity, and majesty or they can be exalted and given direction. God does not meet someone without a reason. There is always something special He wants that person to do—some specific task to accomplish or some specific message to communicate. For Jacob, it was the message to assure him that despite his foibles and misgivings, the God of his fathers was still with him.

God reiterated the promise, "Behold, I am with thee, and will keep thee in all places whither thou goest, and will bring thee again into this land" (Gen. 28:15). What an assuring promise! The very God Himself gives such certitude to deceitful Jacob.

With such an encounter, Jacob awoke from his sleep astonished by the experience. He acknowledged and extolled God's name by saying, "How dreadful (meaning sacred or holy) is this place! This is none other but the house of God, and this is the gate of heaven" (verse 17).

Whenever sinners come in contact with God's presence, something very spectacular and different happens to them. They are permanently changed. One example of this is the case of King David when he acknowledged his sins saying, "Against thee, thee only, have I sinned" (Ps. 51:4). God heard and accepted David's confession and surrender, erased his sins, and reinstated him to His favor. But another case is that of Uzzah, who touched the ark of God to stabilize it and was consumed instantly.

God knows our motives, our hearts, and our desires toward earthly and spiritual things. He waits to receive us and longs to have an encounter with us. There are many things He wants to communicate to us, and we must make ourselves available to Him. God wants us to feel His presence near. His promise is sure: "He will not fail thee, neither forsake thee" (Deut. 31:8). God is in every place wherever we go, and we must always make room for Him in all our activities. May we seek to develop a love relationship with Him, so we will always be assured that His presence surrounds us.

Day 20

Trust *in the* L*ORD* *with all thine heart; and lean not unto thine own understanding.*
Proverbs 3:5

Humanity is so confident, self-assured, and independent that we are always asserting "I can do it; I do not need your help." Our brain power, skill, intellectual exploits, and physical prowess give us a sense of invulnerability. We feel all sufficient and capable. And that is rightly so, because God made us all in His own image and vested us with power, intellect, and a will to do what we please.

Because of that embedded creative genius, humans feel that there are no insurmountable challenges. To a large degree, we are right because we have not only attempted but have conquered the unconquerable. Historical, geographical, and scientific records attest to the exploits, bravery, and triumphs of the human race. We have conquered Mt. Everest, Antarctica, and we have even seen a man on the moon! We have cloned a sheep and are in the process of making other humans through in vitro fertilization. Is it any wonder that we feel self-fulfilled? It seems as though there is no need for *trust* in the Divine. Humans can do all things—anything we want to do ... or so we think.

Even though we may feel self-actualized, the wisest man that ever lived gives this counsel from which today's erudite scholars could profit: "Trust in the Lord with all thine heart." All one's wisdom, skill, knowledge, insight, and discernment are gifts from the Creator who gives to everyone—men, women, and children—impartially (see James 1:5).

Any human accomplishment is a gift from God. It is God who gives man the ability to grasp, to learn, to interpret, to experiment, and to execute. A thinking individual must put God first because without Him in their life, their mind remains inane and mushy. Without God's Spirit, man can comprehend nothing; he doesn't have the capacity or capability to self-infuse. Man needs to know his position in the universe of things and that he ought to trust the Great God and Creator of the universe.

The more intellectually endowed need not feel superior. God distributes equally, and there is no giftless person. Humanity must depend on God for every facet of their interaction, for all wisdom resides in God's bosom, and He gives understanding to all. Men and women both must desist from boasting about their exploits and native instincts and instead come to completely rely on God. All humanity is able to literally and symbolically move mountains through God. God alone dispenses power, wisdom, and understanding, so we must first acknowledge God and have fellowship and intimacy with Him. May everyone seek God's direction and develop more *trust* in God.

Day 21

Understandest *thou what thou readest? Acts 8:30*

Do you understand what you are reading? This is a fundamental question that is asked of everyone who seeks to learn something by reading. For example, if you are learning a foreign language or doing a math problem and are given a passage and it says, *translate,* the first question the instructor asks is, "Do you understand what the article is about and what is required of you?" In order for any kind of learning to take place, the learner must understand the substance of the text.

The need to understand is basic. One cannot act if he or she does not understand what to do. Whatever the task is, understanding the instructions is primary. The first request for understanding comes from the young King Solomon who was thrust into office unprepared. Knowing his limitations, he prayed to God: "Give therefore thy servant an understanding heart to judge thy people. . . for who is able to judge this thy so great a people?" (1 Kings 3:9). With *understanding,* you have knowledge; without it, you are ignorant.

The case of the Ethiopian administrator cited above focuses on the need for understanding. Returning to his palace duties from his business trip and reading Isaiah 53, he was deeply touched by the content. He did not know to whom or what they referred; he was simply reading words. It was then that the Holy Spirit moved upon Phillip and urged him to take a south bound detour toward Gaza. Thereupon, Phillip met up with this lone traveler and seeker after truth. He then approached him and asked the very potent question, "Do you understand what you are reading?" (author paraphrase).

The Ethiopian administrator's response was trenchant: "How can I, except some man should guide me?" (Acts 8:31). His answer validates the fact that learners need teachers and instructors. That teacher may be a mom, a friend, a trained professional, a pastor or a rabbi. It may even be the Holy Spirit. Speaking through King David, God assures us of understanding. "I will instruct thee and teach thee in the way which thou shalt go" (Ps. 32:8). When the Holy Spirit teaches, we are sure to understand.

The apostle James advises those seeking understanding to consult God, who gives to all men freely. King Solomon also counsels that the person who has understanding is happy (see Prov. 3:13). A person devoid of understanding is like a mule driven with the whip. He or she does not know whether to turn to the right or to the left. Above all, let us heed the wise man's counsel: "Wisdom is the principal thing; therefore get wisdom: and with all thy getting get understanding" (Prov. 4:7).

May we ask the Holy Spirit to teach us so that we may *understand* God's statutes and His laws.

Day 22

Fear ye not therefore, ye are of more **Value** *than many sparrows. Matthew 10:31*

An individual's worth is of inestimable value to God, but most people become filled with angst when trying to determine their self-worth. The striving for self-recognition dictates the social stratification permeating some societies. Once you belong to a certain social stratum, the position that you and your family gain is fixed for generations. Some elite persons often times become crass and emit sound bites like "Do you know to whom you are speaking? No one addresses me thus"

It is very easy for someone to overrate their sense of self and value. Some go to great heights to self-exalt and bask in a sense of superiority. Others drag along a self-defeatist path with a sense of inferiority and pessimism. There is always a hypothetical dark cloud hovering over these kinds of people, and they seem unable to extricate themselves. Life's multifaceted challenges can have a tendency to overwhelm the faint-hearted, and many succumb to its forces.

However, none need be caught in that dragnet of self-pity, low self-esteem, and despair because there is hope. There has always been Hope. More than 2,000 years ago, Jesus responded to the same self-defeatist syndrome by telling His hearers not to lose heart or their sense of self. He wanted them to keep their spiritual foundation and beliefs and remain encouraged because even the tiniest bird is very important to God. There is not a bird that goes without food, a nest, or a resting place. Then He said to them, "Just think about this: you are made in My image; you bear My imprimatur; inscribed on your forehead is the insignia: 'Made by God.' You are valued; you are worthy. You are more valuable to God than the sparrows; He sent Me to die for you" (author paraphrase; see John 3:16). Because God places such value on you, you are never to fear personal threats or trials. God's care for all these tiny creatures cannot shake His love or dislodge His tender and loving care over you. You are highly favored and richly blessed. You are covered by His blood! Christ's blood was shed for every sinner, and each person is very precious and valuable.

In God's sight, we are of significant *value*. Angels are constantly watching over us; we are God's because He created and redeemed us. How much more *valuable* can that be! The Father has said, "Relax my children; I have you under my wings, very near to my heart" (author paraphrase). May you appreciate the care and *value* thus accorded.

Day 23

Wherewithall *shall a young man cleanse his way? by taking heed thereto according to thy word. Psalm 119:9*

The mammoth question is always *how* can it be done? This is one of the six rhetorical questions that an investigator always asks when he or she wants to clarify an issue. Other companion questions are: who, what, when, where, and why? As the answers to these interrogations are fleshed out, some degree of stasis is achieved, and the seeker gets the answers to their inquiry.

Here David is asking a very poignant question: How shall the youth—the young men and women—clean up their acts? The question begs the answer: the direction the youth are taking is not clean, but filthy and murky. The many distractions facing them have made it impossible for the youth to maintain purity, uprightness, and integrity amid a sea of impurity.

David identifies with the youth's dilemma having been a victim of licentiousness and other self-defeating practices. His is a plaintive plea for the youth, who face the alluring and enticing temptations of the world, to bring God into their lives. How to preserve their innocence and maintain their integrity is the daunting question and magnificent challenge!

This self-evaluative text has overtones of the lost son in Luke 15. He left home and squandered his inheritance living the supposedly good life only to realize that he was lost in the quagmire of decadence. He no doubt asked the same question: how can I regain my integrity, my purity, and my innocence?

Pondering over the question: HOW? The Holy Spirit answered, "By taking heed thereto according to thy word," the youth will achieve insight or self-realization. The youth will hopefully come to recognize that their spiritual and moral life is on a downward spiral, and see that they must halt the course. But how will they get to this point? The Word of God gives the only safe answer: they must live according to the Word and hide God's word in their heart that they might not sin against Him (see verse 11). It is only by studying the Word and praying daily that the youth will be able to resist the charms of the world. Studying God's Word is the only failsafe proof they have against a sinful life.

This question challenges every human being; each of us must confront self and answer three questions: who am I? How did I get here? What must I do to turn around? Self-realization is the first sign of a conscious need for change. The second half of the text states the need for strong, vigorous, and positive action provided only by the Holy Spirit. Each person must engage in self-analysis to ascertain his or her spiritual and moral status. We must study the Word, apply its principles to our lives, watch unto prayer incessantly, and focus on Jesus who alone has the power to keep us unsullied amid the onslaughts of the present world.

May the youth seek for a daily anointing of the Holy Spirit to keep them pure and chaste.

Day 24

Except *the LORD build the house, they labour in vain that build it: except the LORD keep the city, the watchman waketh but in vain. Psalm 127:1*

This is a great text about relying on God. It shows humanity's utter futility of trying to do everything based on their strength, so-called might, ingenuity, and wisdom. Whatever structures humankind erects, whether it be physical, intellectual, moral, spiritual, economic, mental, or emotional, they cannot expect a strong building unless the foundational principles are based on God's Word.

Families establish homes and watchmen guard cities, but all of these activities are futile unless God is the foundation of all their plans. A family without God can never experience and enjoy the spiritual bond that happens when God is a part of the relationships. And a city without God's leading and direction will soon crumble from the inside out. There will be no moral principles to be upheld so there will be chaos in the city chambers and halls of assembly. Corruption in all areas of government will prevail, and everyone will be their own boss, doing what is right in their own eyes. Rulers of cities need to let God guide their operation. If God is left out of our lives and any operational event, then all that we do is wrapped up in futility.

God oversees and directs every activity, but humanity feels capable to direct their own lives and do not desire God's intervention. David deflates that idea, stating, "The steps of a good man are ordered by the LORD: and he delighteth in his way" (Ps. 37:23). King Solomon adds, "A man's heart deviseth his way: but the Lord directeth his steps" (Prov. 16:9).

It is God who brings all of humanity's plans into fruition. He is everywhere directing the courses of our lives, the affairs of nations and of society. We cannot do anything without God's approval, so whatever your challenge is, whether it's to establish a family, to purchase a house, to pursue a certain course of study, to travel, to lead a country, all humankind must seek God first. His counsel is just, and He will lead us into paths of peace.

Engage in no act, small or great, without first consulting your omniscient, heavenly Father. People and nations survive at God's bidding. May we engage Him in all our building activities—whether structures or families, states or unions, kingdoms or palaces. Except God lays the foundation, the structure is sure to topple and fall.

Day 25

> **Yea**, *though I walk through the valley of the shadow of death, I will fear no evil: for thou art with me; thy rod and thy staff they comfort me. Psalm 23:4*

This is a text that speaks belief, offers hope, and engenders faith. It disannuls fear and dread because it exudes assurance and confidence. I am not afraid of anything or anyone because the Lord is with me. It speaks to the Lord's continuous watch over His creatures both as our Protector and Provider.

We bask in this confidence and surety because the True Shepherd is always at our side. Despite the severe challenges of illness, insurrection, strife, loss, betrayal, rejection, alienation, or even death, I am comforted that the Lord is always there walking by my side, holding out His mighty arms, and enfolding me to His bosom. What joy and peace and heavenly calm to just rest your head upon His gentle breast! The joy that attends it is that despite these life challenges, you are not alone on this journey; there is always Someone who is walking beside you.

The "yea," or in other words, "even though," suggests that certain conditions may be present, but we can take heart because it is going to be OK. Other trials, troubles, and tribulations may come, but the sword—the Word of God—and the shield—His holy presence—will see us through the deep shadows of illness and through the dark valley of death. Jesus conquered death, so it shall not have supremacy over our mortal body. Jesus has the last word on death, and in all our shades of grief, He will always be with us. God's Word provides stability, comfort, and confidence. Let us be comforted in this one thing: our God is able, and He will be there when needed.

Amidst the many challenges we face, be encouraged that God is always with us enabling us to carry on. Just like the shepherd goes to the field fully armed to protect his sheep from attackers and marauders, so the Lord, our True Shepherd, protects us from all potential harm. It is a very comforting and consoling thought that this Shepherd is with us all the time. There is no need for fear because He is more than capable; we are well protected.

God is always beside us providing the solace and security we need. Therefore, each of His children can go through life knowing full well that they have a True Shepherd, Guide, and Protector who is filled with love and compassion for His creation. As a result we can go on any journey confidently and boldly. May we come to recognize that *even though* the enemy tries to intercept the sheep's pathway, the True Shepherd has gone on ahead of us and cleared the path. With God leading the way, we need to trust Him and follow His steps. Jesus has had the last word on death, so there is no need to be afraid. Praise God, for He is life!

Day 26

> *For the **Zeal** of thine house hath eaten me up; and the reproaches of them that reproached thee are fallen upon me. Psalm 69:9*

In this dialogue with the Lord, David feels that he has been God's fall guy. He is referring to his sufferings and the insults he has received for standing up for the Lord. His enemies have threatened him, and he thinks it is all because he stood up for what was right. They have not let him forget his past sin with Bathsheba. He has become an alien to his own family, and once again, he has been thrust into a state of despair and isolation. But he still treasures the relationship he has with God, so he decides to go out on the limb to protect God's name.

David had cultivated sensitivity toward the Lord and was overjoyed to meet Him in the temple. While there, he encountered some ridicule from those who were disrespecting the Lord. This enraged David. In another situation Elijah, when confronted with Jezebel's threat, blamed his zeal for the Lord as his reason for fleeing. God wants us to cultivate a *zeal* to communicate with Him, to meet with Him in His temple, and to enjoy sweet communion with Him.

David seemed to have been overly passionate in his worship, especially since God had granted him a reprieve for his sin with Bathsheba. He had now become God's defender. David complained to God that those who reproached God were also insulting him, but he was happy to be the one to bear the brunt of the reproaches they were heaping upon God. However, David was overjoyed that God had reinstated him into His fellowship. The passion to be in the presence of God was like a consuming fire, and David was overwhelmed by the second chance given him. He would spend a lot of time in God's presence singing, shouting, and praising God for all His great mercies. David was passionately at one with God again.

Like David, may we cultivate a *zeal* for God, His Word, and all the wonderful things He represents.

Abide With Us Today

Day 27

But they constrained him, saying, **Abide** *with us: for it is toward evening, and the day is far spent. And he went in to tarry with them. Luke 24:29*

After Jesus' resurrection He joined the company of two discouraged followers and talked with them on their way to the village of Emmaus. They were going to meet the other disciples to discuss the happenings of the weekend. These two, Cleopas and another, were like the other eleven and a host of well-wishers that had been saddened about the occurrence in Jerusalem. They were unsure of their life's spiritual direction now that their beloved Teacher was dead. He was gone, and no one even knew where His body was. They journeyed on very disheartened and hoped that a session with Peter and the others would bring some relevance to their lives and their mission. They would reflect on the events and strategize their next move. Amid the confluence of thoughts that flooded their minds, they were joined by an unexpected guest who shared in their conversation and retorted, "O fools, and slow of heart to believe all that the prophets have spoken: Ought not Christ to have suffered these things, and to enter into his glory?" (Luke 24:25, 26).

The Stranger, "beginning at Moses and all the prophets, he expounded unto them in all the scriptures the things concerning himself" (verse 27).

As the company of three traveled on, they came to a little village at nightfall and fearing for their lives, entreated their guest to spend the night with them. For whatever reason, they seemed to crave His companionship. His conversation intrigued them, and they wanted more. He agreed and settled in with them. As they were about to share the evening meal, He did the accustomed thing—blessed the meal, broke the bread, and distributed it to them. They then recognized the familiar pattern. Their eyes were opened, and they recognized that it was Jesus, their Lord and Master, the Risen Lord who had joined them.

The invitation to "abide with us" was the most tender and passionate request. It is in the evening time that loneliness creeps upon us. At that time the shades of night are portentous, and we need the company and the comfort of another human being. It was during the night season that Jesus asked three of His disciples to *abide* and pray with Him before He was crucified. From the example above we see that these two travelers felt a need for the Master's presence and begged for Him to abide with them.

Jesus is available now—today, this afternoon, morning, or mid-day. Are we going to invite Him to abide with us? Do we want Him near? If we invite Him, He will tarry with us and teach us things we need to know. Contemplate on the words of the evening song: "Abide with me; fast falls the evening tide, The darkness deepens; Lord with me abide" (Henry F Lyte, "Abide With Me").

May we invite Jesus, the King of kings, to come into our lives and *abide* with us.

Day 28

The next day John seeth Jesus coming unto him, and saith, **Behold** *the Lamb of God, which taketh away the sin of the world. John 1:29*

John the Baptist identified Jesus, his cousin, amidst the crowd as he was baptizing new converts in the River Jordan. Some were questioning John about his role and mission, how he defined himself, and who authorized him to preach and baptize. The crowd had heard about the coming of Elijah, whose message would transform their society, and they were curious to know if John was Elijah. As a young preacher, he was calling men and women to repentance and to accept God through the sacrament of baptism. He told them that he was neither Elijah nor the Christ; he was simply a voice preparing the way for the Messiah. The next day Jesus appeared at the site, and once John looked up and saw him, he declared, "*Behold!* Here he comes; here is the Lamb of God who takes away the sins of the world" (author paraphrase).

We do not know if the crowd understood John's allusion of Jesus being the Lamb of God. Jesus did not come to live forever or to perpetuate life as was expected. He came to offer Himself as a ransom for all. As a lamb was used for burnt offering in the priestly services, so Jesus was the pre-ordained Lamb to be slain on sinners' behalf. He came to live out his mission and then be sacrificed.

John knew Jesus was the foreordained Sacrificial Lamb. His life would be offered to end the daily sacrifices of goats, rams, bullocks, turtle doves, and pigeons. Jesus was the *real* Lamb, but so few knew of it. What a privilege it must have been to see Him–to behold Him!

Jesus asked John to baptize Him, but John refused. Jesus humbly retorted: "Suffer it to be so now: for thus it becometh us to fulfil all righteousness" (Matt. 3:15). The Holy Spirit alighted on Jesus' head at His baptism, which confirmed that Jesus was God's Son. John knew that Jesus was indeed the Majesty of heaven having received the Father's approbation: "This is my beloved Son, in whom I am well pleased" (verse 17).

Jesus came and was baptized. He then preached, healed, and lived an unsullied life all while being mocked, derided, reviled, buffeted, rejected, betrayed, and finally, crucified. But He rose and returned to heaven to His rightful place at the Father's right hand where He now intercedes on humanity's behalf. The slain Lamb now lives as a Victor over death and the grave. Saints, may you quickly come to *behold* your Intercessor!

Day 29

Cast *thy bread upon the waters: for thou shalt find it after many days. Ecclesiastes 11:1*

This promising text exudes hope, risk, certitude, and strong faith. It exudes economic overtones of investment and trust while negating self-centeredness. Two scenarios come to mind: first, there is the rich young ruler who came to be enrolled in Jesus' school of discipleship, but when Jesus told him the curricular requirements, "he went away sorrowful: for he had great possessions." (Matt. 19:22). Jesus told him to *cast* his wealth to the poor and then return to follow Him. Uncertain of how his life would continue after such transaction, the rich man left the Master's presence sad and forlorn with all his possessions intact. He missed a great blessing of interacting with the disciples and Jesus as well as the possibility of accumulating more wealth. He refused to cast his bread upon the waters of obedience and faith.

On the other hand, the widow of Zarephath did cast her bread upon the waters of obedience and faith. When the prophet Elijah came and asked that she make his meal first, she did not argue but immediately began preparing the final meal she could make, which she had originally planned to give to her own son. Even though she did not know Jehovah's plan, she willingly did what was requested. The prophet assured her that as long as the famine lasted, she would have enough food.

Rather than cast their bread to the poor, widowed, and orphans, people like the rich young ruler would choose to build larger barns, store the glut from their farming, and then relax and enjoy their treasures. These kinds of people are possessed with unbounded selfishness.

Selfishness rules society, but Jesus spoke of the need to exercise and extend charity, especially to the widows, orphans, dispossessed, and the disenfranchised. Boaz, Naomi's kinsman, instructed his workers to leave enough standing stalks that the widows could come and gather after they had reaped the full harvest. As a result of his action, Ruth went and gathered in his field. He fell in love with her, married her, and they became the progenitor of our Lord, Jesus Christ. Thus Boaz *cast* his bread of selflessness on the water and reaped an immortalized place in sacred history.

What is your response to the admonition? Many respond by looking at the needs of those who are helpless. We need to help provide for those who are struggling to eke out a living: the aliens, the foreigners, the refugees, and those on the margins of society. In doing so, the donor will not be left bereft of goods. The promise is sure: "thou shalt find it after many days." It is not what and to whom you give that produces reciprocity. Everything belongs to the Lord, and He has a thousand ways to repay you. His storehouses are never empty. May you act as He commands and *cast* your bread upon the waters. Surely, you shall find it later.

Day 30

Do *thy* **Diligence** *to come shortly unto me. 2 Timothy 4:9*

The aged apostle Paul was alone in a Roman dungeon. He was sick and suffering from coldness, alienation, isolation, and possibly exhaustion. He urgently needed the comfort and assurance of his friends and especially his son in ministry, Timothy. His mind, body, and soul cried out for human companionship and solace.

Writing to Timothy, he pleaded, "Do your diligence to come soon; I need you. I am indeed longing to see you. I want to embrace you; I want to see a familiar face. Come as you are–do not tarry; come now" (author paraphrase).

Paul's isolation and need for companionship is akin to Jesus when He came from the Garden of Gethsemane needing comfort, only to find His three friends sleeping. In desperation and disappointment, He said to them: "What, could ye not watch with me one hour?" (Matt. 26:40).

Loneliness and ennui almost overwhelmed Jesus, but angels came and ministered unto Him. Demas, one of Paul's followers, became besotted with the world and left the faith. Spiritual things did not appeal to him anymore, so he left the aged and suffering apostle to the wiles and vagaries of the Roman prison authorities and returned to Thessalonica. In light of the betrayal, Paul said, "Demas hath forsaken me, having loved this present world" (2 Tim. 4:10).

Paul knew Timothy's reliability and had proof of his fitness for the ministry. Thus Paul urged him to leave everything and come to his aid. The young minister obeyed and rushed to his mentor's side.

Preachers, evangelists, teachers, and missionaries in the mission field need the prayers and support of their friends and family at home. To the worker in the foreign field, his or her mission may be likened to the troops in Afghanistan, Iraq, Iran, Somalia, or Syria, who are engaged in combat and fighting to preserve the peace of the United States. We must show them *diligence* by our letters, care packages, and prayers, for they are at the forefront challenging enemy forces: spiritual, mortal, physical, moral, and martial. We at home must let them know and feel our communal concern. May we *do diligence* and pray for all those in active service–military or missionary.

Day 31

Enter *into his gates with thanksgiving, and into his courts with praise. Psalm 100:4*

This text suggests our manner of worship. The gates could be the church gateway, the courts, or the main entrance. For King David, the gates alluded to the several entry points at the temple at Jerusalem.

Whenever we approach the precincts of the church, synagogue, tabernacle, or temple, we are coming to meet with the King of kings, heaven's Monarch, Creator of heaven and earth. This is a joyful occasion for several reasons. First, we have the opportunity to come into His presence and to experience His glory. Second, we come with thankful hearts because He has spared our lives and has showered us with an abundance of blessings. Third, we have the opportunity to offer thanksgiving and praise for the eternal sacrifice that makes eternal life possible. Consequently, we enter humbly, reverently and peacefully.

Our lips should be filled with praises; let us join the psalmist in song: "O come, let us sing unto the Lord: let us make a joyful noise to the rock of our salvation. Let us come before his presence with thanksgiving, and make a joyful noise unto him with psalms" (Ps. 95:1, 2).

Some people enter the house of worship with a ruffled spirit; they have no joy or reason to be thankful. They forget that the purpose of their assembly is to meet with Jehovah God, to worship and adore Him, and to praise and render thanks unto Him. The psalmist intones: "Oh that men would praise the Lord for his goodness, and for his wonderful works to the children of men!" (Ps. 107:15). Whenever we *enter* into His courts, may we remember that our lips should continually utter the Doxology: "Praise God from whom all blessings flow; Praise him all creatures here below" ("Praise God, From Whom All Blessings," *The Seventh-day Adventist Hymnal*).

Day 32

Fret *not thyself because of evildoers, neither be thou envious against the workers of iniquity. Psalm 37:1*

We live in a fretful and uncertain age where people are constantly measuring and comparing themselves with others. Often times, if they do not measure up to the standards of another, they lose interest in their ventures. They think less of themselves and make such self-defeating statements: 'I am suffering from low self-esteem.' They will take upon themselves the monstrous demon of the inferiority complex, engage in a self-dialogue, and begin complaining: "Why not me? Why them?" or "I wish ... I wish ... I need ... I want ... I must have ... etc."

Longing inordinately for what others possess is covetousness—an age-old sin. Both Adam and Eve longed for and coveted God's glory, His knowledge, and His perfection. They wanted to be like their Creator, and so they yielded to the tempter's wily craft. The same principle existed among ancient Israel, so God inscribed in the tenth commandment that one should not covet anything that belonged to his or her neighbors (see Exod. 20:17).

Sacred and secular history teems with accounts of people who were discontented with their life's station and engaged in all kinds of devious machinations to get what they desired. For example, Ahab coveted Naboth's vineyard, adjacent to his property. Because he refused to part with his inheritance, he went home, pined, and *fretted* until his evil wife devised a plot to have Naboth murdered in order to give the vineyard to her husband. Covetousness often leads to theft and murder. It is a deadly sin and should not be nurtured. Ahab and his wife were no doubt unfamiliar with this counsel: "Wait on the Lord, and keep his way, and he shall exalt thee to inherit the land" (Ps. 37:34). If we wait on God, we learn to be content with what He gives us. The apostle Paul said, "For I have learned, in whatsoever state I am, therewith to be content" (Phil. 4:11).

King David found himself in a similar dilemma. He questioned God why the wicked were constantly prospering and the righteous were not. It was not until he went into the sanctuary of God that he understood their ultimate end (see Ps. 73:17).

In the temple, the revelation of God's magnificence and glory completely awed David, so he documented this very comforting counsel: "Fret not ... it is not worth it; their lives are short-lived anyway. Do not be bothered or perturbed by their seemingly flourish; God has a better plan and course of action for His people. Trust in the Lord your God and look to Him always" (author paraphrase).

God is trustworthy; His character is unchanging. Each of us can face life fearlessly with the undying affirmation that God will take care of all our problems. May we commit the keeping of our lives in His wonderful, strong, and everlasting arms and *fret not*.

Day 33

> **GOD** *is our refuge and strength, a very present help in trouble. Psalm 46:1*

This text exudes strength, promise, and assurance. It presents the weary traveler with God's stronghold, His consistency, and His power. He is our refuge–a secure hiding place.

Cities of refuge were built and set apart in ancient times as safe places where a murderer could flee and feel safe and secure. As long as the criminals remained in that city, they were safe and free from judgment. Those cities were man-made designates, and the magistrate or any board member could change their mind at any time and lift the ban. If that was done, the wrongdoer would have to return to their original city and face whatever penalty the behavior designated.

Unlike those man-made structures, we are affirmatively told that God is a place of security when all else is insecure. He does not change His mind or "alter the things that are gone out of his lips" (Ps. 89:34), hence He is both dependable and reliable. God is the one constant that we have in the universe. If all nature goes awry, God remains strong, unshakeable, and unmovable. If we abide in Him and let Him be our guide, we cannot be tossed to and fro by any sort of wind, gale, or hurricane. In whatever form they come: physical, material, moral, social, political, economic, aerial, watery, or spiritual, we shall remain sturdy and unshakeable if God is by our side.

God has the anchor; in fact, He is the Anchor. In Him, we remain unmoved because He is not only our refuge, but He is also our Strength. King Solomon attests, "The name of the Lord is a strong tower: the righteous runneth into it, and is safe" (Prov. 18:10). The Lord God is our refuge and our strong tower.

These images of God conjure up safety, protection, security, and confidence. A tower is meant to be an impregnable and safe structure. After the flood the descendants of Nimrod began building the Tower of Babel, their city of refuge, as a safeguard against a second flood.

No man can out do God; He is omniscient, omnipresent, and omnipotent. There is none to compare with Him, and there is no one else like Him. It is not only when troubles arise that He is available because He is always there. May you find joy in knowing that God is the great I AM, the unmovable and unshakeable Rock.

Day 34

> **Hear**, *O Israel: The* LORD *our God is one Lord Deuteronomy 6:4*

In this verse Moses affirms God's authority to those he led out of Egypt. They are at Mount Sinai, and he feels it is time to let them know about the God who had been leading them since their departure from Egypt. God had forcibly wrenched them out of Egyptian slavery and Pharaoh's domain with a strong and mighty hand, and the Israelites needed to recognize His power. Moses reminded them they were God's special people and should render Him their worshipful obedience.

Summoning their attention, Moses speaks, "Listen, hear O Israel—all you God-fearing people: the Lord our God is one God. He is not like the many other gods of the nations that surround you; neither is He like the gods of the Egyptians that you left behind. This is Jehovah. The LORD is His name, and He is the one and only true God, the Creator of the heavens and the earth; everyone ought to listen and obey what He commands" (author paraphrase).

That Moses and Aaron felt the need to call their attention to the absolute authority of God suggested that the Israelites may have equated Jehovah with the gods of wood and stone. The two leaders demanded that they recognize the supremacy of Jehovah—that He is a God above all gods. He is not in the same category as lifeless creations and carvings from a human's hands. He is to be the sole object of their worship, allegiance, and affection.

Although the clarion call was made to ancient Israel, it is also for all who inhabit this current earth. God is to be the sole object of this generation's allegiance, worship, and affection. God has not changed since the days of Israel's deliverance from the throes of oppressive slavery. He is the same yesterday, today, and forever and is still intervening in the affairs of families, society and nations. He calls upon all men to "fear God, and give glory to him" (Rev. 14:7).

God alone holds up worlds and sustains all life. Humanity's singular obligation is to obey, revere, and respect Him. Every generation, including ours, must heed the trumpet call: "The LORD our God is one LORD" (Deut. 6:4). He is the God of gods. May we render to Him our worshipful praise.

Day 35

> *And God said unto Moses, I* AM THAT I AM: *and he said, Thus shalt thou say unto the children of Israel,* **I AM** *hath sent me unto you. Exodus 3:14*

I AM hath sent me to you. This is the strongest and most assertive power of God and Jesus combined. Jesus declared, "I am the True Vine and my Father is the Husbandman" and "I and My Father are One; and believe me that I am in the Father and the Father in me" (author paraphrase; see Exod. 3:14; John 14: 11; 15:1). Thus everything that is true of God, the Father, is also true of Jesus, the Son.

God exists in the present. He is always I AM—never I *was* or *used to be* or *will be*. Today, He is I AM. When tomorrow morning comes, He is I AM. It is His constant, unchanging condition. God always IS. That is why we delight in David's assertion: "God is ... a very present help in trouble" (Ps. 46:1). In Him there is no shadow of turning. As the clocks tick away and the world turns, He is I AM. His ever presence provides hope, assurance, satisfaction, and joy.

When you take leave of family and friends, they usually say, "I'll see you soon." This is not the case with God. Anytime you call upon Him, He is there. He is the one constant that humanity has. He is always I AM. Neither time nor age changes God's condition or agenda. He is always in the NOW. He is continually recreating and reshaping humans in His own image and after His likeness.

When the Israelites cried out to God for deliverance from their enslavement, God chose Moses and Aaron to go to Pharaoh and claim Israel's release. Moses asked God, "What shall I say to the enslaved ones who has authorized me to do this great feat?" God answered, "Tell them that I AM hath sent me unto you" (author paraphrase; see Exod. 3:14). Not that Moses doubted God, but he wanted clarity and identification. To this God replied, "I Am That I Am" (Exod. 3:14).

Thank God for I Am. There is no need to be fearful of attempting any venture for I Am, the indefinable God, is always with us. Moses vouchsafed, "The eternal God is thy refuge, and underneath are the everlasting arms" (Deut. 33:27). If I Am has been doing that for 6,000 years of human history, why should He now withdraw His care from us? He is still the great I AM and will be throughout all eternity. He is the only self-existent Being possessing essential life and permanent existence. That is the great I Am! May you grow to trust Him.

Day 36

*The **Just** shall live by faith. Romans 1:17*

This text sustained Martin Luther's faith as he sought peace for his restless soul while remaining committed to Romanism. Following Jesus' injunction: "Search the Scriptures ... which testify of Me" (John 5:39), he came upon this Pauline text–the "just," i.e. the righteous ones, shall live by faith and presumably not by works. This discovery changed the course of Christianity, religion, and Romanism in the sixteenth century.

The Biblical discovery opened the door to religious freedom and freedom of conscience for all Christendom. Luther refused to continue following the dictates of Rome and the Papacy. Instead, he totally accepted the righteousness that Christ offered through the efficacy of His spilt blood. Luther's findings, activities, actions, belief, and promulgation of the truth changed the course of religion in the world as it opened a new understanding of sacred truths to scholars, clergy, and laity.

The just are those who are accorded righteous and have neither sin nor deceit in their mouths. They can only attain a perfect level of commitment by believing in and practicing the faith and lifestyle of the Christ Jesus. They must have an unshakeable faith anchored on Christ, the solid Rock.

The faith that the just live by manifests a vision and a practical existence of what God alone can do. It lifts the believer above sin. The Bible says without this kind of faith, man cannot please God. "But without faith it is impossible to please him: for he that cometh to God must believe that he is, and that he is a rewarder of them that diligently seek him" (Heb. 11:6).

The believer must claim the promise "I will never leave you nor forsake you" (see Deut. 31:6, 8; Heb. 11:5) and do the works that Jesus did. It is our privilege and responsibility to seek and find out how best God can use us to show justice, mercy, and love to those in need of our help. May we seek to live *just* (meaning blameless) and upright lives and depend on the Savior who is the giver of life. As we trust God, we are saved; we find life both now and forever. As God declares us righteous through faith and faith alone, we are justified.

Day 37

*What? **Know** ye not that your body is the temple of the Holy Ghost which is in you, which ye have of God, and ye are not your own? 1 Corinthians 6:19*

Did you *know* that this body, which we take so much pride in, does not belong to us? It is lent to us while we are earthbound. It is God's property, the living residence for the Holy Spirit. Many do not actually know this.

Even though you invested in it and kept it in tip-top shape, you are simply a steward. Nothing in it belongs to you. You did not build it; it was vested to you. At death, the body goes back to the earth from whence it originally came; the breath goes back to God who gave it. What do you have left? Nothing ... zilch. The physical disintegrates, and the moral, spiritual, and social elements are all silent. King David asks the existential question, "What is man, that thou art mindful of him?" (Ps. 8:4). In his discussion with the Corinthian brethren, the apostle Paul gives the answer. The human body is God's property; each person belongs to God through creation and redemption.

How is it by redemption? It is Jesus' blood that makes possible the efficacy of a soul set free from sin's condemnation and death. It is the blood that sanctifies; without the blood, there is no remission of sin. So when Paul brings ownership to attention, the people are now able to understand that they belong to God.

Paul invites us to consider the body more sublimely. He says this slender, athletic, or curvy figure that we tote around is not ours at all. It is sanctified. It is not like a temple where congregations meet to worship and give honor and praise to God. It is, indeed, God's dwelling place. God wants to reside in us. It is where He chooses to dwell and have His Holy Spirit installed. As Christians, our bodies cannot be engaged in any licentious behaviors or demoralizing practices, they are to accommodate the Holy Spirit. Your body is sacred and precious; God cannot reside where there is drugs, alcohol, swearing, and cursing. He cannot exist where there is evil surmising, malice, envy, hatred, covetousness, or sexual orgies. He dwells in a high and lofty atmosphere where there is no taint of evil. How careful one has to be in keeping that body pure and undefiled! We must always remember that God wants to inhabit it.

Your body is that residence; make room for the Holy Spirit. What a privilege for every believer to have the third person of the Godhead, the Comforter, residing in his or her body! That is indeed joy supreme. May you share that piece of good news with those you meet so that everyone can be informed and *know* that their body is God's temple.

Day 38

> **Let** *both grow together until the harvest ... gather the wheat into my barn.*
> Matthew 13:30

In farming communities, farmers and laborers face the boon of seeding and reaping strong, sturdy, healthy plants or the bane of stunted, dwarfed plants and terrible weeds.

Many weeds have stubborn roots and do not yield easily to uprooting. Sometimes, the true plants and the weeds end up looking alike. Recently, my neighbor brought some very tall, stately-looking green plants from her garden for me to help her determine if they were plants that would produce flowers. I had seen some of the same luscious plants in another neighbor's garden. I mused, *Those certainly do not look like flowers.* That plant was a weed. It is easy for the real and the false to look similar, and it is only upon keen scrutiny that I was able to identify the weed.

This scenario is akin to the parable Jesus told: the keen-eyed laborers identified the weeds and requested permission to uproot them so that the good plants could grow and be properly nourished. However, the weeds had been so intertwined with the good plants that to extricate them would endanger their life and survival. Extreme care was needed to prevent the good ones from being pulled up with the weeds. The farmer assessed the situation and told them, "Let them both grow together. At harvest time the separation will take place" (author paraphrase).

Jesus had a profound lesson to teach His followers. He knew that He was going to leave them soon, and they needed all the skills, insight, and discernment necessary to practice effective ministry. He had a profound object lesson to teach His followers: focus on the great gospel and minister it to the world.

In this society all kinds of people continue to live side by side. There will always be some false professors among true Christians, but they must continue to live together until the day of harvest and judgment. The good must continue to let their light shine. Judgment belongs to God. God will judge everyone in the end, and the "weeds" will get pulled and burned in the mighty fire. The good plants that yielded fruit will be gathered, bundled, and taken to a place where they can truly grow. So what is the message?

The world is the field; the enemy is anyone who intercepts our path and tries to infuse errors and bad habits in our minds. We must be alert and discriminative to discern truth from falsehood. We have to be keen-eyed in accessing information because all that which is false will look like the true. Only the Holy Spirit can make us discern truth. Jesus will return and give every person their just reward according to how well he or she sowed and cared for the seedlings. Sometimes error creeps into the congregation, and the established leaders might be quick to extricate the bearer of such a dogma, but may we choose to stand on the truth and *let* God guide His church.

Day 39

My house shall be called a house of prayer. Matthew 21:13

How careful one has to be in reverencing the sanctuary or any house of worship! It is a holy, consecrated place where God meets His people. He always wants a special place to have communion with them. He commanded Moses while Israel was traveling in the wilderness, "And let them make me a sanctuary; that I may dwell among them" (Exod. 25:8). God longs for and wants to dwell among us; He actually wants to dwell in us. That is why Paul told the Corinthian brethren that their bodies are the indwelling of the Holy Spirit—a temple in which the third person of the Godhead resides. God is very particular about His temple, whether it is your body or a consecrated place.

The temple is not a place for secular jocundity; it is place for prayer, meditation, and worship. That is why no secular transaction operates within its walls. Offerings are lifted in special receptacles so that there is no clinking of coins or rustling of paper. God requires that all things be done decently and in order. God's house requires reverence in everything. Sometimes people get carried away and misconstrue the real purpose and reason for the tabernacle.

When Jesus walked the earth, worship had lost its spirituality having descended to secularism. People had little regard for the symbolic rites pointing to the atonement and the projected death of Jesus. They acted mechanically; they came and purchased cattle, turtle doves, etc., for their sin offerings totally oblivious of its deep significance. Greed, stealth, and the desire to make an extra buck at the expense of the most vulnerable were regularly practiced.

As the crowd thickened and the fervor intensified, every trader sought to see how he could capitalize on the weak and poor and swindle their money. It was on one such occasion that Jesus, on His way to the temple, came upon this melee. He became enraged when He saw the merchants practicing injustice. He condemned their betrayal of justice, chastised them with His tongue, and overthrew their change tables. I can just imagine Him saying something like: "My house is a place for prayer, reverence, and honesty!"

By this singular act, Jesus restored order and reverence to the temple. They had commercialized the sacred ceremonies and brought disrepute to the sacrificial system. God would not be mocked by these selfish, unsanctified, and greedy traders, especially since the rites pointed to Jesus, the very Lamb who entered in the temple precincts.

Today's worshippers must guard carefully how they utilize the temple, or any meeting place where God meets His people. His presence fills the place and only order, dignity, and reverence ought to be practiced there. Where God's presence is, it is holy ground. He wants to meet with us, and we ought to make such convocation a place of holiness and sheer delight.

Day 40

Then he answered and spake unto me, saying, This is the word of the Lord unto Zerrubabel, saying, **Not** *by might, nor by power, but by my spirit, saith the LORD of hosts.*
Zechariah 4:6

These words were pregnant with assurances for King Zerrubabel, who was facing a severe challenge and would have given up but for Jehovah's watchful eyes. God sent him this very poignant and assuring message that he was not alone—that his God was with him and would see him through as He had done for the other nations.

The Word of the Lord distinctly says, "Not by might, nor by power, but by my spirit." God is in charge. It is not by any strong-arm tactics, prowess of humanity, skill, or agility; it is not by the mighty trained and armed militia, cavalry, or infantry; it is not by any person's artistry, machinations, intrigues, or strategies that you are going to be victorious. God is the one who dictates, orchestrates, and directs the world through the power of the Holy Spirit. It was that Spirit that breathed upon the earth and brought everything to life at Creation (see Gen 1:2).

The same Spirit is available to us today. God will interfere, intervene, and guide you if you ask Him to do so. All the residents of the heavens move at His commands. He orders their paths, and there is no collusion. It is His will and His way. Therefore, let man everywhere bow before the Lord of heaven and wait on Him as He directs all their paths. It is the omniscient God who raises up and levels down. He says, "I am God, and there is none else" (Isa. 45:22).

"I am the Lord: that is my name: and my glory will I not give to another, neither my praise to graven images" (Isa. 42:8).

Our God is the God above all gods; nations and leaders need to acknowledge the supremacy and primacy of the Ruler of heaven. If they would subject themselves to His divine authority and kingship and learn meekness and justice from Him, confrontations would be replaced with more peace and common understanding. But as long as people think that they are in charge of their life and the actions that govern civilization, there will always be conflicts.

Amidst all the throes of life, God is still in control, holding and managing the affairs of humanity. We can do only as much as God allows us to do.

Not by the might, skill, or prowess of men and women are nations governed, but by God's Spirit. God has all the power, and He distributes it as the need arises. May we soon realize that we do *not* have anything of value from ourselves. Let us pray for the strength to acknowledge God's might and power so that we will choose to obey Him every day.

Day 41

Oh *that men would praise the LORD for his goodness, and for his wonderful works to the children of men! Psalm 107:15*

This is an exhortation to the entire human family to acknowledge God's majesty and power. This plea implies people's reticence in ascribing praise to the Creator of the universe, and asks the question—why? David wishes that the entire creation could understand and appreciate the grandeur and awesomeness that emanates from such gratitude and praise.

How does one praise someone? You offer compliments to them while they can hear and appreciate them. King David constantly offered praise avowing: "In the grave who shall give thee thanks?" (Ps. 6:5). Why should one say praiseworthy platitudes to the dead?

Again reflecting on God's goodness, tender mercies, and lovingkindness to him and to humankind, David counsels us to praise God for "his goodness and His wonderful works to the children of men." God's wonderful works include: watching over us day and night, guiding us when we travel, providing safety and security on the highways, waterways, and air ways, supplying all our needs, bringing success to our plans, and answering our prayers by delivering us from trouble and distress. In every area of our life, we ought to praise the Lord for it is He who is directing our steps.

Whenever you call, He hears and answers. He provides food for the table, so you are never hungry. He rescues you from the enemy and preserves the children and their children. He heals the sick and keeps us sane. He is the God of gods—caring, compassionate, and omnipresent. Praise Him!

Is there anything else to be thankful for? Think of your existence and the condition of your health. You are alive, able to drive a car, independent, and hopefully employed or retired. Many whom you knew are no longer with us. Praise Him for life!

Let men, women, children, and youth everywhere lift up their hands and voices and give God His encomiums:

"Praise waiteth for thee, O God, in Sion [Zion]: and unto thee shall the vow be performed" (Ps. 65:1).

"Let every thing that hath breath praise the Lord. Praise ye the Lord" (Ps. 150:6).

"Let them exalt him ... and praise him" (Ps. 107:32).

Everyone has something to be thankful for. May we be continually engaged in ascribing thanks to our God and Father.

Day 42

Pray *without ceasing. 1 Thessalonians 5:17*

The shortest verse in the Bible consists of two words "Jesus wept" (John 11:35). Later, the apostle Paul challenged believers, "Pray without ceasing." That order connotes meanings such as do not stop, never take a break, and do not slack up. We need to be continuous in the process of prayer. Praying is analogous to breathing; Ellen White once aptly described the process: "Prayer is the breath of the soul" (*Gospel Workers 1915*, p. 254). Its power is unrivaled. One does not cease from breathing, for it is an involuntary action. Breathing goes on incessantly; our prayer life should follow suit.

Why is prayer analogous to the respiratory function? In the physical world, no human can go longer than three minutes or so without air. Without the supply of oxygen, he or she would soon swoon and experience respiratory difficulty, and ultimately, they may even die.

Similarly, in the spiritual world, no Christian can survive without connecting to God through prayer. Even though we live in an age of super-sonic telecommunication, we do not have the luxury to text or send an e-mail to God. Heaven's super highway is not so wired. But the means of communicating with and reaching God beats out today's best and most advanced electronics. Long before the invasion of fibro optics and the electronic super highway, God told us that communicating with Him supersedes any of humanity's creations: "And it shall come to pass, that before they call, I will answer; and while they are yet speaking, I will hear" (Isa. 65:24). This process far outstrips instant messenger.

In today's society, with its many allurements, snares, and pitfalls that daily besiege us, we must guard the avenues of the soul, heart, and mind by keeping the prayer fires burning. Satan, the arch deceiver, is always prowling; he knows he can stop us from communing with God in prayer. He can create situations that keep us flustered, angry, frustrated, and preoccupied to the point that we cannot "find" the time to pray.

We need to have the spiritual muscles to fight him because he will do all he can to sever our connection with God.

Jesus, our Elder Brother, knew the importance of prayer. He entered upon no activity without first connecting with His Father through prayer and taking the time to seek His approbation and direction. After forty days in prayer and fasting, the Tempter approached Jesus. Had He not been in constant communion with His Father, who knows how the course of sacred history would end? Jesus is our model in everything: in prayer, in living, in loving, in caring, and even in dying. He wants us to know that we are no match for that once heavenly angel, Satan; therefore, we are urged to pray incessantly.

If Jesus was God in human flesh and He still needed to spend such long hours in prayer, how about us? What should our prayer life be like? While here on earth, Jesus did not use any of His divine power to navigate life's crises. He lived as a man so that He could nurture and succor us. He faced every crisis any human would ever face, and He overcame it all to show us that by close contact with the Father through unceasing prayer, we can be overcomers, too. May we be like our Elder Brother and begin now to *pray* continually.

Day 43

It is good that a man should both hope and **Quietly** *wait for the salvation of the* L<small>ORD</small>
Lamentations 3:26

The prophet Jeremiah gives us sobering counsel. Humankind is in a dead hurry. We make requests, and we are anxious for the answers. God has all the answers, and He will answer in His own time, according to His good pleasure and what He knows to be our own good. We were recently counseled to never cease praying, so now that we have accomplished this, we have been advised to wait in silence until God comes through for us.

God is not on a time schedule. He has no bus to take, no class to attend, no speaking or preaching engagement or board meeting. God is never in a hurry. It is we—human beings—who are hurrying to an uncertain location or event. We want the answer before we are through praying. Even though God assures us that "before they call, I will answer; and while they are yet speaking, I will hear" (Isa. 65:24), it does not mean that our request will be answered instantaneously. Our wise Creator will respond in due time; He knows how best and when to answer our request, even if we want an instant reply. That is God's prerogative. Functioning in the here and now, our vision is circumscribed. God is the all-seeing, all-knowing One, and we must wait on Him. Therefore, we must learn to wait *quietly* on the Lord for our time is not His time.

How shall we wait? We must most assuredly wait patiently with the expectation that whatever He does is well done. We cannot dictate to God; we may ask, but if our request is not in keeping with His plans for our life, it may not be granted. He said, "I know the thoughts that I think toward you ... to give you an expected end" (Jer. 29:11). Our request should be that everything happens according to His will so that His will be done (see Matt. 6:9, 10). Many times when we ask, we do not receive because "we ask amiss" (James 4:3). We must wait *quietly*.

It is in the quietness that God speaks to us. Elijah heard that voice only after the Mount Carmel experience (see 1 Kings 18). If we want to receive God's salvation, we must sit and wait quietly. Only then will we hear His voice saying, "This is the way, walk ye in it" (Isa. 30:21). David instructs us to "wait on the L<small>ORD</small>: be of good courage, and he shall strengthen thine heart: wait, I say, on the L<small>ORD</small>" (Ps. 27:14), and "truly, my soul waiteth upon God: from him cometh my salvation" (Ps. 62:1).

Waiting involves patience and watching. God has the only answer you need. Therefore, sit and watch Him work while you wait *quietly* for His glorious manifestation. God is never late; He is always on time. May you allow Him to perform His strange and mighty acts in your life.

Day 44

Create in me a clean heart, O God; and **Renew** *a right spirit within me. Psalm 51:10*

David's prayer request is every Christian's. Each of us needs a renewed heart. We each need a spiritual makeover.

In this prayer is the recognition of our spiritual miasma and the need for redemption. We feel unclean in the presence of the Holy God and need cleansing and freedom from the calamitous path ahead. We are unable to change our spiritual condition, hence the petition. David pointed out that the heart (as well as mind and spirit) is desperately wicked and cannot be trusted; it is only through the Holy Spirit residing in our minds that can bring about a renewal.

God has provided the complete makeover for each of us through His Son's sacrifice and the efficacy of His blood. But we must be awakened to our own spiritual condition, so that we may then cry out like the prodigal son: "I will arise and go to my father" (Luke 15:18). Once we have reached that point, we can plead with our Savior to *renew* us.

God is willing to renew in us His Holy Spirit. He is "able to do exceeding abundantly above all that we ask or think" (Eph. 3:20). Why delay in asking His forgiveness? David had recognized his heinous errors and with the urging on by the Holy Spirit, he humbled himself before the Majesty of heaven, confessed, repented, surrendered, and sought forgiveness. God saw his genuine repentance, honesty, and sincerity and granted him his request. David knew that he was at the nadir of degradation, and if he was going to fulfill God's mission, he needed a thorough and complete makeover. Hence the cry for a renewed mind, body, and spirit.

Many of us have wandered far away from God, and if the Holy Spirit is pleading with us to forsake our un-Christ-like ways, let us heed His urgings and reject those dishonorable practices. Let us wrestle with Him as Jacob did until He recreates a pure heart and a renewed spirit focused on righteousness. Only then can we ask for a full and complete reinstatement into His favor. He will give us a new heart, mind, disposition, and a whole new self. God can, and He will. Seek Him today–this very moment. May you bow your head in silence and ask Him to come within and *renew* you.

Day 45

If you do not **Stand** *firm in your faith, you will not stand at all. Isaiah 7:9, NIV*

This clarion call is to ALL Christians. When one has adopted the name of Christ, he or she cannot be a wishy-washy observer or believer; one has to take a stand. When sin and Satan entered this fair, unsullied creation and despoiled it, God could have destroyed the perpetrators, eliminated sin, and recreated a whole new creation. But in the councils of heaven, Jesus stood. He became humanity's surrogate and offered the supreme and ultimate sacrifice so that all could have the chance to be reconnected to God–to be atoned with Him.

Thus Jesus, a co-creator, divested himself of His regality, innocence, and purity and took humanity on Himself. He came as a babe, grew as a child, lived as a man, and then readily gave up His life for humankind. This entire act is incomprehensible; no wonder John recorded Jesus' exact words, "Greater love hath no man than this, that a man lay down his life for his friends" (John 15:13). This love far transcends the love of a man for a woman, a parent for a child, a sibling for a sibling, or a citizen for his or her country.

Jesus stood up against Satan after His wilderness fast. Amid the throes, loneliness, and histrionics of Gethsemane, Jesus could have yielded to the physical and emotional pressures. He could have just walked away from the agony and alienation that pressed upon His mortal frame, but He did not. He *stood.* He even dialogued with His Father whether He should execute the plan, but He heard not a sound from the Father. No answer. He had to stand alone in that cold and lonely garden. Even His friends, who should support him in prayer, were all overcome with sleep; they did not *stand*.

Jesus chose to cast in His lot with humanity, so He stood. He stood alone in Pilate's judgment hall. He stood alone before Caiaphas, the chief high priest. He stood alone as His mockers derided him and demanded He prove that He was the Son of God. He stood there unmoved, unshaken by their screams. Yes, Jesus stood alone. He stood for all humanity—for every person—He *stood* for you and me. He stood because He came with a mission and remained true to it until it was complete.

Jesus is the model for all Christians. He came and taught us how to stand. He stood in obedience to His Father's commission. He stood because if He had not stood, what would become of humanity? We would have no hope of eternal life. Yes, Jesus stayed the course even when under agonizing pressure of isolation, betrayal, and rejection. He cried out to His Father, "My God, my God, why hast thou forsaken me?" (Matt. 27:46). Silence reigned supremely. Bowing His head, He breathed his last, but He still stood! Yes, the Son of God *stood* for you and for me. And because He stood, we must also stand firmly in what and in whom we believe. May we stand, stand, and stand again for the truth and the faith!

Day 46

Show me thy ways, O Lord; **Teach** *me thy paths. Psalm 25:4*

This is a prayer of submission and contrition. The speaker recognizes his waywardness and longs to be reinstated in God's favors. He also knows that he was enrolled in the wrong school and wants to learn God's precepts, statutes, and laws. This is the first sign of conversion when one recognizes his or her errors and wants to change. This prayer is from a heart yearning for redemption and renewal. Thus, he calls out to God because he knows he can find help from Him during his time of need.

God, the giver of all good gifts, has given man the ability and the power to understand spiritual and secular things. The psalmist attests, "The entrance of thy words giveth light; it giveth understanding unto the simple" (Ps. 119:130). By studying God's words, the learner can have all wisdom. In this particular scenario, the speaker seemed to have lost his way and wanted to come back. Like the prodigal son in Luke 15, he wanted to reconnect with truth. He might have forgotten that truth, justice, and verity are Jehovah's attributes, and he yearned for them. He came to himself, recognized his need, and pled with God: "Teach me what I am supposed to do—where I am supposed to go" (author paraphrase). He is now willing to give God free rein and not follow his own way.

It is only when many of us reach the nadir that we remember that God is there and has been there all the time waiting for us to acknowledge His guidance. King David intones, "And call upon me in the day of trouble: I will deliver thee" (Ps. 50:15). How wonderful it is to be able to fall back on the Word!

The Word is full of exhortation, admonition, and counsel on how to reconnect with the Source of true knowledge. David, the recalcitrant one, spent a life time agonizing with God to grant him complete restoration. His prayers are loaded with conditional requests and pleas. We are very fortunate because we have the examples of David's pining, longings, and need for a wholesome relationship with the Father and His Word. David desperately wanted forgiveness and the power and strength to live a victorious life. We have the Word to guide us—to be the "lamp unto my feet, and a light unto my path" (Ps. 119:105), so we do not have to stumble as he did. His prayer ought to be ours, too: God, please teach me, show me, lead me, so that I can be equipped to help others find Jesus. That is our mission. We are all spiritual mentors and role models of what it means to live the perfect life. May we yield ourselves to God so that the Holy Spirit can teach, show, and lead us on the right paths.

Day 47

The eternal God is thy refuge, and **Underneath** *are the everlasting arms.*
Deuteronomy 33:27

These words of comfort and assurance carry promise and hope to every sin-sick soul. In the morning when I wake, these are some of the first words that come from my lips. All throughout the day, they remain my guide; they keep me focused, stabilized, and spiritually anchored.

These words connote fearlessness and engender bravery and faith, which helps one to stand and not be intimidated by any extraneous forces. They exude confidence and security. God is eternal—from time's beginning to its end, God has been there. God cannot change; that is a defining characteristic of His personality. He is a refuge and a stronghold. He is the one constant in the universe. He declares, "For I am the Lord, I change not" (Mal. 3:6).

Since God is constant and unchangeable, we have no need to fear. In secular terms, He is ubiquitous, but in sacred terms, our God is omnipresent—He is the ever present I AM. We can always fall back on Him. Just as a sick child will place his or her head on their parent's bosom to find comfort, so is our God there to provide similar comfort to the needy, forlorn, or depressed. None can remove us from His bosom while He cradles us. The beautiful consolation is that He has room for every head—yours and mine included.

Like the eagle, the king of birds, God stretches forth His tireless and everlasting arms to shield us. They buoy up the weary, the very tired, the frustrated, and the angry traveler. All adults, youth, and small children can find comfort in Him. God's hands are strong and powerful. When He is near, we need not fear nor faint, for He is a strong tower. He is the hiding place, the place of security. He is our refuge. We can rest assured that under His wings we can safely abide though the storms: rage, hunger, famine, hardships, loneliness, pain, suffering, isolation, brutality, betrayal, rejection, and even death. My God and your God can protect; He is able.

I hope that you can find in God your refuge today, this very moment. Cling to this promise: God cannot and will not change. He will be with you in trouble, in sickness, and in death. He will be by your side to see you through, Come to Him, and you will find safety. The apostle James solidifies this premise when he says, "with whom is no variableness, neither shadow of turning" (James 1:17). Here again God's constancy and permanence are validated. Let us go forward with our hands placed in His. He knows the way, for He is the way. May we seek and find shelter *underneath* His everlasting arms.

Day 48

I am the true **Vine**, *and my Father is the husbandman. John 15:1*

Jesus, in addressing His disciples' overt inquiry about His origin and status, introduced the familiar agricultural imagery of the grape vine in the orchard. "I, Jesus, Son of God, Son of man, am the Vine and my Father, God, is the Vinedresser" (author paraphrase). Jesus referenced a heavenly connection: the vine cannot bear fruit unless it is connected to the main stock.

Jesus, though God himself, still had to draw strength and sustenance from His Father. Having divested Himself of His divinity and assumed humanity, there was need for Him to remain continually connected to the branch—the main tree. He wanted His first disciples as well as all those alive today to understand the significance of the divine/human relationship. Only as we remain attached to the main trunk can we grow and be nurtured. He wanted all to know and understand that as He maintained a constant, living, and abiding relationship with the "husbandman," so should they with Him.

This was very deep theology. Although the disciples knew of Jesus, lived with Him, and went wherever He went, they had no idea from whence He drew His power and strength. There were factions among them relating to their possible position and title in Jesus' prospective kingdom. They all had political ambitions, and Jesus wanted to help them see the bigger picture, which was that they needed to be connected to Jesus, His mission, the ministry of His Word, and their relationship to one another.

They needed to understand the deeper things of God and seek His kingdom first. In their present mindset, they were not ready to grasp the deep things about God and their own mission. Each needed the indwelling of the Holy Spirit. Jesus told them that He had many things to share with them, but they were not ready to receive them. These twelve men were with Jesus daily, but they had not grasped the importance of their calling: to be fishers of men. Jesus told them that each of them had to abide in Him. They had to have a living, active experience with Him before they could catch any fish and make converts. His exact words were "Abide in me, and I in you. As the branch cannot bear fruit of itself, except it abide in the vine ... abide in me" (John 15:4).

If we, like His first disciples, are to be productive in our ministry, we must remain connected to the main branch, the Source of knowledge, power, wisdom, and truth—Jesus. We must constantly draw strength and power from Him because without this living connection, there can be no fruit. He says, "You must abide in me and I in you for without me ye can do nothing" (verse 5, author paraphrase). May we seek to remain attached to Jesus, the True Vine.

Day 49

> **Whither** *thou goest, I will go; and where thou lodgest, I will lodge: thy people shall be my people, and thy God my God. Ruth 1:16*

This text shows the tenacious quality of a daughter-in-law toward her mother-in-law and speaks well for their relationship. After the loss of the men folk: a husband and two sons, Naomi was forced to return to her homeland, but the two daughters-in-law refused to leave her. Both wanted to accompany her. She, however, entreated them to return to their kinsman and country and restart their families.

After much persuasion, one daughter-in-law, Orpah, yielded to her pleas and returned to her family, but the other, Ruth, refused to go back to her previous lifestyle declaring that she was going to stick it out with this lonely mother-in-law. This latter young lady saw more than the need for physical, social, and marital satisfaction. She liked what she saw in her mother-in-law, namely her tenacity to things spiritual and her love for Jehovah. She wanted to find some of her mother-in-law's godliness and be a woman of faith and courage as Naomi was. Besides that, she felt an unswerving commitment to the widow. Why would she leave this poor widow to go and fend for herself back in a land where she was now an alien? Ruth chose to abide with her.

Despite Naomi's sufferance, Ruth did not yield. She responded, "I am going to be with you all the time; I want to experience your godly life with Jehovah. I will live wherever you live, and I will be buried there also. I will not leave you alone so do not force me" (author paraphrase).

This story is an excellent model of the Christian motherhood relationship. It speaks to how a mother-in-law and a daughter-in-law should operate. God honored Naomi's faith and Ruth's courage and blessed both tremendously.

Every mother and daughter would do well to read the story, study the implication, and take cues as to how a healthy Christian mother/daughter-in-law relationship can be fostered and practiced. When God is in the home and He is shared with the uncommitted Christian, much harmony, love, and common understanding can develop. It was the godly life of Naomi that endeared her to Ruth. Naomi became a missionary, and her outreach to the young widow changed the course of sacred history.

God expects mothers and daughters alike to let their lights shine wherever they are. Who knows the workings of God? May Christian mothers everywhere set the right tone so that if young ladies who are not Christian join their families, they may experience God and become Christians themselves.

May Christian families everywhere let their light shine so that others may see their good work and glorify our Father.

Day 50

Then said Jesus unto him, **Except** *ye see signs and wonders, ye will not believe.*
John 4:48

These words were Jesus' retort to the nobleman who came requesting an urgent audience with Him in order for Jesus to come and heal his dying son. Jesus' response seems uncharacteristic of Him, but Jesus did this because there seemed to have been some deference given to women whose testimony did not bear much credence. This gentleman wanted to have His own spiritual epiphany. Jesus sensed His attitude and replied to him, "Do you have to experience for yourself to believe? You cannot act on the woman's report; is it not reliable enough?" (author paraphrase). Jesus showed no eagerness to visit the man's house, and once the man sensed Jesus' lack of urgency said, "Sir, come down ere my child die" (verse 49).

Jesus had just performed His first miracle at the wedding in Cana, and others were anxious for Him to do some more miraculous deeds. In order to accept that He was the Son of God, they needed ample proof. They wanted visual evidence additional to Cana's miracle. So this man coming to Jesus was a kind of quasi test—to see if Jesus would be able to do other marvelous things. Jesus read through him and acted accordingly with the retort cited, "Except you see a sign and a wonder you are not going to believe. Well, I am not on show" (author paraphrase).

The nobleman came to Jesus not as a believer, but with the simple belief that Jesus could heal his son. Jesus read his mind and saw his urgency and faith. The man believed that he stood in the presence of the One who could restore and heal. Thus Jesus said to him, "Go thy way; thy son liveth" (verse 50). Holy Writ says that the man believed the words of Jesus and left and went to his house. On nearing home his servants came and told him that the child was well. When he inquired about what time the change took place, they told him, and he recognized it was the same time that Jesus made the profound utterance: "Thy son liveth" (verse 50).

The nobleman knew full well that when he confronted Jesus, he had confronted divinity, and when humanity confronts divinity, the lower must bow in obeisance to the higher. When Jesus gave the response "Thy son liveth," the father did not ask, "Are you sure, or are you not coming with me?" He just left and went home. This man had asked in faith—believing that Jesus was able, and He was.

Jesus is not here on earth literally walking with men as He did more than 2,000 years ago, but He has sent His Surrogate, the Comforter, the Holy Spirit, which can be at every place attending to everyone's needs simultaneously. Therefore, it is imperative that we earthlings cultivate and nurture a believing, action-oriented, and living faith in Jesus, who alone has the answer to our every need.

May we trust in faith and believe in Jesus as the nobleman did so many years ago.

Day 51

> **Ye** *shall fear every man his mother, and his father, and keep my sabbaths: I am the* LORD *your God. Leviticus 19:3*

God gave two injunctions to the children of Israel: respect and revere your parents and keep His Sabbaths. They were called out from among the heathen, whose influence had seriously affected them. But now they had to follow a new lifestyle of obedience. One of the commands that God gave to Moses to hand down to them was "All ye and all of your children shall fear (meaning respect or reverence) his parents and in that demand for respect include the need to keep the Sabbath of the Lord holy" (author paraphrase). The Sabbath is a day of rest and holy convocation unto the Lord. It is the time when God has a special appointment with His people. At the end of Creation week, God blessed the Sabbath, hallowed it, and set it apart for worship (see Gen. 2:1–3).

God desires wholeness of living for His people both in the social and moral realm. God thunders from His heavenly courts, "Say unto them [the congregation], Ye shall be holy: for I the LORD your God am holy" (Lev. 19:2). Without holiness, no man can see God. Filthiness cannot stand in the presence of the Holy God. He says, "I dwell in the high and holy place, with him also that is of a contrite and humble spirit" (Isa. 57:15). Thus, they who had been released from Pharaoh's grip were enjoined to practice wholesome living and show respect and deference to their parents.

That injunction still stands because it is the only charge that has a promise attached to it–long life. This is important because parents are God's representatives on earth. They are to teach their young children the ways of the Lord. By respecting their parents, children will also respect and honor God's Sabbaths and turn away from idolatry.

Children are reminded to respect their parents and keep God's Sabbath because God is holy, just, and good. Parents have a sacred responsibility to train their children in the fear of the Lord. Sabbath observance and parental honor seem to be equated in God's eyes; they are on the same continuum. If children do not revere their parents whom they interact with, how shall they respect and fear a God whom they cannot see? A parent is the closest thing a child has to knowing God. In children's undeveloped and uninformed minds, their parents are the only God that they know. How onerous is the responsibility that lies at a parent's door!

This passage posits double obedience: first, to the earthly parent and second, to Jehovah, the heavenly parent. If everyone obeys God's statutes, then peace, harmony, love, and contentment will pervade the family environment. May we all pray that God keeps our families together so that children can come to know and respect God.

Day 52

> *As many as I love, I rebuke and chasten: be* **Zealous** *therefore, and repent.*
> *Revelation 3:19*

This is excellent counsel given to Christian churches living out the Laodicean church age. This church represents the lifestyles and behaviors of those people living in the last days just before Jesus returns. The second and third chapters of Revelation describe the seven periods of the church.

Because the Christians of today have seen it all, experienced the expansion of the Gospel truth, seen the implosion of technology and cyberspace on their lives and on society, live in an almost war-free society, own huge bank accounts, possess large debt-free homes, and have their names on the church's attendance roster, some have this grandiose feeling that these are the best of times, and they eventually foster this inflated sense of self-sufficiency; they lack nothing.

The prophet of Patmos has a different message from Jesus for all who fall into that category. They are either totally oblivious of their spiritual dearth or are misguided and suffering from spiritual misdirection. The path that the Christians are taking is really a downward spiral, and there is need for a halt. The call is for repentance.

When people feel very capable and secure, it is then that they are most vulnerable. The prophet states that these people are oblivious of their true condition. It is as if they are drugged, besotted, or blind. He counsels them to purchase the righteousness of Christ, to plead for the Holy Spirit, and to get a proper perspective as to where they are and in what condition they exist. All must listen as He points out our weaknesses. Each must be *zealous* to forsake the ways that do not lead to peace, longevity, and righteous living. He appeals to all latter day people. It is as if He was saying, "Get your act together. Turn away from evil, for I will chastise you if you continue in that downward spiral to the murky waters of extinction."

A total rejuvenation is needed–a passion for uprightness in all that we do. Each must see that he or she lacks the graces of the Spirit. Christians living under a false sense of security and righteousness need to wake up. The Holy Writ counsels, "Woe to them that are at ease in Zion" (Amos 6:1). Unless we turn around and do what is right, God, the great and just Judge, will reject us totally. He says, "I will spue thee out of my mouth" (Rev. 3:16). Let us catch the *zeal* and repent before it is too late. If not, we shall hear the pronouncement "I know you not" (Matt. 25:12).

The saving message of salvation is based on repentance and remission. John the Baptist, Peter, and the rest of the apostles called men and women everywhere to repent of their sins and seek righteousness. Let us examine ourselves and turn from our sinful habits and seek God while He may be found. It will be a fearful thing to receive God's anger and His rejection. What agony it would be if we were thrust out of His presence! We must act now before it is too late. Let none say, "I have much time" because we do not know God's timetable. It is our moral imperative to become aware of our true spiritual condition. May we always remember to be *zealous* about where we want to spend eternity.

This Is the Day the Lord Has Given

Day 53

> **Arise**, *shine; for thy light is come, and the glory of the Lord is risen upon thee.*
> *Isaiah 60:1*

This command is a call to the sleepy, slouchy, disheartened, discouraged, downtrodden, and depressed. To the hopeless, there comes the trumpet peal: there is hope, joy, gladness, and a beautiful future ahead of us. At one time enemies and ferocious warriors encompassed the Israelites, and they felt that their God had forsaken them. Needless to say, a feeling of despair, discouragement, and defeatism prevailed among them. David's question seems appropriate: "Why art thou cast down, O my soul? ... hope thou in God" (Ps. 42:5). However, Isaiah's comforting words offer real hope to Israel; it presages the coming Messiah and Deliverer.

Arise and shine for deliverance is here! Light has shone through the darkness; the living God has come through for you. His light of love, peace, and direction has arrived, and you will be set free. You are no longer a slave to your past.

Additionally, Isaiah reinforces the promise by saying, "Darkness shall cover the earth, and gross darkness the people: but ... his glory shall be seen upon thee" (Isa. 60:2). Despite their oppression the prospect of a better and more glorious day emerged. This prophetic promise was fulfilled when Jesus, the Messiah, came. And because Jesus came, the entire world, not only the Jewish domain, has received light and hope. Jesus is Savior of the world. The prophecy was that He shall save all people from their sins.

Current day Christians need to embrace this promise. Jesus is here with us in the form of the Holy Spirit. The eternal God is with us. He never leaves us; He is always available. When we summon Him, He answers, Here am I; what can I do for you? Consequently, we need not lie and wallow in self-pity and mope about our condition. We have hope and a future. Jesus made that possible. Let us arise, shake off our despair, and shout for our God has extended mercy, compassion, and loving-kindness to us. You will neither be the joke of your neighbors nor receive their derision or mockery. Instead, they will wonder in awe at your success and deliverance.

This universal assurance is for all who tend to dwell in the valley of the shadow of fear and uncertainty. Everyone has access to God through Jesus Christ. Let us extol this one fact: God is in control of all history and our lives. Whenever and wherever God's light shines, no kind of darkness exists. His light shatters the darkness of despair, confusion, sickness, and disease, etc. , because He brings light, hope, and healing. May you rejoice in this news today.

Day 54

> **Believe** *in the Lord your God, so shall ye be established;* **Believe** *his prophets, so shall ye prosper. 2 Chronicles 20:20*

This text extols God's majesty and immutability and summons belief in His word and His messengers. His words are infallible. Humanity must believe that God exists and that He is a Sustainer. Much artificiality invades our lives and makes the genuine almost indistinguishable. The short story "The Lady and the Necklace" is a case in point. The heroine badly wanted flair, so she borrowed a diamond necklace in order to look regal at the ball. Somehow, she lost it and spent a lifetime of drudgery working to pay for the loss. Upon returning the lost treasure, she learned the futility of her toil by the lender's words: "Oh, my poor Mathilde, it was only paste." The heroine did not believe in her natal beauty.

God made men and women for worship. It is the Creator to whom worship and adoration belong. If we do not worship the true God, we worship our own creations. The Old Testament scriptures teem with examples of those who denied God's existence and worshiped the Baals and Ashtoreths, lifeless objects of their own making. On their way to the Promise Land, ancient Israel had Aaron melt their jewelry in order to form a golden calf for them to worship. In their impatience and delusion, they declared, "Up, make us gods, which shall go before us; for as for this Moses ... we wot [know] not what is become of him" (Exod. 32:1). They had lost their belief in Jehovah, their Leader.

Though Israel had intermingled and intertwined themselves with the heathen nations around and lost connection with Jehovah, God still guarded His chosen people zealously. The Holy Spirit empowered the prophet, Jehaziel, to promise them a great deliverance: "Thus saith the Lord unto you, Be not afraid ... of this great multitude; for the battle is not yours, but God's" (2 Chron. 20:15). Later as they prepared for combat, Jehosaphat called their attention to their mission and uttered this injunction: "Believe in the Lord your God." They were to go fearlessly to war for their God would fight for them. They only had to believe in the Lord God, who was and had been their Deliverer. The people acquiesced and directed by the king went out singing the victory song: "Praise the Lord; for his mercy endureth for ever" (verse 21).

No man can be established in any venture he attempts unless God leads the way. The psalmist says it very eruditely: "Except the Lord build the house, they labour in vain that build it" (Ps. 127:1). Only when we are totally established in the Lord can we have success. The call is to *believe* in God alone and His messengers' messages; God speaks through them to us. May we take God at His Word, for He is all truth.

Day 55

*Why art thou **Cast** down, O my soul? and why art thou disquieted in me? hope thou in God: for I shall yet praise him for the help of his countenance. Psalm 42:5*

At this juncture, King David is despaired, isolated, and lonely. He faces the enemy's onslaughts from all quarters. All he sees is darkness; there is none to help. Thus, he is severely depressed. He may have even reached the end of his tether and is already throwing a pity party. The case of Job surfaces; he had every reason to be cast down because friends and family rejected and chastened him for his evil deeds and his pretensions to godliness. When he searched his mind, he could not find any deficits even though his dear wife told him to give up and that he is better off dying–"Curse God, and die," she said (Job 2:9). What advice from the wife of his bosom! She had lost faith in God's ability to help, but Job replied, "What? shall we receive good at the hand of God, and shall we not receive evil?" (Job 2:10). With his condition and the negative influences around him, Job should have been cast down.

To many a struggling soul like Job, when tragedies come, God seems far away. There is neither help from friend, family, nor foe. The individual soul is depressed and expresses an intense longing for companionship–physical and spiritual. What ensues is an outburst of depressive harangues. David seemed to have reached his limit; he was in complete turmoil. For a moment, he forgot that God can send help and relief; he was completely *cast* down.

Eventually, he got a respite and engages in a self-dialogue. When questioning his behavior, he posed several questions: *Why are you so disquieted in me? What is the problem? What is the loss? What is the reason for such tremor and shaking?* David searched deep down but could not find an answer. Then in the silence, the Holy Spirit whispered to him and brought calm assurance: "Hope thou in God: for I shall yet praise him for the help of his countenance" (Ps. 42:5). This parallels the still small voice that spoke to Elijah in the cave.

David's struggle is every Christian struggling with life's challenges: health, security, shelter, and companionship. The Word assures that God is going to intervene, calm the troubled nerves, revive the withered soul, and reinvigorate the shy, timid, weary, and forlorn soul, so He can arise and shine within us.

God is ready and waiting to aid His children; therefore, humanity need not despair. The soul that leans on Jesus for repose will never go without assistance. God is always there overtly keeping watch over His own. When depressive thoughts present themselves on the horizon of your life, turn to the Word and find comfort and strength there. Do not sweat the small stuff; our God is a huge, magnificent God, and He is always in control. Do not be cast down; *cast* all your cares upon Him for He cares for you.

Day 56

*And if thou **Draw** out thy soul to the hungry, and satisfy the afflicted soul; then shall thy light rise in obscurity, and thy darkness be as the noon day. Isaiah 58:10*

This is a conditional message based on reciprocity. It addresses the social context of reaching out to society's marginalized—the dispossessed, disenfranchised, poor, orphans, widows, and the homeless. Those who have a better life situation must *draw* out their possessions to the oppressed so they will be relieved. The Bible promises that if they do this, they will be physically and spiritually rewarded.

When Jesus lived among men, His mission was to the marginalized of earth. He declared that He came to extend Himself to those sitting in the prison houses of darkness, poverty, ignorance, and superstition (see Luke 4:16–19). To those bound by physical, economic, moral, and demonic forces, He brought freedom and liberty. This deliverance message extends to all bound by the shackles of sin and selfishness. The rich young ruler who came to Jesus seeking eternal life was unwilling to draw out his soul to satisfy the needs of the hungry, the widows, and the orphans. He wanted eternal life on his terms, but he remained in darkness and left Jesus' presence sorrowful.

This counsel is very potent. It speaks to all classes but especially to the more richly endowed, who must extend, reach out, embrace, and attend to the needs of the oppressed. When that is completed, the donor will be richly rewarded: the good deeds will cancel out the bad, and everyone will know because the donor will prosper. Their kind actions will shine as brightly as the noonday sun. There will be no darkness or obscurity in their pathway for the Lord will be their Guide. By attending to the needs of the poor, the donor will be blessed and will therefore radiate the purity and goodness of God the Creator. Hopefully, other wealthy people will emulate the donor's action.

The text warns against selfishness, covetousness, and greed. It purports lovingkindness, compassion, mercy, and tenderness. This is a model in community ethics, and those who continually draw out to others will in due time draw in so much that their physical, emotional, and economic nets will be full. God will richly repay their unselfishness with contentment, joy, good health, safety, patience, and an effulgence of good and essential things. Above all, they will be securing a place by the Savior's side after manifesting His character in all that they did. May we continually *draw* out to the needy.

Day 57

He that hath a bountiful **Eye** *shall be blessed; for he giveth of his bread to the poor.*
Proverbs 22:9

This text extends the previous day's premise, which addressed kindness to the needy and the benefits received for selfless acts. Anyone who overreaches himself or herself and gives an outstretched hand to the needy will be abundantly blessed. People must not become so consumed with their own needs and wants to the point of being oblivious to the needs of others. Jesus stated that the needy will always be with us; therefore, we must be on the continual lookout—using His *eyes*—to see how best we can use what God has given us to draw out to the needy.

The eye, as the light of the body, identifies and directs an individual's path. A bountiful eye is one that is filled with goodness, generosity, and kindness. The eye is also symbolic of the heart. If you see a need and the heart—mind—is touched, it reacts in a positive way. This kind of heart, mind, and eye connection is constantly looking out to see the neediest and to satisfy that lack. It is a mind-set of blessedness—a passion to reach out to the least of these. This bountiful eye principle guards against selfishness and promotes selflessness.

The text also implies the need for everyone to cultivate an open eye principle toward members in our society. Each of us has, at one point in time, had a tight-fisted, selfish grasp in which we try to hoard things for ourselves and our family. However, the more generous care about the widows, the homeless, the battered, and the abused. With bountiful and compassionate eyes, they seek to satisfy the needs of the dispossessed. We should all aim to maintain these generous eyes.

Such people also have bountiful eyes. They know where to find bread and direct the seekers to the storehouse. God pronounces abundant blessing on those helpers. After all, the needy help form society's beautiful fabric. God's eyes are on all of us: the "haves" and "the have-nots" as well as the seekers of fodder for the needy. Generosity, not selfishness and hoarding, is how Jesus lived His life, and it is suggested we do the same. . .

May each of us receive the blessing because we choose to make the needs of others a priority. If we shoot for the blessing, it will come down in copious showers. Let us all pray for that special anointing *eye* salve so that we may really see the needs of others.

Day 58

For *God so loved the world, that he gave his only begotten Son, that whosoever believeth in him should not perish, but have everlasting life. John 3:16*

This text forms the bedrock of Christianity. It is the most studied, rehearsed, memorized, and repeated text in all Scripture. It begins with a simple conjunction or a conjunctive adverb—for—which translates into "because" or "since" God so loved ... that He gave. And so the reason is very clear from the start—because God loves so much, He gave. Love is the all-encompassing factor that rules the secular, emotional, moral, social, and ethical world.

Satan led Adam and Eve into deception about God's love for them and was able to gain control of their wills. By deceiving them, he also made a travesty of humanity's psyche, their will, and their ability to perform with any soundness. After this occurred, humanity was doomed to die and should have died. God could have easily recreated new holy beings. However, the Great Creator had other plans.

In the Council of Peace, the Father, Son, and the Holy Spirit consulted on how to treat the sin factor. Jesus, the second person of the Trinity, offered His life as a way to intervene saying, "Father, I will go and be man's substitute; I will leave Your company, the holy courts of heaven, the presence of all the holy angels, and I will yield myself for their sake." Jesus offered Himself to be the supreme sacrifice, but it took more than 4,000 years for this promise to be fulfilled.

Jesus chose to be born among humans and live as they lived—just without partaking of any of their sinful practices. He was able to reveal God's love and His plan for all humanity. He restored the broken breach that sin had caused. God listened to his Son and accepted His preparatory sacrifice. This separation from His Son caused the Father great pain and anguish, but He sanctioned the plan. What love! Love beyond compare—love unequaled.

Jesus' unselfishness and intense love for the human race made Him abandon His divinity. He came, lived, and died so that He could redeem and reconnect man to his Father. With painful sorrow God parted with His Beloved Son, but Jesus assured his Father that His creation would be harmoniously reconnected with Him soon. Once Jesus was sent from God to the world, every man, woman, and child now has access to the opportunity of the saving grace offered by God's gift—yea, even eternal life. Because God loved, He gave His only Son to save you. What is your response to the supreme Giver and His ultimate Gift? I have accepted the Gift. May you also accept God's Gift—Jesus—today.

Day 59

*A **Good** name is rather to be chosen than great riches, and loving favour rather than silver and gold. Proverbs 22:1*

What is in a name? Your name is your identification. When a baby is conceived, even before its birth, a name or a number of names are chosen for the infant. I read a long time ago that a person's name is the most important bit of data he or she possesses. One should always attempt to remember someone's name, even if it is only an acquaintance.

If we forget a person's name, it shows an uncaring, unfriendly attitude and that neither the person nor their name has value. Some names evoke strong and beautiful memories: ecstasy, joy, grandeur, intellectual greatness, sophistication, reverence, awe, success, strength, sagacity, boldness. Others evoke fear, dread, trembling, pain, shame, and death. Consider the names of some Bible greats: God, Jesus, Elijah, Moses, Samuel, David, Solomon, Jonah, Ahab, Jehu, Job, Paul, and Peter. Think of literary names: Shakespeare, Donne, Frost, Bunyan, Plato, Socrates, and Aristotle. Now, think of those evil doers: Hitler, Edi Amin, Sadaam Hussein, and Benito Mussolini. A name emits all kinds of emotions. The text says a *good* name transcends all earthly acquisitions. Is your name good?

Let us see what some names evoke. Holy Writ says, "That unto me every knee shall bow, every tongue shall swear" (Isa. 45:23). Of Jesus, it was said that His name shall be called Jesus because "he shall save his people from their sins" (Matt. 1:21). The name of God evokes awe and reverence because He is good. He is our Shepherd and the Lord of lords. He is our refuge, strong tower, Healer and Prince of Peace. Aren't those good names? No wonder that "at the name of Jesus every knee should bow?" (Phil. 2:10). Jesus is God, and He declared, "I and my Father are one" (John 10:30). When Jesus came down to live and die for humanity, God also came down. What goodness! What love! What a God!

David's name evokes two conflicting ideas. The first is wickedness, which concerns his adultery, murder, and wars, and the second is holiness, which revolves around his prayers, contriteness, repentance, and reconnection with God. God referred to him as a "man after mine own heart" (Acts 13:22). When Solomon's name is called, you probably think of a sage, supreme wisdom, proverbs, humility, and wealth. At Paul's name, you think of a persecutor, missionary, evangelist. Stephen makes you recall martyrdom. Joshua's name brings up strength, courage, and successful leadership. The list could go on for quite a while. Names are truly impactful—they *mean* something. Is your name good?

When your name is called, what is triggered? Maybe people think of excitement, joy, holiness, a praying saint, a truth seeker, a holy person, a youth leader, or a contentious member, shame, and revulsion. Do what you can to let people think good of you and not ill. May your name always reflect uprightness, dignity, and the beauty of Jesus.

Day 60

> **Ho**, *every one that thirsteth, come ye to the waters, and he that hath no money; come ye, buy and eat; yea, come, buy wine and milk without money and without price. Isaiah 55:1*

This text posits a universal call; it is offering free mercy to all. Listen to the prophet's message. He invites everyone who needs a drink to quench their slaking throat to come; it is free. You can come without money. You don't need credit cards. You will not find any strings attached or tricky fine prints.

This gift of water is the free gift of grace akin to what Jesus provided and offered the Samaritan woman. It is for all, and when it is received and drunk, it will continually nourish and slake one's thirst for the gaudy and transient things of life. The prophet sent out a message to those who felt a need for continuous, nurturing, refreshing life-giving, and life-sustaining water. Those who are spiritually malnourished can have access to salvation and do not have to pay penance to be acceptable in God's sight. God's mercy, grace, and lovingkindness are all free. The seeker only needs to recognize their need. Then all they have to do is reach out and access it. The invitation is to seek the Lord and call upon Him. Thankfully, this step is easy; it only takes a prayer.

This call, though given some 600 years ago to Israel–long before Jesus' time–has great relevance for us living in this century and facing mighty social, emotional, intellectual, spiritual, and political challenges. All peoples of the earth–Jews, Gentiles, Muslims, Christians, and the unreligious–are spiritually thirsty and are searching for something a little better. They all want truth, beauty, and a life free of anxiety, doubt, and sin, but these things are only found in the water offered with the free gift of salvation.

Everyone is thirsty, but have you thought about what are you thirsty for? Is it for success in business, education, commerce, technology, or social relations? Whatever is the nature of the thirst, Jesus can quench it. God provides for all humanity freely and bountifully; there is no shortage in His storehouse. More assuredly, if you are seeking spiritual rejuvenation, just reach out and freely grasp the cup of salvation. The woman grasped it at Jesus' hand and said, "Sir, give me this water, that I thirst not, neither come hither to draw" (John 4:15). All her desires were quenched: spiritual, psychological, emotional, sexual, moral, mental, and physical were now under the control of the Master. She left His presence a changed woman–a missionary who invited her entire village with the message, "Come, see ... the Christ" (verse 29).

The flag of freedom in Christ is redemption through His blood. All who want that freedom must accept the free drink whose infusion changes life's direction. Come, all who lack or feel need; it is free for you. Once we taste the living water Jesus offers us, we shall never thirst again; all our needs will be satisfied. Won't you take a drink now?

Day 61

> **If** *my people, which are called by my name, shall humble themselves, and pray, and seek my face, and turn from their wicked ways; then will I hear from heaven, and will forgive their sin, and will heal their land. 2 Chronicles 7:14*

This is a conditional proposition that the Lord presented to King Solomon in a challenging covenant to his people, who had to meet certain requirements in order for God to answer their requests. They were plagued with all kinds of challenges and had called upon God for deliverance and healing; thus God retorted with His condition. They first had to do as He said before He would give them anything.

Ever since Adam and Eve's transgression, humanity has been doing what pleases them best. We continuously engage in all kinds of debaucheries and tout flagrant disrespect for God's laws and statutes. We are unwilling to change, yet we want all the good things from God. Our affliction is the problem of disobedience, selfishness, and self-service. We are exposed to every kind of sickness and disease that plagues humankind, but we are stubborn. We should know full well that God alone has the solution, yet we continue on this downward path. God will help *if*....

There is no unconditional solution to our problems. The recipients of God's favor must do their part. God has already done His; He has emptied Himself of the only precious thing He had—His Son—and He will not accept coercion or forced obedience. We must act our rightful role in this regenerative process. "If my people, which are called by my name" ... what is the name by which you are called? Child of God, sons and daughters of God, Christian? Whatever you are called, God's children must be humble, pray often, and seek Him; that is our responsibility. We must act because God is waiting for us to become engaged. When we do our part, God will do what He has promised: hear, forgive, and heal.

If you are known by God's name, then do what a son or daughter of God would do: represent your Father well and do not bring shame or reproach on His name. Since we know what the consequences are, we must obey.

God is willing and waiting to give His children restorative health and forgiveness for every errant act. He wants to listen to all of our sincere confessions and petitions, but we must act NOW. We remain the only hindrances and obstacles to our own regeneration, freedom, and salvation. God has spelt out His condition in clear tones; He will not act until we do our part. This is righteous reciprocity, and God knows no partiality.

There is no free lunch even in God's dining room. *If* the children obey the Parent (God), they will receive the promised blessings: longevity, total healing, and oneness with the Father. May all the children come to fulfill their obligation.

Day 62

Therefore, being **Justified** *by faith, we have peace with God through our Lord Jesus Christ.*
Romans 5:1

This is a very comforting and assuring thought to the new believer who has chosen the name Christian. When a sinner comes to Christ and accepts Jesus' full pardon, he or she is made *just* for his or her sins and obfuscations are cancelled out. The sinner is given another chance and a new beginning. It is as though he or she is newly born with no imperfections. Jesus' blood justifies all of us and makes us clean.

This regenerative act is what Jesus does for everyone who willingly yields himself or herself to Him. Jesus gives us the best treatment. He erases our sins, gives us a fresh start, and renders us justified. The new believer must accept this by faith alone. We must believe that Jesus alone has the power to change and transform our lives. That is the greatest gift that anyone can receive at the hands of a righteous God. When Jesus renders you justified, peace settles in the mind, and you are free.

We cannot take our spiritual condition and change for granted; the sinner must do something if there is to be any difference. We must believe and have faith that God is able to empower us to live above sin. Once we accept that proffered gift, then through Christ, we are both justified and sanctified; we are on the way to living a sin-free life.

Recently, we studied that "the just shall live by faith" (Rom. 1:17). Those are the righteous ones who practice right living and do so by the power and the belief that Jesus is able to keep them from backsliding to old habits and behaviors. To do so, they must exercise the belief that God's power alone can keep them steadfast in the faith. They have to believe in the efficacy of the blood and its power to save. It is by believing that we are changed, become transformed, and evolve into new creatures.

Being justified is God's doing, not ours. When God justifies us, the sinner and God are in sync. There is no longer any enmity between us and God because the blood cleanses and reconciles. There is, instead, unanimity between us and God. Consequently, we now have free and direct access to God through Jesus functioning as our Advocate.

Undoubtedly, this is a peaceful and uninhibited experience. Gone are priestly interventions; the path to God is open and free, and the sinner stands before God–*justified*–as though he or she never sinned. Jesus freed us. Praise God! Everyone can live in peace because we are *justified*.

Day 63

> *For I know him, that he will command his children and his household after him, and they shall* **Keep** *the way of the Lord, to do justice and judgment ... that which he hath spoken of him. Genesis 18:19*

"They shall keep the way of the Lord" is an assertion of hope and a future reference to the justified ones–the children of the King. Being justified by faith in Jesus Christ, they shall *keep* the way of the Lord and render Him obeisance. The Lord's way is one of peace, joy, obedience, worship, and witnessing.

Humanity has not always been obedient to God (see Mic. 6:8). Through self-will and the power of choice, we can do what we want and not what God desires or approves. Nevertheless, God is staking out a bet on some of His children that He can rely on and who will walk in the "way of the Lord." That means you and me. God has chosen us before we were in the womb just like He chose John the Baptist, Jeremiah, David, or Samuel. You are not here by accident; God chose you, and He knows that you will do all you can to keep, observe, and preserve the Lord's way. His doings will be taught and talked about throughout your generations and your children's generation; it shall continue perpetually as long as He lives.

God has taken a gamble on you; you cannot defer, and you cannot let Him down. This keeping must be a perpetual process, as long as humankind exists and we choose to fear and honor Jehovah God.

God knows His dependable ones, and He is counting on them to keep that which He has committed until that day. God cited His relationship with Abraham–the Father of the faithful. God could depend on Abraham to establish the principles of the High Priest in his household. We are spiritual sons and daughters of Abraham. Can God say that He knows where you live, what you do to maintain healthy relationships, and that you will encourage others to keep the way of the Lord?

God has committed the keeping of those who confess His name to Jesus, our Elder Brother. If you will say "Yes, Father, You can count on me," then join with David in saying, "I will meditate in thy precepts, and have respect unto thy ways. I will delight myself in thy statutes: I will not forget thy word" (Ps. 119:15, 16).

Dear reader, I have pledged to keep God's laws and His statutes. What about you? May we together say: "I will not forget thy statutes; You can count on me."

Day 64

> *Peace I* **Leave** *with you, my peace I give unto you: not as the world giveth, give I unto you. Let not your heart be troubled, neither let it be afraid. John 14:27*

Jesus' disciples were befuddled about their welfare and manageability after He returned to His Father. They were troubled about the social, economic, political, and military might of the Roman powers and how it would impact their mission. Jesus perceived their concerns and in His loving, caring, and consoling way sought to quiet their anxious hearts.

Like Martha, Mary and Lazarus' sister, these newly commissioned disciples were troubled about many things: who was going to restore the earthly kingdom? Who was going to stand up against the various warring sects of Pharisees, Sadducees, and opposers of truth? Would they be able to go out and speak with authority when there was no leader? How would they survive? Many of these unsettling themes were present in their thoughts, so Jesus gave the assurance cited above.

What does it mean to have the peace of Jesus? Calm assurance, control, security, fearlessness, and even a holy boldness ensue when the peace of God fills your very soul. The Master is in control of everything. He assures us not to worry, doubt, or fear anything, anyone, or any situation, for His peace is always with us.

When Jesus gives you something, it is yours to keep. When He leaves you a gift, it is yours permanently. It cannot be shared with any other person, for it is solely yours. The question is, have you experienced or are you experiencing the peace that Jesus left you?

We are His disciples. Though the first ones walked, talked, and lived with Him for just over three years and bore testimony of all that He did, we, His second set of disciples, are walking with Him by faith for seventy, fifty, forty or fewer years. But do we feel the peace that Jesus left with the first disciples when He ascended to heaven? Like His first, we also have the assurance that He will be with us until the end of our walk with Him or to the end of the age.

We have nothing to fear for the present or the future, for Jesus always delivers what He promises. His words are verity and truth, not one fails. If your life is full of stress and anxiety, allow the Holy Spirit to fill you with Christ's peace; it has the property to guard your heart and mind in Christ Jesus. Jesus left us His peace, which is still with us today. Let us harness it and move fearlessly into the future with the full understanding that Jesus' *peace* transcends all human knowledge. May it keep you calm.

Day 65

> **My** *son, hear the instruction of thy father, and forsake not the law of thy mother.*
> *Proverbs 1:8*

Although the text addresses the son, it does not negate the importance of the daughter. The counsel is implicitly addressed to children and shows the importance of both parents' role in training and molding their children's lives. When the stories were told, most of the language used posited a patriarchal point of reference, so it makes sense that the addressee is the son.

King Solomon's counsel to children and youth shows the importance of their heeding parental instruction. The home is the first school for introducing the child to knowledge, thus making it a parental responsibility. This task was primarily that of the mother whose first duty and charge was committed the nurture and training of the child; however, both parents were to be congruent with the God-given instructions. Nurturing and training begins in the womb. During those gestational months, it is mother that must teach the fetus all that is morally good, pure, and upright. It is what she infuses in the baby's mind that shapes the child's character and future.

Numerous studies tell of the impact of pre-natal musings and influences on the unborn fetus. The Chinese and many other cultures use music to stimulate the fetus, and often times, the child comes out with a sharp desire for music and gravitates to that discipline as he or she matures. Many people marvel at the adeptness and adroitness of some children's accomplishment and many ask: how did they learn so much at such a young age? It is the pre-natal exposure. To the mother more than the father is the colossal challenge given to make that child become all that he or she can become.

King Solomon knew a lot about child rearing. In fact, his very first test as a young king had to do with family life; he quickly understood the throes of motherhood and nurturing and was able to make a very wise decision that connected a mother back with her baby. He also knew that training children and bringing them up to maturity and accountability was tricky business (see Prov. 22:6). The youth did not always want to listen to the advice given to them from older folks. Many thought their ideas were outdated and would rather listen to their peers.

The young are usually headstrong, so wise King Solomon wrote copious amounts of warnings to them about heeding their parents' counsel and wisdom. He told the children that they needed to listen to their mother and father because they had lived and had gained many experiences. Their parents would know what is best. Fathers can also counsel daughters as well as mothers to sons.

There is none like a father who can counsel his daughters about the wiles and subtleties of men. Mother always knows best and is capable of counseling and instructing both sexes. Therefore, children should heed the counsel of godly parents whose experiences can guide them as they navigate life's dangerous shoals. The king's advice is potent. May they adhere to it.

Day 66

His compassions fail not. They are **New** *every morning: great is thy faithfulness.*
Lamentations 3:22, 23

As I read this text, I am brought back to my elementary school days when we sang the lyrics of a song called "New Every Morning is the Love" by John Keble for daily morning worship.

New every morning is thy love,
Our waking and uprising prove;
Through sleep and darkness safely brought,
Restored to life and power and thought.
New mercies each returning day
Hover around us while we pray;
New perils passed new sins forgiven,
New thoughts of God; new hopes of heaven.

Those were the "good ol' days" when God was a regular part of a child's education; now, He is un-sacrosanct.

In a world of endless changes, it is hard to find the one Constant. God is the only constant factor we have in the universe; He does not change. There is no *new* God each morning when we awake. Remember He declares, "I AM THAT I AM" (Exod. 3:14). God is always in the present tense. Every sunrise brings a new day. It is a fresh start—a new challenge for us mortals, but not for God. He declares, "For I am the Lord, I change not" (Mal. 3:6). He is the unchanging God, yet He brings us new graces every day as well as new opportunities to get right with Him.

Isaiah said they shall stand and ask for the old paths because the new lead to places that do not foster spiritual growth. In his lamentations, Jeremiah assures us of God's *new* and fresh graces every morning, and His unfailing mercies. This magnificent God, whose faithfulness is great, wants us to know that we have a never-failing Father who cares and watches over us every *new* day. His compassion, mercy, and loving-kindness are bestowed and are available every day. In the mornings when we open our eyes to greet the day, we are recipients of God's fresh grace.

With each awakening, we face new challenges, new graces, new assurances, and new promises. With the Father's great love, we remain strong and bold, for we know who holds the future, and we know who holds our hands. He is compassionate and demonstrates those qualities every new day. Surely, we can vouch that every morning is a new bouquet of love. May we embrace it. A couple of lines from "Great Is Thy Faithfulness" from *The Seventh-day Adventist Hymnal* celebrates the newness: "Great is thy faithfulness, Lord God Almighty ... All I have needed, thy hands have provided; Great is thy faithfulness day unto day." Every *new* day brings surprises, blessings, challenges. and opportunities. May you be blessed.

Day 67

> **O** *Lord my God, in thee do I put my trust: save me from all them that persecute me, and deliver me. Psalm 7:1*

David's prayer for deliverance from one of Saul's radical kinsmen exudes confidence, trust, and hope. Being constantly beset by enemies, his life was imperiled. Consequently, a significant number of his forty-one psalms are prayers for deliverance. They evoke certitude in God's ability to hear and His power to deliver.

David has a desperate plea—O, please hear me! David feels that God is far away from him, so he summons Him to come near, to help and deliver him. He is fearful while he is being persecuted because he remembers that he has not always lived uprightly, so there seems to be a twinge of guilt even as he prays. However, he knows that God in His lovingkindness will not forsake him. God will listen to his cry and respond. To David, this utterance feels as if it is the last call, the last hope. In his desperation, he assures God that he trusts Him and knows that the Lord will come to his aid. The prayer affirms God's power and acknowledges that timing is in God's hands.

The prayer is not a license to go about living our lives recklessly so that when trouble comes, we fall at the Savior's feet for help. Rather, we should take counsel of the Word of God, and if we are persecuted for righteousness' sake, He will save and deliver us.

Our God is ready to help, deliver, and save. He is only a prayer away. He assures His children: "And call upon me in the day of trouble: I will deliver thee" (Ps. 50:15).

As a prayer for deliverance, David is assured that God will vindicate him, and his pursuers will fall in the same pit they have dug for him (see Ps. 7:15). In praise for the answered prayer, he declares: "I will praise the Lord according to his righteousness: and will sing praise to the name of the Lord most high" (verse 17). Consequently, he could finally lie down and sleep, for the Lord had both answered his prayer and sustained him.

Day 68

> **Praise** *waiteth for thee, O God, in Sion: and unto thee shall the vow be performed. Psalm 65:1*

This is a glorious approbation attributed to God as man comes to offer praise and thanksgiving for all the bounties God has bestowed through nature to His errant children. All humanity should offer praise, for it is because of God's lovingkindness, tender mercies, long suffering, and patience that we are still alive.

Our sins continually stock up before Him, and it is Jesus, our Paschal Lamb, who continually intercedes on our behalf and is the reason why we are not obliterated. Thus, people everywhere and at all times ought to give thanks and praise to God, the Father as well as to His Son, Jesus, for their willingness and commitment to bear with us and our many infractions and misdemeanors.

God is everything to all flesh: humans, birds, and beasts; even nature rejoices in His presence. The psalmist says, "Let the floods clap their hands: let the hills be joyful together" (Ps. 98:8). He provides rain to water our land and refresh the grass of the fields; He hears our prayers, petitions, and entreaties, and He answers them; He mends the broken hearted, heals our diseases, forgives our sins, and wipes out all our infractions. He guides our feet in the right path so we do not misstep or misspeak. He intervenes in the history of nations so that His will is done. God is in charge; He is the Captain of the ship, and He ensures that every member of His crew is well-served.

Additionally, all the creatures of His creation are well provided for: birds, fish, and reptiles are all fed and well-nourished. Every morning He greets us with a new breath of fresh air. Every night He watches over us like the mother bird over her nestling brood. There is no other God; He is the only God. He is, indeed, the magnificent, magnanimous God, and all praise and honor belong to Him. Isaiah said, "I am the Lord, and there is none else" (Isa. 45:6).

Let us join with the psalmist and offer our praise. "Let every thing that hath breath praise the Lord" (Ps. 150:6). He is good and His mercies are revealed and extended to His entire creation. Let men and women everywhere praise the Lord. Praise ye the Lord! If you have something to shout about, lift up your voices and offer praise all the time. Here are King David's utterances: "I will praise thee with my whole heart" (Ps. 138:1); "O give thanks unto the Lord; for he is good: for his mercy endureth for ever" (Ps. 136:1); "O praise the Lord, all ye nations: praise him, all ye people. For his merciful kindness is great toward us: and the truth of the Lord endureth for ever. Praise ye the Lord" (Ps. 117:1, 2).

May everyone *praise* the Lord with every waking breath.

Day 69

What do ye imagine against the Lord? he will make an utter end: **[Iniquity]** *affliction shall not rise up the second time. Nahum 1:9*

This is one of the most forceful and poignant utterances of Jehovah. Speaking to the prophet, Nahum, regarding the destruction of Nineveh, this verse has implications for the end of the age–the end of humanity's existence. The destruction of the city was referenced directly, and Nahum's predictions came to pass for the wicked city was destroyed in 612 BC and was never rebuilt. It remains a desolate ruin even today.

Nineveh's iniquity epitomizes the conditions of this current age. When God acts this time, it will not be as it was with Sodom and Gomorrah or with the antediluvians of Noah's day; none will be spared except the righteous. God says emphatically and most assuredly, "Affliction shall not rise up the second time." Sin will not rear its ugly head again. Can you imagine an environment where there will be no one to tempt, annoy, cajole, lure, encourage, or entice to do wrong? There will be no sinful desires. There will be no more tears; we will be a new, sin-free creation (see Rev. 21:4; Isa. 35:65, 66).

Imagine what it will be like to live in a sin-free, unpolluted, untainted atmosphere! Gone are pollution, miasma, filth, corruption, and distortions. When writing to the Corinthian people, the apostle Paul told them that when all things are made new, they shall see Jesus face-to-face. Jesus Himself will be there, and no darkness will exist because He is all Light (see 1 Cor. 13:12). Think about this with your spiritual eyesight of faith and holiness!

I invite you to meditate on a world without infractions, a world with God, Jesus, and the holy angels. May our prayer be: "Come Lord Jesus, come quickly; quicken me with thy Spirit that I may live a holy life before You. Come quickly and restore to us the lost kingdom. Please give us freedom from sin." There will be no more pain, death, funeral corteges, surgeries, amputations, kidnappings, and loss of vitality and stamina. Everything will be new.

With the old order having passed away, there will be peace and harmony throughout the entire universe (see Isa. 65:25). *Iniquity* in all its variant forms will never more be seen in this vast creation. We shall then bask in heavenly beauty and purity of God's eternal atmosphere where there will be nothing but immeasurable peace, holiness, and joy. Won't you plan to be there?

Day 70

> *Then Peter said unto them, "***Repent***, and be baptized every one of you in the name of Jesus Christ for the remission of sins, and ye shall receive the gift of the Holy Ghost."*
> Acts 2:38

Peter's altar call has a threefold urgency: repent, receive remission of your sins, and receive the gift of the Holy Ghost. This is the call from Peter, the impulsive, insightful, and most discerning disciple. He was the rejecter of Christ, who at the watch denied knowing Him; he is the one whom Jesus prayed for and the angel sent a direct message to after His resurrection, "Tell his disciples and Peter …" (Mark 16:7). This is the same Peter who said after the crucifixion, "I go a fishing" (John 21:3). This same Peter—now converted, commissioned, and empowered—is speaking with such power and authority based on the Word of God. He speaks with a holy boldness.

The converted Peter, now unashamed of the cross of the risen Savior, stood before the motley crowd and spoke in thunderous tones calling men and women to repentance. Is it any wonder that Jesus gave him the commission to feed His lambs and sheep (see John 21:15–17)?

Jesus knew Peter's heart. He knew his weakness and his strengths and that he could count on Peter to take charge of the mission he had assigned the eleven. Peter was the most impulsive, intuitive, and aggressive member of the group. It was he who made most of the declarations about Jesus and was quick-witted and insightful to answer many of Jesus' challenging questions. "Whom do men say that I the Son of man am?" (Matt. 16:13). The disciples gave different answers. Then Jesus asked them directly: "But whom say ye that I am?" (verse 15). It was Peter who confessed, "Thou art the Christ, the Son of the living God" (verse 16). It was Peter who accepted the challenge to go to Jesus on the water. "Lord, if it be thou, bid me come unto thee on the water?" (Matt. 14:28). Jesus saw Peter's heart and knew what kind of ambassador he would become. Jesus assayed Peter saying, "I have prayed for thee, that thy faith fail not." (Luke 22:32). When the Holy Spirit took control of Peter, he became a transformed man. As a converted disciple, he was fulfilling Jesus' wish and prayer for him—"When thou art converted, strengthen thy brethren" (Ibid.).

When the Holy Spirit takes control of those human traits and transforms them, we can only bow in obeisance to the great I AM. Peter, thus emboldened by the Holy Spirit, preached about Christ to the entire assembly. At the quickening of the Holy Spirit on their hearts, many in the crowd were convinced and asked, "Men and brethren, what shall we do?" (Acts 2:37). To this inquiry, Peter responded that first they needed to repent. Then they needed to turn and forsake their wrongdoings, seek God's forgiveness, and be prepared to receive the Holy Spirit. He told them these steps were important because once they were followed, their sins would be blotted out and they would be justified in God's sight and would be ready to receive the anointing of the Holy Spirit.

Peter's message is the universal message of repentance and remission; it is the only one to be preached. It is calling men to forsake their evil, selfish, headstrong, and stubborn ways and respond to the voice of the Holy Spirit urging them to give their heart to Jesus. This universal altar call will not cease until all humankind have heard and either accepted or rejected it. The door remains ajar while Jesus is in heaven interceding on our behalf. May men and women accept the invitation to *repent*.

Day 71

Search *the scriptures; for in them ye think ye have eternal life: and they are they which testify of me. John 5:39*

Speaking about His validity and relationship to His Father and the Scriptures, Jesus boldly told the disciples and His hearers that if they had any doubt, they should go to the Word. Moses, David, Isaiah, and other prophets had given testimony of Him, so if they wanted the truth, they needed to intensely search the Word. The prophet Isaiah states, "For precept must be upon precept ... line upon line; here a little, and there a little" (Isa. 28:10). That is the basic guideline for studying the Scriptures. Thus, the Bible is its own interpreter and concordance.

Several Old Testament writers prophesied of the coming Messiah's birth, life, and manner of His death. Moses spoke of His coming. David in the book of Psalms spoke of the treatment at His death, and Isaiah spoke of His suffering and death. The Gospels bear witness and validate His existence.

To cite a case in particular: Jesus entered the synagogue for worship on the Sabbath day and was given the Scripture reading taken from Isaiah 61:1–"The Spirit of the Lord God is upon me." Having read it, He closed the scroll and said, "This day is this scripture fulfilled in your ears" (Luke 4:21). He was referring to the passage whose citation pointed to Him, the Savior. They just looked at Him in astonishment and disbelief and retorted, "Is not this Joseph's son?" (verse 22).

The clarion call is to us, our children, and to all God-fearing people who want to know more about this Jesus, the Redeemer, Intercessor, and soon-to-return Savior. With so much misinformation about Jesus, God, and religion, one can only have clarity, wisdom, and true knowledge if he or she turns to the Word. Jesus' advice is very potent and urgent. Each person must seek and find the truth for himself or herself. We cannot depend on what others say or interpret; we must go to the Word directly and search its truths for ourselves. Thank God, the Book is available for all to read.

Search the Scriptures diligently, for in them are the eternal words that attest to the Sonship and Lordship of Jesus Christ. In response to this challenge, the prophet Jeremiah wrote, "Thy words were found, and I did eat them ... I am called by thy name, O Lord God of hosts" (Jer. 15:16). The apostle John said, "Thy word is truth" (John 17:17).

God's Word can withstand any test. May you *search* it yourself. Thank God, we have free access to the Word.

Day 72

> **Train** *up a child in the way he should go: and when he is old, he will not depart from it.*
> *Proverbs 22:6*

This is a clear and vivid injunction given to all parents, educators, and child caregivers.

Child training is the most important task given to parents. Children are vulnerable and need training from the womb. When Pharaoh's daughter found Moses on the bank of the river, his sister asked the princess if she needed a nurse for the infant, and upon the affirmative answer, she went and got the babe's mother, Jochebed. When the nurse-mother arrived, the princess gave her the baby saying, "Take this child away, and nurse [train] it for me, and I will give thee thy wages" (Exod. 2:9). Thus Jochebed reared and trained Moses. She got the opportunity to teach him the fundamentals of the Hebrew law and God's requirements for His chosen people. He was so entrenched in the Hebrew doctrine that when He became a grown man, He chose God, God's people, and God's ways over the glamour and glitz of the Egyptian palace. It is said that "by faith Moses, when he was come to years, refused to be called the son of Pharaoh's daughter; Choosing rather to suffer affliction with the people of God, than to enjoy the pleasures of sin for a season" (Heb. 11:24, 25). Child training pays huge dividends.

Moses' early training speaks directly to parents and demonstrates the impact of a godly Christian home influence on the upbringing of children. Parental training is to help children develop a desire for the things of God such as reverence for God and holy things, obedience, and maintain a respect for parents and the elderly. It should not be authoritarian or permissive. Child training requires a steady balance of love and discipline as well as discipleship. Parents should not engage in or present challenges that will provoke the child into rebellion, disobedience, or disrespect. The apostle Paul concurs with the wise King by giving additional parental guidelines (see Eph. 6:1–4).

"When he is old" i.e. when the child is matured, he or she will have been so rightly trained, that he or she will not depart from the principles learned. Children cannot make salient decisions, which is why God gave them parents. Parents are to observe their children's individual's strengths and weaknesses, then develop the positive and delete the negatives. They have to present them the respective options and consequences. In this process, all who come within the child's purview—parents, grandparents, and teachers—have the responsibility to train them to be selective. Thus instructed, they will know what is right, true, and beautiful, for children live what they learn. This child speaks to all:

I am the child;
You hold in your hand my destiny.
You determine largely whether I shall succeed or fail
Give me, I pray you,
Those things that make for happiness.
Train me, I beg you,
That I may be a blessing to the world. (Anonymous, "I Am A Child")
May we all engage in training the children in the Lord.

Day 73

> *Though he fall, he shall not be* **Utterly** *cast down: for the Lord upholdeth him with his hand.*
> *Psalm 37:24*

This text offers assurance to the heavy-laden, the downtrodden, and the discouraged. As I write, there is a case that causes a mother to be completely cast down. As I reflect on the Word, I find comfort therein to share with her. God orders and directs the steps of a good man or woman, for He is constantly watching over them. Even through discouraging situations, the Lord promises that the individual who trusts in Him will not utterly fall. Instead, he or she will be lifted up, for God is holding him or her with His right hand. The mother having difficulty has found solace in those words.

God knows how to raise up the fallen: in spirit, emotional, physical, social, mental, and financial. This text provides comfort: "Why art thou disquieted within me? hope thou in God: for I shall yet praise him, who is the health of my countenance, and my God" (Ps. 42:11). What a glorious answer and assurance! What joy there is to find solace and comfort from the Word! No wonder the psalmist declares, "Thy word is a lamp unto my feet, and a light unto my path" (Ps. 119:105). Also, "wait on the Lord, and keep his way, and he shall exalt thee to inherit the land: when the wicked are cut off, thou shalt see it" (Ps. 37:34). "Wait I say, on the Lord" (Ps. 27:14). Proverbs 3:5, 6 also tells us to "trust in the Lord with all thine heart; and lean not unto thine own understanding. In all thy ways acknowledge him, and he shall direct thy paths." These words offer promise, assurance, and hope in the face of any crisis. Let us embrace and internalize them, for God upholds us with His mighty arms and His words are truth.

The Lord assures the oppressed freedom and victory. God is in the midst and He will comfort, guide, and direct with His own hands and lead with His own eyes. Hope thou in God! He is our Helper in trouble; He is holding you up with His strong right hand; He is our strong Tower. God is able. He will give you the strength needed to continue on. God has the power to raise, elevate, resuscitate, resurrect, rejuvenate, and recreate. He can do all things. So if He says that He will uphold you in His righteous hand, He will do it repeatedly. Go forward and trust His amazing power. Leave all in His mighty hands. He will raise you up and hold you so you will not fall again.

May every struggling soul in *utter* despair find comfort in this beautiful psalm. Commit it to memory. You will never be left alone; God says it and He means it.

Day 74

I have seen all the works that are done under the sun; and, behold, all is **Vanity** *and* **Vexation** *of spirit. Ecclesiastes 1:14*

Solomon, the wisest, richest, and most famous of men and kings had seen and possessed everything there ever was to have. He had wealth, wisdom, honor, glory, fame, and every comfort available at that time; he lacked nothing. He obtained these because God bountifully bestowed them upon him. When God gives, He gives copiously. He promised, speaking through Malachi, that He can give so much that you will not have space to accommodate it, and the apostle Paul concurs. "Now unto him that is able to do exceeding abundantly above all that we ask or think" (Eph. 3:20). We have a God who is not tight-fisted or frugal in His offerings. When He gives, He showers and inundates.

Now as a young king, God appeared to Solomon and posed the universal question: "Ask what I shall give thee" (1 Kings 3:5). Solomon responded and asked for wisdom, knowledge, and understanding so that he could use those qualities to execute the task assigned him. God listened to his request and told him that because he did not ask for worldly acclaim, He would grant him all that he requested and more. God decided that He would add riches. And Solomon was very aptly endowed. He became and remained the wisest and wealthiest man as well as the most famous, most learned, and most quoted man under heaven.

He spent a significant portion of his life in indulging his sumptuous desires: wine, women, and hedonism. He enjoyed a royal fling. He had seen all that anyone's eyes could see. He enjoyed all that heart, mind, and body could accommodate, and he acquired and practiced all the wisdom and knowledge far beyond his ken. Later on, he reflected on the reality of life, his future included, and left these immortalized words: "Life is a fable: all this acquiring, extending, grasping, satiating amounts to ashes—there is no substance in it. All is "vexation of spirit" (Eccles. 1:17). Life is like grasping for the wind.

When the Queen of Sheba visited him, she remarked upon leaving, "It is a true report which I heard in mine own land of thine acts, and of thy wisdom: Howbeit I believed not their words, until I came, and mine eyes have seen it: and, behold, ... the fame which I heard" (2 Chron. 9:6). What she saw, heard, and experienced so bedazzled her that she returned home mesmerized, transfixed, and glorified. She had nothing but praise for the great and magnificent God of Solomon. She affirmed, "Blessed be the Lord thy God, which delighted in thee to set thee on his throne, to be king for the Lord thy God ... made he thee king over them, to do judgment and justice" (verse 8).

Jesus, referring to the effulgence and aura that surrounded Solomon, looked at the simple lily and remarked that Solomon's glory was incomparable to the beauty and simplicity residing in that simple field flower. Jesus wanted to draw our attention to the beauty and the purity that are in simplicity rather than in the gaudy and showy things of life. It is not the abundance that one possesses that creates happiness. Solomon left us an immortal lesson on moderation, temperance, and contentment. May we heed his counsel.

Day 75

> **When** *thou sittest to eat with a ruler, consider diligently what is before thee.*
> *Proverbs 23:1*

This text posits a cautionary lesson in social relations, especially to people of a certain social standing who are invited to fraternize with society's high-born. This involves presidential dinners, CEO's parties, administrators' retreats, and other forums where the rich and famous gather. The message calls for the invitee's self-control, self-discipline, and self-examination; the guest must have standards. Who you are as a person, what you believe, what you partake of, and your ethical standards are all crucial elements in this kind of social interaction. Simply put: watch what you eat or drink.

Daniel and his three companions faced that crisis of appetite and food, but they chose to honor God in their food and drink. They flatly refused to partake of any of the delicacies from the king's table and chose pulses, grains, nuts, and water. It was food that cost us Eden and its bliss. Satan tried the same trick with Jesus thinking he could get the Son of God to succumb to his temptations, especially the first—to make bread out of stones—having just ended a forty day fast. It was also appetite and the craving to be satiated that caused Esau to lose his birthright blessing. Based on the record, King Solomon's counsel is very appropriate.

Today's Christian will always be invited to dine with important people. Their tables and ballrooms will be copiously filled with all kinds of delicacies and rich wines, etc. King Solomon knew that some people in the presence of prestigious people will compromise their standards and principles just to fit in. They will not want to be thought of less than they really are; they have to keep up appearances and join with the crowd. Solomon points out the need for caution and the invitee's alertness. Otherwise, by being over satiated, he or she will lose his or her sense of reason and engage in foolish chatter and/or make unsound decisions. History is replete with the stories of men and women who made many unsound decisions around the dinner table or in the ballroom.

When you are invited to fellowship with important people, the guest should think about how his or her involvement honors God. This body is not yours; it is a loan from God and is the temple of the Holy Ghost who dwells there. Therefore, whatever is ingested ought to glorify God. "Whether therefore ye eat, or drink, or whatsoever ye do, do all to the glory of God" (1 Cor. 10:31) is the Pauline counsel.

Whatever is your station in life and in whatever circumstances you find yourself, you must be able to honor God in your body, in your speech, and in your food. In this, compromise is not a safe route. We must know our weaknesses. Under no situation should we allow the vice of gluttony to rule and or control our senses. We must refuse to let it mar our integrity and high social standing. Above all, we are God's workmanship, and we must always aim to honor Him in everything that we do. May we be aware of *when* our weaknesses are tested so that we may honor God fully and completely in all that we do.

Day 76

For I have given you an **Example**, *that ye should do as I have done to you. John 13:15*

What a beautiful epitaph of Jesus! You should follow in the footsteps of Jesus—what a wonderful charge and commission! They were told to walk in His steps, go where He went, and do what He did. The same challenge is ours, his second disciples. Do we have this ability? That is the question we must answer. Think about where His feet went and what they did.

Steps also mean actions. Jesus' feet took Him to places where people were always waiting for something: to be healed of an incurable disease, to be fed, to be preached to, to have their babies blessed, to restore the dead to life, or to sit in a boat and calm the raging billows; wherever there was a need, His footsteps took Him there.

Jesus' first disciples no doubt were quite familiar with the saying of Isaiah: "How beautiful upon the mountains are the feet of him that bringeth good tidings, that publisheth peace; that bringeth good tidings of good, that publisheth salvation: that saith unto Zion, Thy God reigneth" (Isa. 52:7). So in their commission, they knew their mission; they were now going to be those prophetic feet—walking in His steps—bringing the good news of the Gospel to the then known world.

To walk in the footsteps of Jesus meant that they had to do the works that He did, had to pray as He prayed, suffer as He suffered, be persecuted as He was persecuted, preach and heal as He did, spend long nights in prayer as He did, and pray alone as He did. They had to be sensitive to all human needs. I think I hear Jesus saying:

"I am the Model man. Say what I say and do what I do. Live how I have lived—in total communion with the Father. Next, love as I loved. Love one another and remain connected to God and to Me. Help the poor, answer the cry of the needy, heal the sick, and cast out demons. Preach, teach, and baptize one another; be My hands and feet. Touch people everywhere, and don't forget that I will be with you all the way even unto the end of the age. Follow Me; I know the way. I am the way, the truth, and the life. The peace I have, I give unto you all. Let there be no strivings for headship or leadership. Follow my example and be willing to serve rather than be served. If need be, give your life for the cause; I am your *example*. Follow Me."

This is a challenge to all who have taken up Christ's cross and have chosen the path of discipleship; it can be done. Jesus did it, and He said that the disciples would do greater things than He had done. For one, they had access to the Holy Spirit all day, every day. Jesus had their backs and whatever He asked the Father to give them, He would grant it. The disciples then and now have had more resources with them than when Jesus was here in person. He prayed that His followers be granted the precious gift of humility to do the things He did (see John 17). No task was too menial for Him to do, and the disciples were to follow their Leader's cue: love and work harmoniously. May we also follow Jesus' example.

Day 77

*I have been **Young**, and now am old; yet have I not seen the righteous forsaken, nor his seed begging bread. Psalm 37:25*

David's reflections on his long life and God's goodness to him and his children call for praise and thanksgiving. Having gone through all kinds of threats, dangers, and vicissitudes of life, and on approaching the nearness of his life's end, he could honestly say that his God had been a great God. David ascribes glory, praise, and honor to the great God of all humankind.

No one goes without a heavenly service. No one passes God's eyes uncared for. In essence, God takes care of all creation: humankind, beast, and birds. He even cares for the flowers and the trees; He sees everything in this world and provides for all. The naked are clothed, the homeless are sheltered, and the hungry are fed. All of His creatures find shelter under His everlasting arms and outstretched wings. This is a message of hope and consolation to those who feel that their needs are not being met and that no one cares for them. Even the needs of the disobedient are fully supplied.

God is non-discriminatory and unbiased. His sun, rain, warmth, hot, or cold is evenly distributed and extended to all humankind. But especially to those who walk uprightly and maintain the standard of holy living, they will always ultimately be amply supplied. God cares; His sustaining power is available to all. None need worry, languish, or pine if his or her table is not well spread and the pantry is not overflowing. Each of us is in our Father's care, and who knows how best to take care of His children than a loving, caring Father? Our Father knows just what will satisfy our several tastes. He is our Supplier, Shepherd, and Husbandman. Leave it all to Him.

If you think David wants to get one over on us then speak to your grandfather or great grandfather. Let them share with you how God has provided for their families during the very, very dark days of their lives. God, the eternal One, never leaves His children uncared for and has all under control. None under His care will go without.

Isn't it wonderful that King David could reach his senior years, reflect on all his life stages, and still offer praise and thanksgiving to God for all the bounties He so wonderfully and graciously gave to him? That affirmation speaks well for God. It shows that God is a Caretaker and that from youth to old age, God is a Supplier. No one who trusts and depends on Him will ever go without or suffer any lack. Those who depend on the Lord God of the Ages will never have to beg for bread, for He is the Living Bread.

Day 78

*Who gave himself for us, that he might redeem us from all iniquity, and purify unto himself a peculiar people, **Zealous** of good works. Titus 2:14*

This is the missionary Titus' exhortation to the Christians in regards to living the Christian life. In his discourse, he brought back to their minds who Jesus was and what it meant to have Jesus' name affixed to them. He reflected on Jesus Christ, who lived a sin-free life. Christ offered Himself to redeem humankind and bring us unto Himself. He wanted to purify us and keep us unspotted from the world. His mission was to give us a life without any trace of sin. That is awesome! Can you imagine that the Son of God would do this for you and me? But that is exactly what He did.

Jesus especially wants a peculiar people whose primary focus is to be *good* and to have a passion for righteousness. He wants us to be dedicated to right living, right thinking, and upholding right standards. Titus says that Jesus cannot take in His abode anything that is corrupt or has a trace of sin or iniquity with it. That is why He will put an utter end to sin. Remember that iniquity in any form shall not rise up the second time (see

Nah. 1:7). So He is searching for these people—Christians who want to live above sin. He is looking for people who will take a stand for the right above all else; he is looking for people—for men and women, children, and youth—who will stand like the three Hebrew youth who took a gamble on God. Whether or not God chose to intervene on their behalf, they would not bend or bow to the nuances of King Nebuchadnezzar. Those three stood for truth, uprightness, integrity. They stood for God. Consequently, God reciprocated and stood up for them and vindicated them and His holy name.

Today, God is looking for the kind of youth whose zeal or passion is for Christ and for holy, righteous, and upright things. He wants people who will choose Him over the sensational and transient. Their zeal is to honor God and make Him known to their peers. He is searching for these peculiar Christian youth. Can He find you? Will you make yourself available?

The question is: do you want to be purified, have your sins erased, classed as just in God's sight, and have Christ's righteousness imputed to you? If you do, Christ is waiting with out-stretched arms to embrace and enfold you into His bosom where nothing but love is found. Christ offered himself to give you a second chance of life. May we this day accept the gracious offer and let Jesus know that His sacrifice for us was not in vain. We appreciate and value it and so we yield to Him. Let the purification begin today—now! And let us continue to be *zealous* after those things that lead to uprightness, dignity, and wholesome, unsullied characters.

Listen to His Voice

Day 79

He that is slow to **Anger** *is better than the mighty; and he that ruleth his spirit than he that taketh a city. Proverbs 16:32*

Several texts address the human dilemma of self-control. The continual management of one's behavior is urgent. This text speaks specifically to one of the most dangerous emotions that plague humankind—anger.

Anger is one of the seven deadly sins. It carries in its path death, dismemberment, and destruction. There is no law negating the display of anger. Jesus was angry when He came to the Temple and saw the disrespect and disregard for the holy place as well as the theft and deceit that were practiced by those merchants. As a result He overthrew their entire transaction and chased them out of the temple precincts. He stated that they had converted His Father's house from a place of worship to an abhorrent market place.

When it is under control, anger is a healthy emotion. No wonder the text enjoins that if anger exists, one should proceed cautiously in its use. An angry person is someone who is out of control.

The emotion of anger bears many unknown issues. People who are angry cannot think straight. Their thoughts are convoluted because they are being driven by blind reason. They cannot be trusted to act intelligently because they lack discernment. Neither do they recognize right from wrong. Anger is an impulsive psychic trait, and like the others, it must be subdued or eradicated. However, a healthy dose of anger is good because it balances out the emotions of love, peace, and joy.

King Solomon advises caution in igniting our anger strain: go slowly. The self-controlled man or woman will be more revered and respected than the abrasive and impulsive one. Self-control beats pugnacity every time. Replace anger with righteous indignation, controlled action, and decision making.

We must recognize the superiority of self-control over combat. Success in business, education, marriage, or any other enterprise can be ruined by an angry person or disposition. It is a great personal victory to control one's temper. If and when your fuse is getting short, do two things: breathe a silent prayer and think of the loss or forfeiture you might sustain. May we abide by the Pauline counsel: "Be ye *angry,* and sin not" (Eph. 4:26) and save ourselves and others needless pain, misery, and heartache.

Day 80

Behold, *I come quickly: blessed is he that keepeth the sayings of the prophecy of this book. Revelation 22:7*

In the revelation of Jesus to John on the lonely isle of Patmos, the heavenly Messenger said that He was coming quickly and that everyone who understands and obeys the prophetic sayings recorded will receive blessings.

This call is summoning men to the imminence of Jesus' return. How quickly, we do not know. God's time is not computed as ours is, but "Behold" calls one's attention to its urgency.

In speaking of readiness, Jesus quoted the parable of the thief breaking into the master's house during the night and his unpreparedness for the intruder. Since the day of Jesus' return remains unknown, all have to maintain a state of vigilance. We need to be ready to act and move at a moment's notice. There will be no time to get dressed, grab a bag, put on shoes, or say goodbye. We have to be fully clothed (see Eph. 6:10–18) and ready to move into action.

The closest earthly situation akin to constant readiness is the Swiss Army. There is no sitting army, but within four hours, the army, cavalry, infantry, equestrian, air force, and marines will be ready. Every Swiss citizen is a trained person and must be ready to report whenever duty calls. This is what you call preparedness—ready for duty at a moment's notice. Similarly, the citizens of the kingdom of heaven are to be ready and waiting for their Lord's return. They are to be fully dressed for at any moment, behold the Master comes!

Today, Christians live in a world of expectancy and anticipation. How soon Jesus will return, we do not know. But the vision and the prophecy were given more than 2,000 years ago, and even though God does not compute time by human measurement, there is certainty that Jesus' return cannot be ere long. According to Galatians 4:4, when the fullness of time came, Jesus, the Son of God came, lived, and died and returned to His Father's right hand. That is more than 2,000 years ago. In God's time, He will send Jesus to gather His righteous saints.

All Christians who read and listen will understand the prophetic announcement: "Behold I come quickly," as well as Jesus' entreaty, "he that hath an ear, let him hear what the Spirit saith unto the churches" (Rev. 2:29; see also Rev. 3:13, 22). None can claim ignorance; each must live soberly and godly in today's world, for at any time the Master will come. Christians, *behold*! He comes. May we be ready.

Day 81

Casting *all your care upon him; for he careth for you. 1 Peter 5:7*

Jesus is our Rock of defense. He is our Shepherd, Sustainer, Provider, and Keeper. He is everything. He knows our every need, and nothing in any way that concerns our peace and happiness escapes His eyes. Wonderful Savior! Magnificent King! Precious Redeemer!

Our habitation is plagued with severe challenges: serious illnesses, life-threatening diseases, poverty, famine, and displaced families. All around, people are concerned about how to stay afloat amidst the challenges, and many become depressed, despaired, discouraged, bent out of shape, and are cast down. Some can barely raise the head to see the light of day; no help is in sight. As a result of these pressures, many blame someone or something else for their angst. But we all must *cast* all our cares upon God.

These have been humankind's age-old challenges; however, the Christian should not be too discouraged. The Word of God provides counsel and certitude about our welfare. God has promised to supply all our needs according to His riches in glory, for He is very rich. Everything on planet earth belongs to Him. "The earth is the Lord's, and the fulness thereof; the world, and they that dwell therein" (Ps. 24:1). So if we are hungry, naked, thirsty, or poor, it may be due to our own lack of thrift and industry and we have not accessed God's precious gifts. Peter's message should resonate with us.

If God has made provision for all His created beings to have ample supply, how is it then that we are faced with these respective challenges: hunger, starvation, famine, and extreme poverty? It has to be the inequitable distribution and management of wealth and resources. Social, geographic, and agricultural conditions affect the distribution of supply and demand, and people in certain geographic zones face very serious lack. They are downcast, despairing, and defeated.

However, there is hope in God's word, and Peter assures all to not be so anxious about bearing all your problems because Jesus has the cure. Casting our burdens is an active, continuous process that we should not stop. We need to pile them upon Him, for He can bear them. He is the only One who can solve our problems. He can open up closed doors. He has the key and cares. You are His by creation and redemption, so do not take life's blows so hard. He holds up worlds.

We are God's children. He is our Papa and no good and kind Father abandons His children. Rest assured that God will never leave us to languish. He is concerned about our daily existence and survival and does not want us to be burdened. Give all of our problems and concerns to Jesus. He cared enough to live an exemplary life, died to save us, and ascended to intercede for us. What more can He do for us? Our Beloved Brother and Father God would never leave us alone to flounder amidst all of life's crises. At this moment Jesus is looking down on our condition and is addressing our respective needs. Do not be disheartened, troubled, or discouraged. *Cast* them at his feet. Help is here!

Day 82

*Seest thou a man **Diligent** in his business? he shall stand before kings; he shall not stand before mean men. Proverbs 22:29*

Continuing his instruction and counsels to the young and the enterprising laborer, Solomon exhorts them to be earnest and adroit in their economic exploits. Any businessperson of integrity, fervency of spirit, and commitment to any given task will succeed. If this is coupled with astuteness as well as industry and business knowledge, they will gain a position of esteem and high social standing; they will excel.

If you are that person who gets up early and goes about your task with exactness, monitors your hours, and expends a great amount of effort, you will surely reap an abundant harvest. In order to make this happen, an investor or entrepreneur must practice constancy, consistency, and commitment to the given task. Such deed will produce envious results, but they will be revered among the great men and women of the area. They will not be found among the lazy and uncharitable men and women, whose lifestyle is voracious for its profligacy. Rather, they will be a model entrepreneur and an upright and wealthy person. The abhorrent life practices of the others lead only to extreme poverty and beggary. This is because they were not *diligent* in acquiring a trade or a skill, so they remain unskilled, poor, destitute, and devoid of vision and direction.

On the contrary, the man or woman who has learned several skills will always have a job. When the opportunity presents itself, he or she will get the job and be promoted. The other individual, because of lack of vision and insight, will remain unskilled and do only menial work. Consequently, he or she cannot change his or her social status, and his or her children and spouse cannot enjoy the company and association of a richer social environment. The entire family must suffer with the one who lacked diligence in his or her unpreparedness for life's challenges. He or she cannot take that giant step into the future, so he or she will continue to work as well as associate and live among the careless and the indifferent. This text carries an exhortation and a warning. It is an exhortation to the insightful, discerning person, who is constantly searching for opportunities that lead to social mobility. But it is also a warning to the slovenly to acquire adeptness and a good skill. If the latter's attitude remains unaltered, he or she will remain at the nadir of the social ladder. May we all practice diligence so that our families and futures will be blessed.

Day 83

*The Lord shall cause thine **Enemies** that rise up against thee to be smitten before thy face: they shall come out against thee one way, and flee before thee seven ways. Deuteronomy 28:7*

How great and marvelous is our God! He watches perpetually over every one of His children. None will ever suffer at the hands of their enemies or those who disfavor them. The eyes of God are constantly open and are keeping watch over His own.

This text promises safeguard, assurance, and security to all of God's obedient children. More specifically, it was the announcement to the Israelites who were constantly besieged by enemies. But Jehovah God assured them that if they remained obedient to His precepts, the enemies who rose up to attack them, their dwelling places, their cattle, and their children, will die, giving His chosen people a long-awaited for deliverance.

The bestowal of God's blessing is conditioned with obedience. We are of Abraham's seed because we are spiritually aligned to Abraham by virtue of Jesus. The Word says, "And if ye be Christ's, then are ye Abraham's seed, and heirs according to the promise" (Gal. 3:29). The promise made to them is also our promise. If we but serve the Lord and obey Him, our enemies also will come in and attack us from one gate, door, or avenue, but they will take flight much faster than they came in. The Lord Jehovah will open many paths to deliver us if we obey His commands. God said, "For my thoughts are not your thoughts, neither are your ways my ways, saith the Lord" (Isa. 55:8). And the wise man concurred, "The wicked flee when no man pursueth: but the righteous are bold as a lion" (Prov. 28:1). Wickedness and evil cannot stand in the presence of the awesome, pure, and holy God.

God is in the midst of us. Psalm 91 gives deep assurance of protection from all kinds of *enemies*: human, beast, and nature. "A thousand shall fall at thy side, and ten thousand at thy right hand; but it shall not come nigh thee" (verse 7). Our God is able. He is the ever present I AM–our Champion and Deliverer. Give praise unto our God! Our enemies can have no power over God's children. May God's people trust in Him and have no fear.

Day 84

Fear *not, little flock; for it is your Father's good pleasure to give you the kingdom.*
Luke 12:32

Jesus addressed the care and anxiety that had welled up in the disciples' psyche. They had the Martha syndrome. They were careful and anxious about many things: their role in the kingdom they had hoped Jesus would set up, preaching, healing, and casting out demons, following His footsteps, and the people's acceptance of them after Jesus' absence. What about their families' livelihood? Would they have to go back to doing their original trade? These issues weighed heavily on their minds. Thus Jesus, reading their thoughts and feelings, told them, "But rather seek ye the kingdom of God; and all things shall be added unto you" (verse 31). They were to submit themselves to God, their Father, and let His will be their primary focus. When that occupies first place in their minds, every other concern will fall into place. They would have no *fear*.

Just in case, they did not quite get it, Jesus told them to not be afraid and that God had already planned to give them the kingdom. He told them that the Father had a plan for them, and they needed to be patient and let Him work out His will in their lives. When Jesus speaks, He utters the Father's words–truth, wisdom, and assurance. He had no reason to mislead His new followers. He declared to them and to us, "I and my Father are one" (John 10:30). He speaks the Father's mind to us; therefore, children, *fear* not!

The comforting message was not only for the eleven, but is also for all those who would come after them, including you and me. Additionally, Jesus cited God's care for the birds and flowers, making the point that we–made in His image–are much more precious and valuable than they. He counsels us to have neither doubts nor fear; we need to let God be God!

Disannulling fear, Ellen G. White states, "God never leads His children otherwise than they would choose to be led, if they could see the end from the beginning and discern the glory of the purpose they are fulfilling as co-workers with Him" (*Ministry of Healing*, p. 479). Let us go forward fearing less and trusting more. God is still the same today as He was yesterday and will be tomorrow. Do not forget that He is God and He cannot change. He is the ever present I AM. Let us be brave and move forward knowing that Jesus is in front.

God has already planned to give us the kingdom and to usher us into a realm of peace, happiness, and joy. Why are we suffering discontent, disease, fear, and anxiety? Don't you know He delivers what He has promised? May we cry out like the father of the child possessed by a spirit, "Lord, I believe; help thou mine unbelief" (Mark 9:24). *Fear* not; our God is in charge!

Day 85

He that **Giveth** *to the poor shall not lack: but he that hideth his eyes shall have many a curse. Proverbs 8:27*

Jesus states that the poor will always be among us. They are a part of our social DNA; they are an integral part of the fabric of our lives. They are there for us to show compassion, kindness, and sympathy.

The wise man says, "He that hath pity upon the poor lendeth unto the Lord; and that which he hath given will he pay him again" (Prov. 19:17). If one reaches out and satisfies the needs of the poor, he or she is saying, "See, Lord, I have taken care of the needy." We need to show generosity and put our treasures in the bank of heaven. The Lord will repay us for all of our unselfish acts.

The poor live in a state of expectancy and anxiousness not knowing how their hourly needs are to be met. They revel in worry and self-pity. However, the Lord has empowered the wealthy to have compassion to the destitute. King Solomon aptly confirms that if you give to the poor, your storehouse will be continually replenished. The donors will receive God's continuous blessing because they showed pity to the poor. Jesus affirmed their beneficence: "Inasmuch as ye have done it unto one of the least of these my brethren, ye have done it unto me" (Matt. 25:40).

Those who turn a blind eye to the needs of the poor shall surely receive many curses. What condemnation! Do what you can for the poor by helping the weak if you are strong. By reaching out and satisfying their needs, we are laying up treasures in heaven and the Lord will honor our commitment.

The poor are here to test our generosity, mercy, lovingkindness, and goodness. In reaching out to them, we show how much of God's love, goodness, and tender mercies reside in us. God wants us to identify with the needy. In helping them, we are being the hands and feet of Christ. May we continue to *give* to the poor and needy.

Day 86

Honour *thy father and mother; which is the first commandment with promise; That it may be well with thee, and thou mayest live long on the earth. Ephesians 6:2, 3*

What a challenge for all children! Laden with perpetuity within its phrases, it is the first commandment purporting a reward.

To honor is to fear, respect, revere, nurture, uphold, care for, and protect. This is a solemn duty accorded to each offspring. This promise offers longevity and prosperity. Inferred in this command is a curse. It is either a bane or balm. If you honor and respect your parents—father and mother, respectively—you are guaranteed to do well physically, morally, economically, socially, intellectually, and spiritually. You will be well fortified, and your ventures will be successful. However, the promise is conditional (as all God's promises are). If you honor your parents, you will receive all the blessings, but if not, the reverse consequences are steep—a short, brief life, shortened youth, no prosperity, and you may even become a stumbling block to others.

Emphasis on each parent separately is important because some children might be biased to either parent. Here, both are very important. Each parent has a different set of values to give their offspring, hence the need for this acute counsel. King Solomon has written several pieces of advice calling young people to listen to the advice and law of their mother and to stick closely to the instructions of their father. Parents are the patriarchs and have the experiences with which to guide the feet of their children. This is a cyclical pattern, for those who are children now, will become parents tomorrow. It was the poet laureate, William Wordsworth who penned this generational factor aptly: "The Child is the father of the Man."

This fifth commandment of the Decalogue is very crucial inferring both outward and inward deference to parents. It promises success in every endeavor. No other Old Testament commandment has a promise. This is special to God, to children, and to parents. Children, by obeying and honoring their parents, are assured a long life on the earth. Who doesn't want to live long and enjoy the blessings of our Creator?

May all children obey and *honor* their parents so that they may live long and productive lives.

Day 87

> **In** *my Father's house are many mansions: if it were not so, I would have told you. I go to prepare a place for you. John 14:2*

What words of assurance and tranquility that issued from Jesus' lips! Those words must have been a soothing balm to the troubled and fearful minds of the twelve borne down with anxiety and worry. To those who live in tenements, log cabins, make-shift houses, clustered- pigeon-hole like houses, tree houses, caves, and caverns, the assurance is that our Father has titled mansions for each of the redeemed to dwell therein and call their own.

The Queen of England and many of earth's great rulers own mansions and live sumptuous and comfortable lives. There are many times when those who are less fortunate begrudge their affluence and luxury. However, there is hope and a bright future for those who put their trust in God. Jesus says to us today: My Father has not one but many great mansions. They will be ready for each of us to inhabit when we reach the new earth.

Jesus indefatigably states, "If it were not so, I would have told you." What certitude! Then He continues, "I go to prepare a place"—He is creating a mansion for every one of us. This task of preparing and erecting is not given to angels; it is Jesus Himself who is doing the job. Don't feel self pity if your abode here is not the most commodious for living and entertaining. These abodes are temporary, replaceable shelters; they are simply holding places. God has acres for each of us. When writing to the Corinthian brethren about the glories in the new earth, Paul said, "Eye hath not seen ... neither have entered into the heart of man, the things which God hath prepared for them that love him" (1 Cor. 2:9). Our abodes will be permanent and will never need repair, for nothing shall decay in the City of God—*De civitate Dei*.

Let us accept the invitation; God's word is true and dependable. Whatever He promises, He delivers. Plan today to receive the keys to your mansion. Jesus said, "And if I go and prepare a place for you, I will come again" (John 14:3). He is now with our heavenly Father, and we anxiously await His return, for everyone will have a plot in and on the Father's compound. May we all be anxious to move *in* to our heavenly home.

Day 88

> *I the Lord thy God am a **Jealous** God, visiting the iniquity of the fathers upon the children unto the third and fourth generation of them that hate me. Exodus 20:5*

Is it all right to display the emotion of jealousy? What does it really mean to be jealous? God declares that jealousy resides within His bosom, which shows us that it is a good emotion to possess. God possesses only that which is pure, noble, and upright. Here, God is saying that He is very particular and wants worship to be ascribed to Him alone. He also said, "My glory will I not give to another" (Isa. 42:8).

God reminds us that He is the Creator. He deserves worship, adoration, praise, and obedience. He gave these commands to His chosen people—the Israelites—whom He alone delivered from the yoke of oppression and the bondage of Egyptian slavery. We, too, are spiritual Israelites by adoption, and God has provided for our deliverance from the bondage of sin. Because of this, God can surely state, "For I am God, and there is none else; I am God, and there is none like me" (Isa. 46:9). He repeats that worship, obedience, and honor belong to Him. You shall have no other gods before Him; He must take first place in your life. Do not give His praise to idols. If you do so, you are reflecting and remembering the Egyptian customs and practices. He brought our deliverance, and He desires your praise and worship. If we renege, He will let our children pay for our intransigence—not only those who came from our loins but also their children and their children's children. It will be generational bane. Dear reader, is it not better to have the generational blessing rather than the curse of iniquity?

Human beings tend to be *jealous* over many things: husbands are jealous over their wives, parents over their children, employees over the success of other employees, etc. Jealousy is regarded as the green-eyed monster emanating from covetousness and envy. That kind of jealousy is evil, and if allowed to go uncurbed, it may produce harmful ends such as insecurity, desertion, separation, annihilation, abandonment, or even death.

God's jealousy is neither evil nor adversarial, but it carries with it a passion and zeal for honor, obedience, and reverence. Having come from Egypt where there were many gods and idols for each aspect of life, God seemed to be just another god to add to their list. But God wanted them to know that He was the only true God. He was their Deliverer, and He was *jealous* in their adoration. If they could not accept Him as supreme above graven images, then He could not be their God and they could not be His people. God demands that we make Him first in our choices and give Him guarded reverence and honor. In that regard, He is a *jealous* God demanding all worship and adoration. May He have first place in our lives.

Day 89

> *I will give unto thee the **Keys** of the kingdom of heaven: and whatsoever you shalt bind on earth shall be bound in heaven: and whatsoever you shalt loose on earth shall be loosed in heaven. Matthew 16:19*

This is a great challenge that Jesus placed upon His disciples' shoulders. Peter had just affirmed to Jesus that He was, indeed, the Son of the living God in response to Jesus' inquiry as to whom they thought He was. Upon Peter's response, Jesus replied that His answer was not spontaneous but that it had been divinely inspired. Based upon Peter's response, Jesus told the group that He was giving them the authority and power to continue ministry in His name. He was giving them the keys to the kingdom.

What does it mean to be given the keys to the kingdom? Jesus' time with them was now short-lived, and He had to empower them for ministry. They would be commissioned to continue the work of preaching the Word that their Master had begun.

The good news of the Gospel would now be for all humanity—Jews and Gentiles alike. Peter was the first commissioned disciple to lead people to the kingdom of God. It was he who received the vision to adopt Gentiles into the faith. He preached on the Day of Pentecost and called men and women to repentance. He also presided at the first administrative council in Jerusalem. Is there any wonder why Jesus said to Peter, "When thou art converted, strengthen thy brethren" (Luke 22:32)? Jesus knew He could depend on Peter. After Jesus' resurrection, the visitor at the tomb told the women to go and tell the others and Peter that Jesus was indeed resurrected. Peter needed the assurance that Jesus was indeed alive because he was going to be the spokesperson for Jesus and the Gospel.

Peter was very blessed. He led the fledgling church and the ten disciples, and he presided over the selection of Judas' replacement. He had a tender heart, an inquisitive mind, and an assertive spirit needed for the growth of the new church. He was insightful, sensitive, and discerning. Jesus commissioned them to preach, teach, baptize, and heal whoever they thought worthy and led by the Holy Spirit.

Their first miracle was the healing of the lame man who sat daily at the temple gate asking for alms. The Scriptures say that Peter, who was with John, said, "Look on us.... Silver and gold have I none; but such as I have give I thee: In the name of Jesus Christ of Nazareth rise up and walk" (Acts 3:4, 6).

Peter and the others, infused with Jesus' full authority, had now become His hands and feet. They were carrying out the work He had begun and taught them. They were preaching the forgiveness of sins, teaching the liberating power of Jesus' sacrifice, helping men and women get ready for the kingdom of God, and providing access to God by opening the doors of the church to all.

We Christians have received the keys from our forbearers; we are here to open the doors to the kingdom so that all men and women can find Jesus. May God help us to be sensitive to the spiritual needs of those we seek to lead. May He help us find the courage to take the *keys*.

Day 90

> **Let** *the words of my mouth, and the meditation of my heart, be acceptable in thy sight, O Lord, my strength, and my redeemer. Psalm 19:14*

This benediction is my solace and daily prayer. It is the request that God would allow him or her to live a life under His total control. It is for the Holy Spirit to control the mind so that in the communication process every thought, idea, and notion that surges into the mind as well as every expression that is uttered through our lips may meet God's approval.

How can this be done when the psalmist declares that "in sin did my mother conceive me" (Ps. 51:5)? Even in that procreative process, there is sin; every child is conceived through sin because we are all sinners. Thankfully, we have the opportunity to surrender our wills to God and pray, "Dear Father, I want to be wholly thine; take control of my mind, desire, emotion, feelings, and actions." It is possible, for our God is able to keep the things that we have committed to His keeping. The apostle Paul exhorts us to "let this mind be in you, which was also in Christ Jesus" (Phil. 2:5).

The mind of Jesus contained only pure, holy, praiseworthy, noble, and unadulterated love. He had a love for every living soul—born and the still unborn. There was no malice, hate, jealousy, or envy at all in Him. He was purity through and through, so when Paul exhorts Christians to let the mind of Jesus be the master of their mind, it is a very admirable feat. Our attitude is to be like Jesus': loving, humble, respectful, unselfish, caring, and watchful. Thus, if our thoughts and attitude are in submission to the Holy One, then what we think and do will be holy and pure and noble. In everything, we will be reflecting Christ's behavior, and God will accept all that we think and do. We can confidently and sincerely utter a prayer like "May my words and thoughts find favor and be praiseworthy to You, my God."

If the mind of Jesus takes hold of our minds, there is nothing that we cannot do: "With God all things are possible" (Matt. 19:26). May our thoughts, ideas, and oral expressions be sanctified because the Holy Spirit is in control.

We must *let* Christ fill our mind, heart, attitude, emotion, and feelings with good things. May we *let* Him live within us.

Day 91

My son, give me thine heart, and let thine eyes observe my ways. Proverbs 23:26

This strong and wise counsel from the wisest man that ever lived is a clarion call to children and youth. The son was the addressee because of the patriarchal system that prevailed then and because the son was to be the head of the family dynasty. But both sons and daughters were to be God-fearing and Godlike providing different kinds of leadership within the family. Thus, although the commission is given directly to the son, both sons and daughters were to yield themselves to the promptings of the Holy Spirit.

Since the human heart is desperately wicked and prone to be self-willed, it is only the Holy Spirit's power that can cause a stout heart to bend and yield to God's directions. The injunction is submission to God and giving Him your heart. Your heart is the seat of your emotion, mental faculties, and your decision-making core. If the heart and mind is under the control of the Holy Spirit, then your eyes, ears, and mouth will be as well. The counsel Solomon gives is voluntary, not forced.

This entreaty is a deterrent to the son and daughter wondering off into strange paths of debauchery and worldliness or anything that entices and lures him or her away from the path of rectitude and uprightness. One reason for the emphasis on the eyes is that they are the windows to the soul. It is the eyes that first catch a glimpse of whatever is out there. The eyes see, and the mind acts. They tell the mouth to speak, the hand to touch, or the ears to listen. How important then are the eyes! That is the reason why the children are often taught these lyrics very early in life:

Oh, be careful little eyes what you see
Oh, be careful little eyes what you see
For the Father up above is looking down in love,
So be careful little eyes what you see.

The words of the other parts of the body are repeated in this song: ears—what you hear, hands—what you do, feet—where you go, mouth—what you say, and mind—what you think. Then the final stanza brings the body together with the heart:

Oh, be careful little heart what you love,
Oh, be careful little heart what you love,
For the Father up above is looking down in love
So, be careful little heart what you love.

If all those faculties are controlled by the power and authority of the Holy Spirit, then the possessor will most assuredly observe the paths of rectitude. This is a failsafe plan for living a beautiful, wholesome, God-approved life. Who knows better than the king who declared that his exposure to and acquisition of all earthly things amounted to vanity and emptiness? May every son and daughter heed the advice and let these words be their guide.

Day 92

> **Now** *unto him that is able to keep you from falling, and to present you faultless before the presence of his glory with exceeding joy, To the only wise God our Saviour, be glory and majesty ... now and ever. Amen. Jude 1:24, 25*

This benediction constitutes Jude's final words of exhortation to the new Christians. Having faced many challenging situations, his primary purpose was to reintroduce them to the Triune God, who would erect a fortress around them and anchor them in their new faith.

Jude's message, though addressed to those Christians exposed to all kinds of temptations toward immoral living and false teachings, is universal and speaks to Christians globally. Apostasy was high among the believers, so he encouraged them to live above sin, for God would be able to preserve them and keep their feet, minds, and heart in the right direction. If they practiced Christian brotherhood: caring for the less fortunate, holding up each other in prayer and praise, practice their faith, and refuse to engage in sensual behaviors, then holy angels would be their attendants and direct all their behaviors. Jude further assured them that God would not leave them alone. They were to trust Him, for He is able to preserve and protect them from falling back into sin. Jude encourages all believers to remain firm in their faith and trust in God's promise for their future.

Christians living in these last days are now faced with similar challenging temptations: pornography, sexual permissiveness, and internet seduction. Sin is in high places; godlessness is in the land; hypocrisy and the elevation of the secular above the sacred is more common than not. How relevant is the counsel for today's Christian! Despite all the doom and gloom, the Christians' charge is to live soberly and godly in this present world. We are besieged by multitudes of religious voices; sin is more inviting and available to us than ever before, and we have been bombarded on all fronts. It has invaded the sanctum of the home, and our young children are held hostages to media frenzy, exploitation, and seduction.

God, who is the same yesterday, today, and forever, will not forget His promise. His eyes are watching all His children, and He will keep them under His wings and guard their steps. We must trust Him and yield ourselves to Him. We must follow Him all the way. He is able to keep us from falling back into sin of any kind and will ensure that we remain faultless and faithful and bring us into His presence joyfully. May you never again give into fear or despair for our God is able. He was able then for the first Christians, and He is able *now* for today's Christians. We must hold onto this promise—He is Able.

Day 93

> **O** *Lord, thou has searched me, and known me. Psalm 139:1*

This utterance expresses pity and lamentation, a kind of helplessness. It is as if to say I have reached my exhaustion point, and I am in utter despair; there is nothing else I can do. So Lord, since I cannot do anything to modify my behaviors, take charge. You know it all; I can hide nothing from you.

This is a grand moment for King David. The acknowledgment of one's true condition is classified as moment of insight or self-realization. It is the place where the struggler recognizes their utter helplessness. The struggler has come face to face with their demon-self and must choose to either fight or take flight.

Gone are the shams, pretenses, and charades or even the self-dialogues. This is the real thing. We are calling for self-disclosure and ownership.

In the parable Jesus told and recorded in Luke 15, the lost son reached his nadir when he found himself forced to eat the husks of swine's food. He had nothing and no one gave him anything. He came to himself, turned around, and said, "I will arise and go home to my father" (see verses 17, 18).

David reached that point of desperation when the prophet Nathan confronted him about his twin sin of adultery and murder. David declared, "I have sinned against the Lord" (2 Sam. 12:13). He took ownership for his wrongdoing and paid heavily for his recalcitrance. This act trickled down to his children and children's children. However, God accepted his confession, repentance, and surrender. As a result of this chastening, David wrote Psalm 51 in which he asked God for cleansing, forgiveness, renewal, restoration, and for a continuous indwelling of the Holy Spirit.

None of us can be helped until we realize our helplessness and the need for intervention. Then we can truly ask the Lord to take over because we cannot manage on our own. It is then that Jesus will reach down as He did when He grasped Peter's hand and gently raise us up. But we must recognize our limitations and reach out to the One who is always available and able to raise us out of the pit. God knows everything about us; we cannot hide from Him because He is everywhere. He is constantly aware of the activities and actions of all His children. God is omniscient, omnipresent, and omnipotent.

God knows each of our melting points, and He knows the real you. May we allow God to take charge of our lives and make sure all our secrets are wide open before Him.

Day 94

Peace *I leave with you, my peace I give unto you: not as the world giveth, give I unto you. Let not your heart be troubled, neither let it be afraid. John 14:27*

God is a God of peace. Jesus is the author of peace. There is no vengeful anger or wrath in Him. The text is a consoling affirmation He gave to the disciples and to us. What calm words of assurance! He gives us a peace that we will always have—not just tentatively, but permanently—as long as you remain connected to Him. If you become disconnected, there will arise turmoil, anxiety, intolerance, and disconnect in our lives among families, communities, societies, and nations. Knowing Jesus is having peace.

If Jesus promises have given us peace, why is there so much trouble, despair, antagonism, fear, distrust, and uncertainty pervading our lives and society? Why are human beings so bent out of shape trying to make peace? Jesus has given it to us; all we have to do is to access it. But where is it? Where can it be found? Certainly, the peace that He gives is a different kind of peace. He said that it is not like the peace the world offers. Peace is what takes place when we offer to pacify and create accord with the other. How is Jesus' peace different from the world's peace? Let us see what Jesus' peace entails.

The peace of Jesus has no uncertainties; it is all certitude. It calms boisterous and raging seas, and it casts out demons and restores the insane mind. It calms the windstorm, cools down the fevered body, deletes doubt and anxiety, and suppresses sinful desires. His peace offers comfort, ease, and serenity. All of that is available in the package if we are willing to accept Him and His gift. Jesus' peace is permanent and unchanging.

The peace of the world is transitory and limited and is based on a contractual principle of conditional agreement. World peace is an idealism that will never be realized as long as rulers, dictators, and heads of governments continue to vie for supremacy and militaristic ascendancy. Not so with the peace that emanates from the lips of our beloved Pilot, Jesus. He said that He came to bring peace and not confusion. Jesus is our peacemaker, and He left peace for us. We must not allow the enemy to continue to sow discord and doubt in our minds so that we remain in a state of flux and turmoil. Jesus' peace is one of the greatest gifts that He can bestow on mortals, and we should access this great virtue.

Speaking to His disciples from the Mount, Jesus pronounced a blessing upon the peacemakers. We should seek to cultivate and nurture the abiding peace that He left for us. "I leave with you, my peace I give unto you" were His last words. May we treasure this prized possession so that it remains constantly with us,

Day 95

The earth shall **Quake** *before them; the heavens shall tremble: the sun and the moon shall be dark, and the stars shall withdraw their shining. Joel 2:10*

The prophet Joel cites portentous future events. At the heart of these revelations is the call for repentance, revitalization, and renewal. Humanity, in its vileness, has forgotten God, the Creator, and has replaced Him with the created. Consequently, God will speak through His creation so that men and women may acknowledge His Lordship. Whenever nature speaks, our attention is awakened and redirected. Only then will we call upon God. Many people only call upon God in the face of calamities: tsunamis, earthquakes, fires, floods, hurricanes, and acts of terrorism. We have to lose something before we call upon the name of the Lord. No sooner than the problem is resolved, and we go back to our regular routine.

The prophet says that there will be earthquakes and the heavens will tremble with loud thunder and lightning. The sun, moon, and stars will withhold their warmth, brilliance, and light. We must acknowledge that the Most High rules this world.

Some of these events have already occurred: the Great Lisbon earthquake of 1755, the "dark day" in 1780, and the falling of the stars in 1833. Various eclipses of the moon are all portentous acts of the mighty Power, who says that He will "ariseth to shake terribly the earth" (Isa. 2:19).

Today, we have more frequent occurrences of earthquakes, tsunamis, floods, and fires. Our God is still speaking. He wants everyone to know who is in charge–"the earth is the Lord's, and the fulness thereof; the world, and they that dwell therein" (Ps. 24:1). Joel's prophecy is only partially accomplished. Part two of the prophecy (Joel 2:28–31) is yet to be fulfilled. As God's Spirit is gradually withdrawn from the earth, evil forces will cause devastation and destruction to move in, and there will be calamities upon calamities. In the midst of all this, God is still keeping watch over His people. None need fear for God is in control. He controls all nature and has the whole world in His hands.

The Lord God will have a people who will acknowledge, fear, and revere His holy name. He will continually make His presence felt among the nations. He is God. May all the earth praise Him.

Day 96

Remove *not the old landmark; and enter not into the fields of the fatherless.*
Proverbs 23:10

From time immemorial, the acquisition of land has been a challenge to many. Land is and has power. It has ownership and shows that the possessor has some clout. In the past, the more land you possessed, the more established you were. It carried with it certain rights and people were accounted rich based on the number of hectares or acres they possessed. This practice led to cheating, especially from those unable to manage: widows, orphans, and the fatherless.

The original Israelites were each given boundaries and territories in the new homeland marked off according to their tribes. In many cases it was not unusual that a more defiant and greedy owner would seek to get more than his share, so he would remove the original landmark-boundary. The plan was implemented primarily around the males so as to maintain male hierarchy and dominance. However, there was an example when a father died and had no sons to inherit his portion, so the daughters came to Caleb, one of the leaders after Moses and Aaron's death, and asked for their father's portion, and it was given to them.

Many family disputes have been about land ownership. In order to have more and extend borders, one would engage in all kinds of chicanery such as shifting the line posts so as to get a few more feet or square yards added to the plot. The sad irony is that the possession of land is transient; no one takes any part of his or her inheritance with them to the grave.

The removal of the line posts was common practice among ancient Israel, so Solomon addressed this baneful practice demanding that people respect and revere the landed territory and not *remove* the old landmark. Twice he counseled them: "Remove not the ancient landmark, which thy fathers have set" (Prov. 22:28), and then again: "Remove not the old landmark; and enter not into the fields of the fatherless" (Prov. 23:10). Even today, people are obsessed with the acquisition of more land. They may possess any number of acres, but they only truly occupy one or two acres.

This potent advice compels each person to be content with his or her own property. There is absolutely no reason to defraud the poor. The aggressor's action is greed, and we should remember that none should alter the deed to the plot or overreach our limits.

This problem still operates in many families. The more one has, the more one wants to access. People who swindle and rob the most vulnerable should make restitution in a very tangible way. It is the godly thing to do. The stronger and more able ones ought to care for the fatherless and not rob or defraud them. Isaiah 58:7–10 gives instruction on how to treat the fatherless. Rather than being aggressors and oppressors of the poor, the greedy and selfish ones should practice true religion, so they can receive God's approbation.

Lest any forget, "The eyes of the Lord are in every place, beholding the evil and the good" (Prov. 15:3). May His eyes see you doing only good.

Day 97

But Jesus said, **Suffer** *little children, and forbid them not, to come unto me: for of such is the kingdom of heaven. Matthew 19:14*

These are Jesus' remarks to His disciples because they saw the children as a nuisance and unimportant. To them, Jesus had more pressing matters to address, so they sought to control His responses to the people's needs.

As mothers brought their little ones to Jesus to be touched and blessed by Him, the disciples saw them as utilizing too much of the Master's precious time. They rebuked the mothers and told them they should not bother Jesus with such mundane matters. However, Jesus looked above and beyond what they were saying and took time for the children. Jesus rebuked the disciples and told them that if He had time for anyone, He had time for the children. Anyone who comes to God and yields to Him must possess the humility, simplicity, and naivety of a child. God's kingdom is established for such as these. Jesus is not seeking the pompous, proud, and upright. He came for the earnest seeker of truth. He will accept these seekers first, even if they are children. This is the greater lesson: adults must come to Jesus with the same humility, simplicity, innocence, and deference as children have when they come to learn. ; We must be ready to hear the Gospel story and accept it as present truth. Jesus declared that He came not to call the righteous but to bring sinners to repentance. Those recognizing their spiritual need, hunger, and thirst will find the Savior and possess the simplicity of the child because they are searching for truth, wisdom, and knowledge. They want to know the Savior and be changed by Him.

Even though He is now in heaven, Jesus is still accepting little children. Jesus is available to the children, and through His ministers and clergy representatives, He is blessing them. Children at different ages can decide to follow Christ. Let them be exposed to Him at home, at prayer meeting, and at tent and evangelistic meetings in their early years and when they reach the years of accountability, they will not forget the God they had learned about in their formative years. According to Isaiah, "All thy children shalt be taught of the Lord" (Isa. 54:13). Let them be brought to Jesus, and let Him teach them. He is the best Teacher they could ever have.

Not only will the children have peace from His teachings, but there will be joy and happiness in the family circle because everyone will know the Lord. Let everyone, babes, infants, and toddlers and those with childlike faith be brought to the Lord! *Suffer* them all!

Day 98

And all thy children shall be **Taught** *of the Lord; and great shall be the peace of thy children. Isaiah 54:13*

This text was mentioned in the previous day, but it is such a beautiful promise that it deserved its own day! Children cannot be taught of the Lord unless the parents take them to Him and prepare an atmosphere where Christ occupies first place in their lives. Fetal preparation is advised for all potential mothers. The children are so important to Jesus that He took time out for them. At their earliest, they must be taught about the Great Creator of the universe. They shall know of Him through His mighty created works: birds, trees, flowers, the seas, springs, rivers, creeks, fish, animals, and all humanity. They will know what He has done, can do, and is doing for them on a daily basis, and they will be taught to talk to Him through prayer.

Children live what they learn, and parents have the responsibility to nurture and train them by exposing them to good, beautiful, and upright things. That is why King Solomon counsels to "Train up a child in the way he should go: and when he is old, he will not depart from it" (Prov. 22:6) is potent. The major question is: what shall they be taught? In Deuteronomy 6:6–9 we find the instruction manual and the curriculum that God gave Israel for the children. Those instructions are eternal and are just as relevant today as when God spoke from Sinai.

Children still need to be taught about the Lord. Teach them love, obedience, respect, and reverence for God and holy things. Teach them to honor their parents and to be obedient to God's voice. Baby Moses was taught of the Lord through his godly mother in infancy and in childhood. When he grew up in Pharaoh's palace, he was thoroughly entrenched in the principles and laws about Jehovah. He had all the militaristic exposure to palace rules and regulations, yet he chose to go with the people of God than to enjoy the pleasures and glory that came along with his princely demands and requirements. The Bible says that he chose God over worldly fame and power (see Heb. 11:24, 25).

This commission is for every parent and prospective parent. The task of raising a child is great and noble. To children in their formative years, the parent is the only God they will know. How important it is then that they be taught that there is a God to whom they owe allegiance! All caretakers, including grandparents, are to heed the injunction. This is a generational principle: when these children become young adults, they will not forget what they had been taught, but in turn will teach these principles to their children and perpetuate its mission. If these truths are embedded in their minds at an early age and reemphasized as they grow, they will not ask for the right paths because they will know them. They will enjoy a good and upright life that honors God, for His knowledge will be in their hearts.

God has covenanted to personally teach the children. What a blessed privilege for your son and daughter to have the Creator of the universe impart knowledge to him and her! God says, "These words ... shall be in their heart" (Deut. 6:6). David concurs, "I will instruct thee and teach thee in the way which thou shalt go: I will guide thee with mine eye" (Ps. 32:8). There is no greater affirmation! No wonder the prophet Isaiah reminds all that the children must be *taught* of the Lord. May parents accept the challenge.

Day 99

> **Unto** *the upright there ariseth light in the darkness: he is gracious, and full of compassion, and righteous. Psalm 112:4*

Here is another of Jehovah's great promises to the obedient. There is the assurance that even in their darkest hours, God's light will shine forth, give direction, and provide deliverance.

God will never leave His people by themselves to flounder in a sea of troubles, uncertainty, and doubt. As He was with ancient Israel leading them out of Pharaoh's Egyptian bondage—a cloud by day and a light by night—so He will be here today for all those who call upon His name and willingly obey Him. The prophet Malachi speaks for God and records His exact words: "For I am the Lord, I change not; therefore ye sons of Jacob are not consumed" (Mal. 3:6). You ask, how are we related to the sons of Jacob? We are all related through the covenant God made with Abraham, which promised his seed will be blessed. We are all spiritual Israelites, hence the promise is ours, too. Paul, quoting the prophet Isaiah, avers God's promise: "Jesus Christ [is] the same yesterday, and to day and for ever" (Heb. 13:8). He also says, "But thou art the same, and thy years shall not fail" (Heb. 1:12).

Unto the obedient, there will be protection for He that promised is righteous, compassionate, tender-hearted, and full of goodness. There is not evil, retribution, or revenge within Him. To those who walk humbly with their God, there will always be a way out of the surrounding darkness. God has promised that the "Sun of righteousness [will] arise with healing in his wings" (Mal. 4:2), and "they that dwell in the land of the shadow of death, upon them hath the light shined" (Isa. 9:2). Peter was locked up in the dark prison, but an angel of light was sent to loosen his chains and release him. Daniel was in the lions' den, but light shone through and sealed the lions' lips so that no harm came to him. The three Hebrew youth were thrown in the fiery furnace, but Jesus, the Light of the world, stood and walked among the flames, which immediately lost their power and intensity. The king was forced to acknowledge that the fourth person "is like the Son of God" (Dan. 3:25). Yes, unto the righteous and upright, light will always shine out of the darkness and deliverance will come. They beheld His glory, and it was well with their souls.

Since God controls, leads, and guides, only beauty, truth, light, holiness, and purity can emit from Him. Our God is a Manager, so let the upright be strong. Trials, tribulations, harassments, and harangues will come, but underneath them are the everlasting arms of Jehovah El Elyon—the most high God—in whom light, love, and righteousness dwell.

May everyone in His creation walk uprightly and give praise and honor to the God of all ages. Praise Him because His mercy and goodness never fail. Go confidently with your hands in His strong and mighty hands.

Day 100

And he was clothed with a **Vesture** *dipped in blood: and his name is called The Word of God. Revelation 19:13*

Speaking of Jesus, the prophet of Patmos saw Him return and sit on a white horse with the inscription "True and Faithful." That is what He is, has been, and will be for time and eternity.

The description reflects a holy one: His eyes are a flaming fire and on His head are many crowns, which indicate His regality, sovereignty, and total authority. He has an unknown name that indicates the mystery and greatness that surrounds Him. Because His robe of vesture was dipped in blood, it indicates the sacrifice Jesus made when He shed His blood for sinners in order to make them pure and white. Red blood purifies and makes sins white. A line from "Whiter Than Snow" in *The Seventh-day Adventist Hymnal* reads: "Wash me in the blood of the Lamb and I shall be whiter than the snow." The robe dipped in blood signifies His coming to execute judgment on the nations.

Jesus' name is synonymous with the Word of God. John 1:1 reads, "In the beginning was the Word, and the Word was with God, and the Word was God." Verse 14 says, "And the Word was made flesh, and dwelt among us, (and we beheld his glory, the glory as of the only begotten of the Father,) full of grace and truth." It is the same person referenced here. His name is the Word of God. Yes, He was the Word made flesh, and He dwelt among humanity for just over thirty-three years, and then He offered His own precious blood to save humankind. Upon his return, He will wear the bloodstained robe symbolizing His sacrifice for the human race.

This bloodstained vesture bears the imprimatur of holiness: "King of kings and Lord of lords." This shows that Jesus has universal sovereignty over all the kings and lords of the earth. We shall know Him, for He shall be clad in a bloodstained robe—a symbol of the eternal sacrifice. No one can imitate that appearance. All the saved will be dressed in robes that are white as snow because they will have been washed and made pure in the blood of the Lamb. All their character flaws will have been straightened out, and they will stand before the Lamb as righteous. The blood of Jesus Christ is the world's greatest purifier because it removes the stain of sin and leaves the sinner spotless. His red blood transforms evil into purity.

When Jesus returns, humanity will recognize Him not as the crucified one, but as the reigning Monarch. His blood-covered robe is the affirmation of His sacred fire. At His first coming, He revealed God's love and His grace. At His second coming, He will reveal God's holiness, justice, and judgment. He is coming in majesty and power, and we shall know Him, for we shall see Him donned in His *vesture* bearing Calvary's blood stains, the marks of His eternal sacrifice. May we welcome the King of kings and worship Jesus Christ our Redeemer.

Day 101

Whoso *keepeth his mouth and his tongue, keepeth his soul from troubles.*
Proverbs 21:23

We live in an age of abundant knowledge. There is an alarming amount of chatter. Everyone seems to have something to say, and there are always people willing to listen. For the past two decades talk shows have taken over the airwaves; you can find these kinds of programs on the television, the radio, and the Internet. Now there is Facebook, Twitter, YouTube, etc. People are using these respective social media channels for several purposes; however, though the wise person thinks that talking is good, it is good to remember that there is need for prudence. We need to be selective in our exchanges and vituperations.

To be a charlatan is not a virtue but a bane. Many times people talk without being asked to contribute to the exchange, but chatter is cheap and can be divisive. Talk that is uplifting, energizing, and informative is magnanimous. Many times it is often damaging because it is used to mock, cheapen someone's reputation, or cause death through an evil witness.

Solomon admonishes the "blabbermouths" to treasure silence. If you do not say or join in the conversation, you cannot be accused of or charged with misbehavior. He further points out that the tongue is a dangerous and desperately wicked organ. It should be well guarded. As a child I often heard my mother repeat some adages: "The cow reads his law in its belly" and "I have oft regretted my speech—not my silence." And then there is this one about the owl: "The wise old owl, the more he sees the less he speaks; why can't you be like that owl?" Of course, the owl is partially blind and has only night vision. As I became older and reflected on these statements, they formed the guiding light for my verbal expressions.

Many other texts in the Bible address the problem of controlled speech. David says, "Set a watch, O Lord, before my mouth; keep the door of my lips" (Ps. 141:3). Solomon enjoins that our words should be like "apples of gold in pictures of silver" (Prov. 25:11). Whoso adheres to these counsels will be less inclined to utter painful and hurtful words that leave deep, unsealed wounds that cannot be healed. Let us remember that a spoken word cannot be retrieved; you may say, "I am sorry," but that word has already had its effect, and no amount of apologies can soothe the pain.

Solomon also says, "a word to the wise is sufficient." If you practice to hear more and speak only when directly addressed, then your words may be well chosen and fitly spoken. All people should be constantly mindful of what, how, when, where, and why they speak, for it is out of the abundance of the heart the mouth speaks. May your words be gracious and or choose to be silent on many things. Doing so may preserve your life as well as many other lives as we follow David's counsel: "Let the lying lips be put to silence; which speak grievous things ... against the righteous" (Ps. 31:18). May God always delight in our speech!

Day 102

For I say unto you, That **Except** *your righteousness shall exceed the righteousness of the scribes and Pharisees, ye shall in no case enter the kingdom of heaven. Matthew 5:20*

This text is Jesus' greatest statement of true Christian living. It warns against pretense to godly living, uprightness, and hypocrisy. Prior to this counsel, Jesus outlined the characteristics of those who pursue the kingdom: the poor in spirit, the merciful, the pure in heart, the peacemakers, the meek, the mourners, and the upright. These would be happy people because they made God first in their lives, and each would be accorded respective healing graces. He stated that some would experience suffering, persecution, and even rejection from their families, but if it happened to honor Christ, then it would be worth it all.

The major lesson Jesus wanted to communicate was about their relationship to God: heart righteousness versus self-righteousness. The Pharisees and scribes believed in and practiced an outward show of self-righteousness, but Jesus pointed His followers to the genuine practice of faith. The current belief was that a public display of righteousness was qualification for entrance to heaven. Jesus saw their outward profession of righteousness, but inwardly, they had no real heart connection with God. They did not have any desire to have an experience with Him or to have Him change and transform their hearts. Thus, Jesus told His followers that people need a different kind of righteousness. What they saw in the Pharisees and scribes was not the real thing; what the disciples and we today need is real love and obedience—not legal compliance. Jesus wanted us to realize that our righteousness must come from what God does in us and not what we can do by ourselves.

Isaiah averred that all humankind's righteousness is like filthy rags; we are incapable to render ourselves righteous; therefore, our actions, worship, and praise must be God-centered and genuine.

God judges our hearts, motives, and deeds, for it is in our hearts where our real allegiance is found. We cannot be on the outside what we are not on the inside. Jesus pointed out that the righteous deeds of the Pharisees were like tinsel: their examples were not models for the young flock to emulate, and they should not be passed on to His potential followers. Consequently, the disciples had to ensure that their religious practices, commitment, lifestyle, and utterances followed the Master's rather than those of the professors of religion. Theirs had to exceed what those teachers and writers of the law professed if they really wanted to share in God's manifold grace and lead others to the kingdom.

Jesus' final words reminded the disciples to look to and follow Him. They should always do what He says, for He is the way. He wanted to make sure that His disciples then and now practiced genuine Christianity and be a model to the world. Let us today and every day be like Jesus everywhere—at home, at school, and at the workplace. Let the life of the Man of Calvary be seen in us every moment, in every transaction, and in every activity. May we be genuine followers and not pretenders!

Day 103

Yea, *my reins shall rejoice, when thy lips speak right things. Proverbs 23:16*

This text expresses the parental expectation at the accomplishment of their offspring. Children do not always do right by their parents, and many parents are saddened by the ethical behavior of some children. The precursor to this wish says, "My son, if thine heart be wise, my heart shall rejoice" (verse 15). It seems as the parent here is somehow disappointed in the actions and activities of the offspring and is expressing a desire for right thinking and prudent behavioral practices.

When this is done, it brings happiness and contentment to the parent. And not only will the heart rejoice, but the very reins of the parent, the inner most being, will be astir as their children's lips speak truth. Thus, from deep within comes forth joy because the parent has seen the good the offspring has achieved and is satisfied. It is the joy of seeing a child achieve success in all that he or she attempts.

If one's offspring achieves a high place of honor in the state, government, business, or in the church, that gives the parent special joy. By reason of this achievement, the family is elevated and gains recognition. Parents can thrust out their chest and say, "That is my son (or daughter)! He (or she) sits among the high ones of the society!" All their expenditures, sacrifices, and labors have not been futile, but glorious.

What is also more rewarding is if he or she sits or stands in legislative assemblies and gives prudent counsels. Out of the child's mouth comes eloquence, justice, truth, and uprightness. The parents or relatives are enthralled because their child stands up for integrity and is respected in the land and among the nations.

There is a call for rejoicing because their child is now counted as one of the upright and in whose mouth dwells wisdom and truth. In their eyes he or she may even be classified as a Solomon or a Daniel. Yes, even though at the beginning, it seems as if there would be failure, God takes what seemed to be bad and makes it into something praiseworthy.

This vignette reminisces the expectation in the verse. While at a health retreat luncheon, I met a couple who shared with us the joy of the achievements of their son, who is a doctor. He is not just an ordinary doctor, but one who has gained renown for having invented the Tissue Plasminogen Activator, which can be given to a stroke victim within the first three hours of the accident and thus avert massive brain damage. She was extremely proud and said, "Yes, that is our son. He invented something that can thwart serious damage, maybe permanent paralysis or even death."

When such feats are performed by one's offspring, there is indeed rejoicing to where even their reins have rejoiced. May there be continuous praise for our children's success, especially when they have consecrated their talents to be used in and for the Master's service!

Day 104

> *For I bear him record, that he hath a great* **Zeal** *for you, and them that are in Laodicea, and them in Hierapolis. Colossians 4:13*

Paul, while a prisoner in Rome, wrote several letters to the saints in Asia. In this letter Paul addressed the brethren at Colossae. He counseled and entreated the more stable brethren and the leaders to exhort the new believers. Its contents reflected the elders' report of the group's status, so it brought him some comfort. He was unable to visit them as previously due to unforeseen circumstances and political overtures. In this letter he reflected on his past relationship with the brethren and sent his personal greetings.

Paul also referred to the passion, zeal, and commitment demonstrated by Epaphras, as he was holding up the preeminence of Christ. Paul felt assured that this minister was doing an excellent job under the Holy Spirit's leading. He told the saints to trust him, for Paul knew him and his zeal for the church and all its members. As chief minister, Paul was able to comfort and admonish the brethren to support their pastor, for he cared passionately for them.

Whenever the president of the world church can commend his co-leaders or colleagues in ministry, that is praiseworthy; it means he has great supporters, and the work is sure to continue according to plan. When every member has zeal and is passionate about the success and growth of the organization, then there must be a rich harvest.

Regarding spiritual things, each of us must be passionate about sharing the truth and communicating this passion to all we know. The question is: can our co-laborers attest to our commitment and shared responsibility in ministry? Is it possible for us to bear our part of the burden to share Christ with others or are we willing to fold our hands and let others—pastors, elders, deacons, and other elected officers—do the work while we look on and give only lip service? The example of Epaphras' leadership that Paul referenced is a model of Christian brotherhood and leadership.

All Christians must share in the responsibility of holding up the church's programs and ministries. It is not one person's responsibility, but all of ours. We must be so united in the church that we are like a body, where each part works in tandem so that the organism can function fully. Together, we must generate zeal in ourselves and in others. God is depending on each member to do their duty; we cannot fail our commander, Jesus Christ. And more than all, what do you not want to hear from His lips: "Well done, thou good and faithful servant ... enter thou into the joy of thy lord" (Matt. 25:21), or "I never knew you: depart from me, ye that work iniquity" (Matt. 7:23)? May we have a great zeal for the Lord and His church so that we may receive His approval!

God Speaks

Day 105

In Gibeon the Lord appeared to Solomon in a dream by night: and God said, **Ask** *what I shall give thee? 1 Kings 3:5*

Solomon, Israel's newly crowned king, was overwhelmed with the kingly responsibilities. Traditionally, the kings went up to offer sacrifice, so Solomon went up to Gibeon to offer his sacrifice to Jehovah God. God saw His unpreparedness for the task, so He appeared to him in a dream and posed this question: "Ask what I shall give thee?" That exchange could have evoked two emotions: fear and awe of the great God of the universe or sheer delight that God chose to commune with him.

Fearlessly, Solomon entered into a conversation with God. He recounted God's dealings with his father and why he was made king (verse 7), and then he confessed his ignorance and insufficiency for the task of leadership. He told God that he was a child and did not know what he was doing, so the most critical thing God could give him was wisdom. "Give therefore thy servant an understanding heart to judge thy people, that I may discern between the good and bad: for who is able to judge so great a people?" (verse 9).

God saw Solomon's heart, which was pure and noble. He knew his yearnings and desires and understood what the young, fledgling king wanted. God came to his aid, for He wanted to use him as an example of obedience, uprightness, and wisdom. Then God responded, "Behold, I have done according to thy words: lo, I have given thee a wise and an understanding heart; so that there was none like thee before thee ... And I have also given thee that which thou hast not asked, both riches, and honour: so that there shall be not be any among the kings like unto thee in all thy days" (verse 12, 13). God gave what He promised conditionally based on obedience to His precepts, statutes, and commandments.

God is willing to grant youth and extension of life to us today. He gave it to Methuselah, Adam, Enoch, and a significant number of the patriarchs. All we have to do is to ask. Today we have many seniors living to their ninetieth birthday and beyond; some have reached a century and are still holding.

Are you willing to take everything to God and to ask for His direction, or are you waiting to hear His voice? Like the young king, each of us must see our own limitations and approach God in sincerity and meekness and ask for what we need that can bring honor to His name. Sometimes we wonder why we lack. It may be that we did not ask, or even if we *asked,* we might be asking for the wrong thing?

Ask God for what you want, and He will give you what you need. No sincere request goes unheeded or unanswered. Ask, ask, and ask! Jesus assured us that whatever we ask for in His name, the Father will grant it. May we continue to *ask* of the Father the things that we lack and do need!

Day 106

Bless *the Lord, O my soul: and all that is within me, bless his holy name. Psalm 103:1*

Psalm 100:4 opens with an affirmation and an admonition: "Enter into his gates with thanksgiving, and into his courts with praise: be thankful unto him, and bless his name." It immediately calls the reader's attention to action: be thankful and give praise! Whatever situation you are facing, give thanks to the God of the universe and bless His name. His many names encompass the entire panoply of our being. He is our refuge, our strong tower, everlasting Father. He is our strength and our mighty healer. He is the Lord of lords and King of kings; He is the sanctifier, and He is the Lord of all the earth.

But how does one bless the name of God? And what constitutes blessing? To bless is to invoke divine favor upon or to sanctify and to confer well-being or prosperity upon someone. During the days of the patriarchs, the act of blessing was very popular. Parents blessed their children, especially the firstborn son. In the case of Esau, he exchanged his blessing for a mere pot of lentil stew. When he came in and found that his brother, Jacob, had usurped his right, he wept sorely and said, "Hast thou not reserved a blessing for me?" (Gen. 27:36). That blessing was his authority and power to stand as the leader in his family and among God's people. While on his deathbed, Jacob called his sons and gave each of them a blessing. Even today the custom is still practiced among many nations. Every child wants to be endowed with favor from his patriarch. It was so widely practiced that Dr. Luke, quoting an old custom, wrote: "As it is written in the law of the Lord, Every male that openeth the womb shall be called holy to the Lord" (Luke 2:23). That means he is sanctified and set a part for holy purposes. He is blessed.

Now, how does one bless the Lord? It is by extolling His mighty name. Blessing also connotes thanksgiving and offering praise to the Most High. When we say, "Bless me, O my Savior, bless me," we are asking for favor. But when we bless the Lord, we are expressing gratitude for all His goodness, tender mercies, and compassion meted out to us. So when we say "Bless the Lord, O my soul," we are literally saying, "Praise Thee, O God, for all You have done." Humankind cannot bless the God of the universe; it is the other way around. It is God who blesses; we give Him praise.

Our lives should be one of continuous praise and thanksgiving: Thanks for prayers answered, for victories won, for deliverance from dangers known and unknown, for protection, for food on the table, for a sound mind, for a modicum of good health, and for success achieved. Because of God's complete control over our lives, not only should our lips, mind, and heart but every fiber of our being should extol praise to the Almighty. King David ascribes several praises to the Lord (see Ps. 107).

Blessings are a generational factor. Parents teach their children to hallow, respect, and revere the name of God and to be always thankful for His gifts. They in turn teach their children, so the principle perpetuates. We must always be appreciative, for God is everlasting, and His watchful care is available as long as time lasts and human beings need His blessings.

May your soul *be thankful* and praise the Lord God, Rock of Ages!

Day 107

Create *in me a clean heart, O God; and renew a right spirit within me. Psalm 51:10*

King David's lamentation and petition is every sinner's plea for deliverance from the throes of sin and infidelity. David met himself, and he did not like what he saw: an adulterer, a murderer, a thief, a manipulator, and a usurper. In submission and repentance, the guilty king threw himself on God's mercy, fell at his feet, lay prostrate on the ground, and wrestled with God for renewal and reinstatement in His favor.

As king, he thought he could get away with these respective devious acts, but Solomon tells us that the "eyes of the Lord are in every place, beholding the evil and the good" (Prov. 15:3). He knew that as king, he was beyond humanity's scrutiny; no one had the audacity to question the king's actions; no one dared confront him. He reveled in his secret deceit until Nathan, God's prophet, came and confronted him with the analogy of the sheep narrative. Upon hearing the story, David was filled with indignation and adroitly used his kingly posture and wisdom to pronounce judgment on that evil and wicked fellow: "As the Lord liveth, the man that hath done this thing shall surely die" (2 Sam. 12:5). The prophet listened to the king's harangue, analyzed his response, and then replied: "Thou art the man" (2 Sam. 12:7). David was flabbergasted and confounded; he did not know how the prophet knew his secret.

Daniel said to King Nebuchadnezzar, "But there is a God in heaven that revealeth secrets, and maketh known to the king Nebuchadnezzar what shall be in the latter days" (Dan. 2:28). "He revealeth the deep and secret things: he knoweth what is in the darkness, and the light dwelleth with him" (Dan. 2:22). That is our God; that is David's God, but David had not known that. He had not had an experience with the Omniscient One. When he did, he could not stand up with a straight form, he had to bow low. He confessed his sins like the prodigal son in Luke 15:21: "I have sinned against heaven."

King David had one saving grace about him; he knew where, when, how, and why he had slipped into God's disfavor. Upon recognizing his folly, he quickly turned to God and sought forgiveness. In all his sins, David was not arrogant, but humble, penitent, and contrite, which is why God could say that he was a man after His own heart. David recognized his problem and sought healing.

David had a sensitivity to sin. He knew he was not perfect, and he quickly sought to amend his imperfections. That is all that God requires of us—ownership, confession, repentance, and forsaking the sins that plague us. We must surrender our all to Him. As we read Psalm 51, we get an insight into David's condition. We understand his sorrow and his pleading to be reconnected to God and to receive His approval. Look at the strong verbs he uses: wash, purge, restore, renew, forsake not, and hide not thy face. These show deep contrition and the need for reinstatement.

Let us daily pray the Davidic prayer: "Create in me a clean heart, O God" (Ps. 51:10). When God creates in us that new heart, there will be no trace of evil lodging there or the desire to sin. May we pray for a clean, pure heart, for Jesus is waiting to give such a heart to the penitent and contrite seeker!

Day 108

*O **Death**, where is thy sting? O grave, where is thy victory? 1 Corinthians 15:55*

This is a very sobering rhetorical question. The addressee cannot respond because of its permanent silence. The apostle Paul speaks to this monstrosity that robs one of life, yet death will not have the last word. There will be a victorious song of triumph, for Jesus brought victory and triumph over death even though it seemed to have taken over His body. But He burst the tomb and came forth alive. When the angel came down and called for Him, death had to loosen its deadly claws and set God's Son free. Jesus' triumph is our hope and promise.

For two brief days, death seemed to have triumphed, but that was only a temporary control. Death has no power over the righteous, and it had no power over the Creator of life. Death is but a cessation of breathing and bodily operations. Jesus declared that this pause is but a sleep. He proved this in the case of Lazarus, Martha and Mary's brother, who had died four days before Jesus and his team arrived at the village. Jesus said, "Our friend Lazarus sleepeth; but I go, that I may awake him out of sleep" (John 11:11). Also in the case of Jairus' daughter, who lay dead in the upstairs room. Jesus simply took her hand, called her name, and she opened her eyes. Both Jairus' daughter and Lazarus were simply asleep.

Death to Jesus is the loss of eternal life. It is more appropriately titled the "second death." When that happens, a person has no more hope. Their eternal salvation is forever fixed. Now, none need fear the first death, which is simply sleep. When the righteous dead are awake at the Lord's second coming, the first person's face they will see is Jesus, who will bestow eternal life and immortality on them. They knew they went to sleep and are now awake. Death can and will have no power over them. John Donne, a seventeenth century poet, spoke very aptly about death:

"One short sleep past, we wake eternally, and death shall be no more; death, thou shalt die."

No one placed in the grave is now dead; they are all asleep waiting the call of Jesus, the life-giver. Death and life are on the same continuum; death is the second phase of life. All that lives shall die. Sin made that our reality. Paul says, "For all have sinned, and come short of the glory of God" (Rom. 3:23), and in Romans 6:23, he points out that "the wages of sin is death; but the gift of God is eternal life through Jesus Christ our Lord." Death is the result of sin; it is humankind's nemesis.

Paul's exegesis brought his hearers the reality and totality of life. Death to some is the final aspect of their life, but to others, it is only a temporary cessation of the physical, bodily functions. He assures the living that death does not and will not have the last word. When Jesus returns, the sting of death will be obliterated. There will be victory and triumph! No more funeral trains, no more weeping and lamentations. Only inexorable joy! Praise God! Jesus made it possible for life to triumph over *death*.

Day 109

But with thee will I **Establish** *my covenant; and thou shalt come into the ark, thou, and thy sons, and thy wife, and thy sons' wives with thee. Genesis 6:18*

To establish is to set forth and enact. God called Noah and told him that the end of all flesh had come up before him; they had corrupted His way upon the earth, and He was going to destroy them. God found Noah's family to be the only righteous ones, so God promised them that He would save that household of eight people: Noah, his wife, their three sons, and their wives.

God established His contract with them. When God establishes something, it cannot be abrogated. He is the eternal God; His words and plans are unalterable. There is none greater than He, and He is subject to no one. God is still searching for earthlings with whom to establish His covenant and who will be obedient and willing to carry out His action plan. God covenanted with Noah and used him to preach the message of grace to the antediluvian population. Unfortunately, all rejected the call of mercy to change their lifestyles and turn to the Lord. Consequently, everyone except his family was swept away in the deluge.

Can God say of you and me as He did of Noah, "I am making a covenant with you; I know you will bring up your household after me to obey my precepts, statutes and laws"? Furthermore, can God depend on us to be His spokesperson to call men and women out to repentance as Noah did? He has commissioned us to go into the entire world and tell men everywhere the good news. God is still searching for such men and women and families with whom He can establish His covenant. Are you one of them? Is your family such a family?

Today, God is calling men, women, children, and youth to come into the ark of safety—His church—and find refuge and security from the throes and anxieties of life. Above all, Jesus is there waiting to give them entry. Open your heart to Him today and say, "Come into my heart, my home, my life, dear God, and set up Your covenant with me." God does not coerce nor cajole; He invites. Make sure that your life, your home, and your family is one with whom the Lord can establish His covenant.

After that antediluvian deluge, God again established His covenant with the current generation: Noah's children. He would never again destroy the earth with a flood. He set His rainbow in the sky as an everlasting covenant with the people of this age. Every time the bow appears, it reminds us of God's covenant with humankind. God is still keeping His promise, but can He count on you? May He be able to *establish* a covenant with each of us!

Day 110

For Ever, *O Lord, thy word is settled in heaven. Psalm 119:89*

Forever connotes eternity—a timeless period. David affirms that God's words are well-known and established among the heavenly hosts. There is none to deny that. His words are unchanging in the heavenly arena and equally on earth. It is only our presumptuousness that makes us thinks that we can change God's words. Daniel's prophecy points out that there will be a force that will think itself able to change times and laws (see Dan. 7:25). They may succeed on this earth, but God's words surely stand fast. We may attempt many things, but it is the eternal God who controls. What God has written with His own fingers, no man or woman can change.

If the angelic hosts that minister around God's throne bow in obeisance to His authority, why does finite humanity think they can alter God's fiat? David aptly assures humankind that God's words are established forever in heaven, and His faithfulness is to all generations as long as time shall last. That is an indefatigable and unchanging fact.

God never argues with us. He is the Almighty. Omniscience resides in Him; therefore, when He speaks, He does not need our approval. He told Noah that He had established His covenant with him and his house. Who can alter that? King David, who knew God very well, says that when God says something, He means it, and He ratifies it with His seal. God said He would send Jesus, and He sent Him. He said He will deliver us out of our troubles, and He has. God already knows the end from the beginning. He has told us that He will send back Jesus to this earth to gather His saints. We are waiting for that event.

Certainly, God's word is settled in heaven; there is no inkling that it will be different. He commanded and everything stood fast. His Word is solid in heaven and established on earth, and it stands fast. God's words are truth and verity; not one fails. He has the first, last, and best word. We cannot alter or change the things that have come out of God's lips; His words are unalterable.

God declares, "My covenant will I not break nor alter the thing that is gone out of my lips" (Ps. 89:34). Yes, *forever*, God's words are written and they remained sealed.

Day 111

The Lord is **Good**, *a strong hold in the day of trouble; and he knoweth them that trust in him.*
Nahum 1:7

"God is good; all the time, and all the time, God is good" is a choric praise used by many worshipers to ascribe honor to God for His watchful care, protection, and preservation of His children. This is an affirmation of their gratitude to the Almighty for all His goodness in dealing with them. King David says we are not consumed because of the Lord's goodness. Thus the choric praise is very appropriate in the assembly of the saints who recognize God's majesty.

Our God is not only good but He is also a stronghold and a fortress, especially when His children face trouble. One is admonished not to panic when trouble comes, for God will stand up for and by His people. In Psalm 34:19 David avers, "Many are the afflictions of the righteous: but the Lord delivereth him out of them all," and in Psalm 46:1 he says, "God is our refuge and strength, a very present help in trouble." All of Psalm 46 is an assurance of God's illimitable strength.

Our trust and abiding faith in God's sustainability empowers us to proclaim that He is good. His watchful eyes and outstretched arms are constantly available to us. God knows the needs of each of His trusting children. Peter advises, "Cast all your care upon him; for he careth for you" (1 Peter 5:7). King Solomon states, "The name of the Lord is a strong tower: the righteous runneth into it, and is safe" (Prov. 18:10). Isn't that pure goodness?

Coupled with God's goodness, is His everlasting mercy, compassion, and loving-kindness. God is all goodness and knowledge; He knows whether you are faking or sincere. His eyes are on everything and everyone beholding the good and the bad.

Can you attest to the goodness of God? Do you have a story of how good He is to you? If God has been good to you, do not keep it; bring it to the front and share it. May you spread the news of how God is *good* to you; your testimony will bless many lives!

Day 112

> **Hearken** *unto thy father that begat thee, and despise not thy mother when she is old.*
> *Proverbs 23:22*

This is another of Solomon's salient advices on family ethics directed especially to one's offspring. When children have grown and begin to establish their own family, they tend to disregard the counsel of their parents or view lightly what they have to say. In many instances, they leave their elderly parents to manage on their own. It seems to be an age-old phenomenon and not just a characteristic of twenty-first century children. King Solomon, who was writing more than forty centuries ago, had to call children's attention to their lack of duty to their aged parents. They had a careless and indifferent attitude toward the aged much like that which is seen today.

God knew of people's fickle attitude, so in the Decalogue's fifth precept, he instructed children to honor, respect, and show deference to their parents. The apostle Paul concurs with the fifth law (see Eph. 6:1).

As sons inherit the patriarchy, they too become fathers and establish their own dynasty. In many cases, they are less inclined to listen and take counsel from their male ancestors, thinking they know more than their elders. They forget that the elders have experience. The sons have not yet lived; therefore, they are not exposed to the rudiments of life. The conflict between youth and the aged rages in today's society. God granted Solomon the wisdom he requested. When the Holy Spirit inspired him, he was equipped to make such fundamental statements regarding family dynamics.

Beside the rebellious attitude toward the father, children tended to disrespect the mother and reject her counsels. That behavior is common even today among teenage boys who often refuse to take instruction from the women in their lives, whether it be teachers, mothers, or any female in high or low standing. King Solomon's advice is very cogent at this time when the youth are hearing so many voices claiming their attention. They must not forget that it is the father who engendered them and that his wisdom and experience surpasses his sons'.

Children were expected to esteem their mothers; this was especially important in a society where women were looked down upon as the handkerchiefs of the world—to be used and discarded. It was the mother who nurtured the child and trained him or her in the womb and passed on to the unborn fetus all the character traits needed to develop into a well-rounded person. Therefore, mothers deserved as much or even more respect than the fathers. The king understood the dynamics very well, and he was able to transmit counsel across forty centuries that still has relevance today.

Children should not reject or despise their elders because they are old. It is during this period of their lives that they need tender care. They have expended their energy, skill, and resources to nurture and bring up the children, and they should not be abandoned and placed in homes of the aged while their offspring continue to enjoy their lives. God holds the children accountable for taking care of their aged parents; they must learn wisdom from them and protect and care for them in their twilight years. All children would do well to heed the call of the wise man. May we all *hearken* his message and remember to respect our parents, grandparents, and the elderly in our society.

Day 113

I can do all things through Christ which strengtheneth me. Philippians 4:13

This is the greatest affirmation of faith, trust, confidence, and wholehearted commitment to the mercies and saving grace of Jesus Christ. It infers that if one stays connected with the power of the Holy Spirit, there is nothing that one cannot do. Without Christ, no strategy, scheme, or plan will work; it's all about Christ abiding in us.

When anyone gives himself totally to the Holy Spirit's control, there is nothing that he cannot achieve. With such commitment, men and women are able to accomplish great things because God has given them His mind, which was made in His image. "Let this mind be in, which was also in Christ Jesus" (Phil. 2:5).

Both Matthew and Mark declared that everything is possible with God. One only has to yield to the will of the Lord, and the Holy Spirit will empower the believer to do great things. When the will is submitted to Christ, there is no limit to one's ability to achieve magnificent feats. May we attempt great things for God! He is there to strengthen and uphold us.

The Almighty empowers us, so why are we still so languid about many things when every possibility is within our grasp? Humanity has been given the mind of Christ. God made us in His image and imbued us with a mind to think and a will to act. If we do not achieve, it is because we have not accessed God's gift.

A person's reach must exceed their grasp and surpass their limited vision. We must stretch the muscles of our mind and soar like the eagle. Whatever the task is: physical, emotional, intellectual, moral, social, or spiritual, we can do it. Resiliency resides in our psyche and physique. We are not alone in these endeavors; the Holy One is with us. Therefore, every one of us can do everything through Jesus. God gives us the strength because our wills are united with His.

Even amongst challenges and temptations, the promise stands. We might not be given super-human strength to climb mountains and sail across the continents, but we will be given enough strength to face the enemy from all fronts. The enemy will not be able to overpower us because we are aligned to the power house—Jesus, our caretaker, shepherd, and protector. We must be careful to lay our plans before Him and align our wills with His. Only then can we triumphantly aver, "*I can do everything through him for he gives me the strength.*" May you talk yourself into believing and acting on that premise? Yes, you can. Yes, you must! God makes that possible.

Day 114

But why dost thou judge thy brother? or why dost thou set at nought thy brother? for we shall all stand before the **Judgment** *seat of Christ? Romans 14:10*

God is a fair God. With Him, there is no partiality or deference. All people are given equal opportunity to accept or reject Him. Christ came, lived, died, and returned to His Father's right hand to execute judgment and justice to humanity. All will be evaluated and assessed according to our actions and our hearts. We earthlings cannot become discriminative and consign people to hell or heaven. That is not within our prerogative.

God and Jesus are the eternal judges. Therefore, we cannot now sit in judgment on others. That is God's domain, and if we try to attempt at His job, we are simply playing God.

Our responsibility is to know God and to make Him known to others. We should not be judgmental, for God is doing that work and does not need our help. What He requires of us is a clean heart, pure motives, and worship. "That unto me every knee shall bow, every tongue shall swear" (Isa. 45:23). Our responsibility is worship, praise, and adoration. Cease from judging our brothers and sisters and help them toward the kingdom. In God's eyes we are all equal; we are all sinners in need of Jesus' redemptive blood. Our current mission is to heed the apostle's counsel: "But let a man examine himself" (1 Cor. 11:28).

Since judgment, justice, and reward are in God's purview, and all of us must bow before Him and every tongue must confess that He is God, when we stand before God's judgment seat, our concern will be self-centered and not other-centered. Everyone will receive his or her fair reward. No sentence will be punitive; there will only be unsullied justice. One's life must either magnify or minimize Christ. When that premise becomes life's motivating force, we will know who the true judge is. Until then, let God be God.

If we are still unsatisfied with this premise, go to the Word and read thoroughly Matthew 7. It should bring clarity and insight to our minds. May each person seek God and not be *judgmental* of others, for it is God who has the last word!

Day 115

> *Now Samuel did not yet **Know** the Lord, neither was the word of the Lord yet revealed unto him. 1 Samuel 3:7*

Samuel was a child, and he had not experienced what it meant to know the Lord. The question is: how does one get to know the Lord? And still deeper, how does an individual get to know someone? This is not obtained in a cursory, fleeting moment with the person. One has to spend time with and in the presence of the other to get to know him or her. Being an acquaintance with someone does not mean you have true knowledge of them. If you want to know what is in a text, you have to spend time leafing through its pages laboriously, grasping the details and technicalities; you have to study it. Only by doing so can we have thorough knowledge of the contents.

Young Samuel had not yet received the revelation of God's will and plan for his life. All he knew was that he was special and that his mother, Hannah, had lent him to Jehovah to be used as Yahweh saw fit. But of his mission, he knew nothing. He had to wait on God's revelation. God came to him in a soft voice. Samuel did not recognize the voice, so he went to his preceptor to ascertain if he had called him. Eli had not summoned the youth, and since he heard the calling twice before, then it must be significant. He told Samuel to return to his bed, and if he heard the voice a third time, he should answer, "Speak, Lord; for thy servant heareth" (1 Sam. 3:9). Eli knew that God was calling the youth, but Samuel did not know that it was God's voice. He had known about the true God, for his mother had introduced him to Jehovah since his birth. Upon Eli's advice, he listened and heard God's voice.

It was then that Samuel's journey to know the Lord began. He listened to His counsel, obeyed His commands, and followed His instructions. He and God established a partnership, and Samuel found that he really was getting to know the Lord.

Here are a few questions to consider if we desire to know the Lord: can we recognize God's voice when He is calling us? What kind of relationship must we have so that He can speak to us? How long does it take for one to know the Lord? When does the knowing process start? Paul said of young Timothy, "And that from a child thou hast known the holy scriptures, which are able to make thee wise unto salvation" (2 Tim. 3:15). Knowing God begins in infancy and before. Hannah's example is a good model for parents.

Parents must teach their children to listen to hear God's voice. By spending time with Him in His Word, through daily prayer and meditation, lingering in His presence, talking with Him, and hearing His directives, we will get to know God. Let us today determine to know nothing else except God's will for our lives. Knowing Him is obeying Him. May our lives continually demonstrate that we *know* the Lord!

Day 116

> **Lift** *up your heads, O ye gates; and be ye lifted up, ye everlasting doors; and the King of glory shall come in. Psalm 24:7*

This trumpet peal calls people everywhere to raise their heads, arms, and hearts in adoration to the King of kings, for He is worthy of praise and worship. As David reflected on the magnificence of the great temple in Jerusalem and as the congregation came in to worship, he could not but think of the Majesty of heaven's presence filling that entire magnificent edifice.

The ark of God had come home and found its rightful place in the Temple; it was a time for celebration. Thus he summoned the entire assembly's attention to recognize and accept the presence of the Lord. God had come back to physically dwell among His chosen people. It was a time for jubilation and thanksgiving.

The ark had been away from Israel's presence for a long time. It had unfortunately been with the Philistines, but now the presence of the Lord was returning to its rightful heritage. Unspeakable joy filled the atmosphere. Here is the antiphonal praise: "Lift up your heads, O ye gates." You can just hear David say, "Open them; throw them wide open, and let everyone from everywhere come back to worship for the ark of God, the Shekinah glory, is with us once more! It has found its resting place. The presence of God will once more abide with His people." Then comes the question: "Who is this King of glory?" (verse 8). The jubilant answer is "the Lord strong and mighty, the Lord mighty in battle" (verse 8). In response to the question a second time comes the answer: "The Lord of hosts, he is the King of glory" (verse 10).

People from every corner of the earth must come and bow in adoration and worship this King. Worship, praise, and adoration belong to Him alone. He is the Creator, the Lord of lords and King of kings. He is the all-seeing, all-knowing, all-powerful God. Our existence comes from Him alone. We must let Him take up residence in our lives.

This is also a futuristic adoration pointing to the time when Jesus will return bringing peace and righteousness to the earth. Then the proclamation: "Open ye the gates, that the righteous nation which keepeth the truth may enter in" (Isa. 26:2) will be realized. The King of glory and all the redeemed will enter into the gates into the city of God, and then the gates will be lifted up and be forever opened. The redeemed shall lift up their hands and shout, "Glory hallelujah to the Lamb that was slain and is alive forever more!"

May you plan to *lift* up your head in celebration when Christ shall be crowned King of kings and Lord of lords!

Day 117

> *Let this* **Mind** *be in you, which was also in Christ Jesus. Philippians 2:5*

What an exhortation! This is a universal appeal is to every Christian in every age. As an ageless counsel, it is not constrained by class, race, ethnicity, culture, status, color, achievement, wealth, or rank.

Do you know what characterized the mind of Christ? What was His attitude? If you do, then follow His example; if not, seek to know. What were Jesus' constant thoughts, His meditations and concentrations? If you are young in the faith and have limited knowledge of Jesus, and like young Samuel, you did not yet know God, then you need to spend time seeking to know what was in His mind. Jesus advises, "Search the scriptures ... they are they which testify of me" (John 5:39).

Holy Writ tells us that his mind harbored no sin or utterances of vain repetitions. He had no malice or hatred for even those who sought to kill Him prematurely. He was free of curses and malignity, and He did not strive for supremacy or equality with God. He was all humility and was always choosing to serve rather than to be served. He exercised true love to all who came across His path and constantly sought to do good: healing, teaching, blessing, releasing the bound, and feeding the hungry (see Luke 4:16–18). His attitude reflected the Father's mind. Thus, "I and my Father are one" (John 10:30).

The mind of Jesus nurtured no pain. Instead, He relieved pain and suffering. Wherever He went, people were healed of every kind of malediction. He either touched them, or they touched Him and power emanated from Him to the sufferers, and they were healed. Jesus was all about healing, blessing, and forgiving.

Jesus occupied His mind in doing His Father's business. When we get to know Christ, He imparts to us His character, His mind, and His will, and we move in the direction of perfection. Like Christ, we should manifest a servant attitude and be willing to serve others first out of love rather than guilt or fear. Christ's mind was all purity, love, and perfection. Pray that the mind of Christ invades your mind so your character and attitude will be like His. His mind is full of holiness and wholeness. May you cultivate His presence, dwell on His completeness and righteousness so that your *mind* becomes like Christ's!

Day 118

And he went a little farther, and fell on his face, and prayed, saying, O my Father, if it be possible, let this cup pass from me: **Nevertheless** *not as I will, but as thou wilt.*
Matthew 26:39

This is the most agonizing prayer that Jesus prayed while in the Garden of Gethsemane. He petitioned the Father three times for the release as the guilt of sinful humanity weighed heavily on His soul.

The garden was His favorite spot, for it was where peace, quietness, and solitude abode. He felt safe and private and could be in His Father's presence and unburden His concerns. But this time it was different; it was time for Him to face the dreadful task of yielding up His life. The pain, burden, and the sorrow almost overwhelmed Him. The first time He agonized with the Father, there was no answer. He went a second time and prayed again pleading for relief, but again, no answer. His Father seemed out of reach and hearing. The third time He went a little farther to a sequestered spot in the woods and there poured out this plea. He was more ready to yield to the Father's will. Still, there was no response. Then, as if reading the Father's mind, writhing in agony and deep contemplation about the mission for which He came, He prayed, "Nevertheless, not as I will, but as thou wilt." Having said that, Jesus yielded to the authorities.

His agony was maddening because although He had taken His three most dependable disciples for spiritual support while He went alone to pray, when He returned to them, they were always fast asleep. What was it? Were they overwhelmed with fear, uncertainty, and discouragement? Did the enemy put them to sleep so that they could not watch and pray for their beloved Teacher and even for themselves? Whatever was the cause, Jesus had to pray alone. Yes, alone. There was none to stand with Him. Sheer agony! Alone!

Jesus came to do His Father's will and would not renege on it. Humanity's fate hung in the balance; it was either His life or their total loss. He decided and offered Himself to pay the penalty even though He had never done anything wrong. He took the insults, the whipping, the abuse, the curses, the mockery, and yes, the death. He gave up His life because it was the Father's will. What sacrifice!

Like Jesus, our prayers should be prefaced with "according to the Father's will." We have no will of our own and do not know what we want. God knows what is best for us; therefore, let our requests be according to God's will.

"Thy will be done" or "according to Your will" ought to be the core of our prayers. May the Lord help us to say our prayers with resignation and always accept God's will for our lives.

Day 119

O give thanks unto the Lord; for he is good: for his mercy endureth for ever. Psalm 136:1

Praise waiteth for thee O God in Zion, and unto thee shall all flesh come; thy praise shall be continually on my lips, for I incline my heart unto wisdom. This is a song of praise for all people; O, that they would lift up their voices and utter praise and worship for the God of the universe, the maker and sustainer of everything that breathes!

Because of God's tender mercies, lovingkindness, constant watchful care, and the love He bestows, and ultimately because He emptied heaven and divested Himself of His only Son, our logical response is to offer praise to Him.

God's mercy has been extended to humanity since the creation of the world and will continue as long as humanity needs grace until the day when God says that the end has come.

For all that God has done and is doing for the human family, all should come and show appreciation. Join King David and give thanks. David extols God's name three times in Psalm 107:

Verse 8: "Oh that men would praise the Lord for his goodness, and for his wonderful works unto the children of men!"

Verse 15: "Oh that men would praise the Lord for his goodness, and for his wonderful works to the children of men!"

Verse 21: "Oh that men would praise the Lord for his goodness, and for his wonderful works to the children of men!"

Verse 22: "And let them sacrifice the sacrifices of thanksgiving, and declare his works with rejoicing."

This is our solemn obligation for great and mighty is His name and His work. It is because of the Lord's mercy why we are not consumed.

God is faithful and gracious to His children, and His steadfastness causes rejoicing among the righteous. May men and women everywhere lift up their voices and offer praise unto the great God of the earth for all His goodness!

Day 120

*He giveth **Power** to the faint; and to them that have no might he increaseth strength.*
Isaiah 40:29

What a mighty God. He is an ever-caring and loving Father whose eyes oversee all! No one needs to fall into despair; no one facing any arduous circumstances needs to throw their hands in the air or fall into a fit of depression because God's word says that our loving Father gives power to the weak and fainting. So, stand up and take hold of God's hand!

The Sovereign Lord tells us that He can hold us up, for He made us. We can draw our power and strength from Him, for he is the Omnipotent One. He cannot fail. All we have to do is reach out and ask Him for help. The Word says that God gives to all people freely and that God is more willing to give than we are to ask. When God gives something, it is permanent. He did not give Jesus for a time (though He spent only thirty-three and a half years among us), but it was a gift for all eternity. God gave His all—His love, His patience, and His Holy Spirit. He gives the angels charge over each of His children to watch, protect, and guard everyone who calls upon His name. He cares for all.

By giving power to the faint, every nerve, every fiber of one's being is strengthened and energized. Through power, Jesus performed mighty miraculous works that gave strength to the limbs of the paralytic, stopped the thirty-eight years of hemorrhaging in the sick woman, strengthened the withered hand, and many more. To Martha and Mary, He revitalized their fainting hearts by restoring their brother, Lazarus, to life.

Our God is a strong tower and a fortress. He possesses all power and strength. If you tend to be weak and your knees shake, He will revive you; He will increase your power, and He will give you the strength you need. All the power of the universe resides in His strong and mighty arms.

God is omnipotent; He is all-powerful, and He is able. He can do everything. He will bring to pass all that He wills. He desires to give strength to the weary and increase the power of the weak. Even the strongest person gets tired at times, but God's power and strength never diminish. He is never too busy or tired to help and listen; His strength is our source of strength, and it is constantly available to us. And when you feel life crushing down upon you, and you know you cannot make another step, you can call upon God, and He will renew your strength. He has done it several times for me. He has done it many, many times to others, and He will do it for you, too. Remember He says, "Call on me."

God gives and gives and gives again and again! Grasp His outstretched hand and experience the new you! Feel the power surging into your veins and pulsating your muscles. May you praise the Lord for this unspeakable gift—His *power*!

Day 121

*It shall not be **Quenched** night nor day; the smoke thereof shall go up for ever: from generation to generation it shall lie waste; none shall pass through it for ever and ever.*
Isaiah 34:10

Here, the prophet Isaiah apocalyptically points to the end of the world when the Son of righteousness will be enthroned and sin and sinners will be forever eradicated. In the first destruction of the antediluvian world, God used water, but when He saw the remains of the deluge, he covenanted through His bow that He would not bring destruction by water ever again. Next time, He would use fire.

The remains of fire are impotent ash. No root or branch of anything will remain. According to the prophet Nahum, God will make an utter end of everything. "Affliction shall not rise up the second time" (Nahum 1:9).

The text does not elicit fear about the future, the end of the world, or God's rule of justice and judgment. It actually tells us that this loving and merciful God will eradicate every trace of evil and sin. God will universally wipe out every form of sin. The unquenchable smoke that rises does not intimate a constant and continuous phenomenon, but as long as there remain traces of sin, the smoke will continue to rise. This is analogous to the continuous burning and rising of smoke at Ground Zero in New York City after the terrorist attack in 2001. The cinders and smoke remained unquenched for several months. After all was consumed, the smoke ceased. However, once the smoke ceases, the destiny of the human family will be forever sealed. It will be God's uninterrupted final act.

After the fire cleanses and purifies the old earth, a new earth will emerge wherein righteousness prevails (see Isa. 66:17). There is no eternal burning hell, for God shall wipe away the old things and create a new home for the redeemed of the earth. Never more will iniquity mar God's holy atmosphere. Satan will be extinguished, and peace will reign supremely. Fears, anxieties, illness, disease, dysfunctional minds, funeral trains, and mourning will be gone; there will be immortal and immeasurable joy. May we rejoice in this wonderful hope!

Day 122

*God is our **Refuge** and strength, a very present help in trouble. Psalm 46:1*

What consolation and assurance this text brings to us! A refuge is a safe place wherein no one can enter and disturb the peace of those who are hiding. When one is hiding in God, the enemy cannot enter that place. One is secure if they trust in God.

Cities of refuge were established for the safety and protection of a convicted murderer. He or she could stay there until the problem had been resolved or the judge was dead. As long as the individual remained in that special place, he or she was safe.

Our God is bigger than any city. He oversees the cities of the earth. He is our safe place—our hiding place. He keeps us under His wings and upholds us with His powerful hands. This act of God is awesome and incomparable. It is so magnanimous that finite minds cannot completely grasp its enormity or even the simplicity of the great act of God. How He does it is beyond our ability to understand.

When trouble comes, the first thing we ask is for God to help us and have mercy on us. When sickness comes, one turns to God. The wonderful thing is that our Father is always just waiting to help. Even right now at this moment as you are reading and meditating on the greatness and goodness of God. He will not turn anyone away.

Certainly, we can all depend on God. He is a place of security when all else is insecure. His divine assurance is to "call upon me in the day of trouble; I will deliver thee" (Ps. 50:14). What more does one need? Absolutely nothing. When God speaks, the entire earth trembles in awe at His presence and the sound of His voice. His words assure and comfort, so we need not be fearful or despair when faced with seemingly insurmountable challenges. Our God is real; He is there and will come through for us every time. His all-seeing eyes are everywhere.

We should be comforted that we have safe places: under his wings and the strong tower where we can harbor and be safe. God is not like a city of refuge; He is our refuge and our strength. In a previous day's meditation, Isaiah declared that God gives strength to the weary, the weak, and the faint. He is our stronghold. He is the Almighty, and He is everything to all humankind. Whatever you want Him to be for you, He is: deliverer, leader, protector, provider, and He is even a shelter during the stormy times. Call on Him, and He will answer. He is God, the great I AM, the all-knowing, all-supplying, and eternal God. What a God! Who can fathom Him or His ways? Job declares, "Which doeth great things past finding out; yea, and wonders without number" (Job 9:10). They are out of our purview. Let us rejoice that in Him we have safety. May we all find a *refuge* in God!

Day 123

*My **Son**, if sinners entice thee, consent thou not. Proverbs 1:10*

This clear and distinct message addresses sons, but it is meant for all children. None is exempt from the enticement that lures children off the path of rectitude and uprightness. Coincidentally, this was the very first Bible verse I learned in elementary school. During those days every child had to commit to memory several dictums from the Holy Bible. Thus, this text has been etched in my memory since I was six years old. Who were the sinners to entice a little six-year-old girl, I have not a clue, but we had to memorize certain salient verses as a safeguard against evil thoughts and actions. At that time the Bible was an instructional subject in the curriculum; very early in their lives, the school-age children were taught to honor and respect God and His Holy Word.

The teachers had done a good thing, for as I grew older and assessed the text denotatively and connotatively, new meanings developed and served as a deterrent against evil actions. One should learn very early to have control, to hide God's word in his heart, and to listen to the promptings of the Holy Spirit.

The text is about choice and self-control. It informs the innocent that there will be temptations and enticements to go in the wrong path. Childhood is a fragile and vulnerable period when one's judgment is tenuous. Consent not is the advice. That is why Solomon counsels parents in Proverbs 22:6 to "train up the child in the way he should go." The Lord also said to the children of Israel "to teach them diligently unto thy children" (Deut. 6:7). Raising a child in the Lord is so appropriate and urgent.

When those counsels are adhered to, the children will know what is right from that which is wrong. They will have the strength, power, and resilience not to yield to whatever is presented to them no matter how alluring, dazzling, or enticing it might seem. They will become discriminative and selective learners, for the words will have been hidden in their hearts and mind. They will know truth and not deviate into forbidden paths that destroy body, mind, and soul.

Evil people will seek to lead the unwary child or youth into unsavory paths. Parents must teach them to be strong and not yield to the enticing and seemingly innocent actions and activities. Above all, they must teach them to make Christ their stronghold; He understands their challenges, for He also was challenged. Paul assures that He is able to succor those who are tempted: "But [He] was in all points tempted as we are, yet without sin" (Heb. 4:15). There is hope! The enticed one needs to "come boldly unto the throne of grace ... obtain mercy, and find grace to help in time of need" (verse 16). The tempted is never alone; Christ is always available every step of the way. Reach out to Him and claim the assistance He offers.

Let all children be on guard, for there will always be evil men and women seeking to entrap the innocent and naïve ones. Look out for them! Study their snares and flee from them. When you run, God will dispatch angels to assist you; you are never in this alone. Only be strong and be firm. Stand up for the right always, and do not consent to sin. Aim to be like Joseph, who said, "How then can I do this great wickedness, and sin against God?" (Gen. 39:9). May we all remember that we are the *sons and daughters* of God, and if we cling to Him, sin will lose its power over us.

Day 124

I will instruct thee and **Teach** *thee in the way which thou shalt go: I will guide thee with mine eye. Psalm 32:8*

This is a very precious text to me. It was the mantra for my children's worship in the early days of their spiritual training. When I discovered this verse, I knew it was a text I wanted them to learn, digest, and internalize. It became our daily benediction at the end of morning worship. It was sheer delight to have my four young boys commit this text to memory and hear them repeat it after a short time. The text was not only for the boys, but it pointed to my commitment and responsibility as a mother in charge of the children's spiritual growth. I am reminded of Pharaoh's princess's charge to Jochebed: "Take this child away, and nurse it for me" (Exod. 2:9). That order became my child-rearing spiritual mantra.

Now that I am a grandmother, I realize the magnanimity of the verse. It is really God's promise to us. He will instruct, teach, and guide our children. It is very comforting to remember that His eyes will always be on us watching what we do, where we go, and whose company we enjoy. He will show us the paths of righteousness. How delightful to have the Creator of the universe condescends to be our teacher, mentor, and counselor! Is it not awesome to know that our heavenly Father cares so much that He makes a covenant to be with us? And do not forget that the unchangeable God says, "I will." This is not a statement of wish or expectation but one of determination: I will. I can just hear Him saying, "You can depend on Me."

This is very reassuring. God's eyes are over us, and His hands are guiding us and directing our feet individually. We should not worry about the curriculum when He is instructing us. He knows your intellectual needs, your limitations, your strengths, and your weaknesses. He is the Teacher par excellence! Let Him carry on His work in your life. He will not only instruct us but He will also provide the appropriate workplace so that all His children can grow and have success. God has our entire life under full control. Do not panic. Feel safe. Our God is real. Surely, His Word stands fast! Be open to His direction. Even now, may we all let Him guide, instruct, and *teach* us so that we may be more like Him.

Day 125

Mark the perfect man, and behold the **Upright**: *for the end of that man is peace.*
Psalm 37:37

This is great counsel to anyone searching for a model man or woman whose companionship brings happiness. There is an abundance of wicked people traversing the land practicing wickedness; some even believe their evil and insidious acts are purported as good.

This text summons the believer to develop spiritual sensitivity; one must be able to discern between the false and the genuine. Much pretense has characterized life's actions, and there is a fine line between the genuine and the superficial. Where are all the real people? Everyone seems to be an actor who is performing rather than being.

It is easy for one to be deceived with the tinsel and glitter, for even in the Christian life, there are wolves dressed up in sheep's clothing. Unless the Holy Spirit guides and instructs and gives the power of discernment, it may be hard to see the blurry lines because the false looks so much like the real. Will the upright men and women of integrity, please stand up!

The Bible enjoins its readers, especially the Christian: "Study to shew thyself approved unto God" (2 Tim. 2:15). Jesus advises, "Search the scriptures; for in them ye think ye have eternal life" (John 5:39). It is the Holy Spirit that will guide and lead into all truth. It will teach you how to identify the pretense and hypocrisy, sift it out, and reveal the truth. It is the Holy Spirit who will lead you to connect with the like-minded traveling on the road to uprightness and righteous living. When you have been guided by the Holy Spirit and have identified a fellow sojourner, then you are to connect with him or her, for this individual is practicing wholeness and holiness in living. Stay with this person, and walk closely to him or her. Keep their company, for he or she is blameless and upright. Hang out together, for you will be able to strengthen each other and together will have a peaceful and satisfactory end.

Divine power is a discerning mechanism. Jesus promised that when the Holy Spirit, who is the Spirit of truth, comes, He will lead the seeker into all truth (see John 14:17, 26). The artificial and unreal cannot stand in the presence of the real thing, for the truth is a cleaver. The upright are obedient; they hear and know the voice of their Leader and will be guided by Him. Jesus said, "I am the good shepherd, and know my sheep, and am known of mine" (John 10:14).

Our daily prayer ought to be: "Lord, lead me away from the feet and company of those who love, cherish, and practice evil." May we all be given a clear vision of the *upright*–those who have integrity, pursue peace, and walk in obedience!

Day 126

Be sober, be **Vigilant**; *because your adversary the devil, as a roaring lion, walketh about, seeking whom he may devour. 1 Peter 5:8*

Vigilance calls for constant alertness. There was a group who titled themselves "The Vigilantes." Their aim was to search out and crack down on all the wrongdoers and violators of the law.

So to be vigilant means that one has to always be aware of their surroundings. In the Christian walk, as well as the physical and social walk, one has to be constantly on the alert for pitfalls: moral, sexual, fiscal, estranged women, debaucherous men, and the unchaste. There are all kinds of challenges lurking outside just waiting to pounce on the unsuspecting victim. While Jesus was here with His special twelve, He warned them about these different kinds of prowlers. King Solomon in Proverbs wrote profusely to young men to be wary of those subtle entrapments: "My son, if sinners entice thee, consent thou not" (Prov. 1:10).

As one walks on the paved sidewalks, he or she has to look out for the raised or sunken divisions lest he or she will fall to the ground. I have many such encounters walking in my subdivision. Peter knew about these pitfalls, for he also experienced many. He was not always vigilant; he did not look out for the subtle entrapments that caught him off guard. Drawing on the experiences he had with the brethren, Jesus, the Sadducees and the Pharisees, and the new church administration, etc., he was very cognizant of the enemy's diverse, multitudinous, and multifaceted arsenals. Acting on Jesus' counsel to feed His sheep and tend to His flock, Peter's counsel to the elect is very appropriate and timely.

As sinners awaiting our Lord's soon return, we must always be vigilant. We cannot take our eyes off the cross of Jesus, His Word, and His counsel. We must pray always. Paul says to "pray without ceasing" (1 Thess. 5:17) because the enemy, Satan, is not pretending. He is the roaring lion, and he is hungry for food–the souls for whom Jesus shed His precious blood. Therefore, we must be vigilant. We also need to create the awareness of the danger lurking around; never take your eyes off the enemy! Do not be careless in your meanderings. Remember, he comes in all forms, arrays, and colors. Look out for your adversary and commit the keeping of your heart, mind, and body to Christ. Do not let him devour you; do not let him rob you of eternity. Hold strain; be ever watchful! Stay on guard! May you be *vigilant*!

Day 127

Thy **Wife** *shall be as a fruitful vine by the sides of thine house: thy children like olive plants round about thy table. Psalm 128:3*

This is such a blessing pronounced upon the faithful, God-fearing husband! The text speaks to the beauty of an established family life and a family's dream home. The husband, as the leader, provider, and patriarch of his family, will come home with joy to a healthy, wholesome, beautiful, well-regulated family. The agricultural imagery of his wife as a vine fully flushed with an abundance of fruits, blooming in health, radiance, satisfaction, and contentment while exuding the full sap of life is simply beautiful.

Some may read into this phrase the license to keep the wife pregnant, and it has been said that a woman is most beautiful when she is with child. The house will be filled with children, and it seems to validate the statement: "Happy is the man that hath his quiver full of them" (Ps. 127:5). However, I find that this is not necessarily so. It is not the joy of a "full house" but rather the joy and satisfaction that the husband gets when he returns home and finds his home in good order: the children are contented, and the wife is happy. There is no fretfulness, repining, anguish, or distress. The atmosphere breathes contentment, harmony, cleanliness, happiness, and radiance. The Spirit of God resides there.

The house is full of joy because the children are obedient and cooperative; they respect and honor their mother, so the atmosphere is heavenly. The children are healthy, and their skin is radiant without scars or scabs or recent outbreaks of any kinds of rash. They look like ripe olives in all their lushness and effulgence.

A significant amount of the credit goes to the father. He is a provider, a worker, and a stabilizing force in his family. He knows what fatherhood entails and takes the Divine One's command very seriously—to be the house-band around his family—binding them together in all areas of life: spiritual, moral, economic, social, and intellectual. The Holy Book says that the children will rise up and call their father blessed because he upholds righteousness and the fear of the Lord in his house.

There is homeostasis in the family, for peace, joy, and contentment reside therein. It is a home where the husband acts and bears full responsibility for the care of his family. There is joy immeasurably. These are the rewards for being a faithful and good father. There are blessings on every man who fears the Lord and remains faithful to Him. May God entrust good fathers with a good wife and healthy, respectful, and obedient children!

The text addresses the wife, but it is really about the Christian husband who does everything to ensure that his wife glows with health, happiness, and contentment. His is an enviable role of whom any wife should be proud. The couple in this psalm has a home where God resides and angels love to dwell. The husband is the model husband from whom all prospective husbands should take cue. Prospective wives also learn from the encomiums given to his wife! May all husbands and *wives* keep their family close to God and be truly blessed for it!

Day 128

And he said, Let me go, for the day breaketh. And he said, I will not let thee go **Except** *thou bless me. Genesis 32:26*

This is nothing more than the tenacity for survival. Jacob recognized that he had come face to face with a force mightier than he. It was the very God who confronted Jacob, but he did not know it. As he struggled with the mighty force and power, he realized his own limitations and recognized his inability to forge ahead to meet the foe, his brother. Jacob was stopped dead in his track. He had met the enemy and found it to be himself.

Jehovah God had to confront Jacob in order to let him assess his past behaviors and actions; he had to have a self-dialogue and review his impure motives. As he came face-to-face with the real him, he recognized his own weakness and his unpreparedness to meet Esau.

Jacob lived and practiced a life of deceit, chicanery, fraud, and unfaithful behaviors. He was a usurper. But when he met that uncanny, supernatural force, he knew that what he had found was beyond his ability. He became maimed and partial paralysis seized his groin and rendered him incapable of continuing the struggle. But he would not let go. Somehow he recognized that he was in the presence of a deity, and he steadfastly held his grasp. It might have been quite a scene to see him engaged in that debacle all night. Then the Force spoke: "Let me go, for the day breaketh." The contender held on with all his might, strength, and determination and replied: "I will not let thee go, except thou bless me." Now Jacob realized he needed an affirmation from the heavenly Force. He did receive one—the dislodgement of his thigh muscle.

Besides his physical discomfort, Jacob wanted the assurance that his sins and wayward behaviors had been cancelled. He now craved for the Messenger's righteousness and continued the hold until he was assured of its impartation. He wanted justification. The Visitor saw that his conversion was real: he confessed, repented, and surrendered completely. Then He blessed him and gave him a new name. He was no longer Jacob, but Israel–an overcomer.

To overcome our shortcomings, many of us, like Jacob, have to wrestle with God all night in prayer–maybe even many nights until we get the victory over our besetting sins. Remember that Jesus, the sinless One, spent nights in prayer pleading for strength to face the cross for you and for me. He did not have to do it, but He did. We must follow His example; it is the only way by which we can achieve righteousness. Do not get off your knees until you have the assurance that your prayer is heard, and you are forgiven. May God perform His strange act on you and make you a victor rather than a victim!

Day 129

For thine [**Yours**] *is the kingdom, and the power, and the glory, for ever, Amen.*
Matthew 6:13

This verse speaks of God's sovereignty. Everything belongs to Him. Humanity has nothing; we can create nothing. How foolish for us to boast about our possessions! Humanity tends to be a usurper, often infringing on God's territory. Since everything belongs to God, our rightful duty is to worship, hallow, and adore Him and His name.

David says, "From the rising of the sun unto the going down of the same the Lord's name is to be praised" (Ps. 113:3). That means praise is to be offered continuously: from creation through pre-millennial times to this present age, none is excluded; every tongue must confess the glory and magnificence of Jehovah. Our limitedness and finiteness prevent us from fully grasping the greatness of our God and so rather than worship and adore Him, we deny Him praise. Humanity has neither power nor glory; all our substance comes from God. God deserves all praise and honor.

God's kingdom covers all the created worlds: they are His territory. His power upholds everything, and no one can rob God of His glory. It is His, and throughout eternity, His glory will be fully revealed to us. God speaks, "My glory will I not give to another" (Isa. 42:8). Hence our prayers, supplications, and repentance shows God that we glorify, adore, and praise Him for all His created works.

It is because of His goodness that we are even able to adore Him, for it is through and by Him that all things consist and exist. We give Him the glory for the earth and its fullness. They are His and will be forever. There will be and can be no end, for God is eternal and everlasting. We ascribe praise and glory through "Praise God, From Whom All Blessing Flow":

Praise God from Whom all blessings flow;
Praise Him, all creatures here below;
Praise Him above, ye heavenly host;
Praise Father, Son, and Holy Ghost!

Day 130

The **Zeal** *of the Lord of hosts will perform this. Isaiah 9:7*

This text answered the question of how the Promised One would fulfill the prophet's predictions. Isaiah foretold what He would accomplish and the names He would be called. Each name was an attribute of His character and His work. The child presented here is the same divine child Matthew wrote about: Immanuel.

Other names by which the child would be called are: Wonderful, Counselor, the Almighty, the Everlasting Father, the Prince of Peace. All these names were ascribed to the infant even before He was conceived. He shall be called Jesus and Immanuel. Of His territory and government, there would be no end; it would be eternal, everlasting, and endless. This seemingly impossible feat was enacted by God's zeal, passion, and power.

This is rather enigmatic, and one is caused to wonder how it was all done, but the prophet in vision assures us that the zeal and the passion of the great God was going to bring this into effect. God's plan, though not revealed to humanity, was fulfilled. The virgin conceived, bore the child, and He grew into a man. He lived a model life and was maligned and crucified, but He rose and returned to His Father in heaven from whence He came. He became all that the prophet spoke of Him: King of kings, Lord of lords, Savior, Prince of Peace, Wonderful, and Counselor. Yes, Jesus came with all the glory of the Father and the holy angels and God allowed the mission to be executed. He was also called "Son of the Most High God." God's zeal made it all happen.

God's zeal, power, authority, authenticity, passion, and enthusiasm have fulfilled the prophecy. God rules, and since all power resides in Him, all things are done as He decrees. Let us try and catch a glimpse of God's zeal for us. He has plans for us of which we know not. Wait and watch Him perform His marvelous work in our lives. Catch His zeal!

Allow Him to fill us up with a holy passion for the things that are pure, lovely, righteous, noble, and full of integrity. When God fires you up, you will really be ablaze for Him and communicate this zeal to others. May you catch the vision, the passion, and the excitement! God is at this very moment awaiting your response. Will you give the Creator access to perform what He wants to do in, through, and by you? May we be willing to let His *zeal* transform our lives!

God's Humors

Day 131

The Lord is gracious, and full of compassion; slow to **Anger**, *and of great mercy.*
Psalm 145:8

Throughout the psalms David constantly extols God's qualities and His attributes including His grace, tenderness, lovingkindness, compassion, greatness, patience, magnanimity, and His great unconditional love. Other prophetic writers also attested to God's truthfulness: "God is not a man, that he should lie" (Num. 23:19).

David who had tried God's patience repeatedly said, "I have sinned. I have caused You shame and abomination, but You have not cut me off. You do not get angry and dump me as others have done." David pointed out that God's anger is short lived; it takes a long time to wear out God's patience. Ancient Israel and their offspring sorely tried God's patience by committing open rejection of His laws. He bore with them. He never rejected them, but He stated that He was a jealous God. He allowed their enemies to oppress them until they could recognize their need of Jehovah's guiding hand. When they were severely oppressed and cried unto the Lord, He heard and delivered them.

Another generation arose, and they hankered for and emulated the idolatrous practices of their neighbors. However, God kept the promise sworn to Abraham, Isaac, and Jacob, and He continued to be their God. Consequently, He endured all the insults and rejection they heaped on Him, and He graciously retained His anger.

God's tender mercies still extend to us. Our wickedness has not altered His mood or His care for us. He is still there compassionately waiting for us to repent, revere, honor, and obey Him. Because God does not retaliate instantly when we violate our part of the contract, we tend to think He is asleep, but we need to always bear in mind that "the eyes of the Lord are in every place, beholding the evil and the good" (Prov. 15:3). He does not even wink! Everything is known to Him, and He only gives reprieve because of His great mercy.

God gives us a pattern of how we should treat one another. God treats us with love and patience; we ought to do the same. If He consumed us for every infraction, we would all be obliterated instantly. We are to adopt His patience, understanding, and self-control so that we can manage our emotions and practice the virtues of godliness and godlikeness. The wise man says, "Seest thou a man that is hasty in his words? there is more hope of a fool than of him" (Prov. 29:20). He also said, "Be not hasty in thy spirit to be angry: for anger resteth in the bosom of fools" (Eccles. 7:9). Only God's Holy Spirit given and installed in us can create the right and holy emotion that will stymie the overarching, controlling emotion of anger. God promises help when we need it most; and in every challenge, if we call upon Him, He is there. God's Word says, "He that is slow to wrath is of great understanding" (Prov. 14:29). May we emulate God and show that we are wise and not susceptible to *anger* and folly!

Day 132

Be *ye angry, and sin not: let not the sun go down on your wrath. Ephesians 4:26*

Is this wise and practical counsel? The rationale is that an angry person loses capacity to think and act sanely. A person's emotions are all contorted, and it often causes spontaneous and erratic acts. Yesterday's text warned against the emotion of anger. How are we to reconcile these two ideas?

We have just looked at the attributes of God and found that He is not a vengeful God; He is slow to anger and plenteous in mercy. King Solomon said an angry person causes strife and confusion, but the apostle Paul counsels believers to "be angry and sin not." Is this reasonable advice? Is it possible to be angry and not commit a violation—physical, ethical, moral, or spiritual? The fact that the counsel says to not desecrate yourself in doing evil must be evidence that you can be angry and maintain your cool. This admonition seems to strike at the heart of self-control, and when things go awry, one should act wisely to amend the situation. In Navajo life, when infractions occur, there is call for a peace conference and the elders sit in a circle with the offending one and explain how he or she was wrong. Their lifestyle is hinged on making peace and maintaining homeostasis in the family, the village, and the tribe. Thus, rational humanity is able to control unmanageable situations.

According to the text, it is possible to maintain anger for hours, days, or even weeks. It is anger that makes nations go to war—they are unwilling to sit at the negotiation table and iron out their differences. The same situation happens in families: spousal disagreements, parent-child disputes, and sibling rivalry. This also happens among church members. I have heard stories where people attend the same church, sit in the same pew, and do not speak to each other because of an age-old disagreement. They remain aloof and angry with each other, and in many cases, they cannot recall the incidence or incidences. Such folk have either not read or understood the second half of the text: "let not the sun go down upon your wrath," or they are stubborn and will not allow the Holy Spirit to work upon their hearts.

If there is anger or disagreement, the parties should follow the biblical counsel. They need to get together and hash out the problem before the end of the day. When the sun sets, a new day begins; one does not know if when he or she goes to bed that night there will be an opportunity to see the next day's sunrise. Many people take a risk when going to bed with unresolved issues. Every day brings new challenges and new resolves. No one need tote the bitterness of one day into the next and the next. Besides, we are sons and daughters of God and should reflect our Father's attributes: self-control, love, kindness, humility, peace, and compassion. The apostle Paul knew that disagreements would continually surface among the saints, so he commissioned us to pray for Jesus' mind to be in us. If we possess Jesus' mind, then no wrath, envy, jealousy, or anger will have any place in our heart.

However, if our old emotions surface, we should aim to dismiss it instead of nurturing it. In doing so, we will reveal the God-like attributes of how love conquers all. May you *be* able to calm the emotions by the constant indwelling of the Holy Spirit and by feeding on the Word!

Day 133

Comfort *ye, comfort ye my people, saith your God. Isaiah 40:1*

What words of consolation! What joy to hear God's voice speaking directly to you like when he thundered from Sinai many millennia ago! Before sin marred the face of this pristine and holy atmosphere, God spoke directly with Adam and Eve. Later, He spoke to Moses at the burning bush, "Put off thy shoes from off thy feet, for the place whereon thou standest is holy ground" (Exod. 3:5). God also spoke from Mount Sinai when He gave Moses the Decalogue for ancient Israel. God is always with His people, and He is always talking to them.

Even though God's specially chosen people wandered away from Him, because of His great mercies and abundance in compassion, He always hears their cries and responds to their needs. God sent these words to the prophet Isaiah in order to bring assurance and consolation to those who trusted God but were discouraged and cast down.

The original message informed Judah of God's plan to deliver them and how they should not fear. The same message is for us today bringing consolation and assurance that our God is still the deliverer for those who abide in the covenant relationship with Him. To every faint-hearted Christian challenged by life's uncertainties, the message of consolation is to be comforted by your God, for He is strong and trustworthy. He promised that He would save Judah, and He will come to save you as well.

Jesus comforts and assures the anxious: "I will come again" (John 14:3). The whole air of heaven breathes of comfort; even the angels comforted the disciples at Jesus' ascension (see Acts 1:11). These are words of verity and truth; He will come again. Every waiting, expectant saint needs to find consolation in these words. These are prophetic words spoken by the Master and confirmed by His escorting angels, who set Him at His Father's right hand.

God is a comforter and a shelter. He will pardon every sin and give peace to the restless. As a Shepherd, He shall feed His flock all through the ages. His tender care is always available; there is no lack or easing up in His operation. Isaiah 40:11 gives a vivid but gentle description of the care God gave to his children: "He shall gather the lambs with his arm, and carry them in his bosom, and shall gently lead those that are with young." None is excluded; even those who recently join the family of God. He will guide us all gently and lead us into a haven of rest. Do you know what it feels like to be embosomed in the Father's arms? Allow yourself the vicarious feeling and revel in the experience.

With such a God as our Father, why should His followers fret and be discomfited? May we be *comforted* and happy! God is in the midst of us; we are safe, secure, and assured of His care.

Day 134

Verily, verily, I say unto you, If a man keep my saying, he shall never see **Death**.
John 8:51

Jesus' words express conditional behavior tied to obedience. One has to obey in order to live.

Jesus said "verily" twice giving authenticity to His utterance. There is no gainsaying about this statement. It is all verity and truth. Jesus is life; He came to give life and to give it more abundantly and perpetually. He brought humanity everlasting life. Sin introduced death, so He came to offer something that supersedes death—life. Like many things in life, the offer is contingent on obedience.

God made the provision: He sent His Son, and the Son yielded; now, it is humanity's turn to act. We must say, "I accept the gift" and become engaged by listening, accepting, and obeying the words of the Giver.

Jesus told us that the words He spoke where ones of life and truth. He told us He is the way, the truth, and the life. He told us that He is the light of the world. I encourage you to read Matthew 13 and John 11 for more of what Jesus has told us.

Jesus taught people to love and care for the dispossessed of the earth: the widows, orphans, and homeless. He taught about abiding in Christ, about generosity, blessings, backsliding, and rejecting the truth. He gave us great insight on hypocrisy, self-deception, keeping the Sabbath, God's commandments, meekness, piety, forgiveness, and God's impartiality. In thirty-three and a half years of public ministry, Jesus taught hundreds of topics. No wonder He is called the Master Teacher! His curriculum was inexhaustible.

Whatever subject we need to know, we should first go to the Word. We will surely find it documented in the Gospels. An important comment about Jesus' teaching was this: "For he taught them as one having authority, and not as the scribes" (Matt. 7:29). That was correct, for there was never a man that lived like this Man. All wisdom, knowledge, and doctrine reside in Him. Jesus affirms: if anyone wants life, it is absolutely necessary for him or her to keep My Word. His words are life-giving, life-sustaining, life-retaining, and life-perpetuating.

Do you want the perpetual life that Jesus offers? He cannot present those who refuse to keep His sayings to His Father. Many patriarchs and prophets have spoken about His birth, life, and death, and now they are all sleeping in their graves and awaiting the call of the Life-giver. When Jesus referred to death, He was citing eternal death as in the final extinction of our race. One has to be obedient to the teachings and dictum of Jesus. We must obey the tenets and live a holy life. None can enter the rest unless he or she is spotless. The only way to achieve this is by obedience to the teachings of Jesus. If we cannot do this, eternal death is our only option. Jesus brought life and still offers life. As long as the doors of mercy remain open and you enter, eternal life is guaranteed. May we do what we can to escape eternal *death*.

Day 135

"For the wages of sin is death; but the gift of God is **Eternal** *life through Jesus Christ our Lord.*
Romans 6:23

Eternal life lies at the heart of the Christian's salvation; it is death's antithesis. Everyone who works receives wages. Some may be unsatisfied, as in the case of the story Jesus narrated about the employer who gave out jobs at different hours of the day and agreed on one fixed price for each employee. When evening came and each received his pay, some were satisfied, but some grumbled about the equanimity of the pay because the one who worked for one hour received equal pay with those who began at the first watch. The employer told them that they had agreed about the price, so each worker received his correct pay. Life also pays wages; there is a paycheck for every man, woman, and child.

In life, there are many who court sinful habits with no desire to forsake and repent of their indulgences. There is a payday for them as well, but the reward may not be as they expect. In the heavenly pay roll, there is no falsification of facts and figures; all that we have done is recorded against our names, and angels keep track of our activities and actions. None can say he or she is cheated. In God's accounting firm, all workers stand equal before Him. There is no bias or favor. What you work for is what you get. If you sow disobedience and discord, you will get sorrow and death; if you sow obedience, you will receive life. Jesus says, "I am come that they might have life, and that they might have it more abundantly" (John 10:10).

If we do not forsake our sins, death is our paycheck. We cannot access the heavenly courts where God's holiness resides. The Word says that we are all sinners born in sin and shaped in iniquity (see Ps. 51:5), and we can do nothing to change that status. However, help has been provided through the blood of Jesus, the Lamb slain from the foundation of the world. Because we have sinned, we deserve to die. Death overshadows all humankind. However, the Word assures us that God's gift of eternal life transcends death; the only condition attached is that you have to accept it and receive the gift. You have to open the door when Jesus knocks and invite Him in (see Rev. 3:20).

When Christ enters, He abides with you forever, and the Holy Spirit leads you into all truth (see John 14:20). The Holy Spirit's indwelling will keep you sinless and put you on the path to receiving eternal life. Everyone has access to it. Reach out and freely grasp it; it is yours for the taking. Sin pays wages, and for some it is very costly, but eternal life is free. May you accept this gift of eternal life so that you may live forever with the Life-giver.

Day 136

> *The* **Fool** *hath said in his heart, There is no God. Psalm 14:1*

A fool is someone who is either stupid or self-willed. How can any living person ignore or deny the existence of God? The natural world teems with evidences that God exists, so for those who exude foolish utterances, they are either lying to themselves or are very perverse. For attacking the Deity, God should eliminate them, but God is merciful and is waiting for the fool to become wise.

If there is no God, how does the sun continue daily on its orbital path? From where do we get the air that envelops the atmosphere filling our lungs and keeps us alive? Who and what sustains humanity, beast, and vegetation? Let God now stretch forth His hand and withdraw the air, and we shall see how long any life forms can remain alive without artificial aid.

King David declared that God's goodness and mercy were evidentiary; one only has to look all around to behold the manifestations of His love, which bless every phase and object of creation. How could there not then be a God? Surely there must be a greater power than humanity's trite utterances! David avers, "Surely goodness and mercy shall follow me all the days of my life" (Ps. 23:6). All around us are the unspeakable riches and manifestations of God's existence: the changing seasons and the gushing waters of creeks, rivers, seas, and oceans. You can find His existence in the snow-capped mountain peaks reaching up to heaven and the deep, sonorous valleys. Yet the fool who cannot account for his or her own presence is asserting that there is no God. What an effrontery to the Majesty of the universe! In foolhardiness and ignorance, the fool says that all things continue as they were from the beginning. Who then and where is the beginning and who originates the beginning? The Holy Book begins, "In the beginning God created the heaven and the earth" (Gen. 1:1).

Let the fool show his or her own beginning. We should not give a fool any credence. We should despise foolish utterances. Do not listen or keep company with fools, for they are perverse in their own way. They want to live by their own standards and rules and refuse to obey God's truths. If there is no God, they can have no accountability. They can live freely and do as they please. Avoid foolish people. The fool needs to seek and find the great Creator of the universe and bow in reverence to Him. King Solomon has some very choice words for foolish people in the books of Proverbs and Ecclesiastes.

Let the Word of God abide richly in you and every chance you have. Lift up Jesus, and lift up God! Utter praise and adoration to Him, for He is holy, righteous, and marvelous. Let everything that hath breath praise Jehovah. May our lips continually offer thanksgiving and praise to His holy name, and let no *foolishness* escape our lips!

Day 137

> *But* **Godliness** *with contentment is great gain. 1 Timothy 6:6*

This statement is the key to spiritual growth and personal fulfillment. The world is filled with many unhappy and disgruntled people. There are always murmuring about wanting this and that and maintain a continual striving for what others have. They are never truly satisfied, for they are always seeking to obtain more. Some seek wealth and riches while others seek fame and power. Yet, with all their acquisitions, they are still discontented. They lack God.

Since we are tenants to this world, our striving should be God-centered. We should always aim to be more like God. Jesus counseled His first disciples, "But seek ye first the kingdom of God, and his righteousness; and all these things shall be added unto you" (Matt. 6:33). When God takes first place in our lives, the acquisition of worldly things becomes secondary and tertiary because godliness reigns supremely. Thus we should be content with what God is doing in our lives. The counsel to the Philippians found in Philippians 4:11–13 is also applicable to Christians living in this age. In whatever state we find ourselves, we are to be content, for it is God who works in us to do His will. We truly should want to imitate a Christlike character so that we may exude godliness in all our dealings.

A mind constantly grasping and reaching for worldly possessions is ungodly, discontented, and self-centered. It does not care for the underclass or the marginalized. The aged apostle advised the youthful Timothy not to consider those who possessed much but rather to be content with what he had. Paul suggested that the Holy Spirit will guide people into moderation. If God is directing our life, we will have a contented mind; there will be no competitiveness. When God dwells in our heart, the needs of others will be equally valued, for the possessor has learned to share with others.

The major question for the godless is, "What will you exchange for your soul?" Are the amassing and hoarding of things more important than reaching out to the needy? Jesus, speaking to our greed and selfishness, said, "These ought ye to have done, and not to leave the other undone" (Matt. 23:23). That message connotes true godliness.

Seek God's guidance and direction in everything. Let us be happy and contented with what He has given us and daily practice godliness. The Spirit of God will dwell richly in you directing your heart and your mind. God has promised, "I will never leave thee, nor forsake thee" (Heb. 13:5). So, be content with what He brings to you. The aged apostle says, "I have learned, in whatsoever state I am, therewith to be content" (Phil. 4:11). May *godliness* and contentment be our status and our prayer.

Day 138

*Nor **Height**, nor depth, nor any other creature, shall be able to separate us from the love of God, which is Christ Jesus our Lord. Romans 8:39*

This text extends the previous verse where the writer affirms his commitment to the mission, ministry, and the body of Christ. Paul had resigned himself to martyrdom for the cause of Christ Jesus. That commitment equates with when Jesus chose to come to earth to offer His life to redeem humanity and restore fellowship with God.

Paul's resolve resonates with that of two sixteenth century reformers: Martin Luther, who said, "Here I stand; I can do no other; so help me God!" The second was John Huss, who chose God's word above the canons of the public church: "I shall not die, but live, and declare the works of the Lord" (Ps. 118:17). Such has been the resolve of countless men and women who chose martyrdom for the word of God over human-made creed and traditions. Stephen, the first Christian martyr, chose to die for the cause and the faith of Jesus. I have chosen this text to be my resolve, and it can be found at the end of my first inspirational book, *Stones of Witness*. May your resolve be: "Come what may, I will stand up for Jesus as He stood, yea, hung on a cross for me! He took my place and bore my shame."

It is a Christ-centered affirmation. It is not like Peter, who said that he would go with the Lord to death, but instead denied his Savior three times before he was fully converted. The converted soul that leans on Jesus will never retreat when the battle rages.

Every Christian must also commit to standing up for Christ. They must not allow any earth-shaking power to cause them to release their grasp on eternal things. A Christian motto is: nothing shall separate me from the love of God.

Dear reader, allow yourself to bask in this most comforting and reassuring promise in all Scripture—God will always be with us despite life's challenges. Pledge right now that you will stand with those who have stood for their Lord: the three Hebrew youth, Daniel, Stephen, Jesus, as well as the thousands of Christian martyrs who chose to suffer affliction and death, defied potentates and rulers of kingdoms, and stood for the cause of Christ because He stood for them first. And He stands for us now. May we stand for Jesus today and resolve that no *height* or depth will ever separate us from His love.

Day 139

Let us make man in our **Image**, *after our likeness: and let them have dominion ... over all the earth. Genesis 1:26*

On the sixth day of Creation, God decided to make humanity. To complete the process, God said, "Let us make man in our image." Humanity then is not just different from the rest of what God created but we bear the actual imprint of God's character. Jesus is the express image of the Father. The disciples needed clarification due to Jesus' constant reference to His Father. They asked, "Lord, show us the Father, and it sufficeth us" (John 14:8). He answered, "Have I been so long time with you and ... how sayest thou then, Show us the Father? ... the words that I speak unto you I speak not of myself: but the Father that dwelleth in me, he doeth the works" (verses 9, 10). Jesus also told them, "I and my Father are one" (John 10:30).

It doesn't matter what is our physical form. God created us to look like Him, and we are all His sons and daughters. We possess His DNA, His holiness, purity of thought, peace, piety, meekness, and abundant love. Humanity was made perfect in form and symmetry and bore no semblance of deformity. Originally, humans possessed a clear, unpolluted mind; their faces, resplendent with joy for purity and wholeness, radiated from within. No wonder Satan beguiled Eve and told her she would be like God. Eve forgot that she had already possessed godly qualities, for she was made in God's image.

Humankind must know that they are special: God made us to reflect on His character and nature: pure, holy, loving, forgiving, patient, and upright. We must strive to retain our Maker's characteristics though scarred by centuries of sin.

Because we are made in God's image, we can feel positive about ourselves. When we criticize and find fault with ourselves, we are negating God's handiwork and our God-given abilities. Being of God's unique design should help us to love God even more. It is like we become His hands and feet, imparting His love and caring for the needy.

God is still refurbishing characters and wants to restore His image in us. Will you allow Him to remake you into what He wants you to be—a reflection of His character? Wouldn't it be praiseworthy if someone could come up to you and say, "Brother (or sister), I do not know what God looks like, but you bring Him to focus"? Can the world see Jesus in you? Jesus told Phillip, "He that hath seen me hath seen the Father" (John 14:9). May we always bear the Father's *image*!

Day 140

Neither filthiness, nor foolish talking, nor **Jesting**, *which are not convenient: but rather giving of thanks. Ephesians 5:4*

Paul's counsel to all Christian believers is very timely. We live in a society where coarse arguments, idle chatter, and much filthiness emanates from many lips. Our lips witness to others about the saving graces of our

Lord and exalt His name. A heart, mind, and lips that utter harshness or seemingly vulgar and vain babblings need a complete makeover or a reconditioning, which was what David prayed for in his cleansing oration. A brook cannot expunge clean and dirty water simultaneously. Besides, the mouths of God's children are sanctified, so nothing idle or profane should exit from them.

Christians have but a brief time to share the Gospel and to witness of God's goodness and His saving merits offered through Jesus' blood. We have no time to engage in foolish prattle and cheap chatter. Rather, we should walk, talk, and practice those graces that exalt Jesus' name and life. Having ourselves abandoned a sinful life, we should not engage in any behavior that repels the Holy Spirit's presence in our lives. Paul counsels us to think on those noble attributes and to avoid the company of those who engage in idle prattle, foolish talking, and jesting (see Phil. 4:4–8).

Our society has lost much of its moral values, and speech that was once fit only for the stables has now found itself on the air, in our living rooms, and at our dining tables. Obscenity and coarse joking are so common that we begin to take it for granted and sometimes even hear it coming from sanctified lips. That is why the aged apostle counsels that improper language should have no place in the Christian's conversation because it neither reflects God's gracious presence in us nor edifies ourselves or others. Sometimes we excuse our participation under the guise that it is just to be a part of the crowd, but the Word says it is not convenient or proper. Flatly speaking, it does not fit the Christian's repertoire. Such behavior is inappropriate for any who bears the title of Christian.

Some people do things for jest, but we must never forget that the members of our bodies are consecrated to God and are the temples of the living God and the Holy Spirit, (see 1 Cor. 6:19, 20; 1 Cor. 3:16, 17); therefore, nothing that defiles should either enter or depart from it. Sanctified, holy, consecrated bodies speak as the Spirit gives utterance. "Let no corrupt communication proceed out off your mouth, but that which is good to the use of edifying ... may minister grace unto the hearers" (Eph. 4:29). It is good to remember that evil communication corrupts good manners (see 1 Cor. 15:33). The advice is timely and appropriate, and we should heed these counsels, and in so doing, silence becomes the preferred mode of communication. "O Lord, thou has searched me, and known me.... For there is no word in my tongue, but, lo, O Lord, thou knowest it altogether" (Ps. 139:1, 4).

May we keep our words from *jesting* and remember that we are the sanctified and holy sons and daughters of a King!

Day 141

Ask, and it shall be given you; seek, and ye shall find; **Knock**, *and it shall be opened unto you. Matthew 7: 7*

This is part of the three-fold principle that Jesus gave for engagement in any of life's undertakings. Knock is part three of the command: Ask, Seek, Knock. But all three are interrelated. The first verb–Ask–is the acronym for the complete task: A=Ask; S=Seek and K=Knock, also known as A. S. K.

In any quest, be it spiritual, educational, business, marriage, purchasing a house, or taking a vacation, one must first present it to the Lord and ask for direction, advice, or guidance. The novice needs the wisdom, expertise, and knowledge to forge ahead.

Having taken the first step, the second, is the S–Seek. Go out and search; enquire to see what is available. Here is when the problem becomes challenging. Some people will ask, but they are unwilling to go out and see what options are available. However, they are following the first two tenets of A. S. K–ask and seek.

At the end of the acronym is K–Knock. This is the most challenging level. Our knees begin to shake, our hands sweat, and our brain freezes, for the fear of rejection looms like giants. Most seekers are afraid to take that quantum leap and knock on the first door to gain entrance. But the seeker must knock so that the person on the inside can open the door and say, "Come in."

If the beginner truly believes in his or her mission and seeks God's direction first, he or she will go forward boldly, knowing that the Holy Spirit will be there as a guiding force. The seeker will be empowered, for they will know which door to knock. Jesus guaranteed the effectiveness of this method. He affirmed it! "For every one that asketh receiveth, and he that seeketh findeth; and to him that knocketh it shall be opened" (verse 8). If the Creator of everything gave the mandate, why are there so many unemployed and unemployables? What of the poverty and want? Have they not followed the charge of the Master: ask, seek, knock? This is Jesus' method to combat social disparities in distributing and allocating resources. It is a challenge to the adventurous seeker.

Jesus is Lord and Master. He is the Owner of the world and its possession. He knows where every opportunity is, and He can lead and direct the seeker to the right site. Whatever He says He will do, it will be done. King David affirms God's position: "My covenant will I not break, nor alter the thing that is gone out of my lips" (Ps. 89:34).

Jesus told the disciples to wait in Jerusalem until He sent them the gift of the Holy Spirit. He fulfilled the promise at Pentecost—forty days later. May we grasp the Hand of omnipotence and A. S. K—ask, seek, and *knock*, for you will certainly find! The Master has the keys. Trust Him!

Day 142

And they stoned Stephen, calling upon God, and saying, **Lord** *Jesus, receive my spirit.*
Acts 7:59

These are the last words of Stephen, the first Christian martyr, who died for the truth. This was his prayer as his assailants stoned him until his last breath ebbed away. And dying, he called upon the Lord God to receive his spirit and to forgive them for their heinous act. Like his Master before him, Jesus prayed a similar prayer before his breath also ebbed away: "Father, forgive them; for they know not what they do" (Luke 23:34). Stephen's killers were wicked men who refused to listen to truth. As Stephen recounted God's past leadings in the lives of the patriarchs down to Jesus, the evil men gnashed on him with their teeth, stopped their ears, rushed upon him like mad dogs, and cast him out of the city; then they performed their heinous act.

Stephen was stoned because he spoke up for God and declared to the Jews their complicity in killing Jesus, God's Son. Beside Paul's, Stephen's oration is one of the most magnificent, truth-filled, and provocative addresses recorded in the Scriptures. It says that when they heard the piercing truths and their part in rejecting Jesus, they were "pricked in their hearts," i.e. they saw themselves and their actions, but rather than crying out for mercy, they became hostile, agitated, and demanded blood. They had just killed Jesus, three years prior, and their appetites were sated. They wanted to eradicate any vestige of the truth, purity, and righteousness that Christ proclaimed. They refused to hear or have any remembrance of the recently slain Savior or of His message.

Stephen, being filled and empowered by the Holy Spirit, could not keep silent. His action was a precursor to the apostle Paul's later affirmation: "Neither death, nor life ... nor height, nor depth ... shall be able to separate us from the love of God, which is in Christ Jesus our Lord" (Rom. 8:38, 39) Stephen chose death before dishonor. As he was being stoned, his persecutors and murderers saw the righteousness of Christ unfolded in his face, and their sinful selves could not contain it. They eliminated him to assuage their consciences. Yet the dying man offered a prayer of forgiveness for his attackers, "Lord, lay not this sin to their charge" (verse 60). He felt that their actions were done ignorantly; they had not allowed themselves to hear, accept, or internalize the words of the Master, so they committed murder. But in his last moments, the dying Stephen looked up to heaven and declared some of the most treasured words ever spoken except by Jesus, "Behold, I see the heavens opened, and the Son of man standing at the right hand of God" (verse 56).

What a life and a testament! Stephen paved the way for other Christian martyrdom. During the years of the gospel proclamation, many preachers were attacked, mauled, and slain. Several of the apostles met a similar fate: Peter was crucified upside down; some were sawn asunder; Paul was beheaded. But they chose to suffer and counted it worthy that they could participate vicariously in the sufferings and death of their Lord. Paul said, "Yea, and all that will live godly in Christ Jesus shall suffer persecution" (2 Tim. 3:12). Not surprisingly, persecution has been the primary tool used over the centuries to silence and eliminate Christians. But our gracious, thoughtful, and loving Savior has promised us:, "Be thou faithful unto death, and I will give you a crown of life" (Rev. 2:10). May we stay true to our *Lord* even in the face of persecution.

Day 143

Mark *the perfect man, and behold the upright: for the end of that man is peace.*
Psalm 37:37

David told us that those who are upright are those that practice perfection of character. David was passionate for righteousness, integrity, wisdom, and knowledge. The aspiring Christian should seek the company and camaraderie of such an individual because the person makes God first in his or her life. David's children were obedient and followed his example. Identify with David; let him be your model and mentor. When such a one like David is found, and you walk together, then you will be assured of peace, longevity, right living, and wholesomeness of character. God shall preserve you and deliver you from your enemies. Your enemies will seek to make peace with you because your entire life actions are reflective of Jehovah. King Solomon avers, "When a man's ways please the Lord, he maketh even his enemies to be at peace with him" (Prov. 16:7). The power of the Holy Spirit and the presence of the Lord in the life of one's children is a bulwark against the enemy; evil cannot persist in the presence of the Holy God. May you seek out such a fellow sojourner!

The counsels to the upright are very positive. David advised them not to fret and worry about the prosperity of the wicked, for the Lord orders the steps of the obedient and delights in their actions (Ps. 37:23). He also pointed out that in his brief life, he had never seen the upright in need.

To the anxious, he counseled patience (Ps. 37:34). God's timing is always right—He is never too late or too early. He knows when to satisfy each yearning. The perfect person is obedient to all God's laws and statutes; this person continually exalts the Lord's name.

Upright people are not envious or covetous; they do not compare themselves with others or question their success. They understand the operation of the ungodly and adhere to David's suggestion to not worry about the prosperity of the wicked, for one day they will be destroyed. You will search for them and neither their legacy nor heritage can be found. There will be no trace they even existed; all their possession will have become chaff. However, perfect men and women have integrity that will last eternally.

Let Christians seek the presence and company of those who make God first in their lives; this engenders peace, happiness, contentment, and wholesomeness. Enoch had a perfect walk with God, and God took him. God shall deliver His upright children from the wicked: "the Lord upholdeth the righteous" (Ps. 37:17). May we strive to do right always! The people whom you have marked have latched on to Jesus, so their lifestyle is a reflection of the Man of Calvary.

May you *mark* and follow them as they follow Christ.

Day 144

> **Now** *the Lord of peace himself give you peace always by all means. The Lord be with you all. 2 Thessalonians 3:16*

Not later, but *now*—at this very moment. The message is fraught with urgency and is designed to quell the disorder that was prevalent among the new believers at Thessalonica. Although primarily addressed to that congregation, it is a universal message to all Christian congregations, but it is especially tied to the newly planted churches. It was a challenging environment for the believers who were uncertain about Paul and Silas' new doctrine. Because of their pagan background, they wanted more clarity about the doctrine. There was concern and confusion about whether to accept or reject this new-fangled idea. Hence, there arose many disputes and arguments. When writing about the Thessalonians, Paul remarked that they were less studious and committed than the Berean saints, who went and searched diligently to see if what they had been taught was the truth (Acts 17:11).

Thessalonica was a diverse city of a mixed multitude, and certain Jews refused to accept the teachings about Jesus, the Messiah. So, they assaulted the house of Jason accusing him of harboring people who were sabotaging Caesar's rule. They were now rejecting the Savior's message and His messengers. Satan always interferes with the spreading of the Gospel and incites evil men and women to assault the messengers of God's word.

Our age is no different from Paul's, even though there are two millennia removed. Humankind is the same; our characteristics have not been tamed by 2,000 years of culture, religion, and dogma. We are still as spiteful, hateful, and rebellious as when Adam disobeyed God's instructions. The rebellious DNA saturates our genes, and today's world is ready to assail and attack that which in its judgment seems unclear. Disputes in all areas of life occur over secular and sacred matters. There is little time given for peaceful interactions and negotiations, for there is always rancor. Now there is need for peace and common understanding to settle life's many problems.

Amidst today's various challenges, the apostle's counsel is very cogent. He wants us to know and recognize that God is not the author of confusion, wrath, or discord. He tells us that the Lord of peace gives you—as He gives everyone—His peace. It is His gift to us. May we by all means, strive to accept the gift and live a peaceful life among all!

God's gift is permanent. Just before Jesus returned to His Father's right hand, He told His chosen eleven that He would always be with them through the Holy Spirit. He told them that He was leaving them His peace: "Peace I leave with you, my peace I give unto you: not as the world giveth, give I unto you. Let not your heart be troubled" (John 14:27). A couple of years later, the apostle Paul admonished his new congregants to allow the peace of God to remain with them always. It is also our charge. *Now*, may we let no man or woman spoil our beautiful peace that Jesus alone imparts. Seize it and treasure it!

Day 145

> **Open** *thou mine eyes, that I may behold wondrous things out of thy law. Psalm 119:18*

What a beautiful prayer, plea, entreaty, and petition! It is all-inclusive. This is not only David's prayer. It is for every Christian who recognizes his or her blindness and craves clarity of vision and understanding.

David recognized his deficits and limitations regarding the statutes, laws, and commands of Jehovah. Deep within, he had a longing for the deep things of God: a more profound relationship with the Almighty.

Somehow life may have clouded his vision and skewed his insight. But now he recognized the need to go forward. With partial sight, one cannot engage in any sound decision-making or action-packed direction. One does not know the way, and if his or her peripheral vision is compromised, the individual cannot go forward. In order to act, one needs full vision—clear eyesight. That is why Jesus offers eye salve to remove the scabs that may have blurred the vision field: "And anoint thine eyes with eyesalve, that thou mayest see" (Rev. 3:18). Understandably, the need for such a cry—"open mine eyes."

This cry revealed that David did not want to be excluded from any activities. He did not want to continue to wobble in blindness or ignorance to the things of God. Previously, he declared, "I delight to do thy will, O my God: yea, thy law is within my heart" (Ps. 40:8). That expression conveyed the pleasure derived from walking humbly and obediently according to the Master's requirements. But now it seems as if fame, worldly pleasure, and materialistic, philosophical, social, moral, and political intrigues had clouded his senses. His spiritual sensibilities were numbed; he had sidestepped God's ordained precepts and followed his own inclinations.

However, despite this tentative overshadowing, he had his "prodigal" moment and offered this plaintive and urgent plea to open his eyes so that he may behold! He wanted more than just to see; he wanted to gaze upon, meditate thereon, and internalize the requirements of God's law. This reawakening summoned his need to be realigned to God and to appreciate divine things. He longed for the communion he once enjoyed with his Maker and was desperate for reconnection. "Be pleased, O Lord, to deliver me ... thou art my help and my deliverer; make no tarrying, O my God" (Ps. 40:13, 17). And the final plea: "O how love I thy law! it is my meditation all the day" (Ps. 119:97).

Our merciful, tender and compassionate God hears when you cry. David cried out to him; God heard and accepted his confession. May the Holy Spirit help each of us to reach that prodigal point and cry out for help! Let us reach for the hand of God and have Him anoint our eyes with the heavenly eyesalve—the Holy Spirit—so that we will also see where we are and know what we have to do. Only then will we be able to behold and obey the wondrous things that are in His statutes. Like David, may we pray for a vision and understanding of the Holy Scriptures and that God will attend to our daily prayer: "*Open* my eyes; give me understanding so that I may behold the wondrous things in Your law."

Day 146

*For I am **Persuaded**, that neither death, nor life, nor angels, nor principalities, nor powers, nor things present, nor things to come, nor height, nor depth, nor any other creature, shall be able to separate us from the love of God, which is in Christ Jesus our Lord.*
Romans 8:38

This affirmation has no uncertainties. In his encounter on the Damascus road, Paul knew it was God that confronted him, so when the voice spoke, he asked, "Who art thou, Lord?" (Acts 9:5). He recognized that he was dealing with an ultra superhuman force, for the contact left him sight-impaired, and he had to be led into the city. Amid his humiliation, he must have prayed yesterday's benediction: "Open mine eyes!"

This once haughty, proud, and audacious persecutor was now humbled, sightless, tottering, babbling, and tethered. He had to be led to an alien place and people; his mission all skewed. However, the Lord sent Ananias to go and minister unto his new inductee. He was afraid to go on this mission, but the Holy Spirit told him not to be afraid, for the once aggressive hunter was now "a chosen vessel unto me, to bear my name before the Gentiles ... For I will shew him how great things he must suffer for my name's sake" (Acts 9:15, 16). That was God's plan for the young antagonist soon to become protagonist of the Gospel of Jesus Christ. Saul was going to have a real makeover with Christ—a total reconditioning. God had harnessed all that destructive energy and transformed Saul into a positive force to work for Him.

Having met Jesus, his name was changed from Saul to Paul. Whenever anyone comes in contact with the Savior, their lives are changed. Jacob, on meeting with the divine Messenger, had his name changed from Jacob to Israel—from supplanter to overcomer. Paul's name changed from persecutor to preacher. He spent more than three years in the Arabian Desert learning about the triune God, His mission, and His workings for humankind. God stopped him dead in his tracks and gave him a new name, a new vision, and a new mission.

Though confronted with many challenges on his journeys both from within and without the church family, Paul counted it all joy that he could suffer for Christ's sake. He was never despondent even though he was shipwrecked many times, bitten by a viper, thrown into prison, and charged with heinous crimes, etc. Amid them all, he gladly confessed, "Nay, in all these things we are more than conquerors through him that loved us" (Rom. 8:37). Then with his faith firmly established on the Rock of Ages and the Word, he boldly declared that nothing seen or unseen, present or future could come between him and the Savior. He finally declared his position: "Who shall separate us from the love of Christ? Shall tribulation, or distress ... or sword?" (Rom. 8:35). He had experienced all; he had been tried in the furnace of affliction and knew what it meant to stand for the Lord. He was fully persuaded, and he had surrendered all of himself to Christ.

The apostle could proudly and valiantly say that he was convinced that there was no force that could change his position on Christ. His relationship with God remained fixed. Paul's mantra ought to be that of every Christian: no forces—be they political, social, religious, moral, or economic—will short circuit our relationship with the triune God. Paul gave Christians everywhere a lifeline for spiritual stability. May we be *persuaded* to grasp it!

Day 147

And after the sop Satan entered into him. Then said Jesus unto him, That thou doest, do **Quickly**. *John 13:27*

This was history's seminal moment. The life of the Son of God and humanity's lifeline rested upon one man's action, Judas Iscariot. At the Passover when Jesus offered His cleansing power to the first disciples, He revealed that one among them would betray Him into the hand of the authorities, and He would be killed. His remarks befuddled them. Immediately, each introspectively self-examined himself and asked, "Lord, is it I?"

They knew Jesus possessed superior powers. They had seen Him heal the sick, raise the dead, cast out demons, and perform many miracles, so they knew He had "special insight" into the human heart. Their inquiry was most appropriate; no doubt they were familiar with Jeremiah's text: "The heart is deceitful above all things, and desperately wicked: who can know it?" (Jer. 17:9). Here is reason enough for their insecurity and uneasiness.

As each disciple reflected on his relationship with Jesus, only one could not find that they had committed any infraction. While they pondered, the lovely Master assuaged their anxieties and told them that the one to do the servile act would take the sop. Then Jesus performed His strange act; He gave the bread dipped into sauce to Judas who took it, partook of it, and remained silent. Even at that time, he had the opportunity to cry out and say, "Lord, I have messed up, help me: I am sorry," but he sat stolidly among the group.

Judas sat and resisted the Holy Spirit's urging, so it left him. "And after the sop Satan entered into him." He still had the opportunity to confess, but he resisted—hoping to see Jesus perform an escape. He had seen Jesus walk away from His pursuers, so he imagined it would be the same this time, but it was not so. Judas rebuffed Christ's last offer of mercy, so the Holy Spirit left him. It was then that Jesus uttered His death knell: "That thou doest, do quickly." Are you going to continue with the deal or are you going to retract? The remaining eleven sat silently contemplating, waiting, and watching to see the next step. Nothing happened. Judas alone knew the purport of Jesus' remark.

Having eaten the sop, he left their company. The Word says that "it was night" (John 13:30). Darkness now enveloped his soul, and he could not see the way. He was lost having planned the betrayal and subsequent execution of the Son of God. He knew the arrangement and felt no remorse, so the shades of night came upon him, and there was neither hope nor ray of light. He went out and hanged himself. Satan and the Holy Spirit cannot co-exist simultaneously in the same person; one must yield. May we *quickly* choose to yield our hearts to the Holy Spirit.

Day 148

*The Lord is my **Rock**, and my fortress, and my deliverer; my God, my strength, in whom I will trust; my buckler, and the horn of my salvation, and my high tower. Psalm 18:2*

A song called "A Shelter in the Time of Storm" found in *The Seventh-day Adventist Hymnal* emanates from this verse: "The Lord's our Rock; in him we hide: A shelter in the time of storm." The Rock is characterized as the toughest of all stones. It is hard and solid; it has no hollowness or shale in it. There are neither vaporous particles nor air pockets within it. People continually make reference to something as solid as the Rock of Gibraltar, which stretches out into the Atlantic Ocean, dividing England and France, and has been the cause of many a European conflict. It is very strategically placed, and humanity has referenced it because it remains unchanged, even when beaten by the elemental forces of wind, rain, sea, frost, and snow.

Yet, David, thousands of years before, could affirm that the Lord was his Rock, his fortress and high strong tower. God is all of that and more; He is a stronghold against external and internal forces.

During his lifetime, David confronted many challenging situations; the book of Psalms teem with prayers, praise, thanksgiving, lamentations, and petitions. He faced daggers, javelins, conspiracies, and betrayal such as fleeing from Saul, his son's betrayal, and enemies untold. He was constantly harassed and hunted. Despite these challenges, God stood by, guarded, inspired, protected, and led him like a true shepherd does to his sheepfold. David was God's special man, and so God watched over him; He established, crowned, and anointed him to be king over God's chosen people; God delivered him from all his woes and foes. Because of the wonderful, yea, enviable rapport that David enjoyed with God, God could say of him, "I have found David ... a man after mine own heart" (1 Samuel 13:14).

David performed some abominable acts: murder, theft, and adultery, yet when he was confronted, he repented in sackcloth and ashes and turned his heart back to God. That is all God asks of the sinner: confess, repent, surrender, forsake, and return to God. King David was also a warmonger. He ordered, led, and massacred thousands of his enemies. Yet, God delivered him out of all the snares.

Despite his foibles, David was a very magnificent king. He knew God and had experienced His goodness, lovingkindness, mercies, and grace. David could assuredly speak for God. His psalms are riddled with praises and thanksgivings: "O give thanks unto the Lord, for he is good: for his mercy endureth for ever" (Ps. 107:1; also see chapters 105–107).

Is God your rock, stronghold, deliverer, and buckler? Then write a song of praise to Him for what He has done for you. He imbued David with physical, moral, mental, intellectual, spiritual, and emotional strength so that he could attempt and execute any task. God will do the same for us. May we learn to rely on Him, for He is our *Rock*.

Day 149

> *But the* **Salvation** *of the righteous is of the Lord: he is their strength in the time of trouble. Psalm 37:39*

Every good thing that happens to the righteous is God-given; it is righteousness that exalts a nation. Those who practice holiness will always be strengthened. Isaiah says of them that they will run or be weary; instead, they will walk and never faint, for they depend upon the Lord for their sustenance (see Isa. 40:31). God's will and his powerful manifestation will be seen because He provides them with the tenacity to continue. He is their strength and stronghold. David affirms, "The Lord is the strength of my life" (Ps. 27:1; see also Ps. 73:26). God is the strength for all who trust in Him.

God is a stronghold all the time, not just in time of trouble. He never changes, and His outstretched arms are sturdy and muscular; they can withstand any force. His broad bosom is there for all to find comfort and solace. Every morning He imbues us with a fresh supply of mercies. All that we possess come from the Almighty; He will intervene and outwit our assailants. He knows that He is our only possession, and when we call upon Him, He will deliver us and save us even from ourselves.

The righteous will continue to receive favors from the Lord, for His grace and His strength will be imparted to them so that they can soar like the eagle. Anything you attempt will receive His approval as long as it honors and glorifies His name. He assures us: "Surely as I have thought, so shall it come to pass; and as I have purposed, so shall it stand" (Isa. 14:24).

God has done everything possible to save humankind; He gave His Only Son so that humanity could be reconnected with Him. He daily dispatches angels to protect us as we traverse earth, and He sends the Holy Spirit to comfort, teach, reveal, enlighten, and restrain the enemy's attack. He is Lord of all, and we must make ourselves available to Him. We must yield ourselves fully into His care. He gives overflowing grace. If the weak and debilitated call upon Him and drink from His fountain of life, they will receive the strength He imparts. You will also be revitalized, refreshed, and reinvigorated. God is able; He is all possibilities. Let the weak say, "I am strong!" God gives strength to all. Reach out and make the connection.

As I write these meditations, I am completely overwhelmed how the Holy Spirit impresses my mind with the super abundance of God's goodness. He is indeed mighty to save. Do not wander away from Him. Stay close. Won't you write him a song of praise and thanksgiving? May we fully understand that our *salvation* comes from Him!

Day 150

> *Thus saith the Lord, thy Redeemer, the Holy One of Israel; I am the Lord thy God which* **Teacheth** *thee to profit, which leadeth thee by the way thou shouldest go. Isaiah 48:17*

What an affirmation of the great, universal God, our Creator! Aren't we terribly blessed to have the Lord of all creation be our instructor? We have the Majesty of heaven to teach us how to engage in any business proposition as well as how to succeed. Furthermore, He is there in all we do to direct us step by step? He knows the end from the beginning; all knowledge resides in Him. Nothing escapes His all-seeing eyes. Knowing this is marvelous, and I am truly excited because I know my God is in charge; He is the Divine Teacher!

Listen to His words. He is in the classroom—your home, office, kitchen, boat, or yacht! Whatever the situation may be, He is there, and He is telling you that He is here to instruct, show, and guide you to the places He wants you to go.

Everyone should enroll in this learning institute where the Lord is president and CEO. This is the ideal ivy league school, for no one will make failing grades, and it posits an open enrollment: all people from different races, cultures, and religious affiliations have access! Classes are held all day, every day, all year long. Everyone who attends will succeed. Who wants to miss out on this chance of a lifetime? Who does not want to seek entrance in this institution of learning? The best thing is that no one can or will be denied admission. This is something to shout about: the Lord God himself will be teaching you! Incomprehensible! But again, nothing is impossible with God.

If Jehovah God, who inhabits eternity and whose name is holy, is in charge, then His students are guaranteed a fair and balanced deal. He stakes out His authority and His divinity: "Thus saith the Lord, the Holy One of Israel" (Isa. 45:11; see also Isa. 45:22; 46:9). Thus, we earthlings need not fear the present or the future, for the Redeemer is our able instructor, guide, and leader.

When and wherever God leads, nothing can go wrong. Humanity is guaranteed success in every attempted venture. Are you willing to let God teach and instruct you? Remember in God's university, tuition, books, and everything needed is free. He won't hire substitute teachers or aides, neither fulltime professors. He doesn't even need fulltime professors. This is a unique educational setting—the only one of its kind in the universe. Hurry and get your application in if you want to be instructed by the great God Himself! I do; I hope you will, too.

Here is our president's message, "And all thy children shall be taught of the Lord; and great shall be the peace of thy children" (Isa. 54:13). "I am the Lord thy God which teacheth thee" (Isa. 48:17). Certification complete! Graduation assured! Job offer guaranteed! May you call the office and register for the class from this incredible *Teacher* today!

Day 151

> *In the year that king **Uzziah** died I saw also the Lord sitting upon a throne, high and lifted up, and his train filled the temple. Isaiah 6:1*

Death brings rebirth, a new insight, and a challenge. The New Testament carries a story about the grain of wheat dying before a shoot comes out (see John 12:24). Jesus declared through John the revelator that "I make all things new" (Rev. 21:5), and in the natural world, when an old tree dies, a new sapling emerges. Thus, death and life—the end and a new beginning—are on the same continuum. The king's death forms a memorable occasion in the prophet's life. The Lord chose to reveal to Isaiah in a remarkable manner all His majesty, glory, and power. His robes filled the Temple, and His glory lightened the entire edifice. What a marvelous, earth-shocking, yet humbling event that must have been!

Out of that marvelous encounter, the astonished prophet heard the voice of God assuring him that his sins were forgiven, and his iniquity was pardoned. He now stood justified in God's presence, ready to undertake God's assignment.

With his sins purged, his eyes directed toward God's glory, he found that he had a mind and heart ready to execute God's will. When the question was asked: "Whom shall I send, and who will go for us?" (verse 8). The consecrated prophet responded, "Here am I; send me" (Ibid.).

King Uzziah did not have to die for Isaiah to be cleansed, justified, glorified, and equipped for service, but it was a momentous historical event marking his call to the prophetic ministry. God revealed himself to the prophet, forgave his sins, cleansed him, then empowered and commissioned him: "Go, and tell this people, Hear ye indeed, but understand not; and see ye indeed, but perceive not" (verse 9). God's chosen people had fallen back into sin and idolatrous practices primarily because of the ruling monarch's ill health. After he died they did as they pleased, hence the need for God's cryptic warning. Isaiah was called at the right time to behold

God's holiness and purity; God was reaching out to His children.

Many Christians are like Isaiah. They want to be engaged in God's mission, but they are not ready. Our daily routines frustrate us, and we forget that God is very near and longs to remake us into His image. He wants to purge, cleanse, and justify us, but we must yield ourselves willingly to Him. Only then can we hear His voice. We have to be attuned to hear the divine voice and get a glimpse of God. Isaiah did not only just hear but he also saw a glimpse of God. God manifested himself to the prophet like He did to Saul on the Damascus road; His Presence lightened up the place.

This meeting was an earthshaking occasion for the young prophet, and he responded readily to God's appointment. Like the prophet, we must discern God's voice and be ready to be used by Him. Have you seen Him and had an encounter with Him? If you have not been called, pray that God calls you to ministry. Like Isaiah and young Samuel, we must make ourselves available so that when you hear His voice, you can respond: "Speak, Lord. Here am I; send me."

Day 152

O sing unto the Lord a new song; for he hath done marvellous things: his right hand, and his holy arm, hath gotten him the **Victory**. *Psalm 98:1*

"Praise waiteth for thee, O God, in Sion: and unto thee shall the vow be performed" (Ps. 65:1)! This is enough reason to lift up the name of the Lord and shout out praise. At sunrise, we have a new song, for He has preserved us through the night. At sunset, we have another song for the marvelous things He has executed during the daytime. Our songs of praise should be all thanksgiving and adoration; there is no other God like our God.

Can you count all the wonderful, marvelous, and innumerable acts God has performed on your behalf? It is enough to just be able to sit and read this text and reflect and meditate on His watchful care and the many escapades we have surmounted, but to recount the battles He has fought on our behalf and to see us through is absolutely incredible. Only our God could do this. In our weak and helpless selves, we could not fight our own challenges, but His holy arm has stretched out far and wide and covered a very large expanse. When God's arms are stretched out, no force or power can bend them. He raises His right hand, and the enemy falls at His feet. Yes, it is that outstretched hand and arm that carried us through and gave us the victory. It pulls us into His embrace and cuddles us into His bosom of love and security.

This outstretched arm carried Moses and six million Israelites through the Red Sea as well as Joshua over Jordan. Yes, He carried your parents and their parents and those before them also through and over every difficult challenge they faced. He carries you even at this moment through the affronts you face on the job, at the workplace, and in your home. He gives you insight and discernment on how and when to engage or attack the enemy. Yes, He gives you the victory. He raises your right arm and says, "You are a winner." He is the God of victory; He cannot lose a battle. What magnificence! Every morning we must lift up our voices and sing a new song of praise and adoration for the mighty and outstretched arm of Jehovah, who has preserved us so that we are not overcome or destroyed by the enemy.

"Let every thing that hath breath praise the Lord" (Ps. 150:6). It is His rightful due, and we, His people, must not refrain our praise. Every morning He gives us a new song. Sing it! During the daytime He carries us along and leads us to balmy places. Sing His praises aloud! Shout them over every hill and in every valley and on each grassy plain. Lift up your voices and sing His praise in the car or on the bicycle, even in the bath. Wherever you are, let your lips utter praise and more praise coupled with thanksgiving. Victory is ours! Let our voices lift up and sing the Doxology–"Praise ye the Lord. Praise ye the Lord from the heavens: praise him in the heights. Praise ye him, all his angels" (Ps. 148:1, 2). May you keep a song in your heart—the *victory* is ours!

Day 153

But they that **Wait** *upon the Lord shall renew their strength; they shall mount up with wings as eagles; they shall run, and not be weary; and they shall walk, and not faint.*
Isaiah 40:31

We live in an age where "patience" is an abominable word; everyone is in a hurry. Each wants the activity done yesterday. If it is at the bank or at the clinic, in the supermarket line or wherever there is a queue, people are restless. They want to be on the move. No one wants to wait their turn. This text points out the blessings that come with waiting.

Before Jesus returned to heaven to take up His position at His Father's right hand, He told the disciples to "tarry" i.e. to wait for the descent of the Holy Spirit, which He would send to empower them to continue His ministry. They waited—not in idle jesting or frivolous talk or in lamenting the loss of their Master, but rather went into performing steadfast prayer and confessions as well as reconciling their differences. Then when they were ready to receive God's precious gift, He showered upon them the Holy Spirit, who empowered them to carry out the gospel commission: "Go ye therefore, and teach all nations, baptizing them ... Teaching them to observe all things ... lo, I am with you always, even unto the end of the world" (Matt. 28:18–20).

The Great Commission is for every disciple; the challenge is yours and mine to go and do what the Master has commanded. While we are waiting for Jesus' return, we are to daily engage in replicating the Master's work. Isaiah recounts the benefits of waiting upon God, and the most significant benefit is a renewal of strength. Resting and waiting strengthens and enlarges bone and muscle so that they will have great power and perform extraordinary feats not attainable beforehand. Superb strength and stamina will be accorded the saint who waits upon the Lord Jehovah. Not only will physical strength be restored but also there will be a boundless surge of spiritual energy. This occurs because the saints spend much time in secret prayer, and they draw from God's reservoir, which sustains and replenishes.

While waiting on someone, we are often occupied in some mundane task or activity. In a similar manner, as we wait upon the Lord, we should be continually occupied: spend time in His presence, read His Holy Word, or engage in silent prayer. We draw strength from Him. As we wait, we listen for direction, and we will hear His voice saying, "This is the way, walk ye in it" (Isa. 30:21).

One should wait in the least distracted atmosphere, for silence, a clear environment, and a sensitive ear are all required. When the virgins were waiting for the bridal party to arrive, some of them fell asleep so they could not hear the sounds of the footsteps of the travelers and the horsemen as they arrived. They waited idly, totally disengaged in any productive activity. When the party arrived, they were unprepared to enter the banquet hall. They waited in vain (see Matt. 25). God is not in a hurry; just wait on Him for everything. In one of His prayers, King David says, "Truly, my soul waiteth upon God: from him cometh my salvation" (Ps. 62:1). May we also pray that we become able to *wait* on the Lord in an engaged and productive manner.

Day 154

> **Examine** *yourselves, whether ye be in the faith. 2 Corinthians 13:5*

The apostle Paul is directly addressing the Corinthian brethren, but his message has global impact. It is directed to all Christians and Christian aspirants. This is a call for close self-analysis of the believers' belief system, faith, and reality.

Have you had an encounter with Jesus similar to Paul's on the Damascus road? Or are you hiding behind under someone's creed? Have you discovered truth for yourself? Are you seeking to know the truth? On what does your faith rest? Do you truly believe what you believe? Can you attest to the doctrine of the triune God: Jesus Christ, the Holy Ghost, and God the Father? Can you state like the Ethiopian eunuch to Phillip: "I believe that Jesus Christ is the Son of God" (Acts 8:37)?

We must know the principles we uphold, whether we are a follower of the meek and lowly Jesus or of a religion that is pretentious and hypocritical like that of the Pharisees. Are you just going to church to look good and to be a Christian socialite? What is it that motivates you to action or castrates you into inaction? Have you examined your motives?

Many people join the church just to be hip. The same principle was operative in Jesus' ministry. He told his first prospective follower to eliminate his earthly possessions and follow him. Jesus told another that he needed to attend to needs of the poor and needy. Neither did what Jesus asked. But Zacchaeus, the tax collector, alighted from his post, communed with Jesus, made Him a feast at his house, and then followed Him. Jesus commissioned His potential followers to attend to the needy and follow His mission (see Luke 4:16–18); we should go and do likewise.

We are all in the school of life, and each of us has to be examined to determine our knowledge of the curriculum. God has covenanted to teach us, and if we follow His instructions, we shall pass every test. Furthermore, we must examine our church-going activities and spiritual condition to find out whether we are truly and sincerely following Jesus' example. How well you do determines your scholarship.

Let us be certain of what and on whom we believe. If we are not on the sure Word of God and His promises, then we are standing on slippery ground. Be sure you know the truth. There are tumultuous voices trumpeting all kinds of doctrines and selling all kinds of wares. We need to pray and ask God for discriminating ears to hear the truth and for the Holy Spirit to lead us into all truth. The enemy of our souls is attacking the wary, the careless, and the indifferent because they are not rightly connected to Jesus, the source of wisdom, truth, and knowledge. Seek God, and He will plant our feet on solid ground. May you *examine* yourself!

Day 155

> *Rejoice, O* **Young** *man, in thy youth; and let thy heart cheer thee in the days of thy youth ... but know thou, that for all these things God will bring thee into judgment. Ecclesiastes 11:9*

Who is better able to counsel the youth than Solomon, the wise, pleasure-seeking, pleasure-loving young ruler, who did not deny himself any of the pleasures and fantasies of youth? He advised young people to enjoy their youthful years, for they are young only once and when that period passes, there should be no regret. Though well-advised, the preacher's words in Ecclesiastes 12 recount the travesty of life and that youth does not last eternally. It fades, and in its place maturity, autumnal, and wintry years set in.

Youth is classified as the spring of life when the sap in all its fullness and vivacity is coursing through the veins. It is indeed the proper time to soar, explore, engage, and enjoy life. The young have no sense of vulnerability; they think they are immune to certain pitfalls or accidents. Youth keeps them above those challenges, and nothing is formidable for them.

Youth is the period of unmatched power and advantage. Parents are there to take the free-fall, and they just march on stealthily without any angst or anxiety. This is their privilege, and they should utilize every aspect of it. Life, and especially youth, is but a brief shadowy experience in the continuum of existence.

Based on this expose, the king admonished the youth not to deny themselves of any of the pleasures their eyes craved or their hearts desired. However, he intimated caution to be careful of indiscretion and of any exploits. Though youth is a time to frolic, each youth must know that this is only a hiatus. It will come to an end, for life admits no stagnation; it moves on like the seasons, so youth will pass on. No amount of cream or salve applied or the search for that elusive "fountain of youth" can halt the rushing stream of mortality.

Reflecting on the challenges, excitement, and pitfalls accompanying youth, the king in later years titled those wild uncontrolled, passionate years as "vanity of vanity." I hear many say the old phrase, "that was then; this is now" because today's youth have richer, wider, and more treasured activities that summon their energy, and there are some that think that Solomon's advice was good for his time and not ours. This is the cyber age, and that makes a huge difference between then and now. That may be so, but everyone still experiences the cycle of life.

Let the young be mindful of their "good times," for each is accountable to God. He will assess their behaviors and actions and determine whether they were good or bad. May the *younger* ones enjoy themselves yet still act soberly.

Day 156

*For I bear them record that they have a **Zeal** of God, but not according to knowledge.*
Romans 10:2

Was the apostle alluding to a misguided or misdirected knowledge that his congregants had of God? Speaking to all people of the Christian era, he posed the question: is your knowledge of God real or is it superficial? This question references the previous text calling for self- examination of one's motive, practice, and core belief: let a person examine their heart to see if they are in the faith (see 2 Cor. 13:5).

People can be overwhelmed with zeal or passion to do everything and appear to be busy, but there is no genuineness. There is no real conversion, and the truth does not dwell in them. They have not sought to be born of the water and of the Spirit (John 3:4). They are manifesting the Nicodemus syndrome and are also lacking the birth that Nicodemus needed. They are zealous for God, but they lack the true knowledge of God's capacity and power.

This is humankind's bane: we think that because we are in the church and our names are on the books, and because we faithfully support the local church and foreign missions, we are righteous. Paul references this behavior as having "a form of godliness, but denying the power thereof" (2 Tim. 3:5). Pretentiousness to things of the Spirit is not the same as possessing and being imbued with it. Passion or zeal comes from experience. You cannot be passionate about an ideal; it has to come from within. It is not possible to be zealous for God when they neither know nor have experienced Him.

Elijah had a zeal for God because the idolaters had rejected God whereas Saul had a misdirected zeal as a persecutor of the early Christian church. However, he became zealous for the things of God after he met Jesus on the Damascus road and had an eye-opening encounter with Him. As the converted Paul, he now knew what constituted zealousness for the Lord God. He could analyze his hearers' utterances and know the real from the fake. Sadly though, they could be doing all these supposedly good and excellent things, yet they were ignorant of God's righteousness (verse 3). King David said that the zeal of God's house had consumed him.

Every Christian needs an Isaiah vision—we all need to see the Lord and have our filthy garments washed in order to receive the approbation of the triune God: Father, Son, and Holy Spirit. God will reveal himself to the anxious seeker and will gladly give His righteous character over to those that search for it. Let us study God's Word and search the Scriptures so that God can reveal Himself to us. Let our zeal for Him be genuine and not superficial. What we need is the real thing: a thorough knowledge of God's mercy and His power to save.

May your prayer be: "Lord, give me your *zeal* so that I will teach every person I meet about Jesus' love, His sacrificial death, and His imminent return!"

Your Holiest Is My Utmost

Day 157

A soft Answer turneth away wrath: but grievous words stir up anger. Proverbs 15:1

Many of us become agitated when our ego is bruised. As impulsive and spasmodic creatures, we are quick to defend our territory and space. Often times, the tongue precedes the mind, so we respond harshly, unkindly, and angrily. The writer knows much about the human mind and advises us to think before we speak.

The sage's advice is cogent: if and when we become angry, one method to remain soft is to count to ten before answering. If the situation requires a brash response and we count to ten, a flood of ideas will rush into our consciousness, and we will undoubtedly act differently. The few moments spent in silence breaks the course we would have intended to take. In anger, we might have screamed or yelled or even uttered some uncomely words, but the few moments in silence turn the tide of our thoughts and dissipate the imminent angry outburst. Hence, our intended angry answer is gracefully cushioned, and the intended recipient might wonder at the change in behavior. The gentle response deflates the tension and quells the flames that were about to burst into an open conflagration. Gentleness, one of the fruits of the Spirit, is administered to the smoldering flames and smothers the embers of emotion. In its place it leaves peace and quietude.

If we are faced with a situation requiring a harsh response, we should think before answering. The spoken word, like the spent arrow, cannot be retrieved. The speaker might give copious utterances of "I am sorry; I did not mean it that way" or countless other excuses, but the damage has already been done, and the scar remains permanently; therefore, everyone ought to be careful of the tone in which she or he answers. King Solomon reminds us that the tongue is a deadly thing that needs to be bridled (a strong metaphor drawn from equestrian pursuits). Jesus, the Master Teacher, stated, "For by thy words thou shalt be justified, and by thy words thou shalt be condemned" (Matt. 12:37).

Even before Jesus came on the scene, the Old Testament prophets counseled that the tongue of the wise should not castigate or chasten others, but they should instead issue strong, life-giving, life-promoting, and life-enhancing words. The lips of the wise dispense knowledge, not harsh words. Those who utter hasty, brash, or unkind words are not wise but foolish, and foolish people act without thinking. Their actions excite and incite unseemly behaviors that are detrimental to life. It is incumbent on everyone, but especially Christians to practice human kindness, common understanding, patience, self-control, and to consider the other person as though the situation was reversed.

The ideal behavior is to think before giving any verbal response to any situation. Think of how Jesus would respond; remain calm in your soul and do not fan the flames. May you remember to do this always, for the soft, quiet, untarnished *answer* will cover a multitude of bile.

Day 158

*He that **Believeth** on the Son hath everlasting life: and he that believeth not the Son shall not see life; but the wrath of God abideth on him. John 3:36*

This is a very strong and promising universal note. It reverberates John 3:16–"whosoever believeth in him should not perish, but have everlasting life." This is a voluntary act. You have to believe that Jesus Christ is the Son of God, but what is it to believe? It is implicit trust—acting upon evidence. It is embracing present and valid truth. Jesus said, "I am come that they might have life, and that they might have it more abundantly" (John 10:10). Yes, Jesus offers and delivers the possibility of everlasting life in a clean, sanctified, pristine atmosphere. But you must believe the words He uttered.

Many people are sad and unhappy because of the polluted environment and politics as well as the misery and denudation of the human family. Jesus offers a better way. He says to come unto Him, for He is the way. He came to this world to bring us a new life—a better life filled with joy and happiness. But it is a conditional offering. Though freely given, the taker has to become engaged and declare, "I want to accept; I recognize that Jesus is superior." The taker must fully receive Jesus and believe that all power resides in Him.

What is required is a belief that Jesus is God. A true follower must believe that He is God's Son, the second person of the Trinity. By believing, accepting, grasping, and appropriating the gift, one is guaranteed everlasting life. If you do not believe, you cannot act; and if you do not act, you lose out on the offer and will not have access to the gift of everlasting life. Rather, you incur God's displeasure and His disappointment. Can you afford to disappoint God? And can you afford the loss of the promise—everlasting life—and trade it in for God's wrath?

When Phillip asked the Ethiopian eunuch, who was returning to Queen Candace's business, if he truly believed that Jesus was the Son of God, he responded, "I believe that Jesus Christ is the Son of God" (Acts 8:37). Phillip thereupon baptized him based on his confession and affirmation. Do you believe as the eunuch did? But I hear some say, "That was twenty centuries ago! Get real." And you are correct. Time has not changed; the sun still takes its daily circuitry; night follows day, weeks follow weeks, months follow months, and time continues. God is the only constant in the universe: His spoken and written words still remain unchanged. Its power today is just as potent as when Phillip, the evangelist opened the Scriptures to the traveler.

With the many voices calling men and women to repentance and acceptance of God's free offer, are you willing to accept the gift and earn God's favor or would you rather earn His displeasure? All humanity must choose. We are creatures of choice and to not choose God is to choose the other. Each of us must know and decide what it is we shall believe because belief brings assurance and eternal life. Not believing incurs God's wrath, eternal damnation, and loss of eternal life. May you *believe* in the Son of God!

Day 159

Who can understand his errors? **Cleanse** *thou me from secret faults. Psalm 19:12*

Here is a request to be cleansed from life's foolishness. An individual may be unaware of his or her behaviors practiced in unguarded moments, but if one acknowledges God's requirements, laws, and testimonies as well as the rewards of obedience, he or she is not living ignorantly. Thus, we have this prayer.

Humanity's weakness and sinful nature act as a deterrent to wholeness and holiness. We need to recognize that everyone stands guilty in God's presence. God created us to have communion with Him, but our sins are a thick cloud, and they have separated us from Him. In our sin-stained, muddied, and unfriendly condition, we cannot face the Majesty of heaven, so David pleads on our behalf: cleanse us all from secret faults. This is a prayer of contrition and submission. The goal is to eradicate all that is impure from every corner and crevice of my mind, heart, and body, and bring it to the front.

God alone knows our secret actions. We need to go only to Him to seek cleansing and forgiveness and be rerouted back to the straight path that leads to eternal life. Only the power of the Holy Spirit can make that possible. The Holy Spirit must overshadow us; it must consume and empower us to live above sin. When the prayer is answered, and we are cleansed, we can sin no more. The Holy Spirit will reside in our hearts, for it does so in the hearts of the pure, humble, and contrite.

When someone's character is untouched by the Holy Spirit, it erects a barrier between all that which is holy. The individual is enslaved to ignorance, believing that it is righteousness and truth, only to realize that a barrier has been established between him or her and complete cleansing. There is no cleansing outside of the Holy Spirit. Every trace of error must be erased so that we can receive the gift of righteousness, complete cleansing, and thus experience oneness with God. Every person needs to be cleansed, for it is only the pure in heart that will see God.

Let us access the water; the Holy Spirit alone has the power to cleanse us and make us whiter than the snow. When our thoughts and actions reflect the Divine, we shall know that we are thoroughly cleansed. May we, by His grace, remain pure and spotless! Never neglect secret prayer when the soul lays everything bare to the inspecting eye of God. He can scrutinize every motive and truly cleanse us. Plead with God for deliverance and victory. He promises, and He will come through for the truly penitent. May we be *cleansed* so that we are able to be intimate with God!

Day 160

*He will swallow up **Death** in victory; and the Lord GOD will wipe away tears from off all faces. Isaiah 25:8*

Oh, what joy will it be when we behold God's face! It will indeed be a blissful sight: sin and sinners will be no more, and there will be no more funeral trains. When Jesus comes, death too shall die. It will be swallowed up, never more to raise its ugly head, and the living saints will claim victory.

Besides the total extinction of death, our loving Father God will wipe away tears from all faces. There will be no more sadness or need for house gatherings; His people shall be free—free from every malady that afflicts the body, mind, and spirit. Can you envision that atmosphere? An environment where only righteousness exists! There shall be no more farewells, goodbyes, loneliness, or sorrow. There will only be one great joyous occasion, for once again Eden will be restored, and the sweet ring of harmony that once graced this creation will again be established. That will be joy inexorably.

When God speaks, no one needs to doubt, for the Lord Himself hath spoken it. God says that He will make a clean sweep of everything that defiles. There will be a total cleansing and eradication! He will take away all rebuke of His people from off the earth. My God is about to do something marvelous, and I trust him for He cannot change. His words stand fast.

God spoke to Moses at the burning bush, and then sent him to free His children, who had been long enslaved by Pharaoh. He told Moses, "I AM THAT I AM" (Exod. 3:14). He also gave Malachi the message: "For I am the Lord, I change not'" (Mal. 3:6). What more proof do we need to assure us that God stands by His utterances?

The psalmist declares, "For ever, O Lord, thy word is settled in heaven" (Ps. 119:89). The beautiful and encouraging message is that there will be no more pain, sorrow, death, tears, hunger, famine, loss, temptation, poverty, or any of the social ills that currently plague humanity. God will totally remove everything that despoils us, and we shall bask in the sunshine of heavenly joy, peace, and happiness. I can't wait to enter into that experience. How about you? Let us take God at His word. Let us work to enjoy the eternal bliss that He has for us. Do not miss out on this great occasion of God's promise! Remember, God will remove the sting of death from off this earth, and there will be life forevermore.

Another beautiful and comforting thought is that we shall be reunited with our loved ones now sleeping in their graves awaiting the Lord's return. Death will be forever wiped off their faces, and they shall once more enjoy the company of their families, good health, and vitality. But more than anything else, Jesus will be there. Once He brings life, death must disappear. May we claim His promises so that we can experience eternal life and not eternal *death*.

Day 161

And this is the promise that he hath promised us, even **Eternal** *life. 1 John 2:25*

John, who wrote all the epistles that bore his name, was very close to Jesus when He chose, taught, and led the twelve disciples. John took on an affixation to Jesus and is named the "disciple whom Jesus loved" (John 21:7). He was very close to the Master and wrote about how He was the divine Son of God. God revealed to him the apocalypse found in Revelation.

John's writings speak very affectionately and passionately about Jesus. He declared that he and the other eleven bore witness of Jesus, and what he wrote was a direct result of what he had seen, heard, and witnessed: "That which was from the beginning, which we have heard, which we have seen with our eyes, which we have looked upon, and our hands have handled, of the Word of life" (1 John 1:1).

It is this John who wrote about Jesus being the Word and established His origin: "In the beginning was the Word, and the Word was with God, and the Word was God" (John 1:1), and "I saw, and bare record that this is the Son of God" (John 1:34).

Based on his record, John is very qualified, competent, and able to exhort all believers. He wants all his readers to know that Jesus' words are true and reliable. Jesus declared, "I am come that they might have life, and that they might have it more abundantly" (John 10:10). These are not words spoken in jest, but words of the Creator. These words constitute the promise that all who believe in Him have life.

When Jesus or God promises something, neither reneges on it; they always deliver. His promises are sure. Jesus said, I will send "the Comforter, which is the Holy Ghost, whom the Father will send in my name, he shall teach you all things" (John 14:26), and He delivered forty days after His ascension. Pentecost was the fulfillment of the promise. Since then, He has been pouring out the Holy Spirit on several generations and congregations that need and seek the power.

There are only two ways for travelers: one leads to eternal life and the other to eternal death. Jesus has already paved the way to eternal life by offering His precious blood. He now sits with His Father interceding on our behalf to ensure that we access the eternal life promised and offered. The concept of eternal and eternity is alien to us, for all we know is this life, so it can be challenging to envision the future and everlastingness. But Jesus promises this will take place, and besides, He has declared that He is life. If we have Christ, we have access to eternal life.

Jesus will deliver His gift to all who seek it. May we all seek that which is freely offered to us–*eternal* life!

Day 162

Fear *thou not; for I am with thee: be not dismayed; for I am thy God: I will strengthen thee; yea, I will help thee; yea, I will uphold thee with the right hand of my righteousness.*
Isaiah 41:10

Can you imagine the Creator and Majesty of heaven making such a declaration to His earthbound children! This is indeed magnificent and awesome: God affirming His plans and His covenant with His children! I am totally overwhelmed.

God declares, "I AM THAT I AM" (Exod. 3:14). God has neither past nor future; He is always the I AM. And because of this factor, He knows and does everything. He does not need an assistant or a secretary, for He is self-sufficient. He upholds worlds and promises to strengthen the weak areas of our physical constitution as well as our spiritual debilities. King David said, "God is our refuge and strength, a very present help in trouble" (Ps. 46:1), and He will hold us up with His hand of righteousness. Imagine God holding up His right hand! When you see the right hand raised, you know that both help and victory are in sight. What assurance! What magnificence! What care and concern! Only the great God could assay such a phenomenon.

We can all go for a ride on the King's highway; our God is there with us; He is beside, before, and behind us as well as at our sides. He totally encompasses our being.

Our prayer can be: "Glory and thankfulness belong to You alone, great God of the universe! You are with us all the way; we have no fear—only gratitude, trust, and confidence."

Let everyone come before our God with thanksgiving, praise, and worship. Our God is truly a God above all gods. He is the Almighty! Love Him with all your heart, and bow in His presence. He is worthy to be praised. Give thanks for such a Father! Be brave, be valiant, be courageous. Go forward! He is at your back, so you are free to soar, climb, and fly! Take the plunge; He is the I AM, and He is always present. Never forget that!

Jesus is your best friend; He will hear you when you call and will help you when you fall.

May we go forward *fearlessly* into the future for our God surrounds us!

Day 163

God *is our refuge and strength, a very present help in trouble. Psalm 46:1*

God, our Father, Creator, and Shepherd declared that He is God and will never leave us at any time. Hear Him: "I will help thee; yea, I will uphold thee with the right hand of my righteousness" (Isa. 41:10). Here the psalmist affirms experientially that God is our refuge and hiding place; He is our strength. God is there all the time saying, "Before they call, I will answer; and while they are yet speaking, I will hear" (Isa. 65:24). He surely is our very present help—not only when we are in trouble, dissatisfied, or disturbed but also He is available to us all the time. God can be relied upon; in Him there is no shadow of turning. He does not change. He is there for those who acknowledge Him as well as for those who do not. He is the God of all. It is God who made all and by Him all things consist. Therefore, rejoice and be glad! It is He who hath made us, so He knows us and our needs individually.

Let us never be weary or become faint-hearted or flustered. God is in the midst of us; He is our stronghold, refuge, and our fortress. With such a balustrade around, before and behind us, why should anyone fear or become restless? Our God protects, hides, comforts, settles, and continuously hovers over His children. Let us be calm in our souls; our God is in charge. He holds the reins and shall lead us into our own resting stall where there will be only peace, harmony, safety, and quietude. Lean on His strong and mighty arms; they are well able to support everyone.

Are you looking for a place to hide? Are you weak and disturbed? God has all that you lack. If it is covering and security you need, He offers it to you. If you feel weak, tremulous, debilitated, and faint, He is our strength. He will renew and reinvigorate your sagging muscles. If you are hungry, His storehouses are never empty; there is always a bountiful supply. Remember, He owns everything. Yes, God is a wonderful Father. He knows all about your sorrows, pains, weariness—your everything. You cannot hide anything from Him; your entire life is as an open book before Him. He cares and wants to help you. Run to Him! Cast every anxious care on Him. He has all the secret caverns, and He knows the clefts and crevices and the strong places where you can find shelter. Do not be fearful, for He is here to know, protect, and shelter us.

The more I discover about the awesomeness of my great God, the more excited I am. His greatness and watchful care totally befuddle my mind. I am very grateful and thankful for the enlightenment the Holy Spirit brings to me. I share the enthusiasm with you that you may also catch a glimpse of what it means to take God at His Word, to know Him, to trust in Him, and to find refuge in Him. God is always there for us. He is real! He cares, and He listens and answers our questions. I do not know what some of us would do if we could not communicate with Him through secret prayer. It is during those quiet moments when we come closest to Him that He can cuddle us and draw us unto Himself, so we can have some private time together. God cares; He is real. He loves you and longs to enfold you in His bosom. Won't you help someone find God so that they can develop a relationship with Him as well?

This Father, our mighty and faithful God, is waiting with eager anticipation to receive His children into his arms. May we not let our *God* wait in vain!

Day 164

> **Hear** *my prayer, O Lord; give ear to my supplications: in thy faithfulness answer me, and in thy righteousness. Psalm 143:1*

The Lord has declared that He is not far off from any of us, and He is always available to us, especially when we are faced with a crisis, calamity, or a challenge. David prays the universal prayer, for all who feel need to call upon God in critical life situations. David's prayer is ours: God is my refuge and my strength. Grasp it!

At this time David is surrounded by enemies; he knows he can fearlessly trust in his God, so he entreats the Lord: "Hear my prayer, O Lord; give ear to my supplications." God says His ears are not hard that He cannot hear. But King David's urgency requires immediate action, so he asks God to stop and listen—to understand his unique circumstance and to attend and respond as soon as possible. David does not doubt God's ability to help him, but the cry came from a deep sense of his own unworthiness and his need to know that God is right there. He wants instant validation.

David affirms God's faithfulness, his righteousness, and his promised deliverance. David is assured that his request will be answered. Confident that God hears, David adds a clause of submission, "Teach me to do thy will; for thou art my God ... lead me into the land of uprightness" (Ps. 143:10). Here is the model plea—total willingness and submission to be used by God.

God is looking for people with a willing, contrite, and submissive heart. He says, "And call upon me in the day of trouble: I will deliver thee" (Ps. 50:15). Thus, we need not be shy to come to Him and pour out our wants and our needs; He is waiting to hear from us because He knows we have acted upon faith, knowing full well that He will answer. Trust God all the time—every waking moment of your life. He holds up the universe, and He knows our needs. He is not a seasonal God; He is always available to hear and answer our prayers.

When was the last time you spent a long time talking to the Lord and poured out your heart to Him? God wants to hear from you in the same way you want to hear from Him. He longs to have a conversation with you. He wants to be your forever friend. He yearns for more than just a passing acquaintance. He needs a genuine heart connection with you.

Many of us only reach out to God when calamity approaches such as illness, sorrow, death, children in trouble, unemployment, or any other such social or economic ill. That is not good enough. When that occurs, we are using God conveniently to suit our purposes. God requires total commitment and sincerity of heart. He wants us to pant after Him, to reach out for Him and access His sustaining power. Not only in times of seeming distress and disease but also in times of joy and pleasantness. Do not forget that God is our Father. He is only a prayer away. He is there waiting for you to come to Him. Go! Talk to Him right now. May you quickly understand that God will *hear* your prayers!

Day 165

She looketh well to the ways of her household, and eateth not the bread of **Idleness**.
Proverbs 31:27

Idleness is one of today's prevailing conditions. Many people have no desire to be engaged in any productive enterprise. If they do, it is generally only for pleasure. They want to do nothing. If you call up a friend or even your children for that matter, they will say, "I do not want to," or "I am busy." If the conversation continues, you will soon discover that they were engaged in some trivial or meaningless activity.

Somehow, they are not totally responsible for the "do nothingness mentality." The bane of technology has heaped upon us a sleuth of activities that excite the senses, engage the minds and hands, and in many cases, are insubstantial. There are no rewards; people just want to play. When asked the usual answer is "It was fun." Idleness is much fun.

Many of the idle have no jobs and do not want one. But they have an iPod and an iPad or the most technologically sophisticated phone listening to songs and watching music videos or checking on Facebook. The bane of this generation is idleness and pleasure.

However, all is not lost; King Solomon's immortalized counsels in the Good Book are a model for young women (though men can learn from it as well). The well-accomplished woman is constantly engaged. She extols and practices these virtues: insight, discernment, strength, wisdom, kindness, industry, thrift, and sound spiritual values. She does not cultivate the nothingness mentality and uses time efficiently. As a girl growing up, my mother repeatedly warned against idleness. She would say, "An empty brain is the devil's workshop, and your hands are his tools." I became fixated on that statement, and later on I found one even more profound: "Our time belongs to God.... Of no talent He has given will He require a more strict account than that of our time" (*Christ's Object Lessons,* p. 342). This augurs for time management with no place for idleness. Solomon says that none should feed an idle or lazy person. Every person has been given the talent of time and the gift to work. Idleness is a sin, and if it is left unmanaged, it can lead to ruin.

The industrious person does not beg or borrow; they make preparations for a fulfilled life. A woman provides for her household and has no room for idleness or shiftiness. She does not rely on handouts or welfare, for she is a skillful, able, and agile woman. She refuses to eat the bread of idleness. Not satisfied with mediocrity, she is always duty-conscious. Her house is always full of supplies because she practices economy and thrift. Consequently, her children will rise up and call her blessed; her husband also will praise her, and the neighbors will honor and respect her. Idle people are restless; they cannot sleep. Solomon says that the sleep of a laboring person is sweet and that idle people should learn a lesson from the ant—the mother of industry. May we all trade our *idleness* for productivity!

Day 166

For the word of God is quick, and powerful, and sharper than any twoedged sword, piercing even to the dividing asunder of soul and spirit, and of the **Joints** *and marrow, and is a discerner of the thoughts and intents of the heart. Hebrews 4:12*

What magnificence, power, and awesomeness there is in the Word of God! It is a cleaver! Look, consider what it has the ability to do! To bore, pierce, cut, and dissect. Paul uses the physiological imagery to connect to the power that resides in the Word of God. The vivid imagery portrays a butcher carving and cutting away at the carcass of the freshly killed animal to produce choice cuts.

The Word of God has the ability to scrutinize our entire life. The joint is the place where two bones meet or hinge and revolve or rotate around each other. The physical analogy points freely to our spiritual frame. Even where bones meet, the Word can still find entrance there. One, therefore, cannot hide from the Word. Based on Paul's declaration, David's proclamation is indeed appropriate: "Thy word have I hid in my heart, that I might not sin against thee" (Ps. 119:11). The Word of God is a searchlight peering into every nook and cranny of our being and revealing our weaknesses, liabilities, and defects. Nothing is left unturned. The Word renders us guilty or innocent. David said, "Thy word is a lamp unto my feet, and a light unto my path" (Ps. 119:105). Earlier, David had asked a very important question: "Wherewithal shall a young man cleanse his way?" (Ps. 119:9). The answer is found in the second part of the verse: "By taking heed thereto according to thy word." The Word then becomes everything; it is the guiding star of our lives.

The Word acts as a laser beam; it reaches into the inner recesses of our mind and discerns our thoughts and intentions. It is like a flashlight shining into the deep corners of the soul, heart, and mind. God's Word is a discerner.

All of humanity's actions are opened before the Lord, so all stand naked before God. As the joints hinge the body parts to each other, so the Word connects the entire spiritual being. Humanity's life revolves around the Word; it is the ball and socket of our spiritual life. The Word binds, and it separates.

Jeremiah declares, "Thy words were found, and I did eat them; and thy word was unto me the joy and rejoicing of mine heart" (Jer. 15:16). The Word therefore nourishes, sustains, fortifies, searches, and preserves. May we have awe for the Word of God, as it is what keeps even our *joints* together.

Day 167

And then I will profess unto them, I never **Knew** *you: depart from me, ye that work iniquity.*
Matthew 7:23

These words were the most solemn indictment to escape the lips of our tender, loving, and compassionate Savior. They were meant to be a wake-up call to the "do good" professors, who practiced superficiality but lacked genuineness in action. It is a condemnation on a hypocritical life practice.

Jesus was counseling His disciples on how to identify the artificial from the genuine. Referring to work and results, He pointed out that people will be known by the fruit they bear (verse 20). In one of His travels, Jesus came upon a flourishing fig tree that seemed as if there were fruits on it, but when He went looking for fruits, there were none, only leaves. Disappointed, Jesus cursed the fig tree, and it withered (see Matt. 21:19). I understand this analogy very well because I have had a similar experience.

I planted six tomato suckers in a very fertile area of my front lawn. I had never seen tomato plants grow so large; they were constantly in flourish. There was a healthy vine at the end of the plot, and it grew far and wide. It spread huge branches, and at each node there were an abundance of blossoms. But there was not a single fruit. I examined it for three months hoping to find a tiny fruit, but there was nothing! Finally in early September, I uprooted the plant because it wasn't a showpiece; its leaves and vines were inedible. It grew and extracted all the nutrients from the soil, but it produced nothing. In reality, I had experienced one of Jesus' moments. I saw the literal fulfillment of Jesus' reference and action. One has to be careful of the image he or she projects. What is presented or what looks good may be only fluff.

Some people might bear inedible fruits, and others will work for self-glorification. Jesus saw all of this and told the disciples to be always on the alert, for many are pretenders who think they are working zealously for the Lord. However, Jesus said that when it came to accountability and reward, they will recount the noble, unselfish, purposeful acts in which they were engaged, but Jesus will look at their motives. He will tell them that their work was full of iniquity, and He has never known them. They will answer: "Lord, Lord, have we not ... in thy name done many wonderful works" (Matt. 7:22). But this was not the case. Genuine conversion and self-denial characterize the Master's workers.

Be sure that all your works and actions are God-directed and Holy Spirit motivated. Be sure that God knows you and that you know Him. On that last day, Jesus will reject those whose works are motivated by selfishness rather than selflessness. The last words you want to hear from the Savior's lips are not rejection, but an invitation: "Come, ye blessed of my Father, inherit the kingdom prepared for you" (Matt. 25:34). Every Christian should ensure that Jesus approves his or her actions and motives. May we all guarantee that Jesus *knows* us by continually lifting our voices up in prayer!

Day 168

> *The* **Liberal** *soul shall be made fat: and he that watereth shall be watered also himself.*
> *Proverbs 11:25*

This is the language of spiritual, physical, and economic reciprocity. It is life's oxymoron: the more one gives, the more one receives. Who will embrace that principle when all around us are people motivated by selfishness? Inherent in the text is the vacuum created whenever one gives, but the vacuous spot must be refilled. The more one gives ungrudgingly and unflinchingly, the more God gives back.

God supplies of all our needs and gives to all humankind liberally. He does not withhold any measure of the recipient. The apostle James tells us how well God gives (see James 1:5). A case in point of liberal giving is the widow of Zarephath. She used her liberality to share her last ounce of flour and drop of oil to prepare firstly a meal for the prophet Elijah, and she was bountifully rewarded. Her unselfish act preserved the family's life during the remaining days of the famine. Indeed, her soul was made fat—fully watered both physically and spiritually; her selfless liberality staved off death.

Similarly, when we share liberally, our heavenly Father sees and rewards us with a fortune. God's Word says, "Give, and it shall be given unto you; good measure ... shall men give into your bosom. For with the same measure that ye mete withal it shall be measured to you again" (Luke 6:38). Freely you have received, so freely you can give, return, and share.

Let us use our excess to bless others and not hoard in barns, silos, and storehouses. In giving to the needy, the indigent, and homeless, we will be abundantly blessed. The Word authenticates that key principle. We brought nothing into this world, and amidst all that we amass, we can take none of it with us at death. May we use our resources to water copiously as many lives that need our liberality? God told us through the prophet Malachi that if we share what we possess with others, He will be more than liberal to us; He will give us far abundantly more than we are able to accommodate (see Mal. 3:10). May we heed the counsel of the Holy One and give to all *liberally*!

Day 169

> *When a* **Man's** *ways please the Lord, he maketh even his enemies to be at peace with him.*
> *Proverbs 16:7*

King David said that a righteous person will always honor God. His son, the wise and astute King Solomon, commented on ethical, moral, and spiritual issues, and he affirmed his dad's statement. He declared that when anyone does right by the Lord that even his or her adversaries are forced to acknowledge God's evidence in his or her life.

Yes, God turns around the vilest men and women, who must bow in acknowledgement of the presence and manifestation of the Almighty. All practicing Christians must live soberly, godly, and wisely today so that the enemy will have no authority or power over them.

God's power smothers the harangues of the troublemaker. Satan can only come so far and no further. Christians are protected by the power of the Divine, and God must give permission for all the enemy's actions and whereabouts. Thus the enemy can have nothing to say; he can point no finger or find any fault.

When God is in, the enemy is out. They both cannot exist in the same environment. Based on this revelation, we must seek to please the Lord in all that we do. If what we do pleases the Lord, why should we be concerned about whether our actions are in sync with what humankind thinks? Our first obligation is to God. We are to honor, worship, and praise Him. If we act according to God's requirements and expectations, then He will lead the way and will rid us of all our enemies. Strife, hostility, animosity, and all other negative emotive outbursts cannot thrive where God resides.

Let people everywhere permit God to be their guide and teacher. If that is done, there will be a harmonious environment, fewer wars, more peace, common understanding, and good will toward one another. King David reminds us that "the steps of a good man are ordered by the Lord" (Ps. 37:23). Let us remain connected to the Lord so that we can experience peace and harmony and not hostility, fear, or hatred. With God in the midst of us, all is well. May we allow the great God of the universe to direct our step! He will lead us in the right direction.

Day 170

> **Not** *unto us, O Lord, not unto us, but unto thy name give glory, for thy mercy, and thy truth's sake. Psalm 115:1*

Here the poet is giving glory and adoration to God alone and not unto anything made by the created. When the writer penned these lines, the architecture was magnificent. God gave humanity wisdom, skill, and talents to erect some of the greatest and most magnificent buildings that existed. The first and second book of Kings is replete with the aura that surrounded the creation and erection of those mighty edifices. Solomon's temple, his mansions, his palaces, and all the mighty holdings that he built were bedazzling. Consequently, humanity was prone to worship the work of his hands.

When King Nebuchadnezzar surveyed the city of Babylon, which had been directed and built by his architectural skill, he looked at the magnificent construction and exclaimed, "Is not this the great Babylon, that I have built ... my power ... my majesty?" (Dan. 4:30). Today, there are magnificent structures that humankind has erected for its glory. Think of the Taj Mahal, the palaces of reigning monarchs, presidential mansions, and millionaires and billionaires' residences occupying vast territories; humanity has built for its glory and pleasure.

Rather than ascribing glory and praise for what we have done, the poet recognizes that God owns everything and allocates gifts, skills, and talents to everyone. All power resides in Him. Thus, the poet ascribes praise, honor, worship, and adoration to God alone. Elijah's performance at Mount Carmel showed the vacuity of worshipping things made by created beings.

God has endowed men and women with skills and talents to make whatever he or she sets out to do. However, all the grandeur is transient. If an edifice is erected, it remains at the behest of the wind and the rain. It cannot shout and say, "Come in! I have room for you." It is just a structure–a lifeless object. We cannot breathe life into any human form; we cannot raise the dead or restore life. We, therefore, must adore only the name of God.

The clarion call is for people everywhere to glorify God's name because of His great mercy and truth, His character, and His goodness. Our will and character are depraved. Paul says, "I am carnal, sold under sin" (Rom. 7:14), so there is nothing in ourselves to glorify. The Word further enjoins that at the name of Jesus, every knee shall bow and every tongue confess. In doing so, we are in harmony with our Creator and Redeemer. God alone deserves our worship, praise, and gratitude. His name is wonderful! May every *man*, woman, and child praise Him from whom every blessing comes!

Day 171

> **Our** *God shall come, and shall not keep silence: a fire shall devour before him, and it shall be very tempestuous round about him. Psalm 50:3*

This is a great promise and certainty of our Lord's coming. Long before He came to earth as the babe in the manger, David prophesied of His second coming to bring an end to sin. This is the Christian's hope.

In a world saturated with evil, isn't this the great hope–the blessed hope–that God will come and put an end to these corrupting and devastating impositions? Yes, He shall come and with a retinue of holy angels! This is a positive assurance that when He comes, the "great ones of the earth" will shudder at the tempestuous conflagration that accompanies his arrival.

The entire universe will know when the event occurs, for His coming will be a great shout, pealing of thunder, and a flaming fire that will burn out the dross of sin and leave behind a clean, pure element of righteousness.

Yes, our God shall come. It is not probably, or maybe, but the positive assurance that our God whom we have waited for, looked, expected, and hoped for will come in His own time. The important fact is that He shall come, and nothing can deter, hinder, or sabotage that process. This is the most glorious hope and the most wonderful promise. God does not make promises He cannot fulfill. It is this hope that burns within our hearts–the hope of the coming of the Lord.

Just before Jesus ascended to heaven to be at His Father's right side, He promised the first disciples that He would send them the Holy Ghost, and it would empower them to do greater works than He had done. And Scripture is full of the mighty works that Jesus did in three and one half years of public ministry. The Comforter came on Pentecost–forty days after His ascension. He also told them, "I will come again" (John 14:3). And upon His ascension, two heavenly beings appeared to the forlorn disciples and assured them that "this same Jesus, which is taken up from you into heaven, shall so come ... as ye have seen him go into heaven" (Acts 1:11). That is what we are all waiting for–the majestic return in glory of our Lord and Savior, Jesus Christ. David prophesied, Jesus affirmed, and the angels confirmed.

How wonderful it is to have our God reveal His secret things to His prophets and to the upright, even some 2,000 years prior to the event! David saw His arrival in a vision: Jesus clothed in majesty, awe, and regality. The heavens shall rejoice and clap their hands for the King of the universe comes to bring justice, peace, and healing to all humankind; the earth shall tremble and "every eye shall see him" (Rev. 1:7).

Be ready to receive the Majesty of heaven when He bursts the eastern sky with His retinue of angels! Let it not be that you will run from His presence, but you will look up and say, "Lo, this is our God; we have waited for him, and he will save us" (Isa. 25:9). May we all one day behold *our* God in His glory and majesty!

Day 172

> **Pride** *goeth before destruction, and an haughty spirit before a fall. Proverbs 16:18*

Pride, one of the seven deadly sins, has two faces: negative and positive. Used negatively, it is the opposite of humility and posits an egocentric manner: "I am so great, for I am able to accomplish so-and-so." Negative pride is distasteful and belittling, and it tends to put down others. For example, the biblical story of the two men who went up to the Temple to worship demonstrates the negative. One stood out and eschewed a litany of his good deeds. He was full of pride and rudely referred to the other worshipper as a publican. He was showing that in status and class, he was much better. The other lowly, humble worshipper, cognizant of his unworthiness and fully aware and ashamed of his spiritual condition, cried for mercy to the One whom he knew listened to the poor in spirit and contrite in heart. His action espoused humility, and he went home fully justified.

Pride is either distrustful or positive. Distrustful pride is an evil trait producing negative behaviors such as covetousness, envy, hate, and murder. Satan's pride falsely exalted him; he wanted equality with God, and when he was rebuffed, he staged a heavenly rebellion. He coveted Jesus' power, glory, and authority.

Isaiah 14:12, 13 and Ezekiel 28:13, 14 tell us about Lucifer's mind, his prior status among the heavenly host, and his fall. Both writers state that it was his pride that caused his self-exaltation. His privileged position, giftedness, and highest rank among the angelic host made him think he had equality with God and wanted shared rulership. We must be careful how we utilize our God-given gifts. Sometimes, when we achieve much success, we begin to think that we are self-made and deny God's role in our accomplishments.

King Solomon states that pride heads the list of these deadly sins. When it is in full operation, it produces other miscreants creating total spiritual, emotional, social, political, and familial chaos.

However, positive pride is humble, gracious, appreciative, and elevating. It is not showy, and it does not behave unseemly; its possessor walks with an air of accomplishment, yet clothed in humility, gratitude, and dignity. The pride referenced in the above verse is destructive and negative; if cherished and nurtured, the poison it emits will produce only destruction. Let none practice negative pride. Let us instead have pride in being called God's children.

Destructive pride is the inner voice that whispers "My way is best; I am better than everyone." It resists God's leadership, for it maintains false dependency and conceit. It brings one low and ends in downfall. Resist destructive pride. May we all attempt to only possess positive *pride*, for it elevates and lifts the spirit.

Day 173

> *For thus saith the Lord God, the Holy One of Israel; In returning and rest shall you be saved; in* **Quietness** *and in confidence shall be your strength: and ye would not.*
> *Isaiah 30:15*

These words are excellent counsel to the challenged. It is the prophet's response to King Ahab's inquiry about going to war: "Shall I go up to battle or shall I forbear?" (1 Kings 22:6). That inquiry bespoke uncertainty. Responding to the Egyptian alliance, the Lord sent this message through His prophet and thus assuaged their anxieties.

God is assuring the pursuant that their victory does not depend upon the power and swiftness of their steed, but rather it depends on trust and dependence on God. God declared to them as He did to Elijah through that "still small voice" that in quietness and in confidence shall be their strength. God doesn't work through a trumpet blast, a siren, or earth tremors. His works glorify His name. God possesses all might and power. Everything is at

His command, and He wants people everywhere to know who is in charge. He—the Holy One—is in charge. He is everything to everyone, and He guides in all the affairs of humanity ever since the world began.

God gently rebuked Ahab because of his pride; he felt that he could succeed by his own physical prowess: mighty armies, cavalry, infantry, and men of valor. These men even thought that they could escape the enemy and win the battle because of their fleet-footedness: "we will flee upon horses" (Isa. 30:16). They exhibited self-confidence and pride in their own strength rather than in God's saving power.

God wanted them to understand that He always goes before and fights the battles. How great and marvelous is our God. How kind and caring is He! It is at our greatest vulnerability that God's protective hand and eyes are upon us. Obedience and respect for God equates with returning and rest, which translates into true salvation. Hence, victory is assured.

Wait upon the Lord and watch Him work out His great work in and for you. King David's advice is very appropriate and consoling: "Be still and know that I am God" (Ps. 46:10). Yes, it is in quietness and confidence that our God performs. He is in charge. May you allow Him into the *quietness* of your life so that He may take charge!

Day 174

Remember *the former things of old: for I am God, and there is none else; I am God and there is none like me. Isaiah 46:9*

God is engaged in a dialogue with His people, for they seemed to have forgotten who He was and is. Sadly, there was a need for recollection of His prior dealings with them and their ancestors. Thus, He identifies Himself since some may not have heard of him: "I am God, and there is none else." Because the people were surrounded by many idols, they had a problem differentiating between the Creator and the other Baals that were worshipped. So, God declared for the second time, "I am God and there is none like me." That declaration was designed to remove the uncertainty and clarify the current confusion.

God cannot be compared with or likened to idols. He asserts His authority, sovereignty, magnificence, and omnipotence. He told them that there was no other god that could come close to His power. God is the great I AM. He is ever present—the one constant in the universe—the changeless One. Every day He is the I AM and there is no one like Him. Remember!

God is supreme, and He enjoins His people, "Thou shall have no other gods before me" (Exod. 20:3). The Lord is the one and only true creator, sustainer, upholder, and restorer. He declares the end from the beginning from ancient times to the future. The Almighty says, "My counsel shall stand and I will do all my pleasure" (Isa. 46:10). No one else has the power and authority to make such a declaration.

Our God is a God above all the other gods; He is not carved or chiseled. He is the Almighty; His Word stands, and His truth abides forever. He counsels, "Look unto me, and be ye saved, all the ends of the earth: for I am God and there is none else" (Isa. 45:22). Our only task is to accept divine authority. Let us never forget how God has led us in the past, and that even today, His guiding hands and watchful eyes are on us every moment. Remember, He says, "I am God and there is none like me."

Have you accepted the words spoken by God Himself? If so, then teach them to your children and to their children so that they will always remember who is God and live by the word that comes from God's mouth.

It would do us good and God would rejoice if parents taught this precept to their children, so they can grow up to revere the name of God as well. We all need to respect and honor Him and have full knowledge that God is first, best, and last. There is none to be compared with Him. God is superior. Let the children know that God is their Creator and that there is none like Him. May you *remember* to daily create in them the desire to know God!

Day 175

And Moses said unto the people, Fear ye not, **Stand** *still, and see the salvation of the Lord, which he will show to you today: for the Egyptians whom ye have seen today, ye shall see them again no more for ever. Exodus 14:13*

Moses was the leader whom God had summoned to deliver His struggling, oppressed people from Pharaoh's bondage. To human eyes, it was a most indefatigable task, but with God all things are possible (see Matt. 19:26). By God's mighty power and outstretched arm, He delivered them out of the clutches of Pharaoh's stronghold. They were on their way to freedom, but then they came to their greatest challenge—the Red Sea. They had Pharaoh's mighty army behind them, the mighty rushing, foaming waters of the vast Red Sea before them, and mountains and valleys at their sides. What a dilemma and a challenge! There was almost certain death either by their enemy's attack or drowning in the raging tumultuous waters. Panic seized them; complaint, murmurings, and harangues followed, and even ingratitude was expressed. It was a moment fraught with despair, distress, distrust, fright, and forgetfulness. You can just hear them say, "We would have rather stayed in bondage in Egypt than to come out here in this vast unknown—death be upon us! At least we would have a grave there, and our children would have had some place to visit!" Such were their outbursts.

Then Moses called upon Jehovah, who instructed him how he should act. Moses knew his God. He had met Him at the burning bush and was humbled in His presence. He trusted God, and being empowered by the Holy Spirit, he told the frightened, trustless people to not be afraid, for their God would deliver them.

Moses' command assured more than six million travelers that God would bring deliverance to them that day as well as total annihilation and extinction of their pursuers. Could they believe his words and accept their leader's message with sincerity? It was truly a very trying yet trusting experience for the travelers. All the evidences were there: pursuing enemies, the formidable mighty waters ahead, but the leader is saying to have no fear. Only trust the Almighty who they could not see. It was a huge test of their faith. In that moment of crisis, were they able to see God's leading or remember that it was He who had released them out of Pharaoh's clutches? The twin crises of the moment erased all previous experiences of God's leading.

As you meditate on the crises they faced, and as you reflect on the crises you face in your daily walks, how do you compare? Can you trust God anymore than they did? Has He revealed Himself to you in as many ways for you to acknowledge His leading in your life? God declares that He is God. He cannot change, and He is the same yesterday, today, and forever. He is the ever-present I AM; therefore, He is able to do for you and me just what He did for those travelers exiting from the bondage of slavery. We might not now be physically enslaved, but there may be habits, behaviors, and lifestyle practices that keep us fixated with no escape in sight. Help is here! Meet every crisis with Christ. God intervened more than six millennia ago. Trust Him! May we *stand* for Him so that He will *stand* and deliver us.

Day 176

They that put their **Trust** *in the Lord shall be as Mount Zion, which cannot be removed, but abideth forever. Psalm 125:1*

Trust God alone seems to be the focus of this text. Mountains are permanent and immovable fixtures in the earth's structure, so David used the analogy to breathe confidence, stability, and trust in his people. For them, Mount Zion represented stability and firmness, stronghold, and security. Being impregnable, it was the one constant natural phenomenon that gave his people assurance. They daily gazed at Mount Zion, and it was their hope and solidarity. They were able to envision God as the mighty mountain before them.

What a precious analogy that directed his hearers' minds to contemplate on the great and mighty God! He wanted to develop faith and the beauty of trusting in an invisible God. They had to see Him vicariously as they see the mountain that surrounded them. The psalmist assured them then as he assures us today, this very moment, that our God is with us, His children. He is watching, caring, and overseeing all our activities.

God does not change; He does not alter His utterances. He is not a two-faced God. He is the eternal God that operates from the beginning to the end. Because of God's permanence, He boldly declares, "I am God and there is none like me" (Isa. 45:9); therefore, all the children of Christian men and women should take courage and seize the words that come from God's lips. "I am the Lord, I change not" (Mal. 3:6). Our dutiful response to this declaration is to have faith, trust, and belief in that mighty, unchangeable God. He is able. Trust Him!

God shall strengthen and uphold all those who trust in Him. He will deliver you, but you have to let God perform His mighty acts in your life. You cannot help God; all that is required is complete and full surrender to Him. God knows everything; He sees into every crevice and secret places of our minds, even the parts that are hidden from us. He reads the intentions of our hearts. Nothing is hidden from the Omniscient One, so trust Him.

Let God be God; trust Him alone. With this trust, no trial or tribulation shall move us. Not even death will shake our absolute trust in God, our Creator. God alone has the answer. Won't you abandon your concerns to Him and move out in His strength? May people everywhere put their *trust* in God and move forward knowing full well that they are in God's hands.

Day 177

And they were all filled with the Holy Ghost, and began to speak with other tongues, as the Spirit gave them **Utterance**. *Acts 2:4*

This is the beginning of the apostolic ministry as commissioned by Jesus, the risen Lord and now ascended Savior. He told the eleven disciples to tarry and wait in Jerusalem for the presence of the Holy Spirit, which would empower them to carry out their commission.

After days of saddened emotions, disappointment, remorse, shame for their behaviors and self-centeredness, as well as having the time to reflect on Jesus' death and ascension, they finally had their prodigal moment. They came together with one mind, one focus, and one mission to be led by the promised Holy Spirit. Having settled their differences, God honored their sincerity, commitment, and readiness. He gave them the baptism of the Holy Spirit. They were ready to go on the mission that Jesus had been preparing them for during those three and one-half years.

In that upper room, with all their faults confessed, wrongs righted, and hearts pure and free, the Holy Spirit enveloped them and each received the precious promised gift. They no longer spoke impulsively, but as the Holy Spirit impressed their minds. It gave them utterance. Now, they could carry out the mission they were chosen to do: not only to be followers of a Teacher but also to be messengers of the risen and ascended Lord. They had a story to tell to the world.

When the Holy Spirit controls the heart and mind, God's power is limitless. He will empower each of us to utter the things that God wants us to say. David's prayer is very appropriate here: "Let the words of my mouth, and the meditations of my heart, be acceptable in thy sight, O Lord, my strength and my redeemer" (Ps. 19:14).

A heart and mind filled and empowered by the Holy Ghost will continually speak the thoughts of God. Our duty is to let the Holy Spirit take control of our lives, guide our tongues, and make us utter God's word to the hearers. A little side bar is appropriate here: once I was presenting the Word, and when I got up to speak, a devoted sister sitting beside me whispered in my ear, "God be with your mouth." I was very inspired and knew then that someone was praying that the Holy Spirit would use me to deliver the message and interpret it to the hearers.

Let us seek God and put away sin and differences from among us. May our hearts and minds be ever ready to receive the gift that God has promised! That gift will empower us to execute the mission. May we all pray for the gift of the Holy Spirit in our life and that He will give us God's *utterance* on all occasions.

Day 178

When thou tillest the ground, it shall not henceforth yield unto thee her strength; a fugitive and a **Vagabond** *shalt thou be in the earth. Genesis 4:12*

Hard words of condemnation: this is the curse ascribed to Cain after he killed his brother, Abel. When God confronted Cain and asked him to give an account of his brother's whereabouts, he should have come clean and confessed his wrong deed. Rather, he became very arrogant, aggressive, and defensive and asked God if he were his brother's keeper. His exact words are: "I know not; Am I my brother's keeper?" (Gen. 4:9). Cain seemed to have forgotten that God is omniscient and that all God wanted was His confession.

However, sin makes sinners presumptuous and aggressive. Thus, God did not continue the discussion, but denounced him for his murderous act (Gen. 4:10–12). God told Cain that he was cursed and that his labor would provide little fruit. He would forever be a wanderer and a fugitive and will never have a place to call his own.

Cain replied, "My punishment is greater than I can bear" (Gen. 4:13). Cain never acknowledged his wrong act, and he never sought forgiveness. He only tried to blame God for acting too harshly. At no time did he try to repent of his heinous crime. Even when God said, "The voice of thy brother's blood crieth unto me from the ground" (Gen. 4:10), Cain expressed no remorse, regret, or sorrow. He felt justified in his action and felt that God had judged him unfairly.

Cain's behavior foreshadows Judas' betrayal of the innocent Master. When given the opportunity to confess and own up his wrong, Judas remained unmoved. Such seems to be the behaviors of people who have sold themselves to doing wrong. They have made a pact with the evil-doer, and nothing can deter them from pursuing their path.

One must be careful how he or she relates to God and His righteous people. To hear the curse of God is a death sentence in its entirety. No one wants to hear that condemnatory response. In the light of this discourse, parents ought to assume the responsibility to teach their children at their earliest to respect God and His Holy Word. Children need to learn to love each other and not to engender hateful or retaliatory attitudes to either their kin or strangers because if this goes unchecked, none will care for them or love them. They will be rejected by the wider population. Above all, they will displease their heavenly Father in whom only love and righteousness dwell. All caregivers must assume the responsibility to teach the children the precepts of God's great law: love for God and love for others. The Father wants to gather them all to His bosom and not abandon any of them to the rage of the enemy.

Many young people similar in age as Cain have ignored parental counsel, reject and neglect Bible study or prayer, and follow their own desires. They should be reminded that they are God's properties. Their bodies are not their own, and God requires their first obedience. If God is directing their lives, they will make sound decisions and will not be led into paths that can only bring shame, agony, and despair. May we trust and teach others to trust God's Word so that we do not become *vagabonds* like Cain.

Day 179

> **Wait** *on the Lord: be of good courage, and he shall strengthen thine heart: wait, I say, on the Lord. Psalm 27:14*

This counsel posits patience, endurance, and self-control, bringing with it meekness, kindness, and gentleness. This is not counsel for the anxious or impatient person who wants today's tasks executed yesterday. The Lord is long-suffering, forbearing, and patient. His mercies are new every morning, and He knows how to respond to our request in a timely manner. We cannot see into the deep things of God, for we are always in a hurry. Here the psalmist is reminding the hurried that God is not constrained by time elements—the darkness and the light are the same to Him. He has the world in His hands, and He hears our petitions and answers in His own time and pleasure.

We must learn to quietly wait upon God, for His agenda is not like ours, and He is never in a hurry. He has no train to catch or appointment and schedule to meet. He is present any moment of the day or night. While we are waiting upon the Lord, we are learning to trust and say like Jesus, "Not my will, but thine be done" (Luke 22:42). This is true humility, submission, and patience.

Are you willing to meekly sit and wait for God to act on your behalf? Many feel that God takes too long to answer, so they grow tired and languish. They say, "I can hardly wait; I am tired of waiting." Do you have a cross to face as Jesus did? Are your concerns as weighty as His were? Why the hurry? Sit patiently, and wait until God works out His will for you.

With that prayerful attitude, our faith will be strengthened, and we will be a delightful and contented people because we know who holds the future. We know who holds our hands.

While we await God's answer, we should be engaged in some productive activity rather than remaining in a state of melancholia, choler, or repining. In God's own time and according to His good purposes, He will grant us all that we desire and need.

Indeed, waiting can be a tedious, frightening experience because of the uncertainty, but for those who have the Lord Jehovah as their guide, pleasure and a delight is waiting for them. They will utilize the time to help others get ready, for they know that God is in control. God is always punctual; He is never late. Let none who are called by His name release their grasp of His hands and run before Him. He knows the way; He is the way! So wait on Him, for He alone has all the answers to our needs. May you *wait* and rest assured that God will come through for everyone who trusts and hopes in Him!

Day 180

> *For what shall a man profited, if he shall gain the whole world, and lose his own soul? or what shall a man give in* **Exchange** *for his soul? Matthew 16:26*

Jesus posed this dialectical question to His disciples while He contemplated His passion. He knew what lay ahead, and He agonized with His Father about His role in humankind's redemption, as the enormity of the weight of sin bore heavily upon Him. He wanted feedback from the twelve disciples regarding their mindset and commitment to the mission and their ministry.

Jesus read their thoughts; He saw their confusion, trepidations, uncertainties, and angst. He sought to give them clarity about themselves and the tasks ahead. They needed to know what and in whom they believe. Were they prepared and ready to meet the challenges that lay ahead? Much uncertainty roamed through their bosoms; Jesus saw it all written across their furrowed brows. He wanted them to examine their beliefs, so he laid down the ground rules for discipleship: first, self-denial; second, accept the challenge; third, take up His cross; and if need be, fourth, become a martyr.

These were the challenges that weighed upon unschooled minds, and before they could digest the substance, Jesus presented another topic: losing one's life for God and the kingdom. Everyone had already given up their respective trades, families, and careers to follow Him. Did they know that following Jesus constituted such a challenge? What more was He asking for?

Jesus recognized their deep contemplation, yet He posed this soul-searching question above. It is heavily based on choice: what is the better gain, heaven or earth? Which do you prefer, and what are you striving for? Is it life now versus a future eternal life? You have to decide; He presented the disciples as well as people today the options.

Jesus wanted his disciples to focus on the road ahead and their preparedness for the task. They were forced to contemplate on the dichotomy: what will I exchange for my soul? Is my soul of any value? Will I choose life now and death later or vice versa, and what is the worth of a soul? These questions would constitute the gist of their message as they presented the Word regarding Christ. Their message was about repentance, remission, and surrender: choosing life or death.

We are similarly faced with the challenge to choose between the world and its temporary pleasures or life eternal. What do you want? Is it life or death—not the temporary sleep—but the loss of eternity? Whatever you choose, may your *exchange* be a safe one!

Day 181

> *Flee also* **Youthful** *lusts: but follow righteousness, faith, charity, peace with them that call on the Lord out of a pure heart. 2 Timothy 2:22*

Challenges are everywhere and abound as a snare to young people; therefore, they must know themselves, their melting points, and become cognizant of what is out there inviting, entreating, and literally magnetizing them to those "fun" things. It is the fun things—the seemingly innocent activities—that are the most entrapping: "Everybody is doing it."

The prevailing attitude is for all young people to engage in some sort of passionate and delightful activity. The argument is that youth is transient, and they must make the best of the short hiatus known as youth.

Youth is a challenging and exciting time. It is when the desires are rampant and course through the veins, and the world beckons them to adventure. It is the time of high spiritedness and verve. Everything seems possible and available, and the spirit of experimentation is at its highest. It is like the call of the wild. The prodigal son in Luke 15 also heard that call, and he left his father's house to go and indulge in youthful lusts and cravings. However, Paul cautions the youth to assess themselves and to set standards, limitations, and boundaries on their social, spiritual, emotional, and moral activities. The fun things are inconsequential and temporary; they lack substance. Paul was not advocating that young people should find their status miserable, but he did advise the things he felt they should embrace so that their adult years would be profitable.

The lusts, desires, cravings, and inclinations are part of a person's physical, emotional, moral, economic, and mental well-being. Each dimension of the body has its own needs; therefore, young people must bridle themselves, gird up their loins, and run from those things that are deleterious to the human body, mind, and spirit. In youth, critical and lasting decisions are made, and in adulthood, there should be no lamentations or regrets such as "If I had known ... if I had only done so-and-so instead." The counsel is to flee these disabling desires. Long before young Timothy lived, King Solomon stated that the pursuit after youthful desires and lusts is only vanity that effervesces into thin air and leaves the pursuer empty and vacuous.

Taking the king's counsel, Paul advised the young to pursue righteousness, faith, unconditional love, peace, and to cultivate purity of heart. The youth must summon the Holy Spirit to sustain and empower them to rise above sinful desires. It is available every hour of every day of every week, and the youth may pray as King David did: "Create in me a clean heart, O God; and renew a right spirit within me" (Ps. 51:10). That is the only failsafe method for living a godly and consecrated life. May the *youth* flee from disabling desires as if life, body, and soul depend on it!

Day 182

And he said, I have been very jealous [**Zealous**] *for the Lord God of hosts: for ... Israel have forsaken thy covenant, thrown ... thine altars, and slain thy prophets ... and I even I only, am left; and they seek my life, to take it away. 1 Kings 19:10*

Zeal in the midst of discouragement and fear, how challenging! The Elijah story is the bedrock of Christianity. His stalwartness, forthrightness, integrity, devotion to Jehovah, and his commitment to exalt and extol God's magnanimity and authority is unmatched in all of sacred history. Elijah is a no-nonsense prophet, who called sin by its right name. He denounced Ahab's activities regarding the stealth of Naboth's vineyard and declared God's matchless name at Mount Carmel. Yet here he was at this moment succumbing to human frailties of discouragement and fear, especially when he saw that none among God's chosen people chose to stand by his side and uphold God's principles of fear and justice.

Rather than upholding God's requirements, they led out in apostasy and rebellion. They forsook and abandoned their oral contract with God: "All that the Lord said, we will do and be obedient" (Josh. 24:24). They tore down the sacred altars, killed the prophets with the sword, and fought wars. Worship was extinct. Elijah was at his nadir, so he succumbed to the human frailties of depression and discouragement. In dialoguing with God, Elijah pointed out that he resisted the enemy and stood firmly for Jehovah's principles. Alone and despairing, he almost fainted.

God came to the rescue and assured him that he was not the only faithful prophet left in the land. There were still 7,000 who had not bowed their knees to Baal. That was indeed refreshingly good news! Prior to this visitation, Elijah felt that God had not compensated him for his wonderful Mount Carmel feat but was allowing Jezebel to intimidate him and put a ticket on his life. He was God's mouthpiece and could not fathom why he was facing such a dilemma.

Remember, God always protects His own; He never leaves them alone. He will always be their shield and buckler; we only have to trust Him in every situation. Are we zealous for God and his righteousness as Elijah was? Are we passionate and zealous for the things of God or are we just going with the flow? If we are going to stand up for God as the aged prophet did, then we have to cultivate some serious strong faith muscles toned by prayer, daily Bible study, and witnessing. People on the outside must see the passion we exercise on things relating to Jehovah God. May we literally and symbolically be consumed by a *zeal* for God and godly things!

Intimacy With Jesus

Day 183

> **ALL** *they that see me laugh me to scorn: they shoot out the lip, they shake their head, saying, He trusted on the Lord that he would deliver him: let him deliver him, seeing he delighted in him. Psalm 22:7, 8*

This is the psalmist's cry of anguish and lamentation over the loss of friends. He stands alone, for everyone has rejected him. He is not dismayed, for he trusts in the Lord Jehovah, and his faith has become in their eyes a chastening rod. His enemies are laughing and deriding him for his faith in the Almighty asking to see God deliver him now. This open mockery is designed to weaken his faith in God.

David had a great opportunity to recall God's involvement in the lives of those in Israel and how he had delivered them from their enemies. Now alone, David feels forsaken, and in the enemies' presence, he sees himself as a worm, an insignificant, helpless burrowing thing more of a reproach than a blessing. Despite this self-deprecation, he still rehearses God's goodness toward Israel.

David's anguish is a precursor to Christ's and foreshadows Calvary. The elite of society and the lowly mocked and laughed at the Savior, shook their fists at him, and said, "He saved others; himself he cannot save" (Mark 15:31). They rehashed all the symbolic references Jesus made about his imminent death and resurrection such as destroying the Temple and restoring it in three days. The derision continued, "Save thyself, and come down from the cross" (verse 30).

This psalm was the prophetic code regarding Jesus' treatment and manner of death. The mockery, ridicule, pain, opposition, and finally rejection David experienced at the hands of his people were similar to those that Jesus experienced at His trial. The Holy Spirit undoubtedly inspired the prophecy.

On the cross, Jesus uttered the despairing cry of the psalmist: "My God, My God, why hast thou forsaken me?" (Ps. 22:1). David's cry of anguish had affinities with that of Christ. Those last words of Jesus are indeed the cry of rejection, isolation, and alienation.

Even though we cannot literally see God, He is always there. He is like a nurse, for He nurtures, comforts, and attends to our needs. He will never forsake the children whose salvation has been bought with the precious blood of His dearly beloved Son. We are His purchased possession, and He will keep us to the end. May you fortify your minds with the truth so that amidst *all* the derision, scorn, mockery, or abuse, you will stand!

Day 184

> *And they said,* **Believe** *on the Lord Jesus Christ, and thou shalt be saved, and thy house. Acts 16:31*

This text calls into question the idea of faith, belief, and trust. It is the direct answer to the jailer's inquiry: "Sirs, what must I do to be saved?" (verse 30).

Paul and Silas had been preaching and teaching in the synagogues on the Sabbath day and many Jews and Greeks came to hear their words. The response was very good and many returned other Sabbaths to hear more.

This caused discord in the city. Many were converted, which caused much opposition. The magistrates were notified that these two itinerant preachers were turning the city upside down with their strange doctrine about Jesus. They ordered the preachers to cease, but they could not be stopped. To silence them, they beat them and put them in the stocks.

Prison bars with severe locks, shackles, and iron bolts were no deterrent; it did not hold back Peter and these two preachers, for they refused to hold back the truth. While in bonds, they sang spiritual songs and praised God that they could suffer a little for Christ's sake. Then came the ironic twist: a huge earthquake shook the prison stronghold and released the prisoners. Pandemonium broke out! The city became infested with newly freed prisoners ... or so they thought. How can this be? Amidst the confusion, Paul and Silas remained unmoved though they were unshackled. They continued to sing praises to God, and none of the prisoners escaped.

When the prison warden checked the status of the occupants, he saw that the prison doors had been opened. The warden knew that his head would roll for failing to protect Rome's property. Amid the chaos, he drew his sword and would have died like a true Roman, but Paul seeing his intention, cried out to him: "Do thyself no harm: for we are all here" (verse 28). No doubt Paul and Silas were dubbed criminals of the highest order (akin to Barabbas), and their escape would have struck a serious blow to Roman security. For the loss of these valuable prisoners, someone had to pay.

Stunned at such a response, the jailer immediately knew that these two were a different set of prisoners. He wanted to have what they had, who in the midst of crisis and their apparent freedom, remained chained to their post and engaged in a prayer meeting. Consequently, he fell at their feet and posed this immortalized, universal question: "Sirs, what must I do to be saved?" Then Paul and Silas replied with the simple Petrine answer: "Believe on the Lord Jesus Christ."

To all Christendom: safety does not reside in prison walls, chains, and balustrades. It is found in Jesus alone. He alone saves and delivers. May you accept His offer, practice what He says, and *believe* that He has the power to change lives and situations!

Day 185

Children, *obey your parents in the Lord: for this is right. Ephesians 6:1*

It is a given in all child-rearing circles that children ought to respect and obey their parents. Parents also have an obligation to train these children "in the Lord." It is a reciprocal situation. The fifth commandment enjoins children to be obedient, and here the apostle some four millennia later added specific counsel: to be obedient *in the Lord*. The statement infers that parents can train their children without the Lord or out of the Lord's jurisdiction. Let us look at both sides: obey and in the Lord.

What does it mean to obey in the Lord? It means specifically to do the Lord's will and His biddings. It also means to practice correct codes of conduct and manifest right behaviors. There are many parents who have encouraged their children to engage in activities and practice behaviors that dishonor God. In such cases the children knowing what is right from what is wrong are not obliged to obey their parents' commands. Only instructions that synchronize with God's will have a mandatory call to obey. If parents seek to lead their children into unsavory paths, the children must, can, and should refuse to act according to their elders' wishes. This principle applies to all parents–Christians or non-Christians.

If children have not reached the age of accountability, they cannot make sound decisions. Parents have the duty to bring them up in the fear and admonition of the Lord. When that is accomplished, the children will make suitable choices as they mature. If they have been well trained in the principles and precepts of truth, honesty, sincerity, and morality, they can make discriminatory decisions and most assuredly reject that which is censored, even if it goes against parental decision and direction. If the counsel does not honor God, these children must choose between who deserves their best allegiance—God or their parents.

Parents who teach their children uprightness need not fear if they will grow up obeying, respecting, and honoring them. The Word says, "But the path of the just is as the shining light, that shineth more and more unto the perfect day" (Prov. 4:18). Children raised by God-fearing parents will grow up and bless their parents, and by obeying and honoring them, they will be richly blessed with longevity. However, children can choose to disobey their parents if they are asked to do things that dishonor the Most High. Parents should be careful not to elicit forced obedience from their children but to train them that so that when they grow up, they will not turn away from truth (see Prov. 22:6).

As this process is passed on to the children and the children's children, there will be continual generational practice of obedience. May parents guide their *children* in the way of the Lord!

Day 186

> **Drink** *waters out of thine own cistern, and running waters out of thine own well.*
> Proverbs 5:15

This text points directly to the sacredness of the marriage relationship. Though highly symbolic and metaphoric, it is potently practical. It is a strong warning to the man or woman with a wandering and or a philandering eye.

The text is a safeguard against lust, fornication, and adultery. It speaks to fidelity in marriage and advocates a stronghold against sexual sins and desires.

Putting the text in its original context is very important to the modern reader. In desert lands, especially in the Far East, it was common practice for people to steal water from other people's drawing sites. Water here symbolizes life, fertility, growth, and abundance. Without water, nothing can grow, so this analogy has a deep profundity lodged within it. It speaks directly to faithfulness in the marriage; one should enjoy his or her own God-given spouse and not go like ravenous wolves after other wives and husbands, which are signified by the cistern. Though the inference directly addresses the male aggressor, the female is not exempted. In many societies women have become and are the aggressors; the advice is for both sexes.

Running waters refer to a man's sexual virility, which must be preserved and executed for legitimate relationships—specifically for his own spouse. Just like in the Far East, in Old Testament times, it was considered a crime to steal water from someone else' well, just as it was a crime to have intercourse with another man's wife. If the counsel goes unheeded, the offender is endangering the health, security, and stability of the family, the society, and the nation. Besides, someone thus engaged loses respect, integrity, and social standing, especially from the youth and among those who deemed him to be their model.

This counsel, ever so old, is highly needed in this society where family values are almost nonexistent: sexual permissiveness is the norm and both men and women feel they have license to do as they please sexually and are answerable to no one. This society condones and extols the vices and promiscuity of situational ethics: "If it feels good, and I like it, I am going to do it." It is too bad if the person next door does not like it. This behavioral practice demoralizes society and to halt this moral seepage, we must go back and heed King Solomon's counsel cited above.

Society is no better than its families, and families are no better than its men and women, so change must begin there. Each married couple must purpose in their heart that they will maintain the purity of the marriage vow and not go whoring after other watering places under no circumstances. Who knows if the water is not stagnant or polluted? Drink only from your own cistern. Stay with your own wife or husband and be content. Love and cherish your spouse. Faithfulness in marriage is noble and virtuous. With the prevalence of sexually transmitted diseases, the advice could not be more urgent. Every young person should heed this counsel: *"Drink* water from your own cistern." May integrity, honesty, purity, and chastity encircle the family, especially the marriage relationship!

Day 187

For he that soweth to his flesh shall of the flesh reap corruption; but he that soweth to the Spirit shall of the Spirit reap life **Everlasting**. *Galatians 6:8*

Can you imagine having something that lasts forever? It cannot be worn out, rust, decay, or fade. It cannot be extinguished, for it continues perpetually without ceasing. It is like the air we breathe, like the sun that shines every day giving warmth, light, and brilliance. It is an apt metaphor of the everlastingness concept alluded to here.

This analogy is about two states of life and being: life and death. It is about choices. Every man, woman, and youth makes choices each day: what we wear, what food we eat, what job to take, and what university to attend. The idea to be engaged and occupied or to remain idle, to marry or to be celibate is all centered on the choice one makes. Life is all about choices, and the writer addresses an audience that seemed not to have been making the best choices. They seemed unaware about consequences, rewards, and results of actions taken or deeds done. He wanted them to understand that there are rewards for any action taken.

Making a choice is as old as creation: our first parents, Adam and Eve, had to choose while they were in blissful Eden whether they would obey God and live eternally or listen to the wily tempter and die. They chose, and the result is sin and untold misery on the human family. As the children of Israel left Pharaoh's bondage and came to the Land of Promise, they were constantly asked to make choices. On one specific occasion Joshua, the new leader, declared, "Choose you this day whom ye will serve; whether the gods which your fathers served that were on the other side of the flood ... but as for me and my house, we will serve the Lord" (Josh. 24:15).

Like Joshua's declaration, each person, family, and heads of families must decide what choices are good for each individual and the family. If one focuses on the things that are transitory and perishable, then as soon as he or she dies, life is over. There is no hope of everlasting life. The speaker directed his hearers' mind to a quality of life that far transcends the here and now to one with one of permanent qualities.

If one has the anointing of the Holy Spirit, then his or her choices will be God-directed, obedient, and upright. The Word says that when the Spirit of truth comes, it will guide into all truth and that means making proper choices. The Holy Spirit quickens and gives life. If one's focus is on things eternal, he or she is assured of everlasting life. Each person must decide whether his or her focus will be on the temporary things of life or on God's attributes: mercy, truth, compassion, tenderness, and wholeness. Moses reminded his people: "I have set before you life and death, blessing and cursing: therefore choose life, that both thou and thy seed may live" (Deut. 30:19). We have the same option. May we choose *everlasting* life!

Day 188

> *The **Fear** of the Lord is the beginning of wisdom: a good understanding have all they that do his commandments: his praise endureth for ever. Psalm 111:10*

Most people want to be wiser than their peers, so they seek out how they can acquire the most knowledge. No one wants to be called a dummy or to come behind in any gift, so men and women continue this insatiable, unabated quest to acquire more knowledge. The very wise and learned king advised that if men and women wanted to acquire the wisdom of the ages, he or she would need to connect with God, the source of knowledge and wisdom.

To fear means to revere, regard highly, love, and adore. God is the source of all knowledge. He is the data bank and information center. Those who seek wisdom must first acknowledge God's majesty and exude reverence for His wisdom, power, omnipotence, and omniscience. Humankind must clearly acknowledge that God is the fountain of all knowledge and wisdom and that He can supply all we need. The Source is everlasting and continuous; it can never run dry.

The apostle James reminds us that God gives to all humanity freely and does not shortchange anyone (see James 1:5). Humanity must know that if they want wisdom, they must first align themselves with the Source of true wisdom. They must draw their strength, insight, and discernment from the Source. All of our strength, power, wisdom, skill, and adroitness come from God. If God withholds or withdraws His gifts, we are left with nothing; we must fear and revere God.

Every creative activity has a beginning. If it is in learning, one has to learn firstly the ABC's of the craft. If it is a foreign language, one has to learn the rudiments of the language. In trade, the aspirant learner has to be apprenticed to the skilled instructor. The process of acquiring wisdom requires a fear and reverence for God's mastery over all. If one does not recognize that God is supreme and that all knowledge resides in Him, he or she might not acquire true knowledge. Humankind has no power to grasp either secular or sacred truth; people's capabilities are all divinely imbued and without God's approbation, nothing will accrue.

If we do not make God first in everything, even the minutest activity and life decision, our lives will be skewed. We may experience bitter disappointments, failed aspirations, and unrealized dreams, but we must give God first place in our lives. If we place all our plans at His feet and give Him due reverence and respect, He will bless us. The acquisition of knowledge starts with respect for God's name and recognition of His wisdom. May you *fear* Him by giving Him first place in all your endeavors!

Day 189

> *But my **God** shall supply all your need according to his riches in glory by Christ Jesus. Philippians 4:19*

My God owns the universe. He owns absolutely everything—the cattle, sheep, goats, camels, donkeys, steeds, and even the money in the bank; everything is God's.

Humanity is only a steward of the world. None of the money stashed away in foreign banks or the credit card notes and savings belongs to the so-called owners. Every dime, cent, rupee, euro, shilling, and ever dollar belongs to the Almighty. It is all His. I hear you asking, "How? I work to earn wages; God did not work alongside with me. How then can He claim ownership of my substance?" Psalms 24:1 answers the inquiry: "The earth is the Lord's, and the fullness thereof; the world, and they that dwell therein." And that means humankind, beasts and all acquired items—houses, land, and money.

God is the richest of all, for He owns everything. If there is such a rich father, what can he not give to his children? The qualification clause is: all that I need (not all I think I want), God will bountifully supply. God knows your every need; He has provided for all and will supply before we ask. God has no needy or poor children; each is amply supplied. God treats all His children fairly and equitably.

In Matthew 6:33, Jesus advises, "But seek ye first the kingdom of God, and his righteousness; and all these things shall be added unto you." According to His magnificent wealth and our need, we are secure. Be advised that nobody can give you that which God cannot; God owns everything. You do not have to beg, borrow, or take out a loan; all your needs will be sufficiently and richly supplied.

What a wonderful, magnificent, and wealthy Father we have! He is beyond comparison. This promise exudes nothing but confidence. What a Father! May you take every request to our loving Father *God*.

Day 190

Happy *is that people, that in such a case: yea, happy is that people, whose God is the Lord! Psalm 144:15*

Having just been assured that our God has the capacity and resources to supply all our needs according to His riches through our Elder Brother, Jesus, should we not be exultant and joyful? Certainly. That is happiness. We share David's rejoicing and thanksgiving to God for having given him the victory over his enemies.

People who know God and have experienced Him ought to be happy and continually praise Him. If you know God and have experienced His goodness, pardoning grace, success, mercy, and deliverance from many and sundry challenging forces, then certainly you are a happy person. You can face any challenge because your God is with you and will defend you; He will put down your enemies and help you triumph.

More than just knowing about Him, there is much happiness in acknowledging that God, the Father and Creator of the universe, is the Lord. God supervises all His children's activities, so those who acknowledge and adore Him should be always joyous because God lovingly watches over them. Our God is great and good and is worthy of praise and adoration. His magnificence and power transcends our understanding; be happy for such a God!

Let people everywhere be happy that the great Majesty of heaven is their God, for He is the reliable One, and they are His children. That is an enviable, forever relationship. The apostle Paul said, "But covet earnestly the best gifts: and yet shew I unto you a more excellent way" (1 Cor. 12:31). How much more happiness does an individual want than to be aligned to the family of God and have Him as his or her Father! This God, our Father, cares. Be happy; be joyful; shout His name and give thanks, for He is our God and deserves our praise.

I am happy for the Lord is my God, my Jehovah Jireh. Are you happy with the Lord? You have a Rock to lean upon and strong arms to uphold you. Be happy, live happily, and speak only happy thoughts of praise and thanksgiving.

When people meet you and see you overflowing with joy and radiance, they will ask what is up with you. Here is your opportunity to point them to your God. You can give a testimony of the many different ways that God has led, guided, and directed your transactions. You can tell them how He has delivered you out of many tight situations. Let them know that God's care is universal, and you are happy simply because you know the Lord. May you spread the news so that there be many more *happy* people!

Day 191

> *And now, brethren, I wot [know] that through* **Ignorance** *ye did it, as did also your rulers.*
> *Acts 3:17*

In his second sermon, Peter sought to palliate the Jewish rulers and priests by telling them that their part in killing Jesus Christ, the Prince of Peace, was due to ignorance of the prophecies regarding Him and His ministry. Peter's words were caustic, but he cushioned them to shun overt hostility.

If the Jewish people had been ardent students of the Torah, they would have known that the person they killed was indeed the Son of God, their long-looked for Messiah. Peter hoped that the Holy Spirit might have touched their hearts and they would seek Jehovah's forgiveness, but no, they remained stubborn, stiff-necked, and indignant.

He further pointed out that they were not totally responsible for their actions, for Jesus' crucifixion was a fulfillment of the prophetic pronouncement regarding Christ's suffering and death. He appealed to their consciences and told them that they knew about the prophecy for they were all scholars of sacred history. They were being given another chance because of their ignorance, and they needed to repent and be converted. If they did so, they would receive the outpouring of the Holy Spirit to equip them for ministry.

The apostle Paul also referred to the saints' ignorance when he addressed the Athenian crowd on Mars Hill. Both preachers alluded that certain devious acts are preformed because people lack knowledge. In the Athenian case, their inscription showed that they were cognizant of a higher Being, a supreme power far superior to Zeus, but they did not know where He could be found. But in their fervor to worship, created the inscription: "To The Unknown God" (Acts 17:23). That was the window Paul needed, for it gave him the opportunity to present to them the Unknown God—the true God of the universe.

The ignorance exhibited by the two separate classes could be classified: first, as lack of knowledge—the Pauline audience, for they did not know about the God of heaven and earth; and second, the former were looking for the Messiah to come as a deliverer and not as a Man of sorrows, hence He did not fulfill their expectations.

On one hand the Petrine group killed the Just One not out of ignorance but out of fear and jealousy. On the other hand, the Pauline group had no knowledge that there was a God in heaven. Paul was able to point them to the triune God and thus enlightened their minds on things pertaining to the kingdom of God. God winked at their ignorance. However, now that Paul had presented the truth, they could no longer be any ignorance. Paul's message is the capstone of Jesus' power to save. All should accept the gospel of salvation through Jesus Christ. May you grasp at knowledge, for it dispels *ignorance*.

Day 192

> *And my soul shall be* **Joyful** *in the Lord: it shall rejoice in his salvation. Psalm 35:9*

This verse purports joy and gladness, and it signifies release and relief from the oppressors' hand. Here the psalmist seems uncertain of his pursuers' behavior, so he pleads for rescue and asks the Lord for His intervention. In the first verse, he requests the Lord to "plead my cause, O Lord with them that strive with me: fight against them that fight against me." He is engaged in an unfamiliar confrontation, and he knows that he is powerless in the face of those diabolical agencies. His only source of deliverance is in the Lord God.

Though dependent on God, he tries to help out the Lord and so orates a litany of curses to be heaped upon his pursuers' heads: "let their way be dark and slippery ... let destruction come upon him at unawares; and let his net that he hath hid catch himself" (verses 6, 8). When God answers, David will be happy (joyful in the

Lord) because the Lord God hath done great things for him, and he is glad. God has avenged his enemies—what joy of joys.

There is rejoicing and celebration because God's great arm has gotten him the victory. David was a man more pursued and hunted than every other man. Because the hand of God was upon him and God had chosen him to be a leader among his people, the enemy wanted to counter God's plan for the nation and humanity. Confident of God's intervention, he hosts a congregational meeting of thanksgiving: "And my tongue shall speak of thy righteousness and of thy praise all the day long" (verse 28).

Have you ever found yourself in a situation akin to David's where you are being attacked on all fronts and have also called upon God to heap curses upon your oppressors (see Ps. 109)? God knows what trials you are capable of enduring; therefore, it is unlike Christ to employ God's agencies to call down judgment on our oppressors. Both Jesus and Stephen modeled the right behavior toward their enemies. Amid the stones, Stephen prayed, "Lord, lay not this sin to their charge" (Acts 7:60). Jesus prayed the supreme prayer of forgiveness: "Father, forgive them; for they know not what they do" (Luke 23:34). This is the only course open to God's pursued children: leave vengeance unto God.

When persecuted and oppressed, we must let the King of glory intervene on our behalf. When He does, His punishment is just. Let God fight our battles; He is the captain, the legionnaire, and the marshal. He knows the way and has all the solutions. When victory comes, like David, we can rejoice and be joyful because God took control and came through for us. He never fails. May we trust Him and remain *joyful* through every crisis!

Day 193

But Jesus said unto him, Judas, betrayest thou the Son of man with a **Kiss***? Luke 22:48*

The kiss of death! How sad and monstrous! Judas kissed Jesus and sold him into death. Generally, you kiss someone you care about as a form of greeting and affection. In this case, Judas did not show any affection for Jesus but used the kiss as an identifying mark so that priests could seize Him. What calumny! How brazen, cold, and heartless!

Jesus left the door of mercy open for Judas to confess his wrong and seek forgiveness, but he remained silent and asked the same question the other eleven asked, "Lord is it I?" Once Jesus answered the question, the betrayer knew of his transaction with the authorities, and when he kissed Jesus' cheek, Jesus confronted him: "Judas, betrayest thou the son of man with a kiss?" In other words, "Do you know what you have done and are doing?" Before Judas planted that kiss of death on Jesus' cheek, Jesus had been waiting for him to repent and said at the Last Supper, "That thou doest, do quickly" (John 13:27). Judas showed neither remorse nor any desire to stop himself. He sidestepped his prodigal moment thinking that he had outsmarted the priests and rabbis. Judas tried to pull a "fast one" on Jesus but was bested at his game.

How should Christians regard the kiss or embrace of another? Paul enjoins us to "salute [greet] one another with an holy kiss" (Rom. 16:16). That occurs when genuine Christian believers meet each other at holy convocations such as church or camp meetings. The holy kiss is an innocent kiss that is flavored with the love of God and is pure, noble, and without recrimination or pretense. The psalmist also offers another kind of kiss that is wholesome, noble, and virtuous. He says, "Mercy and truth are met together; righteousness and peace have kissed each other" (Ps. 85:10). He is extolling the pure and holy virtues that Christ presented to His disciples in His Sermon on the Mount.

King Solomon states, "The kisses of an enemy are deceitful" (Prov. 27:6); this was Judas's kiss. He tried to deceive Jesus and his companions working under the guise of love and sincerity. He kissed Jesus fully aware of the financial transaction—thirty pieces of silver—and felt he had fooled everyone.

Beware of those you kiss and those you allow to kiss you. Do not kiss or embrace someone: friend, brother, sister, or family member if you do not mean it. May your motives be genuine and pure and your *kiss* sincere!

Day 194

I **Love** *the Lord, because he has heard my voice and my supplications. Because he hath inclined his ear unto me, therefore will I call upon him as long as I live. Psalm 116:1, 2*

What a great reason to express love and adoration to the Great King, the most high! He hears my cries and listens. What a wonderful friend and companion!

This beautiful psalm bears a beautiful testimony. David was constantly pursued by his enemies, and many of his psalms were prayers and petitions for safety, security, and protection from them as well as for their destruction. This particular oration constitutes a litany of praise for deliverance from death; it was very close to his heart and was a personal acclamation of God's goodness and mercy. God loved David, and David relied on God in every area of his life.

Recalling his challenges he said, "I was brought low, and he helped me" (verse 6), so "I will offer thee the sacrifice of thanksgiving" (verse 17). He also said, "I will take the cup of salvation, and call upon the name of the Lord. I will pay my vows unto the Lord now in the presence of all his people" (verses 13, 14). This is a prayer filled with nothing but gratitude and eternal love.

David gave two primary reasons why he loved the Lord: first, God heard his voice and his supplications; and second, God not only heard and listened but answered. Therefore, he knew that He was there and was dependable, so he said, "I will call upon him as long as I live."

God is very near to every one of us. God said, "And call upon me in the day of trouble: I will deliver thee, and thou shalt glorify me" (Ps. 50:15). David heeded that counsel, hence this oration of praise and thanksgiving.

Has God done something lately for which you are thankful? Has he heard and answered your prayers? Are you satisfied, and do you love Him more? He knows our needs, and He hears our cries. He is not indifferent to our utterances. God cares. He deserves our love, adoration, and prayers of thankfulness. Do not just love Him for what He can do for us, but because He is our Father who graciously gives out love, compassion, and tender care as well as supplies all our needs as an earthly father would do. He is more than an earthly father; He is the powerful, everlasting Father whose love saves us and upholds worlds. Love Him; love Him; love Him because as our Father, He first loved us. There is none other like Him.

We are all wonderfully blessed to have the Father of love as our Father. Let us worship and adore Him. When we experience God's wonderful mercies, let us return prayers and thanksgiving offerings to Him. May we *love* Him with every fiber of our being remembering that He first *loved* us!

Day 195

O **Magnify** *the Lord with me, and let us exalt his name together. Psalm 34:3*

This text calls every thankful heart to praise the Lord, especially if He has intervened in his or her life. In yesterday's text, David gives the rationale for loving the Lord. Now, he is calling people to come and share with him the magnanimity of the God who hears all prayers. He is reminding all that it is God who hears and answers all orisons.

David had been redeemed, rescued, and saved from destruction and total annihilation; he was full of gratitude. Thus, he summons his entire realm to hear the marvelous testimony of what God has wrought in his life. It is a blessing that he has recorded it for future generations.

At this convocation, he gives the reason for the celebration. "I sought the Lord, and he heard me, and delivered me from all my fears" (verse 4). Therefore, His name is worthy to be praised all the time—from the rising of the sun to the going down of the same. I want you to share this good news with everyone.

He continues, "O taste and see that the Lord is good: blessed is the man that trusteth in him" (verse 8). You have to be in it to believe it! And everyone who tastes of Him is blessed and satisfied. So, come, let us all lift up His name on high, for He is a God above all other gods. He is the great I AM! Continuing on, he says, "The righteous cry, and the Lord heareth, and delivereth them out of all their troubles.... Many are the afflictions of the righteous: but the Lord delivereth him out of them all" (verses 17, 19). Does one need any more assurance to celebrate? God speaks through His Word, and it surely stands fast. This is enough cause to magnify the name of the Lord!

Is there an event in your life for which you can magnify the name of the Lord? Reflect on His past leadings and current direction for your life. Can you also call a meeting of family and friends and bear testimony of God's goodness to you for healing, rescuing, or delivering you from an addiction or some foul emotion? I am sure you can. If so, then like David, we must proclaim: "Come with me, and let us magnify the name of the Lord our God; let us shout and sing praises to the most High God!" Let every breathing creature praise the Lord! Let everyone exalt His name! The Lord is good, and His mercies, which are new every morning, endure as long as there is a God. May we proclaim it and *magnify* His Holy name!

Day 196

Master, we have toiled all the night, and have taken **Nothing**: *nevertheless at thy word I will let down the net. Luke 5:5*

The bane of the fisherman's toil: no fish in the net. To add to the day's ill luck, Jesus came along and told Peter "to push out from the shore" and place the anchor in the water, so he could teach the waiting crowd. Peter was no doubt put off. Firstly, he was a master of the sea; he knew where the fish were biting. He did understand how Jesus could come and disturb his effort, though fruitless it was? Secondly, that day he was not doing "deep sea" fishing, he was seine fishing, so it was necessary for him to stay near the shore, so he could haul in the net. He felt a little upset, but he complied, and Jesus spoke to the crowd.

Having finished his deliberation, Jesus told the lead fisherman to "launch out into the deep" (verse 4) and move away from the shallow water. Jesus wanted the boat to go out into the deep so that the net could be let down for a draught. This is when Peter became more perturbed and lashed back: "Master, we have toiled all night, and have taken nothing." So Peter and the other seasoned fishermen reasoned in their hearts.

However, Jesus did not relent, and Peter somehow recognized the authority and superiority of the Man in whose presence he stood, acquiesced, and conceded: "Nevertheless at thy word I will let down the net." Peter had not yet learned that Jesus was the Master of the sea and controlled the fishes therein.

The result was a stupendous draught of fish; the nets overflowed, and the boats began to sink. Seeing the miracle performed before his eyes, Peter became ashamed of his behavior, fell at Jesus' feet, worshipped Him declaring, "Depart from me; for I am sinful man, O Lord" (verse 8). Jesus raised him up saying, "Simon, Fear not; from henceforth thou shalt catch men" (verse 10). This became the life-changing moment in Peter's experience; that was his call to missions. Jesus wanted Peter to know that he was in the presence of divinity. We must learn to recognize Jesus' presence in our lives and to know that when He speaks, He expects unquestioned obedience.

There are many lessons to be learned from the fishing exercise: first, nothing can be accomplished by just skimming at the surface, for one has to dig deep to arrive at truth; second, one can accomplish but little, for one constantly needs divine aid; third, one must be willing to seek and take advice from those who can help; and fourth, all must connect with the Source of all wisdom and power to get direction for their aspirations. The presence of the Master at the seaside made all the difference; it turned a frustrating fishing exercise into a fruitful money-making activity and a commitment to follow Jesus. At that place humanity confronted divinity and the latter won. The fishing crew left their nets and followed Jesus. May you let *nothing* stand in your way of following Him today!

Day 197

> O *clap your hands, all ye people; shout unto God with the voice of triumph. For the Lord most high is terrible; he is a great King over all the earth. Psalm 47:1, 2*

Here is another call for humankind to magnify and praise the Lord because of His Kingship over all the earth. Raise your hands all ye people; clap them and shout triumphantly, for He is the God of all the earth. Everything has their being in the Almighty. He is awe-inspiring, and He deserves praise, adoration, and thanksgiving because of His great mercy, magnificence, and power!

Yes, God, the Creator of the universe, rules over all. He directs our coming and our going, our exits and our entrances; He knows every aspect of our being. He is the great King; men and women with possessions, wealth, power, and fame are subservient to the Almighty. He stretches out His hand, and there is none to restrain Him.

Even though this was a hymn of praise for God's leadership, primarily to ancient Israel, He is still a great God today. We are not ancient Israel, but we are also His people—"to all that are afar off" (Acts 2:39). He sent His only Son to die for our salvation and redemption. We are the chosen; we are Abraham's children by proxy and adoption. Through the blood of Jesus, we are grafted into this special inner circle of grace. Today, each of us stands as spiritual Israel through the blood. God, who ruled when Israel wandered for forty years, is still the same God who rules even today, right now, and is by our side on our journey. He is always in charge; He does not need a vicegerent, for He has sole authority. O, clap your hands!

Have you a thanksgiving testimony and need to clap your hands and shout His praise? God made all the known and unknown worlds and keeps everything in orbit; not one planet fails or goes off track. What precision! Who could it be but God? Furthermore, everything in the universe is timed: no tree puts forth its bud untimely; no cows calve before their time; and no person sleeps in the grave before his or her time. All of this happens because of the awesomeness of the Almighty, who keeps the universe running like well-oiled machine or a freshly tuned up car. O, clap your hands!

This text is a solemn call for people everywhere to lift up their voices and sing, to raise their hands in joyous adoration and clap and extol the God of the universe, Creator of everything and sustainer of all. He is to be feared, honored, reverenced, respected, and greatly exalted. O, come let us adore the great God of the Ages, who is the ever-present, constant source of power and strength!

We are not to only clap our hands but testify to others so that they can experience the jubilee. Let us be passionate about God and communicate the zeal to everyone in our purview. Let the excitement be known abroad among every kindred who will also rejoice because they have discovered this wonderful, loving, and caring Father. *O*, may you shout His name before all the earth!

Day 198

The Lord shall **Preserve** *thee from all evil: he shall preserve thy soul. Psalm 121:7*

What comforting words of assurance exuding confidence and trust! Here King David uses the imagery of pickling and canning, which farmers and housewives used in preserving fruits and vegetables so that when the harvest is completed, they will have abundance in their storehouses. Though an ancient practice, it is still widely used today.

This analogy is very clear to even the simplest child. This is the Lord's promise to the obedient and upright. God promises that the righteous shall never be in want; they will not be brought down to penury or beg for bread. All their needs will be amply supplied. Additionally, the enemy cannot even have an upper hand on them because their loving Father will protect them from all evil. David affirms that no evil shall befall thee, "neither shall any plague come nigh thy dwelling" (Ps. 91:10). Your homestead will be protected and preserved. No foreign bodies will be able to enter. Human, beast, encroacher, or prowler will not access the environment of His obedient children.

The Lord shall preserve your body from debilitating sickness and diseases; He will keep you physically fit, mentally stable, emotionally secure, and morally and spiritually grounded. He will keep all your material goods and substances from spoilage of moth or rust. He will restrain the enemy's advance. My God will also preserve your soul. God is ensuring that you and I are saved. Glory!

The certainty of being saved is a conditional factor. God has made provision for each of us to be saved and access eternal life, but we must individually accept the proffered gift. If you remain close to Him, the Source of life, He will keep you from sinning. The seven deadly sins will not overpower you. God will preserve your soul. It is His; He bought you. Jesus died for you to set you free from guilt, fear, evil ideas and plans. He paid with His precious blood. His was no ordinary blue-veined blood; it was sacred, sanctified, and divine blood! Therefore, He will preserve you.

Being bought with the precious blood, we are assured of eternal rest and everlasting life. Since God is the author, creator, keeper, sustainer, and redeemer, when He says He will do something, He does it. Through David's experience with God, he could affirm: "The Lord preserveth all them that love him: but all the wicked will he destroy" (Ps. 145:20). Yes, the Lord will protect and keep the upright; He will set fortresses around you so that you remain unharmed.

Our God will keep body and soul; He will keep also the mind from depression, dementia, or Alzheimer's. The Lord will preserve your body from other debilitating diseases, as also your going out and your coming in all the days of your life. This is great comfort, assurance, and wonderful promise of God's sustaining power. May you claim the promise that our able God will *preserve* you!

Day 199

Behold, I come **Quickly**: *hold that fast which thou hast, that no man take thy crown.*
Revelation 3:11

Inherent in Jesus' direct words to the churches operating in this final church age is a warning and a counsel addressed to God's people. How soon the event of His return will be, we are not privy to, but we know He will come. Whatever God says comes to pass. Jesus tells us to stop and listen, as He will quickly return. And He means it! When He comes in glory with the retinue of heavenly hosts, then we shall proclaim, "Lo, this is our God; we have waited for him, and he will save us ... we will be glad and rejoice in his salvation" (Isa. 25:9).

The message cited constitutes a promise to people living in the New Testament church age who anticipated the return of Jesus (see John 14:1–3). He went up confirmed by the two angels in white and sat at His Father's right hand (see Acts 1:11). He gave the vision to the beloved apostle "to shew unto his servants things which must shortly come to pass" (Rev. 1:1); and for us last day believers, He said, "Behold, I come quickly."

This is an urgent expression even though quickly does not necessarily mean "now or the next few days." With the heavenly intelligentsia, time is not computed. It is not measured by years, days, or months. We do know when He will return to this earth. Jesus, Himself, does not know the day nor the hour, but He said it would happen, and I believe it, even though it is well nigh twenty centuries since that newsflash was given and documented. God and humankind's timepiece do not synchronize. Galatians 4:4 clues us into how God works: "When the fulness of the time was come, God sent forth his Son." He came the first time as a Babe. Similarly, when the message of Matthew 24:14 is fulfilled, God will again dispatch His Son back to earth to gather the faithful, obedient ones.

In God's provenance, quickly does not mean "being in a hurry." Its purpose was to put us on guard. While we await Jesus' return, it is time for a personal, critical assessment of our spiritual standing. In what and in whom do we believe? And how prepared are we if Jesus should appear at this moment? The warning is a call to readiness and watchfulness.

While we are waiting, we need to be careful not to be tossed around by every new ideology. Jesus tells us to hold fast to the truth! Let each stand firmly on the Word of God: "He answered and said, It is written; Man shall not live by bread along, but by every word that proceedeth out of the mouth of God" (Matt. 4:4). These were Jesus' weapons, and they are the only ones with which one can fight the attacker. Let no one rob you of the gift of eternal life. May we be ready and stay ready! May we pray and work for, surely, He comes *quickly*!

Day 200

Remember *the sabbath day, to keep it holy. Exodus 20:8*

This text is the fourth principle of the Decalogue that God wrote with His own fingers and gave to Moses to set before the people as they traveled in the wilderness en route to Canaan. We tend to forget sacred and holy things, especially when things are going well. Sometimes, secular and sacred tasks overwhelm us, so we become miscued and allow things to get befuddled.

God knows us individually; He knows our strengths and our weaknesses as well as our predispositions for the holy and sanctified and for the unsavory and polluted. He knows we have selective attention spans and short-lived memories. And since the Sabbath is special to Him, He calls our attention with the word: Remember!

On the seventh day of Creation, God ended His work and set aside this special day and called it a Sabbath—it was made for rest. He said this was to be a holy day. God wanted to preserve it for honor, worship, rest, and thanksgiving. God sanctified it for holy use and put a special blessing on the day (see Gen. 2:1–3).

God wants everyone to always remember that He is the Creator. Generations before had kept the Sabbath, but after 400 years of enslavement that erased the nature and presence of God from their lives, God had to reestablish His laws and precepts. So He wrote and sent them the message by his trusted servant and leader, Moses. Because their knowledge of God was partially or wholly erased, God called them back to worship using the very forceful word: Remember.

God's unchanging challenge has been passed on to His children living in these last days. He expects obedience; in case we also forget, the message is to remember. There are so many multitudes of issues demanding our attention, time, and energy that to worship God is a distant reality for many. The cacophony of voices and the multitudinous cries make us want to stop our ears, keep a straight face, and say, "Leave me alone." It is amid this chaos that one needs time out and rest. Out of love, God gave the Sabbath as an oasis in this desert-land of existence. We need a day to rest, replenish, and recharge our physical, emotional, and spiritual batteries. God Himself tells us to remember to take time off, refresh ourselves, and worship and adore Him.

God knows that our physical frame is not designed for work and activity all hours of the day, seven days a week. We need time to recoup, refresh our mind, and energize our muscles. We need time for the family. Non-stop work is not the model God intended for us. Thus the day of rest is obligatory on the human family if it seeks to maintain homeostasis. This is yet another reason to remember! God knows what is for our best interest, health, and happiness. May we always *remember* God's design!

Day 201

Set *a watch, O Lord, before my mouth; keep the door of my lips. Psalm 141:3*

This text was my New Year's resolution on January 1, 2001. I wrote it in my prayer journal, and it is only now that I am reflecting on that prayer's significance.

As the New Year approached, I wanted to ensure that God was taking charge of my life. I felt that emptiness and the need for self-control. I was like Peter—impulsive, quick-witted, and ready always to engage in a conversation with or without much deep thought. I did not like that me; I recognized that that path was not an excellent one, so I asked God to take full control of my thoughts so that they would not gallop ahead of me. I needed a different direction, a new way and a new method. I needed to submit all of me to God, and it was my plan to give Him all of me.

As He took control of my mind, my utterances became more God-directed and God centered. David's prayer in Psalm 19 became my daily and hourly recitation. I had to let God's Word infuse my thinking so that I could say the right things every waking hour. That was indeed a mighty challenge—the challenge of submission.

God answered that prayer and is still answering it on a hourly basis. He has made me become more cognizant of how and when I am to engage my mind, mouth, and lips. I asked for God's restraining power to take control, and He has. There is nothing good that one asks of God, our Father, that He will not grant unto us. He wants us to live holy, upright, and unsullied lives before Him, and when He sees us struggling to live right, He sends His ministers, the angels, to guard and keep us. More so, He authorizes the Third Agent of the Godhead, the Holy Spirit, to sustain us, so we are never left up to our own wills and devices.

This experience with God has taught me that if an individual submits his or her life to the triune God, then the Master will answer our request. He sees our contrition and nakedness and rushes to clothe us with His perfect robe of righteousness.

All Christians need to pray that prayer; it needs to be our daily oration. If more Christians prayed this way, there would undoubtedly be fewer arguments, squabbles, and agitations among each other. This verse talks about how we need God to "set a watch" for us. A watchman is always on duty, guarding and protecting the entrance of one's property from intruders and interlopers. Similarly, the Christian wants a watchman to protect his or her thoughts and its utterance. The Holy Spirit is that watchman. What a blessing! Let Him take up residence in our thoughts and mind. He will control, direct, and form a shield so that nothing that is impure or unholy may enter or exit. Let your mantra be Psalm 141:3. May we allow the Holy Spirit to *set* a watch on our minds and lips so that we may become more like Christ in character.

Day 202

Thou art good, and doest good: **Teach** *me thy statutes. Psalm 119:68*

Here is an affirmation of the goodness of God. David felt as I felt when I asked God in that previous prayer—he wanted God "to set a watch" over his mouth. He also recognized his own peculiarities to be miscued. He wanted to do right, so he asked God to be His Instructor and teach him good judgment. The reasons for asking are that God is good, and God does what is good. Based on David's declaration, someone has created this expression, "God is good all the time"; then the listening group responds, "All the time, God is good." This becomes a choric chant, especially when a preacher or speaker wants to awaken his audience to the goodness of God.

Since God is good, David knew that his instruction would also be good. As a king David pleaded for wisdom, understanding, and good judgment. Rulers, CEO's, and men in high administrative roles could take a cue from David's request and ask God to teach them what to do or how to govern, rule, and extend authority. Good judgment is a virtue that those in leadership positions should possess.

Children should be taught very early in life the statutes of the Lord so that as they grow and mature, the principles of truth, justice, honesty, integrity, and uprightness will be embedded in them. Holy Writ enjoins, "And all thy children shall be taught of the Lord" (Isa. 54:13), which includes knowing Jesus as well as recognizing that there is a Higher Power that rules the universe that they should reverence, respect, and obey.

King David also records God's promise to His children: "I will instruct thee and teach thee in the way thou shalt go: I will guide thee with mine eye" (Ps. 32:8). He is a good God who wants all His children to learn of His great salvation. He is pure goodness; let Him teach you through His respective agents: godly teachers, ministers, and parents.

You are in the best and most equipped classroom with the most enlightened teacher—Jehovah God. Sit and learn from Him; may you let Him *teach* you everything you need to know!

Day 203

I will keep thy statutes: O forsake me not **Utterly**. *Psalm 119:8*

This text assures us that God is dependable and reliable. As I read, I hear David's agony of spirit, his alienation and despair. He was in constant fear for his life, and Jehovah was all he had. Was he suffering from the Cain syndrome or was he truly remorseful over his past behaviors and wanted God's affirmation for future interactions and dealings? In this lamentation David wanted assurance that there was nothing between himself and Jehovah.

David was striving for perfection of character, and he extolled God's name and goodness. He promised that when he learned the righteous judgments of God, he would adore and worship Him uprightly. Finally, he issued the promise: "I will keep thy statutes." At this point, David is avowing, but could God really take him at his word? Were his emotive responses genuine and could they be trusted? Would he keep the promise or was he fearful of reprisals?

Uncertainty always accompanies a vow to the Lord. Amidst this new commitment, David feared failure, so he told God that he was weak. He was afraid that God would utterly forsake him because he knew his misdemeanors were repulsive to God. He had reached his melting point, and he recognized that it was only God's mercies that preserved him. Throwing himself on God's bosom, he cried out: "O, forsake me not utterly!"

God never forsakes anyone unless the individual rejects the Holy Spirit's invitation. Jesus felt utterly forsaken on the cross, and He cried out to His Father, "My God, my God, why hast thou forsaken me?"

(Mark 15:34). Isolation and abandonment will cause any individual to feel utterly cast off. None of us wants the feeling of being utterly cast off by God. But there is no need to worry about this, for God has given us Jesus to draw us back to Him. God is very near to everyone through the omnipresence of the Holy Spirit. May we keep our promise to Him as He keeps His toward us!

The struggling Christian must recognize that help is always available; God never forsakes anyone, even when the individual rejects God as Cain and Judas did. They chose. God is still waiting for His errant child to return home. Be sure not to reject the Holy Spirit's urging as it woos us back into the arms of our loving Father; God never forsakes anyone, much less *utterly*.

Day 204

Every good gift and every perfect gift is from above, and cometh down from the Father of lights, with whom is no **Variableness***, neither shadow of turning. James 1:17*

God is the only constant in the universe. He is the Creator of everything: human beings, mammals, beasts, birds, creeping things, sky, sea, birds, and flowers. He is the true owner of everything, so He knows how to distribute gifts and talents. Every good and perfect gift comes from God because He is goodness and knows what sorts of things His children need. A gift is never bad, but it is always useful and practical. God has given a gift to every single person on planet earth.

God alone has stability, solidarity, and dependability. He is more stable than the heavenly bodies because even the stars fell in 1833. With God, there is not even the slightest change. He is immutable saying, "For I am the Lord, I change not" (Mal. 3:6). There is no variation in His habits. He is declared to be the Father of lights, so there will always be light where God is. No tint of darkness is seen anywhere. Light is associated with goodness, so all that God offers is good.

All changes are either for better or for worse. God is unchanging because He is perfect and cannot get better or become worse. The Scriptures declare that God's character, will, and nature are unchanging, fervent, strong, and unshakable. Despite God's fervency, He thinks, acts, creates, decides, and allocates special gifts to special people who will use them to bless His name and humanity. Because of God's unchanging quality, Christians everywhere can depend on His constant love, power, and vigil. All nature obeys His commands: the sun continues on its daily path, day follows night, and the seasons cycle their regular rounds, yet God is more stable than nature.

If we engage in evil practices, it is not of God; God does not tempt or lure anyone into evil. God does not change like shifting shadows but is true and faithful to His Word. His Word stands fast. God wants His children to practice constancy of purpose, reflect His character, and remain true to His Word and statutes. He wants them to take a confident stand in knowing what and in whom they believe. God does not change and cannot change for He is God. God is solidarity, steadfastness, reliability, dependability, and truth. May you trust His *unvarying* ways!

Day 205

My soul **Waiteth** *for the Lord more than they that watch for the morning: I say, more than they that watch for the morning. Psalm 130:6*

The night is usually a long period of darkness and seems longer if one is sick and is suffering excruciating pain. The sufferer cannot wait for the dawn to see that first glimpse of light streaming through the window. Morning and light bring hope, vision, sight, and reprieve. During the night season, people are alone. You bear your pain alone, and you struggle with anxieties alone. There is no watchman or nurse on duty. Sometimes there is not even a pastel light to lighten the room. You are in darkness physically, physiologically, and emotionally. No wonder the speaker mourned and cried out repeatedly that his soul was *waiting* for the morning!

The imagery of suffering bespeaks isolation, sorrow, grief, abandonment, and forsakenness experienced, especially if one is being afflicted by unseen forces. David seems to have been down in the valley of humiliation when he said, "Out of the depths have I cried unto thee, O Lord" (verse 1). But his lamentation is later interspersed with hope. He knows that God will hear and deliver, so he said, "There is forgiveness with thee ... I wait for the Lord, my soul doth wait, and in his word do I hope" (verse 4, 5).

This expression breathes nothing but confidence and certitude. Having thus assured himself of the unwavering, unchanging qualities of his God, he jubilantly exclaims, "My soul waiteth for the Lord ... watch for the morning." Morning brings life, hope, reinvigoration, healing, and companionship. He comes to recognize the power residing in the One whom he trusts will carry him through the night. It is as if he is saying, "I will endure for with the day comes deliverance and release from the Almighty."

This physical, psychological, and mental agony is every Christian's nemesis on his or her journey to the celestial city. This psalm reassures the Christian traveler that in whatever form his or her distress comes, one should not give in to self-pity and despondency, for no one on earth is alone in the struggle. Like Jacob wrestling with the Holy One, we must all cling to and raise high the banner of hope, for those that hope, trust and wait on the Lord will reap their reward.

Humankind must constantly hope, trust, and wait upon the Lord. He is the unchanging One. He never leaves His children to suffer in the overarching darkness; He always sends light and comes through for everyone. He is dependability—neither too early nor too late—He arrives just when you need Him most. Psalm 27:14 sums it up very succinctly: "Wait on the Lord: be of good courage, and he shall strengthen thine heart: *wait*, I say, on the Lord." Never let go; God knows all. May we *wait* on Him, for He will come through for us.

Day 206

Now unto him that is able to do **Exceeding** *abundantly above all that we ask or think, according to the power that worketh in us. Ephesians 3:20*

One version of the same text reads that He is able to do immeasurably more than all we ask or imagine. Can you wrap the latter version around your mind? That which cannot be measured or calculated! That is indeed a wonderful feat. The aged apostle's prayer for the Ephesian brethren is indeed lofty and benevolent, full of care, compassion, and tenderness. He commended them to their heavenly Father's care.

This prayer exudes confidence, sincerity, hope, positivity, and assurance—the full scale of God's unchanging qualities. God is able to grant the request of all who trust Him according to His will for their own good. He will give far more than one can desire, ask for, or imagine. What an awesome God!

Malachi validates Paul's attestations by saying that God will open the windows of heaven and pour out a blessing that you will not have room to contain (see Mal. 3:8–10). Imagine that God will grant to an unworthy, sinful creature more than they desire! Only a father's love can do that. God is our heavenly Father and knows what things we need long before we ask, which is why He gives exceedingly more than we ask for or imagine. We do not truly know how much we need. His storehouse and barns are full and overflowing, and He is waiting to give us some of the overflow. May your faith be increased to ask, reach out, and claim! Then you can share the blessings with others.

God possesses unchangeable goodness and gives according to one's faith and readiness to accept the proffered gift. God can do everything; there is nothing that He cannot do. Three Gospel writers—Matthew, Mark, and Luke all affirm that nothing is impossible with God. And I say that if my God cannot do it, it cannot be done.

We must ask so we may receive. Our God will give us more than we could ever ask for. Sometimes we ask for too little, but our Father gives what will best satisfy our needs. He satiates us. He has illimitable treasures to give all who ask. So, don't be afraid to ask!

Let us then boldly and fearlessly grasp the Hand of Omnipotence because His hands have provided for all that we have needed; great is He that has promised. May you accept the blessings our *exceedingly* gracious Father has prepared and is waiting to release to us!

Day 207

And he answered and said unto him, Master, all these have I observed from my **Youth**.
Mark 10:20

"And that from a child thou hast known the holy scriptures, which are able to make thee wise unto salvation" (2 Tim. 3:15) was Paul's salutation to young Timothy conferring on his discipleship. On the contrary, the rich young ruler came to Jesus to enroll in His school of discipleship, but he lacked the practicality of the Word. When Jesus presented to him the requirements, he rebuffed the Master reciting the above citation. Feeling insulted that Jesus was simply rehearsing with him the practices and principles of the Jewish law, he told Jesus that he could have not achieved all that he had without studying the Word.

This rich, young ruler was blessed and revered in his community, and since he was lavishly endowed economically and socially, he felt a yearning and void in his life. He craved the rapport of Jesus and His disciples. He wanted to be a part of the "in crowd" and share in their aura. He wanted to secure eternal life, to be a follower of Jesus, and possess what the others seemed to have. His dilemma was this: he was selfishly tied to his material possessions and did not think that he should share his wealth with the poor, the needy, and the homeless.

The acquisition and storage of goods is not a precursor for right doing and access to eternal life. This rich young man was besotted with his possessions; they were to him a god—they consumed his life. Thus, when Jesus told him what was needed to inherit eternal life, he said that it was impossible for him to give it all up. He was unwilling to make the slightest sacrifice, even one that would not have scratched the surface of his possessions. The text continues saying that "he went away sorrowful: for he had great possessions" (Matt. 19:22).

The ruler wanted to follow Jesus on his own terms without any sacrifice. Jesus had made it plain to His disciples that self-denial was a requirement for discipleship: forsake father, mother, family, houses, lands, fishing nets, working for the treasury, etc. Each must deny himself some or all of life's comforts and follow Him. This seeker did not know the detailed requirements and thought his possessions were a passport to his joining the group, who should have been elated to have him in their company. He did not take time to learn what discipleship entailed and when confronted with it, he reneged.

What is the lesson in this great story? We may have grown up in the church, have studied and known all its rules and regulations, have become familiar with all the historical and prophetic landmarks, have gotten a good education, and we may have been endowed with riches, but these are not the things that will get us into the kingdom. Jesus wanted all His hearers to know that a person's eternal destiny does not consist on the abundance of the things that he or she possesses (verse 23), but on his or her relationship with others and with God. How one takes care of the poor and needy is the inherent quality that heaven regards and not the size or depth of one's bank account. May we not allow our possessions and acquisitions to rob us of the blessing of serving others and the Master!

Day 208

> *Even so ye, forasmuch as ye are* **Zealous** *of spiritual gifts, seek that ye may excel to the edifying of the church. 1 Corinthians 14:12*

Speaking to the Corinthian brethren who seemed to have exercised some zeal and jealousy over each other's gifts, Paul advised them that their jousting should not be to show power, skill, and authority over each other but to acknowledge their spiritual gifts as lively stones meant to build up and edify the church. If they acknowledged their uniqueness and specialness, their respective gifts could be used to establish special ministries that would ultimately enlarge the church's repertoire and glorify God's name.

Whatever gift the Christian receives, he or she is to use it to build up the body of Christ and the society. The spiritual gifts are to be consecrated to God's service and not for personal glorification and celebration. One should strive to acquire gifts, whether they be musical, linguistic, artistic, etc. They should be used to improve the lot of the miserable and the marginalized (see Luke 4:16–18). Our gifts are to be used productively and not as weapons against the less endowed.

The apostle's counsel to the Corinthian brothers to be zealous *a*fter good works is also for us living in this last church age. We must cultivate a zeal and passion for those things, which are pure, noble, upright, and pleasing to God. Paul told the brethren to ensure that their spiritual zeal coincides with their knowledge, and they should "covet earnestly the best gifts" (1 Cor. 12:31).

Let us be consumed with the zeal, might, and power of the Most High that will enable us to move mountains of difficulty and exalt our Redeemer's name. Use your gifts to strive for God's excellence instead of just showing off. May we all *zealously* guard the gifts that we have received and use them to advance Christ's kingdom on earth!

Avoid Careless Chatter

Day 209

But I say unto you, That every idle word that men shall speak, they shall give **Account** *thereof in the day of judgment. Matthew 12:36*

David in Psalms and Solomon in Proverbs warned against misusing the tongue. They refer to idle chatter and vain conversations as worthless and unfulfilling (see Prov. 14:23; 19:5; 13:3). "Keep thy tongue from evil, and thy lips from speaking guile" (Ps. 34:13). In the New Testament, Jesus counseled His disciples against the use of the tongue, as many prophets before Jesus had also warned against its use (see the books of Jeremiah and Isaiah).

Jesus uses the analogy of the fruit to present His message. Good fruits come from good healthy trees; an unhealthy tree cannot produce good fruit. We speak the things we have meditated upon. Nothing happens spasmodically. What you say is what you are: pure and noble thoughts emanate from a pure and noble mind. The contrary is also true.

Jesus, fully aware of the nuances of the human mind, exhorted His disciples to guard the utterances of their mouth. They were going to be His mouthpiece and needed to speak power, truth, healing, and redemption to their hearers; therefore, they needed to have minds and hearts fully consecrated to the task. Nothing out of their lips should emit that which defiles, spoils, or debilitates. They should only speak words that give life and healing. Thus, the idle, non-essential, unsubstantial, frivolous expressions should have no place in their vocabulary, for they will have to account to God in the latter day for such wasted words.

Jesus told them that His words were power and life. We should all do what we can to imitate the Master. Though Jesus was speaking to His first disciples, the message is for us today as well. As God's children we must reflect on the Father so that the words out of our lips flow with living waters that heal, inspire, and draw men and women to Jesus. Some people are skilled and adept in their use of words; some are less endowed with a few at their disposal. Whatever or however one is endowed, their words reveal the quality of their mind.

Some people use words that negate and destroy the human spirit. Their use is as unproductive as idle, inconsequential words. Words can justify or condemn. One must be cautious and know when, how, and what to speak. Idle words reveal a contemptible, uncultivated, and shallow mind. When the Holy Spirit controls the mind, there is no room for idle, senseless utterances. Instead, one's speech will be well chosen and timely. The speaker cannot say, "I was only joking; I did not mean it that way." The aged apostle Paul counseled us to be of a sound mind. A sound mind will emit productive words, not idle chatter. May we watch what we say, for we will have to *account* for our verbal expressions.

Day 210

Verily, verily, I say unto you, He that **Believeth** *on me hath everlasting life. I am that bread of life. John 6:47, 48*

Jesus authentically, powerfully, and indefatigably told His followers that He, the Son of God, was the representation of the Father. In order to accept the Father, they had to believe and accept Him. Upon that belief predicates everlasting life. When Phillip asked Jesus to show them the Father, His reply was "he that hath seen me hath seen the Father ... Believest thou not that I am in the Father, and the Father in me?" (John 14:9, 10).

Jesus, befuddled at the disciples' lack of comprehension about Him and His mission, asked them how they could not yet understand who He was. Jesus even told them that He was the Bread of Life: "I am the living bread ... if any man eat of this bread, he shall live for ever" (John 6:51).

This principle, which was shrouded in mystery, was what they needed to accept. It is same for us latter day Christians, who must continue to believe that in Jesus is life eternal, and our salvation and future rest on this belief. We need to truly accept and sincerely believe that Jesus is the representation of God.

Today's world has many alluring voices inviting us to believe their script. Much skepticism is parlayed around us. Jesus knew all this, for He warned that grievous wolves will come and enter the sheepfold, attack the sheep and the lambs, and if possible, kill many. The shepherd has to be always on guard. Each person must be sure of what and in whom he or she believes.

The disciples preached the message of *belief* in Jesus Christ. Philip asked the eunuch if he believed, and he said that yes, he believed that Jesus was the Son of God. The Philippian warden saw death for him and his family because of the possible release of the prisoners, but he soon found that all was intact. He asked Paul and Silas what he must do to be saved. They replied that he needed to believe in the Lord Jesus. These disciples followed the Master's footsteps and articulated His message: "Believeth on me."

Jesus' message is the only message we are called to preach. Believe in Him and have eternal life, for Jesus is life; He gives and maintains life. He declares that if anyone believes in Him, they will have everlasting life (John 6:47). His Word is truth, for He is Truth. He says, "I am the way, the truth and the life" (John 14:6); no man or woman can come to the Father if they don't go through Jesus. Therefore, if you can accept the words of the Master Himself, you have accessed eternal life. May you *believe*!

Day 211

Therefore watch, and remember, that by the space of three years I **Ceased** *not to warn every one night and day with tears. Acts 20:31*

This charge is the apostle Paul's message to the Asian convocation gathered at Miletus. These parting words are from a heart severely burdened with the care and welfare of the brethren. He possessed unguarded love for them and desired that they should walk in the path he had shown them. They were very near and dear to his heart, having consumed much of his time and energy for three years.

Asia was a challenging field for the gospel to take root. He was well aware of the pitfalls they would face—pitfalls of skepticism, doubt, idolatry, fornication, all the sinful lusts of the flesh, and opposition to the truth. Having spent two years in Ephesus and one year in the school of Tyranus, Paul was well acquainted with the respective social, spiritual, and moral challenges the new Christians were up against, hence his intense labors. As he spoke to them, he was deeply moved, and thus he appealed to them to recall the intensity, constancy, and fervency that he expended to them. He desired that nothing and no one should interfere with their connection with Jesus. As a gentle, caring shepherd, he counseled, led, taught, and encouraged them to stand firm in the faith.

Moses and Joshua, on the eve of their departure as commander of Israel, also offered similar speeches. Being concerned about the spiritual connectedness of their congregants, both leaders counseled them to choose God first and to stand firm in the faith. The apostle Peter did the same.

If you are a leader, pastor, teacher, or church member, do you have the same burden and care for new believers as the apostles and especially Paul had for the Asian brethren? God expects us to mentor the weak in the new faith and to not only warn them but plead with God to keep and preserve them in the truth. Paul's work with the saints was continuous. That is why he told them to pray without ceasing. May we emulate the apostle's way and never cease to commend them daily into the care of our loving Father!

Day 212

> **Dearly** *beloved, I beseech you as strangers and pilgrims, abstain from fleshy lusts, which war against the soul. 1 Peter 2:11*

We inhabit a world tainted with all kinds of sinful desires: lust of the flesh, of the eyes, ears, and all the visceral organs. King Solomon in Proverbs 6:16–19 emphasizes these desires as pride, idleness, fullness of bread, a lying tongue, hands that shed innocent blood, feet swift to do mischief, and sowing discord among the brethren. Every unconsecrated desire is vile and is at dissonance with purity and holiness.

All sinful desires are anti-God and do not promote Godliness or Godlikeness. Instead, we find putrefaction of the psyche and the spirit, both mind and heart. We sin with the respective parts of our body: the look, wink, gesture, unholy desire, and word. The apostle Peter was very well aware of these kinds of behaviors, so he exhorted all believers—Christians then and now—that they should avoid those practices and behaviors so that they do not tear down their spiritual standing or the body of Christ.

New believers are familiar with those lewd behaviors and practices, which constituted their repertoire before they met Christ. But since they have submitted their bodies, mind, and soul to the Holy Spirit's control, the former practices are now alien to them. They have to begin a new lifestyle that makes them spiritual foreigners.

We are on alien territory because our home is in heaven, God's dwelling place, and it is where we will spend eternity with Him. Peter urges all Christians to shun all sinful desires. We need to be in the world but not partake of its sinful practices. We are all Christ's in whom there is no darkness. Besides, we are His chosen ones—His dearly beloved. Therefore, the key word here is to abstain or cease.

It is very challenging to live pure lives among unbelievers with unholy, unsanctified desires and invitations. We are our Lord's representatives and must live exemplary lives so that our associates will emulate the Christlikeness manifested in us. The apostle Paul enjoins the Roman saints to follow him as he follows Christ (see 1 Cor. 11:1).

As we strive for perfection, we must practice loyalty to God's truth and His way of life. We are called to be light so no darkness of any form or shape is to be found in our actions, speech, and gestures. May you *dearly* beloved focus on the pure, noble, and true!

Day 213

> *Whoso* **Eateth** *my flesh, and drinketh my blood, hath eternal life; and I will raise him up at the last day. John 6:54*

This was a hard saying to a blood abstemious Jewish group. They were astonished at such a dictum and recoiled from it. They did not understand that Jesus spoke symbolically. Earlier on in the discourse, He said that He was the I AM, the Bread of Life, and that anyone who eats thereof would have eternal life (John 6:48), yet the Jewish hearers frowned at the blood concept.

Jesus was offering a very positive and hope-inspired idea that carried a life-giving and propelling force that renewed itself daily. How was one to eat the flesh of Jesus? Jesus said that His Words are life. He said that He is the Bread of Life, so if anyone wants life, they must eat His flesh, which is the Word of God. Jeremiah states, "Thy words were found, and I did eat them; and thy word was unto me the joy and rejoicing of mine heart: for I am called by thy name, O Lord God of hosts" (Jer. 15:16). So, Jesus is the Word. John says that through the incarnadine process "the Word was made flesh, and dwelt among us, (and we beheld his glory, the glory as of the only begotten of the Father,) full of grace and truth" (John 1:14). You can "eat" Jesus' flesh by accepting Him and letting His Word transform your life. We become what we eat, and if we want to be like Jesus, then we must feed on His Word.

Jesus says we cannot only eat; we have to drink also, so He offers us His blood. That blood was shed on Calvary more than twenty centuries ago, so how then can those living in this last church age drink His blood? The blood of any mammal is the life. When a butcher drives their knife into the throat of the animal, it is blood that gushes out. As the creature loses its blood, it dies. Jesus poured out His blood on Golgotha's Hill thousands of years ago so that you and I could have life. The butcher takes the life of the slaughtered animal so that humankind can have flesh to eat to sustain life. Jesus' blood gives life eternally.

Blood is life. It sustains, nourishes, manufactures, and maintains life. Without much rich blood, we soon debilitate and die. We can become a host for all kinds of intractable infectious diseases. Jesus' analogy is very appropriate: His blood provides longevity for all times. Anyone who drinks the blood will not die eternally but will be resurrected to everlasting life. So when anyone accepts Christ, the Living Bread, and allows Him entrance into their life, He becomes united with him or her, just as how the physical bread is assimilated and digested, giving strength and nurturance to the body. So by accepting this Bread, we become embodied with Christ.

Additionally, it is the blood that transports all the nutrients to every nerve and fiber of the muscles. At the Last Supper with the disciples, Jesus prophetically gave them bread, which symbolized His broken body. He also gave them wine as a symbol of His precious blood that would be shed to cleanse us from all sinful acts. That was the covenant He made with them when He said, "I will not any more eat thereof ... I will not drink of the fruit of the vine, until the kingdom of God shall come" (Luke 22:15–18). Today, we celebrate that sacrament as a reminder of the covenant Jesus made with humanity. Humankind is given the freedom to eat God's words and drink of the symbolic wine in order to refresh and renew their commitment to the Father. May we continue to eat and drink of His Word every day of our lives!

Day 214

*The **Fear** of the Lord is the beginning of wisdom: a good understanding have all they that do his commandments: his praise endureth forever. Psalm 111:10*

To God alone belongs eternal praise; He is God, the Creator of everything. God is to be reverenced and feared. He is everything!

Wise people give counsel and exhortation drawn from various pools of experience and knowledge. Both King David and King Solomon gave advice to the wisdom seeker. In Proverbs 1:29 Solomon gives the only true way to acquire wisdom–"choose the fear of the Lord"; and Matthew records Jesus' counsel, "But seek ye first the kingdom of God, and his righteousness; and all these things shall be added unto you" (Matt. 6:33).

True wisdom comes from fearing God (meaning to revere Him). We need to put Him first in everything that we think of doing. God knows everything, including what is best for you. He will guide your thinking and direction. Many people have often left God out of their plans, and doing so decision has worked to their detriment and disappointment. By ignoring or sidestepping God, the Author of all knowledge and wisdom, they follow their own inclinations believing that the pursuit of academic knowledge or any venture is their own responsibility. They argue, "What does God have to do with my pursuit of excellence or wealth access? God is in heaven sitting on His throne totally unmindful of me." They argue this because they have not acknowledged God as the Source of all wisdom and knowledge. They don't realize that by obeying Him, they will receive good understanding and keen insight. Every seeker should first lay all their plans before the Lord for His approval and direction.

Without heaven's wisdom, no man or woman will have a strong foundation on which to make wise decisions. Solomon enjoins that wisdom and understanding are pivotal for one's growth and development. Proverbs 3:13, 26 reads, "Happy is the man that findeth wisdom, and the man that getteth understanding.... For the Lord shall be thy confidence."

The foolish despise wisdom because they think they know it all and that God has no place in their lives. They feel as though they can navigate all their respective waters, so they need not defer to the Creator of the universe. It is God that upholds life and distributes gifts and talents to humanity, so we have a duty to respect, obey, honor, and revere Him. All knowledge comes from God, and we need to fear, hallow, and revere His holy name. Without God intervening in the affairs of humanity, no project or enterprise would ever be successful. Solomon wrote, "A man's heart deviseth his way: but the Lord directeth his steps" (Prov. 16:9). Thus *fear*, along with reverence, is the controlling principle of wisdom. May you let God lead in all your pursuits and endeavors! Put Him first. The result will be abundant joy, satisfaction, happiness, contentment, and a life overflowing with success.

Day 215

Glory to God *in the highest, and on earth peace, good will toward men! Luke 2:14*

This is the greatest, sweetest, most sublime, most glorious, and joyous song that has ever been sung. It is the song of heaven's angelic choir as they burst forth in melodious rapture announcing the birth of the Majesty of heaven, King of kings, and Lord of lords, Jesus, the Creator–the Word made flesh.

Can you imagine a multitude of heavenly hosts praising God for sending His Son as a baby to earth, offering God's goodness to us earth dwellers, Adam's fallen sons and daughters? Yes, the Emmanuel came for us all, the undeserving earthlings.

The Savior of the world was born! God would not have to wonder about the fate of His earthbound children, for Jesus, the Savior, was born! He was part of humanity, as He took on their flesh and blood. All heaven burst into a rapturous song because humanity's chance of being reunited with God was now engendered and inaugurated. Now, there was hope for humankind; there was no longer any need to fear annihilation, for the Son of peace was here. Sin, which brought hate, murder, and death, would soon be eliminated, and a new era of peace, common understanding, and brotherly love would prevail. Each person could now account for their existence and say to their brother or sister, "I know the Lord."

We, for whom Jesus died, must every day express similar joy and *give glory* and praise to God for the unspeakable gift of His Son, our Brother. We can do so through song, prayer, and by studying the Word. Let Him tarry with you, so you can enjoy the peace His presence offers. His appearance brings peace, joy, hope, and forgiveness to all of Adam's children. Glory to God!

This good news is to be shared with every person we meet. We should be constantly lifting up hands of thankfulness and shout, "Glory, glory," for the birth, life, and death of this Son of God. His coming is the joy of humanity's salvation. He brings peace for us. He brings goodwill and allows it to permeate humanity. Even after twenty centuries we can still sing and shout the song of the angelic choir and prepare our hearts, minds, and voices to join in the celebratory choirs of angels as we welcome our Lord back to earth to receive His redeemed. Then we shall sing another glory song: "The King has come; the King has come! Open ye the gates and let the King of Glory come in!" That will be our most glorious and rapturous moment when we see Jesus. May all humankind plan to join in that choric celebration of the *glorious* one!

Day 216

> **Hear** *this, all ye people; give ear, all ye inhabitants of the world: Both low and high, rich and poor, together. My mouth shall speak of wisdom; and the meditation of my heart shall be of understanding. Psalm 49:1–3*

This is a global, generational call to men and women of every clime. None is excluded: "All ye inhabitants of the world." LISTEN! This is a trumpet blast so that none can say, "I did not hear." Everyone is to "give ear." This is like the siren warning that a tornado or tsunami is about to strike. None should take this imminent warning lightly, for it requires urgent and immediate action. If we instantly react to a physical life or death threat, how much more urgent is the divine announcement!

Whether dwelling in palatial mansions or in the lowly hamlets, all must hear and respond to the clarion call. The poor cannot say, "I am too poor to respond." The rich and high-minded might say, "I am too busy, and I am safe and secure in my mighty fortress. This call is for the poor, weak, and lowly." They are wrong, for the Word says that all are called: low and high, rich and poor. All must react to the utterances from the Lord's mouth, for He speaks wisdom. His meditations give understanding and maintain life.

David no doubt wrote this psalm to help God's chosen people rise above the clamor and craving after wealth and fame. Whenever God speaks, men and women everywhere are to hear, listen, and act because to trust in material possessions is futile. One burst of a hurricane, tornado, earthquake, or tsunami can bring instant destitution. The poor need not fret, murmur, or complain about their accursed and deprived lot, for they have nothing to lose. Rather, they should rejoice that they hear God's call and respond accordingly.

In the parable of the sower and the tares, Jesus illustrates to His disciples the final separation of the righteous and the wicked imploring every hearer to take heed: "Who hath ears to hear, let him hear" (Matt. 13:9). Jesus stated that the righteous will shine forth as the sun in the kingdom. Also, John the Revelator, in his messages to the churches, repeatedly called the listeners to hear and respond: "He that hath an ear, let him hear what the Spirit saith unto the churches" (Rev. 3:22).

It is a universal imperative for people to listen and act. The warning is given, and it is incumbent on all hearers to heed the spoken word. May everyone *hear* His call!

Day 217

> *And God saw that the wickedness of man was great in earth, and that every* **Imagination** *of the thoughts of his heart was only evil continually. Genesis 6:5*

This is an indictment on the inhabitants of the antediluvian world, which reveled in all kinds of despicable and sinful activities. Their abominable behaviors caused God to repent that He had even made the world. "Every imagination of their mind, heart and thoughts were constantly dwelling on evil." Competitive villainy was their sport.

The good news is that our generation is not their offspring. All those that did evil and practiced wickedness were destroyed in the raging floods that inundated the face of the earth. Only a family of eight—Noah, his wife, their three sons, and their wives—were saved. We are Noah's family's offspring, so doing the right thing is in our DNA; we are programmed to live, act, and behave righteously.

However, today's generation has freely followed the dictates of our heart and mind, and like our first parents, many of us have disobeyed the laws of God. Many of us are doing exactly as he or she wishes. The Gospel writers have attested to this: "But as the days of Noah were, so shall also the coming of the Son of man be" (Matt. 24:37). Their practices consumed them: drinking and carousing, marrying and giving into marriage, unceasing parties, and engaging in all the vile and sexual orgies that their evil minds conceived. Their life was one continuous practice of evil. They lived the "good life," which was an abomination to God. He hated it and recoiled from those behaviors, so He ensured the end of those practices.

Consider this, every single imaginable thought was to delight themselves in doing evil! What a sad state of affair that must have been. But how different are we post moderns from the antediluvians? What are the things that occupy our thoughts? Are we continually dwelling on evil? The good news is that we have been warned; the Bible documents their evils, so we do not have to fall prey to those sin-sick behaviors and practices. We must heed the warning and examine our motives and our behaviors.

Then there was not one saving grace in anyone. No one had any desire to honor or worship God. It was all about self and the pleasure principle: me, myself, and I–a corrupting practice that produced destruction and finally death. It was evil personified. The Word of God says the thoughts of their hearts were evil all the time. It is a sad existence when evil thrives and flourishes.

When humanity's wickedness superseded God's mercy and love, He intervened and almost completely eliminated the race. But God, in His mercy and compassion, warned them for more than 120 years. Rather than repenting, many persisted in their wrongdoings. Once the world's behavior reaches that level of wickedness–when every *imaginable* thought is evil–then God must destroy the world again. May our thoughts turn to God's holiness and righteousness!

Day 218

*And commanded them that they should take nothing for their **Journey**, save a staff only; no scrip, no bread, no money in their purse. Mark 6:8*

Jesus commissioned and sent His disciples on their first evangelical journey. They were to take no belongings and were to preach and heal. They went on this "trial run" while Jesus was still with them, so He was able to monitor, mentor, and help them to make prudent decisions.

They were to go and accept the hospitality of those they ministered to and be totally dependent on God, who would supply all their physical needs. This was to make the trip a radical exercise in trusting in Faith.

These seventy new and brave men were about to embark on a life-changing task. It was their career, and they had to learn how to navigate the murky waters of schisms, skepticism, and unbelief coupled with Satanic and demonic forces. This was indeed a message and a preparatory mission, and they had to be primed.

They went and returned with glowing reports. They reported to the Master and Commander, Jesus: "Lord, even the devils are subject unto us through thy name" (Luke 10:17). To this Jesus replied, "Notwithstanding in this rejoice not ... but rather rejoice, because your names are written in heaven" (verse 20).

Jesus set a missionary model for the apostles as well as for future missionaries. When missionaries go to the mission field, they must go with God and depend solely on His care. They should make no plans for themselves because God expects them to depend on Him to supply hospitable hosts and audiences.

Onlookers and non-participants may call this impractical and unrealistic faith, but I know of many people who have gone this route and God has honored their faith, commitment, and trust. He has copiously provided for them. If these missionaries are too burdened down with things–chattels, suitcases, tents, sleeping bags, etc. —then their mission and ministry may easily be compromised.

On our separate journeys, God knows what is best, and His way is always right. Like the character Christian in Bunyan's immortal epic *Pilgrims Progress*, we are all on our journey to God's celestial city. Let us be wary of the belongings we acquire that they do not become hindrances and compromise our journey. May we allow Jesus to lead as we closely follow in His steps! The *journey* is all about trust, faith, confidence, commitment, and belief. Let Jesus lead the way, for He is the way!

Day 219

Keep *me as the apple of thine eye; hide me under the shadow of thy wings. Psalm 17:8*

In David's prayer for protection, he went to the field of ophthalmology to engage God's unique care over him. He saw himself as precious in God's sight. David pointed out that just as the pupil (the apple) of the eyes is damaged and there is no sight, he needed God to see his delicate situation and protect him.

David needed God's continual protection and favor, and he further requested that God hide him under the shadow of His everlasting wings. Here he drew on bird imagery. He was fully aware of the span of an eagle's wings, and knowing that God's arms far transcend that of any created bird, he focused on the mightiness of God's ability to act and intervene on his behalf.

As the outstretched arms of the eagle form a covering for its young, David saw God as his eagle and requested coverage and hiding, for he feared exposure to his enemies. The idea of the members of the bird's family protecting the young ones was very real and appropriate for David. All avian mothers know how to protect their young from aggressors, hunters, and other predators by spreading out their wings and covering them.

God's protection does not only deter pain and discomforts as well as removes fear but it also better equips us for ministry. This knowledge gives assurance, comfort, and confidence. It makes us more dependent on God. God guides us when we face painful circumstances; He provides deliverance.

David's prayer is every Christian's daily prayer: "Keep me as the apple of thine eye; hide me under the shadow of thy wings." We should ask for God's daily protection to give us strength of character to face life's many challenges. As he extends His keeping care to us, we shall be protected far more than a mother hen or an eagle protects its young. Our God is the supreme protector; He will guide us all the way to the end of our days. We are all very precious in His sight, and He will keep us as the apple of his eye. What a promise! What comfort and what assurance! May we trust that God will *keep* us and ask for protection every moment of the day.

Day 220

Labour *not for the meat which perisheth, but for that meat which endureth unto everlasting life, which the Son of man shall give unto you: for him hath God the Father sealed.*
John 6:27

Jesus spoke these words of rebuke to His followers, who were satisfied that they had a leader who could provide them with food and other temporal blessings. Jesus discerned that they were following Him not because they believed in Him or accepted His teachings, but to satisfy their physical needs. Having read their motives, Jesus told them that they should not strive for life's transient things but for that which is more permanent and satisfying.

That was an age that lacked refrigerators or any mechanical cooling systems that could preserve their food, so they understood the illustration very well. Christ wanted to move His hearers beyond physical food to the spiritual—He wanted them to recognize Him as the spiritual food, the Bread of Life that came down from heaven (see verse 48). They were invited to take and eat for the Father had approved of Him, the Son, who was indeed "good food."

Everyone should labor to enter the rest that Jesus offers and live according to His precepts. There is more to life than bread and fish; these are only temporary cravings. The ideal is to follow truth and righteousness because Jesus is the way, the truth, and the life. His way is the way to live; people must believe and accept that God has sent Jesus and follow His steps.

Jesus wants to give us both spiritual food and drink. He told the Samaritan woman at the well of Sychar that He had water to give her so that she would never need physical water. Jesus is both food and drink. He is life in all its fullness and the sole proprietor of earth's possessions. Jesus offers rest, peace, and holiness. May we *labor* for it, claim it, and receive it, for it is already ours!

Day 221

*My voice shalt thou hear in the **Morning**, O Lord; in the morning will I direct my prayer unto thee, and will look up. Psalm 5:3*

The NIV rendition of the prayer is equally refreshing: "In the morning, Lord, you hear my voice; in the morning I lay my requests before you and wait expectantly."

David sought out protection early in the morning. He tells us that it is in the early hours of the morning that we should meet with God, for it is when the mind is uncluttered and encumbered with the cares, activities, and challenges of the day.

A significant number of us have been following David's counsel and have found it to be spiritually uplifting and rewarding. In the morning our minds are free of anxiety, and we can commit our whole day to God. As I write what comes floating in my mind is the refrain of the hymn "Give Me Jesus": "In the morning, when I rise, give me Jesus." Give me Jesus. The morning is the best time to consecrate ourselves to God and make our relationship with Him our first priority. Here we submit to Him all our plans for the day to be ordered by His will and purpose. The psalmist states that a man orders his steps, but it is God who directs them (Ps. 37:23), which is why we must begin the day with God and present to Him ourselves and plans to be done. He knows just what we need and will guide us through our daily activities.

For me, the early morning hours are the best times to wake up, read, study, pray, and communicate with my heavenly Father. Jeremiah wrote in Lamentations that the Lord's compassions are new every morning (Lam. 3:22, 23).

We need strength every moment of the day, and we can get a head start when we meet with Divinity early in the morning. On a more symbolic level, we should remember God in the morning of our lives. This is the message in Proverbs 22:6, "Train up a child in the way he should go: and when he is old, he will not depart from it." There is a special call to youth to seek God in their teens. If they start young, they will continue to meet with God early in the morning even into their older years so they can maintain their connection with Him.

Let us seek God early; it is not too late to start a new lifestyle practice of meeting with our Father first thing in the morning. May we plan to meet God in the *morning* and fix our eyes on Him!

Day 222

Who shall separate us from the love of Christ? shall tribulation, or distress, or persecution, or famine, or **Nakedness**, *or peril, or sword? Romans 8:35*

Inherent in the inquiry is not only who but also what circumstances or situations could produce divisiveness within the life of the committed Christian? Paul posed this rhetorical question to his hearers, and today we face the same question individually and as a Christian community collectively.

Physical nakedness connotes disgrace, exposure, and forlornness; no one wants to be in this condition. Jesus counseled His hearers that they should not focus on the transient things of life. Instead, they should focus on Him, for He is life. Here, the apostle Paul asks all Christians to examine their loyalty, solidarity, and purpose in following Christ. Each must know if the love of Christ is the binding principle of their life; if so, then this New Testament text is a good thing to remember: "But my God shall supply all your need according to his riches in glory by Jesus Christ" (Phil. 4:19).

The fragilities of life, physical pressures, and material hankerings should not be the foremost thing to engage our attention. Nothing in the natural or super natural world should take precedence over our relationship with God. Not even nakedness—even if we are stripped to the bones like our brother, Job—should come between the Lord and us and make us lose our commitment to Christ. If we become naked, He will clothe us. When Adam and Eve lost their innocence and made fig leaves to hide their nakedness, God used animal skins and covered them. God will never allow His children to be made ashamed.

Christ's presence is our constant; He never leaves or forsakes us. Even though we may suffer severe challenges, God will see us through. We must abide in Him knowing full well that God is able to keep that which we have committed to Him. Nothing shall pull us apart from Christ's love. He gave His life for us. It is the least we can do to stand up for Him.

God will not have any of His children go exposed: fiscally, economically, socially, mentally, morally, emotionally, spiritually, or physically. He will protect them all the time (see Ps. 91). God has a covering for every situation that would strip us of our clothing. May we refuse to allow anything to separate us from God's loving hand and His watchful care. Under God's protection, we are fully clothed.

Day 223

Before I formed thee in the belly I knew thee; and before thou camest out of the womb I sanctified thee, and I **Ordained** *thee a prophet unto the nations. Jeremiah 1:5*

No child is born by chance. God has repeatedly affirmed His role in the child-bearing, birthing, and conception process. After He joined Adam and Eve together, He told them to go and multiply and make more of themselves. Thus, in the sexual intimacy between a husband and his wife, man comes closest to being like God. Both husband and wife are endowed with the ability to engage in the creative process: hence pro-creation. Thus in every conception, God is there. There is no child of accident; each is ordained because God has foreknowledge.

The Bible has many examples of children born at God's dictates or in response to the mothers' prayers. Rachel's womb was opened, and she birthed Joseph, the deliverer and sustainer of his father's heritage, during the famine in Canaan. He was also a prototype of Jesus, as their lives took a similar trajectory. Think of Hannah who issued forth the greatest judge of Israel, Samuel. Think also of Sarah and the birth of Isaac well into her ninetieth year. There is also Elizabeth, mother of John the Baptist, the forerunner of Jesus. And who could forget the virgin Mary, herself—mother of Jesus, our Lord, Savior, and Redeemer? God ordained when, where, and how they should begin their existence, journey, and mission.

Every child born has a mission. God confirmed that when he told Jeremiah that he was sanctified and ordained before he was even conceived. When I read this particular text, I shuddered at God's magnificence and got a new realization of God's awesomeness in the creative process. No one is here by accident. God has a plan and purpose for every child conceived and birthed.

God is still putting people together and allowing them to engender children that He can use purposefully. All great, wise, and faithful people are of God's devising. Do you recall when Abraham had Ishmael and thought that he was the "promised son," However, God told Abraham that he was not the promised one. God still had a plan to give Abraham and Sarah a son.

Some children are called and anointed from the womb; they are shaped and modeled after God's divine plan and must be engaged in God-directed tasks. Some are created out of wedlock, but God can and will use them all, for it is God who directs their lives. Innocent children do not receive the guilt of their parents' unwise choices or behaviors.

God has a plan for each child before he or she is born. That is good news to prospective parents: God can and will direct the selection of a mate, and He will choose their offspring so that the child conceived and birthed will be ordained for God's purpose. Everyone in His creation is precious and invaluable to Him, and He has a mission for each to accomplish. May we trust that He still *ordains* infants for His purposes.

Day 224

I will both lay me down in **Peace**, *and sleep: for thou, Lord, only makest me dwell in safety.*
Psalm 4:8

This prayer expresses the psalmist's confidence and certitude in God's protection and safety. He is satisfied that His life is on the right path, for God has heard and responded positively to all his pleas. His enemies have been dispersed, and there is now a respite.

There is no more combat; there is rest and peace among nations. David can now sleep without fear of reprisals and being awakened during the night. He praises the Lord for providing a safe haven for him. This peace transcends the abundant harvest. He knows he can lie down and sleep peacefully for the Lord is the one who helps him dwell in safety. The statement, "Uneasy lies the head that wears a crown," speaks to the challenges of leadership. A leader is constantly bombarded with serious decisions of state and nation. The commander is always engaged in strategizing and making agreements for the stability of the nation or the society, so when the CEO can utter such a confident prayer, he or she recognizes God's direction in the affairs of the realm. It is a jubilating feeling to govern with the assurance that God is directing the order of things. This knowledge also promotes longevity of reign and life.

In this case David's enemies are routed out, and holy angels are dispatched to assist him. This is also a prayer of thanksgiving. A few days ago we discussed the morning prayer; however, this oration may best be called an evening prayer, which he offers before he falls asleep at night

Even young children utter a prayer before they crawl under their covers with an assurance that they can sleep safely because God is watching over them. As adults, may the same childish confidence carry us through life's challenges knowing full well that a special Someone gives peace to us, cares for us, and protects us every day. God's tender eyes are consistently hovering over us. Let us boldly, confidently, and fearlessly face the future feeling secure in God's care. May we trust in Him so that all our paths will be *peaceful*.

Day 225

My soul cleaveth unto dust: **Quicken** *thou me according to thy word. Psalm 119:25*

David's utterance was both a prayer and a lamentation. He was cognizant of his wretched condition and was befuddled about his life's path and of Jehovah's direction. He was pleading for clarity.

He saw himself as a borrowing insect. There was no life, no nerve, and no passion to do anything. There was neither strength nor stamina to stand upright. But he knew that he wanted to stand up and be God's man. He wanted to do what God required of him, but there was no strength in his sinews. He claimed the assurance in God's words and asked God to revive him as His Word promises. "Thy word is a lamp unto my feet, and a light unto my path," and "thy testimonies have I taken as an heritage for ever: for they are the rejoicing of my heart" (Ps. 119:105, 111). If we ask God to teach us His paths, we can claim the promises He gives us (see Ps. 25:4). David knew that God would hear his cry and raise him up from his spiritual malaise.

If people find themselves wallowing in despair and despondency, they can look up, for God promises hope, peace, joy, and assurance. He will raise you up and set your feet in the right path. God's Word gives assurance, counsel, power, and light. His peace lightens the bones and strengthens the muscles. It gives direction to right living. Even though one feels lost, he or she can find strength and resolve in the Word.

Like David, we need to ask God to quicken us to our duty and mission and revive in us a desire to study and know the Word. We should ask God to preserve our life and quicken us according to His word and loving-kindness. God promises that He will guide us (see Ps. 32:8).

If you feel spiritually sluggish, go to the Source. Call upon Jehovah, and He will definitely revive you and quicken you with new vision, ideas, or thoughts of how He can use you! Don't forget that God is able to do all things. Leave it all to Him; you will never be disappointed. May our daily prayer be *quicken* our hearts, minds, bodies, and souls!

Day 226

Rejoice *not against me, O mine enemy: when I fall, I shall arise; when I sit in darkness, the Lord shall be a light unto me. Micah 7:8*

The prophet Micah was speaking personally and generally for ancient Israel, God's chosen people, who had intermittently wandered off from His path. Sin and corruption had ruined the family and society, and the only hope for reclamation was God's intervention to restore them from the inside out.

Micah here expresses great faith in God's ability to hear, save, and restore. Personally, "I will look unto the Lord; I will wait for the God of my salvation: my God will hear me" (verse 7). Because of his faith in Jehovah, Micah could tell his enemies that they should not gloat or rejoice or feel as if they had triumphed, for God will elevate His people. He will be a Light for His people when all seems to be enveloped in darkness.

This confidence the prophet expressed should comfort us individually. God brings His people through when times are tough, so we must be patient and wait on the Lord. We must remember that we do not understand the workings of the great I AM.

God will not leave us to the enemy or allow us to sit in darkness and be befuddled. Unless God wills it, the enemy cannot and will have no need to rejoice about taking us captive. God always wins. Each of us must cultivate a relationship with God that exudes confidence in Him, His power, and His love.

As post apostolic Christians, we are stubborn and disobedient, yet God, in His love for us, protects us from the enemy. Our God directs us and subjugates our enemies. We are the children for whom the precious blood was shed, and God will never leave us so that the elements of doubt, fear, disease, mockery, or mimicry overwhelm us. We are protected under His strong and mighty wings. Therefore, rejoice for our God is great, marvelous, magnanimous, and concerned. None shall be left to the winds of strife and vainglory; we are well covered. So rejoice, for God is God! He delivers what He has promised. He is able and is carrying out His side of the bargain that He will be with us always. Here is enough reason to be joyful. May we *rejoice*!

Day 227

Deliver my **Soul***, O Lord, from lying lips, and from a deceitful tongue. Psalm 120:2*

Here is a confession and a prayer for deliverance from petty misdemeanors. Everyone lies or utters half-truths. David knew he had a proclivity to "butter up" statements and recognized that these frailties were unacceptable to God, so he kept his pulse on his utterances. Deep within, he wanted to walk uprightly, hence this very timely prayer: "Deliver my soul ... from lying lips."

Men and women in high positions, especially politicians, tend to speak in deceitful tones. Their tongues are smooth and speak from an insincere heart and execute a contrary action. Most of what they say cannot be taken either seriously or literally.

David, very familiar with the roguery of such a behavior, did not want to follow the pattern of the neighboring rulers. He wanted to live an upright life before God. He knew very well that God was able to read the intents of the heart. He understood that all of humankind's motives are open before God, so he was not about to practice deceit. Knowing his frailties, weaknesses, and obsession, he sought help very early. He sincerely wanted to be a trusted, dependable, and an upright servant, so he asked for purity of thought, ideas, and expressions. He did not desire to be double-tongued. Contemplating on this factor, he asked: "Who shall ascend into the hill of the Lord? or who shall stand in his holy place?" (Ps. 24:3). Which person can stand before the pure and holy God if their utterances cannot be trusted? Then comes the reply: "He that hath clean hands, and a pure heart" (verse 4). Having gotten the response, he vowed to God, "My tongue shall speak of thy word: for all thy commandments are righteousness" (Ps. 119:172).

David's prayer is every Christian's prayer. It is the only safeguard against presumptuous sins, evil thoughts, and a deceitful heart and mind. Even small children should be taught to speak the truth. Because of their impressionable minds, parents have a solemn duty to guard those minds scrupulously and fill them with noble virtues: love, care, concern, simplicity, and honesty.

With that prayer on every lip, the Holy Spirit will reside in the body and sanctify the heart. Let our prayer be: "Keep back thy servant from lying lips and a deceitful tongue, O Lord!" May we speak the truth in love even if it is unpopular and friendless. Deliver our *souls*, O Lord, from the venom of deceit!

Day 228

Thy *hands have made me and fashioned me: give me understanding, that I may learn thy commandments. Psalm 119:73*

The speaker acknowledges their indebtedness to the Creator for having been formed in His own image and being imbued with the capacity to learn and classify everything (see Gen. 1:26). The speaker recognizes that he is God's handiwork; God molded him into the creature he is with limitations and possibilities. He wants to obey God's commandments.

Recognizing humanity's limitations and ambition, he humbly prays to be given understanding in order to learn God's commandments. He does not want to simply memorize them but to actually comprehend the significance and comport of them. This is like a child's request: "Teach me, for I do not know."

God wants us to approach Him with the simplicity and curiosity of a child so that He can teach us. He wants us to be pliable in His hands, so He can fashion and mold us according to His similitude. He wants to infuse in us His Word, truth, and knowledge. This prayer echoes young Solomon's request: "Give therefore thy servant an understanding heart" (1 Kings 3:9). In this prayer he recognizes his limitations and boundaries while acknowledging God's illimitable knowledge, foresight, and wisdom.

We recognize that God knows everything about us and will grant us the things we ask for that will honor Him. This prayer expresses willing submission to His purposes. God is ready to give us more than we are willing to ask for. His Word assures us that He wants to give us understanding. If we draw near to Him and commit our ways to Him, He will give us all that we need.

The two primary gifts we should seek are wisdom and understanding. The Word says that wisdom is everlasting, and the wise shall shine as the stars forever. God has all the possibilities and is waiting to shower them on us. Let us seek understanding that we may live and act intelligently befitting sons and daughters of God, reflecting the image of our Father.

We are God's by creation. Our entire life emanates from and is maintained by Him. May we never cease to acknowledge God's ownership of us, for it is His hands that formed us!

Day 229

When I call to remembrance the **Unfeigned** *faith that is in thee, which dwelt first in thy grandmother Lois, and thy mother Eunice; and I am persuaded that in thee also.*
2 Timothy 1:5

Paul is giving thanks and commendation for Timothy, as he recalled the first time he met him at Lystra (see Acts 16:1). Paul continued by telling Timothy that he remembered his genuineness and sincerity at hearing and accepting the Word.

Paul was able to identify someone who had a genuine interest in the Word. He knew about his upbringing and the devotion and commitment of his grandmother and mother, who were early converts to the faith. He knew that this young man had a connection not only with his Jewish and Greco roots but also had a deep and sincere love for the cause; Paul even claimed Timothy as his son. Timothy's zeal may have mirrored Paul's, for Paul saw him as a potential leader of the fledgling church.

Paul said of him, "Fan into flame the gift of God, which is in you" (verse 6, NIV). Paul laid his hands on the youth, and he received the Holy Spirit. Then he entreated Timothy to "not be ashamed of the testimony about our Lord" (verse 8). Christian families may follow suit by not hiding their light, but they should instead let their children and grandchildren know that they are Christians. Follow the counsel found in Deuteronomy 6:6–9 so that the teachings will follow a generational pattern. That is what God expects of Christian families; parents must constantly uphold God's truths before their offspring.

Paul spotted genuine and sincere devotion in the young man and was not hesitant to enlist him in the Master's service. Elders, leaders, parents, and extended parents would do well to lead the youth to Jesus and teach them to adopt and adapt to Christ's righteous life. We should ensure that Christ's love and helpfulness are seen in the lives of the children and youth, and they should be encouraged to live and practice what they see and are taught. Let Christ be seen in your lives and homes where honesty and sincerity are the watchword. King Solomon's advice in Proverbs 22:6 is an appropriate guideline for Christian families to implement.

An investment in the training of our children and youth is an investment for their eternal life. Let there be no pretense, hypocrisy, or shallowness in presenting the truths to our children; teach them very early what is God's expectation of them and His plan for their lives; help them grow up like young Timothy, passionate for spiritual things and hankering after truth and the Word. May adults help the children to imitate Timothy's *unfeigned* faith!

Day 230

> *And Isaac loved Esau, because he did eat of his* **Venison**: *but Rebekah loved Jacob.*
> *Genesis 25:28*

This text is fraught with meaning and significance. Firstly, it points to the parent-child relationship and how parents show deference to their children. As in the case of Jeremiah, God ordained him before he was in the womb. Similarly, God knew the characters of these twin boys: Esau and Jacob.

In answer to Rebekah's inquiry of the Lord about the children she was carrying, the Lord told her that there were two disparate nations in her womb, and one would have dominance over the other—the older would serve the younger. How God designs these respective innate behaviors and characteristics is beyond us.

As the boys developed, Esau chose the open environment. The grandeur of the hills beckoned him, and he engaged himself in hunting wild boar, goats, deer, and gazelle. Isaac loved his son's venerable spirit, for it no doubt reflected his own youth or what he would have liked to do. Esau exhibited strong and brave qualities and would have been a great provider for his family. Esau's family would always be well fed with meat and other victuals. Besides being an excellent hunter, he could prepare delicious venison (deer meat), which Isaac loved. Venison is the best and healthiest meat. Deer are vegetarians, eating only foods in their natural state, cholesterol and fat free. Esau's bravery endeared him to his father, while Jacob was a mamma's boy, who clung to the more refined and delicate things. The countryside and the rugged hills did not appeal to him, so he stayed in the tent close to his mother's side and learned the art of housekeeping and studying.

Should their differences generate parental preference? Jacob was a schemer; Esau was more realistic and pragmatic, and he could not decipher how one could make a living by constantly staying home and not venturing out to see what was in the wild. Each chose a path (see Gen. 25).

Parents need to question how their divided love impacts their decision-making skills (verses 29–34). Esau was famished after returning from his hunting spree and easily relinquished and bargained off his spiritual and physical inheritance for food—a bowl of stewed lentils—not even venison or flesh of any kind. Isaac was deceived because of his physical incapability—blindness. He was physically challenged, and Esau was spiritually blind. Both were blind-sided.

Since God had already ordained the future of the twins, should he have intercepted Rebekah and Jacob's treachery to the blind father and husband? Esau needed to learn the importance and value of spiritual things. The mother and son's action severed the family, and this action produced irreversible consequences for all their generations even to this day. May none allow *venison* or any other love to impact life's major decisions!

Day 231

> *He that goeth forth and **Weepeth**, bearing precious seed, shall doubtless come again with rejoicing, bringing his sheaves with him. Psalm 126:6*

This text conveys a metaphor drawn from agriculture. Here David likens one's joys and sorrows to that of the farmer who goes out with good, choice, and selected seeds to plant. Why then would he weep unless he was uncertain of the yield? That reaction seems premature, for if the farmer has chosen good seeds and has fertilized the soil, why should he be wary of its capacity to produce the best crop?

This allusion might even have deep political, social, and intellectual overtones; the previous verse says, "They that sow in tears shall reap in joy" (verse 5). If one is engaged in some sort of political, financial, or educational endeavor, there is no need to sorrow because of the uncertain outcome, for there will be triumph and happiness once God intervenes. Here David amplifies the image and makes it into a metaphysical statement. Consequently, he goes out with the precious seeds of trust and confidence that the Almighty will bless the endeavor. When the enterprise is complete, he rejoices because of a successful venture. Just as the sacks are bursting with ripened grain, God brings homeostasis.

In all the unfriendly things we may encounter, God is able to bring us joy. Our tears may be seeds that can grow into a harvest of joy. Whether it is out of a tragedy or challenge, God can bring happiness. When you are burdened with sorrow, know that your times of grief will end and that you will again find peace, happiness, and contentment.

If one sows good seeds and does good works, God honors those motives and rewards justly. He will strengthen, uphold, and give the best result, so there will be joy, happiness, satisfaction, and complete harmony.

This is a promising verse that has a futuristic ring. God has never left His children to their own devices even when they wandered away and disobeyed Him. He is always there like the loving, tender, caring, and compassionate father who says, "Children, I am here waiting for your return; just turn to me and all will be well with you. I will even dry up your tears."

God can and will certainly turn all our *weeping* into joy. May we go forward, trusting in His providence!

Day 232

> *Then said Jesus unto him, **Except** ye see signs and wonders, ye will not believe. John 4:48*

Jesus spoke these words to the royal official who urgently requested Him to come to his house and heal his seriously ill son, who was at the point of death. Though not a believer, this nobleman had such profound faith and respect for Jesus' power that he entreated Him to come and do the doctor's duty—to resuscitate life.

Jesus is always found where and whenever people needed Him. He had just performed His first miracle at the wedding in Cana of Galilee and had provided a very refreshing drink for the guests. The nobleman might have been a guest at the wedding and saw the miracle and marveled at the adroitness of this new preacher, this divine Miracle Worker. What he saw had a phenomenal impact on him.

Jesus knew the mood and mentality of the crowd, their attitude toward His early ministry, and the mind of this official. Jesus' reply seemed deprecatingly chastening to those who wanted to see a physical demonstration in order to believe His divinity as Christ, the Son of God, who came down from heaven. He was born and grew up and dwelt among them, so they were unwilling to accept the claim; they wanted evidence.

Repeatedly, Jesus pointed to their defiance. On one occasion He stated that only a "perverse generation" would ask for a sign. Where was their practical faith and trust in Him? Prior to this, Jesus had performed other miracles in Judea, and His fame had gone abroad. This man, due to his political connection and stature, was less inclined to acknowledge Jesus publicly, but he was desperate to have his son healed. In this, he had affinities with Nicodemus, Jesus' closet admirer and night visitor, who often came to Jesus seeking counsel and dialogue.

Jesus knew this official's thoughts and spoke directly to him. This noble man believed in Jesus' power to heal his son, and Jesus, seeing his degree of faith, commanded, "Go thy way; thy son liveth" (verse 50). The son was not dead, and he would not die from his current malady.

This universal statement is addressed to all who believe in Jesus' saving power. It is designed to engender faith, trust, and belief in the only One who is able. Today, we do not need a sign to recognize the power of omnipotence, for all around us is evidences that the Almighty is in control. All nature reveals the marvelous working of the Trinity on humanity's behalf; it is that power that keeps, sustains, and directs. Let people everywhere move out in faith, believing that God is in control. He holds up worlds and is aware of everyone's needs. A blessing awaits all those who believe without having a public demonstration or evidence.

May we cultivate, nurture faith, and grasp the hand of divine omnipotence! Our God is always very near; He never leaves us alone. Go fearlessly into the future and believe. Believe!

Day 233

*Take my **Yoke** upon you, and learn of me; for I am meek and lowly in heart: and ye shall find rest unto your souls. Matthew 11:29*

What an invitation! Jesus invites His followers to take upon themselves the full measure of His armor and learn from Him. A yoke is a harness used to join two oxen together so they can plough in sync. What then is Christ's yoke? Is it not a burden, a constriction, a device to keep one in subjection to certain rules and regulations? Is it not bondage?

No. Jesus says in contrast to the yoke of sin and the demands of religious leaders, family pressures, and tradition, He offers a light yoke. Firstly, He frees us from all the burdens of this world as well as from all the rites, traditions, and nefarious rules. He takes them from us and carries them, so He now becomes the burden bearer. He is yoked with our burdens. He assures us that His yoke is easy. In order to accept His yoke, we have to do what He asks of us. It is all about obedience. Jesus promises love, rest, and peace with God in exchange for our challenges. Who does not want that yoke?

Jesus invites us to develop a relationship with God and experience a productive spiritual growth and a meaningful life. His yoke brings contentment and tranquility to troubled minds. With Jesus in the boat, we can smile at the storm, for His presence brings peace, safety, and security to the restless and confused. The peace of Jesus comes from looking into His face and realizing the tranquility therewith. His face emits calm, quietude, and security.

Jesus has asked us to bear no heavier yoke than He has carried. He bore the pain and humiliation for the entire world. We do not have to die eternally, for He made the complete sacrifice more than 2,000 years ago. We only need to yield ourselves to His keeping and follow His instruction. It is an open, unrestricted invitation. There is no dress code; take up His yoke.

We must know Him and His mission and then choose to follow Him. He invites us to come and learn about Him. We must study the things He values, the principles He espouses, and the mind He has. When writing to the Philippians, Paul counseled them, "Let this mind be in you, which was also in Christ Jesus" (Phil. 2:5). That is also our thrust. We can learn of Him only as we spend time in His presence, share His teachings with others, and learn how He dealt with humanity.

Jesus extolled the virtues of humility, compassion, kindness, and self-control. None of the seven deadly sins that Solomon cited are found in His character (see Prov. 6:18–19). He daily imparts grace to sustain us, and the reward is happiness, contentment, peace, and freedom from worry, pain, and anxiety. Additionally, there is an abundance of calm assurance. May you accept His invitation today and learn of Him and receive all the blessings and gifts He has promised! Take the peace He gives and appropriate the rest to your condition. May we thank Him, for His *yoke* is indeed easy and His burdens are light!

Day 234

> *My **Zeal** hath consumed me, because mine enemies have forgotten thy words.*
> *Psalm 119:139*

David's outburst echoes the prophet, Elijah, who was both jealous and zealous for the Lord God. God's chosen people had defied His laws and statutes and turned to worship Baals and Astoreth—idols that God forbade them to worship. In this spiritual dilemma, Elijah felt that he was the only one left standing up for Jehovah. However, God quickly reassured him that he was not the only one fighting His cause, for there were 7,000 others who had refused to bow the knee to idolatry and false worship. They had remained true and faithful to the Almighty.

David was acknowledging the truth and purity of God's Word. He was overwhelmed at the insolence and disregard shown for the precepts and statutes of the law of God. David laments, "My zeal hath consumed me." (The NIV translates "consumed me" to "wears me out.") His passion for God was akin to Elijah's Mount Carmel experience.

David's zeal and outrage—his holy indignation—was directed at the transgressors, and he told God: "It is time for thee, Lord, to work: for they have made void they law" (verse 126). He had grown tired of wrestling with them to acknowledge the Almighty's righteous works, laws, and statutes. Their stubbornness grieved his soul, and he wanted God to act.

In frustration, David uttered his last cry for help, but unlike the former prophet who ran when threatened with the loss of his life, David stood up to the challenge. He needed restorative strength and was aware that not everyone who hears the Word will accept it.

We can become so passionate for the things of God and for His worship that we forget that God is the ultimate authority and has final power over everything and everyone. Nothing escapes His eyes. He knows those who are truly His and those that will remain true to Him under all circumstances.

In all our passion and zeal for the things of God, let us be mindful of the quiet working of the Holy Spirit on the heart for not all who hear will accept. God is the judge of all. May we be passionate about what we can control and let the Lord do the rest. He knows all those that are His and His Spirit will gently woo them to His bosom. God is capable of defending His cause and fighting His own battles; we do not need to intervene. God is the Supreme Ruler, upholding worlds and directing the affairs of nations. How then do we think that we can fight for God? If we reject God's principles, we will have to account for our actions. God does not need a defender of His actions—righteous or unrighteous. He is God, the High Priest!

Fix Your Eyes on the Holy

Day 235

And ye, in any wise keep yourselves from the **Accursed** *thing, lest ye make yourselves accursed, when ye take of the accursed thing, and make the camp of Israel a curse, and trouble it. Joshua 6:18*

This was Joshua's strong and repetitious war warning to his people about how to conduct themselves after Jericho's fall. It was the customary practice of invading armies to choose for themselves the best from among the spoils in the besieged city. They wanted booty, but the commander forewarned them that when Jehovah stood up for them, they should not take any of their captors' vestiges. Besides, the city was vile and was to be completely razed to the ground. Nothing should be spared: human, beast, cattle, or fowl. There was to be a total annihilation of the city. To bring in relics of their victory would be insulting to their Commander and Deliverer, Jehovah God.

Thus Joshua told them to throw away everything that they saw, for it was tainted. They should not bring anything from Jericho into their camp or they would bring a curse on all of God's people. Jericho, a rich, powerful, and evil city, was under the divine ban. All the temple treasures consecrated to God's service should be brought into the Lord's treasury. But the city and people would be utterly destroyed because their evil practices had ascended to the Holy God, and He would not have evil contaminate His chosen people–Israel.

Jericho's destruction is symbolic of God's final destruction of sin in this world. He will not tolerate sin, whether it is little or big. The prophet, Nahum, said that God will bring an utter end to sin; it shall not be seen anywhere anymore on God's creation (see Nahum 1:7–9).

Overwhelmed by Jericho's success, Israel attacked Ai, a much smaller city, but they were defeated. Under much humiliation and heart-searching, they enquired of the Lord what could have gone wrong. They had marched up to the city singing the victory song only to be driven back in shame. To their chagrin, they learned that an offensive sin had been committed against God.

Upon searching, they found that Achan had despised the command and took accursed belongings from Jericho. For this, he, his entire family, and all his possessions were brought before the multitude, and they stoned Achan and his family to death. One man's covetous action incurred God's displeasure and Israel's defeat. What God says, He means. And what He means He will do, He does. We cannot successfully contrive with God or His plans or alter His ways.

The lesson for us is that God's commands are unalterable and unchangeable. Whatever is holy and consecrated to His service must remain so. Neither can we appropriate to ourselves the things that are deemed holy. God demands and expects wholeness and holiness from His people as well as perfect obedience in regard to holy and sacred things. If we disobey and disregard those principles, it could prefigure our own demise. God requires perfect obedience now as He required then. May we not touch the *accursed* thing!

Day 236

A false **Balance** *is abomination to the Lord: but a just weight is his delight. Proverbs 11:1*

This text speaks to all people engaged in any kind of business transaction; it asks for truthfulness and honesty in all their dealings. Traders, speculators, and merchants could profit from its advice. The text refers to more than "tipping the scales."

This was a timely counsel in that agrarian economy when people bought goods by weights and measures: linearly cloth by the yardage, gold and silver by shekels, flour by the mynah, etc. It warned against all dishonest measures because the seller was always trying to short change the purchaser. For example, if the buyer asked for four measures of barley, the unjust seller could easily measure three and a half and by sleight of hand charged for four measures. As a girl growing up, I have seen where the haberdasher measuring out a certain yardage of cloth gave fewer inches every time the yardstick reached the 36-inch mark. Unfortunately, the deceit was not discovered until the dress designer went home and began to lay out the fabric to cut the desired pattern she is about to make. It is through such an evil practice that many traders earn a great profit, but it is a profit earned on deceit and falsehood.

This text calls for honesty, uprightness, and integrity in all daily transactions with those around us. All traders should practice uprightness and justness. God frowns upon and hates cheaters. His Word says that such practice is abominable to Him. Everyone who goes into any business does so to gain and not to lose. But gaining at the expense of the purchaser is not success; it is theft and chicanery. Such transactions receive none of heaven's blessing, and the business does not thrive. King Solomon avers, "Lying lips are abomination to the Lord: but they that deal truly are his delight" (Prov. 12:22). It is best to be always honest.

God frowns upon cheaters because they want to obtain wealth at the expense of those who walk honestly and uprightly. It is the latter that God honors. It is therefore incumbent for all traders to deal honestly and uprightly with those in every circumstance and every transaction. Jesus asked His listeners the rhetorical question: "For what shall it profit a man, if he shall gain the whole world, and lose his own soul?" (Mark 8:36). Those who continue to crave filthy lucre at the cost of their eternal salvation are making a very critical error. We cannot take any of our accoutrements to the grave; therefore, we need to spend less time being duplicitous and grasping for the perishable and more on that which is permanent and upright.

God delights in those who practice the Micah 6:8, principle: "Do justly, and ... love mercy, and ... walk humbly with thy God." In all our dealings, let us make every effort to honor God, our Creator. He delights in just weights and measures. May the psalmist's prayer: "Let integrity and uprightness preserve me; for I wait on thee" (Ps. 25:21) be the guide for *balance* of all who engage in any business transaction!

Day 237

> **Come** *unto me, all ye that labour and are heavy laden, and I will give you rest.*
> *Matthew 11:28*

This is Jesus' great invitation to humankind. Anyone who is overwhelmed with life's challenges, come! Jesus is the burden bearer. He is the only one who can carry all the burdens that make us sink beneath the respective loads. He knows each of us; He remembers that we are dust and that we vanish at the toss of a strong wind, so He tells us to come to Him. We just need to trust Him, for He will give us rest.

Jesus can do this and more because He is the model man; He is able! All power resides in Him. In Him, we move and have our being. Without Him, we are nothing. He is the only permanent, constant person in the universe. He is the Creator; He knows all—He knows everything and everyone, and He says to all, "Come."

None need fear or be anxious about responding to the invitation. There are many rooms in the Father's house; the wedding garment is already provided, so you do not need to go and shop for an outfit. He provides it all. No undesirables will be there, for He screens those who enter. All will have clean, pure hearts and no guile in their mouths. There will be no forwardness or perverseness on their lips. They will be the chosen ones—those who have gotten the victory over every kind of addiction, sinful habit, and behavior. These have made their robes white and washed in the blood of the Lamb. They stand faultless before God's throne. They are the overcomers! Jesus tells them to come.

To those still beset with challenges of the flesh, he says, "Come!" He is the solution! Just accept Him into your life. When you come, He has promised to lift all your cumbersome burdens and lighten the load and make it easy for you to travel and go on living. You now have a traveling companion—but He is the kind who helps you carry your load. The prophet Isaiah assures weary travelers that God provides strength. He renews us, for He takes our tired selves and revives us. "To those that have no might, he increaseth strength" (Isa. 40:29). Come!

Weary and worn out with life's challenges, He invites you to open the invitation and accept. Lay your cogitations, anxieties, and fears at the feet of Jesus, and let Him carry them. He is mindful of the least of His children. Jesus cares; His heart is touched by our grief. Why not respond and say, "Thank You, Lord! I accept. Here are all of my burdens; take them and let me enjoy the rest you offer. I can now have peace of mind and contentment that You give."

Jesus has taken all your harassments and heartaches. When you come to Him, you do not leave. The rest you receive is for now and the future; the future rest ushers in God's kingdom and eternal life. Let everyone who reads this day's meditation respond to the invitation: "*Come!*" May you hand over all your cares to the loving Savior!

Day 238

Delight *thyself also in the Lord: and he shall give thee the desires of thine heart. Psalm 37:4*

To delight in something means to be happy and joyous with expressions of gratitude. People delight in many things: material acquisitions, girlfriends, boyfriends, wives, husbands, children, success in business, fame, power, rank, intellectual strength, physical prowess, high standing among peers, wealth, and prestige.

When you are introduced to someone of renown, you usually say, "I am delighted to meet you." When news about a close friend or relative reaches you of his or her accomplishment or achievement, one generally responds something like, "How delightful!"

David tells us that though we can find joy in social things or events that trigger our fancy, one can also find delight—memorable joy—in the Lord. Yesterday we read about the delightful offer that Jesus made to us to come as we are and give Him everything. Who on earth could ever make such an offer and carry through with it? Only Jesus, the co-Creator, CEO, president, and owner of everything can keep such a promise. He can make the offer, for He has everything and everyone at His command. Thus, He grants us freely the desires of our hearts. He gives us all that we think of and want to have. What a mighty, caring, and concerned Elder Brother we have!

Though excited, let us be ever mindful that these gifts and blessings are conditionally related. If you find happiness in responding to the invitation, then you will sit at the table and have a delightful time with your Host. You will spend time with Him to get to know Him well and not just as a passing acquaintance. You can start a forever friendship. How delightful!

King Solomon encourages husbands to delight themselves in their wives. King David intones, "I delight to do thy will, O my God: yea, thy law is within my heart" (Ps. 40:8). We are further advised to delight in the acquisition of wisdom and understanding, for they both give life and longevity. But above the many sensuous delights, our primary delight should be in the Lord and in His Word, for it is the Word that is the lamp lighting the path so one can delight in both the natural, physical, and material world.

The apostle Paul avers, "Now unto him that is able to do exceeding abundantly above all that we ask or think" (Eph. 3:20); therefore, one must learn of the triune God and the things that delight them.

The basic premise is to put God first. We should delight in Him, and He will give you your heart's desires. Lose yourself in Him; revel in Him; spend time with Him in prayer and meditating on His Holy Word. Then watch how delightful your life will be, as He performs His good work in you. He will fill you up with contentment, passion, and love, and you will find pleasure in Him as lovers find in each other's company. Entrust everything to Him. All your life, family, possessions, and plans to be subject to His will and control. As you do this, you will come into a new and rich experience. He will bring you your heart's desires, and there will be mutual delights—you in Him and He in you. What a *delightful* experience! May you begin today!

Day 239

O Lord, Our Lord, how **Excellent** *is thy name in all the earth! who hast set thy glory above the heavens. Psalm 8:1*

The psalmist expressed glory, praise, and adoration to the Lord Jehovah and accorded majesty and excellence to Him. We cannot comprehend the magnanimity of Jehovah God; thus His name is repeated twice: "O Lord, O Lord." This is an expression of high exaltation.

Our limited exposure to God's righteousness and our limited acquisition of secular knowledge still does not enable us to grasp the enormity of the goodness of God. God's name alone defies understanding and none can understand Him or His ways. Our finiteness cannot comprehend the majesty of God's infiniteness because the realm of God's glory is not within the atmospheric heavens. His majesty and glory is set above all.

God dwells far above the starry heavens. He dwells in eternity. We must come to accept and revere the grandeur of the Almighty. Despite His awe, God has chosen to come and dwell among us. That is part of His excellence and goodness as well as the enigma.

God's name is majestic. There is no other name like His. That is why all creatures—great and small—bow, adore, and worship Him. God's glory is set above the solar heavens, so we can look up and offer praise to our marvelous and majestic God, who alone deserves our praise and our worship. One of the astronauts who went into space in the 1980s declared that he did not see God, yet another was overwhelmed by the magnitude of outer space, and he glorified God's creation.

The psalmist concurs, "The heavens declare the glory of God; and the firmament sheweth his handywork" (Ps. 19:1). David again confesses, "When I consider thy heavens, the work of thy fingers, the moon and the stars, which thou hast ordained; What is man, that thou art mindful of him? and the son of man, that thou visitest him?" (Ps. 8:3, 4). Then in the final adoration, he repeats the acclamation, "O Lord, our Lord, how excellent is thy name in all the earth" (verse 9). Read Psalm 8 to fill you up with the glory and majesty of the great God of the universe. God is above all other gods; He is the Creator, and by Him and through Him, all things consist. May all flesh glorify His name? May we recognize that *excellence* and majesty belong to God alone.

Day 240

Watch ye; stand **Fast** *in the* **Faith***, quit you like men, be strong. 1 Corinthians 16:13*

This message is one among the many exhortations that the beloved apostle Paul sent to the saints. This was specially addressed to the Corinthian brethren since he was uncertain of a second visit with them. He wrote this letter of commendation but more so exhorting them to hold fast unto the things he had taught them.

Corinth was very dear to his heart, especially since the city's location was in the metropolis. The residents practiced all kinds of evil and sinful behaviors, and the new Christians struggled to maintain their newly found and established integrity.

Paul had sown the Gospel message, and some had fallen on the respective soils (hearts) that Jesus narrated in the parable (see Matt. 13:1–23). Paul, the new sower, was not about to see the truth snatched by the evil birds of cynicism or scorched by the searing sun of unbelief and sinfulness. At Corinth, some seed did fall on good ground and bore fruits. There were Aquila and Priscilla as well as many others with whom Paul found lodging and plied his tent-making trade. There was also Apollos, teacher and leader, who kept the spiritual fires aflame. Paul said of him, "I have planted, Apollos watered; but God gave the increase" (1 Cor. 3:6).

As founder, teacher, evangelist, and leader, Paul constantly communicated with the fledgling flock through his letters. Even though he had hoped to revisit the church, he sent the letter ahead to counsel and encourage them. He entreated them to be on their guard and to look out for sinister forces and signs that might reenter the church and weaken the members. They were to behave courageously, know what and in whom they believed, stand firmly on the principles of God's Word, arm themselves with it, and not be indifferent to or relinquish their new-found faith. They were to fight the good fight of faith, lay hold on eternal life, and guard well the avenues of the soul.

Additionally, they should act with kindness and love and care for those new in the Gospel. "Stand fast in the faith" is the counsel; they were to be brave, stand up like true warriors, and be prepared to fight and defend their belief. Speaking to the Ephesian brethren, he counseled them to be totally clad with the garments of Christ righteousness (see Eph. 6:10–18). May we also heed the counsel!

Today, we face a different world that is torn by all kinds of irreverent behaviors and practices. Those who know Jesus and have experienced His leading should follow and abide by the same instructions given some twenty centuries ago: be strong in the Lord and the power of His might; know the truth. Stand firmly; stand securely; *stand fast*.

Day 241

Great *peace have they which love thy law: and nothing shall offend them. Psalm 119:165*

This text is primarily for people living in a strife-torn society. Moderns and post-moderns are on a trek of mass confusion, inequalities, and unfulfilled anxieties. There is only war, rumors of wars, strife, bickering, and total displacement of people and things everywhere. There is socio-political unrest on all fronts. Little nations are raising their eyebrows and knitting them at larger nations. There is no common ground for dialogue or peaceful negotiation. The so-called "peace talks" end in national frustration, so there is no peace in the homes, in society, or among the nations. Little and big nations are arming themselves for war while talking peace.

But there can be peace! The psalmist gives specific instruction on how to access this balm: love the Lord, hearken to His instructions, and obey His laws and statutes. Only then will peace come—a wonderful, lasting, permanent peace. Peace that admits no turmoil and suffers no estrangement. To love the laws and statutes of the Lord God is foundational for achieving peace. Jehovah himself said that the peace He offers is neither grievous nor offensive.

If you express any love for the Creator, the natural response is to love and obey. Jesus said, "If you love me, keep my commandments" (John 14:15). Love for God and love for all humankind hangs on the principles of right doing, right practice, positive behaviors, and peace.

Where love abounds and is practiced, there cannot be hate, rancor, discontent, fear, or distrust. Humankind needs to return to God's original requirements: love and obedience. The banalities of envy, jealousy, and covetousness displayed are the enemy's ploys to destroy godly peace. Micah 6:8 spells out very lucidly what God requires of all His created beings: justice, love, mercy, and humility. If all people—leaders, followers, nations, and principalities—observed the Almighty's command, there would be no need to sharpen arrow heads and load guns, rifles, or sling shots. There would be peace, and it would be more than just ordinary and tentative peace. It would be a great peace, harmony, rest, and quietude.

God's laws have in them all the principles for living a happy, satisfied, and peaceful life. Satan chose not to love God's law and so staged a rebellion in heaven. Since then, the peace pact has been broken. Rebellion, animosity, hatred, and discord are rampant on the earth. If people everywhere would return to the law of God and learn from it, there would be less tumult and fewer engagements of armed conflict. God's law guides, instructs, reproves, and leads one into paths of righteousness (see 2 Tim. 3:16, 17). All who delight in God's law experience a great peace; nothing offends them. Therefore, let perpetual peace be on earth. May this *great* peace begin with each of us in our homes, society, and nations!

Day 242

> *And I saw another angel ascending from the east, having the seal of the living God: and he cried with a loud voice to the four angels ... saying,* **Hurt** *not the earth, neither the sea, nor the trees, till we have sealed the servants of our God in their foreheads. Revelation 7:2, 3*

The prophet John saw *another* angel in his vision; there were other angels besides this one, but this angel was empowered to carry out God's mandate. This particular angel had more power than the others and commanded them to stay their hand! *"Hurt not."* The angel told him not to harm any part of the natural environment until God had authenticated His special people with His seal.

When sin entered the world, death came upon everything: humanity, beasts, and the natural vegetation. The trees lost their leaves; the sea lost its calmness; the sun's rays became more intense; humanity became subject to pain, sorrow, and discomfort. Evil ran wild, but God always has a people who are obedient to Him and will receive His seal of approval. They will be sealed for eternal life and the second death will have no authority over them. This is the promise. They are declared righteous before God because they are overcomers. They will overcome by the power of the blood and the testimony of Jesus Christ. They will not be afraid if through persecution and severe trials they go to sleep, for God has already promised eternal life.

The enemy cannot touch any of the sealed, for they are without sin. After all of God's chosen ones are sealed, the avalanche of evil will break loose. There will be uncontrolled disasters, plagues, famines, wars, earthquakes, tsunamis, mass murders, genocide, suicide, and pandemonium. There will be trouble on every hand and from every quarter of the globe coupled with incredible amounts of hedonism. Despite all of this, the children of obedience need not fear, for they are sealed; they will remain unscathed because they will have met the divine approval. God's judgment is final, and humankind will become fearful of all the things that are happening.

Fearful times are ahead, and God's obedient children must not keep silent; they must cry aloud and let people everywhere be apprised of the dangers that are forth coming. We need to tell people that while mercy still lingers, they should seek to find the ark of safety before destruction sweeps this fair planet. The angels are withholding the storm from breaking loose. This message has global perspective. The four angels are holding the four corners of the globe: east, west, north, and south. None is excluded. The warning is to every man, woman, and child living on the face of the earth: rich and poor; high and low; free and captive.

God is still calling men and women to find refuge before it is too late. When the angels receive the command from God, *every* living thing will fall. There is still time to find the safe harbor from the future *hurt*. May we all have our sins confessed and pardoned so that we may receive God's seal.

Day 243

For this corruptible must put on **Incorruption**, *and this mortal ...* **Immortality**.
1 Corinthians 15:53

This verse ends Paul's discourse on the state of the dead. When Christ returns, immortality will be conferred on the saints—both the living and the newly resurrected. He referred to the entire process as a mystery too enigmatic for human minds to comprehend. This condition of humanity in death and the resurrection to immortal life has generated much discussion over the ages. Today, many people believe that the dead are elevated to the heavenly courts where God and Jesus currently inhabit. Paul is setting the record straight that the "conferring of immortality" is a futuristic act. No man now living and dies is ushered into the presence of God. He or she is also not given immortality. If it were so, then all should wish to die, and Jesus need not return.

The learned apostle states under inspiration that we shall all not sleep (meaning "die"), but we all shall be changed (see 2 Tim. 3:16, 17; 1 Thess. 4:16, 17). How and when? Here is the answer: "In a moment, in the twinkling of an eye" (1 Cor. 15:52). The righteous dead shall be raised incorruptible, and they will not be subject to mortality or putrefaction anymore. For this corruptible form that went down into the grave must put on incorruption, and this mortal frame will be transformed and be clothed with immortality. Those that are saved will be given a new angelic body. At His arrival Jesus will transform our bodies into a glorious new thing where death will never more have dominion and control. Every dead person is in his or her grave awaiting Jesus' return; none is in heaven.

Through his cunning, Satan introduced death and thought he had succeeded in Eden and again at the cross, where he tried to keep the Son of God in the grave. But after three days, God brought forth His Son from that contagion of death and called Him back to life. Jesus' body did not see corruption, which was prophesied by David in Psalm 16. Jesus rose and came out. He went in mortal, yet He came forth immortal. He would never again see or taste of death. Jesus returned to heaven to be at His Father's right hand, and when He returns to earth, He will defeat both death and sin and confer immortality on all His trusting and obedient saints. Death shall then die and immortality and incorruption shall reign supremely. We all shall be changed.

Earthy things are corruptible, perishable, and temporary, so they are classified as intangibles. It is only this mortal soul, when transformed and renewed, which has any value. Therefore, we must seek those things that make for permanent happiness—a life lived in perfect obedience to God's will. It is on that premise solely that Jesus will confer immortality on us because we have been found worthy. May we live every waking moment in His presence, clothed in our right mind, and directed by the Holy Spirit. May we be ready to receive the gift of *immortality*!

Day 244

Then shall the virgin rejoice in the dance, both young men and old together: for I will turn their mourning into **Joy**, *and will comfort them, and make them rejoice from their sorrow. Jeremiah 31:13*

As I write these devotional thoughts, I am awestruck at the mercies and goodness of our God. How mighty, merciful, gracious, and caring He is of His children. He bends over backward to satisfy our needs. He is indeed our Comforter and is dependable and trustworthy. He is the Almighty. Is it any wonder that the book of Psalms is full of praiseworthy utterances and adorations? This particular text is the epitome of God's love and promises. Here are some of the praises from David:

"Great is the Lord, and greatly to be praised in the city of our God, in the mountain of his holiness" (Ps. 48:1). "Praise the Lord; for the Lord is good: sing praises unto his name; for it is pleasant" (Ps. 135:3). "O give thanks unto the Lord; for he is good: for his mercy endureth for ever" (Ps. 136:1). Other psalms of praise are 111, 112, and 113 through 117. Then there is a supreme climax of praise in Psalm 150:6: "Let every thing that hath breath praise the Lord. Praise ye the Lord."

If you have much to be joyful about, then lift up your voice and utter praises and thanksgiving to the Most High. God promises that their soul shall be like a watered garden—flourishing and beaming with healthy plants and shrubbery. There will be no more sorrow at all. Purified men and women alike will come to worship at His shrine. Above all, there will be joint praise and no age difference; there will only be a unity of spirit and direction. Consequently, He will turn their mourning into gladness and rejoicing, and they will experience true happiness. There is no reason why there should not be continuous joy.

There is cause for much sorrow in the world, but here the Almighty assures His children that instead of lamentations, He will wipe away all tears from the eyes, wailing from their lungs, and replace their sorrow with hallelujah shouts and joyful songs

When a child is born, it is generally an event that brings joy and gladness to the family; however, the Word aptly points out that we should weep. Likewise, when someone dies, it is generally a sad event, but the Bible says we should rejoice in the hope of the future. God says that He will reverse the process so that joy remains triumphant and sorrow extinct.

The verse also echoes our future with Jesus when He returns to claim all His precious, sleeping and awaiting saints. There will be joy in heaven for the saved, and there will be joy and thanksgiving from the redeemed because they are with the Savior and Redeemer. All heaven will be filled with rapturous joy because sin and sinners will be forever extinguished. The angels will be overjoyed because their Commander has won the battle and has brought His ransomed children home. There will be endless joy. There will be songs of gladness and shouts of hosannas because sin will be forever extinguished. Only one breath of harmony and peace will prevail. Sure enough, there will be joy forevermore, and we will be clothed with immortality! May you experience that *joy*!

Day 245

> *And this gospel of the* **Kingdom** *shall be preached in all the world for a witness unto all nations; and then shall the end come. Matthew 24:14*

This is the great Gospel Commission as exuded from Jesus' lips. All who accept Him have a responsibility to carry the idea of repentance and the remission of sins in the name of Jesus to the world. His power to save and transform lives must be told to every person living in this age. Jesus says to the entire world that wherever people are found and human habitation exists, all must be told that the kingdom of heaven draws near. Every human being must hear the good news of Jesus' saving grace, His substitutionary death, His resurrection, ascension, and imminent return. Everyone must decide whether to accept or reject the gospel message; it is the best news that brings hope and assurance to humankind.

Jesus did not say all will convert or accept, but those commissioned must bear witness so that all can hear and none is without excuse. The unreached cannot say, "I did not hear; no one told me about Jesus and his return or of His mighty power to transform lives." Jesus commissions His followers to proclaim the message to everyone. Their indecisions must not be on the shoulders of God's ministers and teachers. Every hearer is commissioned to share what he or she has heard and learned.

When Jesus commands, He expects compliance. When His followers have shared the Word to every living person then He will come to claim His redeemed. He is waiting on us to execute the command—to reach men and women everywhere and bring this life to an end. Jesus said that the gospel must be preached to all the world and then the end will come. Let not our negligence slow the process by not going forward wherever people are found; each must hear and act. The day of the Lord's return should not come upon anyone unawares. Each person must have access to the wedding garment, receive the free gift, and enter into the marriage supper with the Lamb, Jesus, our Redeemer.

Jesus is waiting for us to come to Him, but we must not come alone. We must lead someone to Jesus. All people within our purview must be introduced to the greatest and best news—Jesus Christ and His saving power. Everyone must know of the Lord, and they will have to decide whether to accept or reject His offer: "Come unto me and be saved." May we share the Word with the world so that all may have the chance to be with our Lord in His *kingdom* when He returns.

Day 246

For I know that my redeemer liveth, and that he shall stand at the **Latter** *day upon the earth.*
Job 19:25

Job has been known throughout biblical and sacred history as God's case study. He is the model of defeat and triumph. Satan confronted God about Job's righteousness and his unique affiliation with Him and accused God of playing favoritism. God gave Satan free access to Job, except his life.

When Satan presented Job's case, God gave him permission to inflict pain, distress, and sorrow upon Job. Job then became the epitome of suffering, untold misery, and disaster. In one day he was reduced from the wealthiest man in the east to penury and near death. The Holy Book says, "In all this did not Job sin with his lips" (Job 2:10). No other person living or yet unborn has had his experience. He possessed patience, integrity, and commitment to his God. He was a man of faith; he believed in his God and implicitly trusted Him. During one of his painful experiences he stated, "Naked came I out of my mother's womb, and naked shall I return thither" (Job 1:21). At another time, "What? shall we receive good at the hand of God, and shall we not receive evil?" (Job 2:10). Job remained entrenched and unmoved in Jehovah. It is said that he "holdeth fast his integrity" (Job 2:3).

Job was the model parent and husband. He continually prayed for his grown children—he hoped God would forgive any infractions they may have committed in their respective sprees. Despite his parental role, Job's greatest asset was his faith. Amid all the vicissitudes of his life—rejection and blame of his friends, instability of his wife, loss of all his livestock, houses and children—Job knew that he could depend on God. He realized that he was God's "lab rat" of sorts, and he stood up to the challenge. Here is his vote of confidence: "For I know that my redeemer liveth, and that he shall stand at the latter day upon the earth" (Job 19:25).

Job knew his God and was confident that his Redeemer would champion his cause. Even though in this disparate condition, he declared that even if worms destroy his body, he would still hope in God. Nothing could deter him from the divine purpose and the union with the Elohim. With strong, steadfast hope and belief affirmed that in the last days of earth's history, he knew that God would vindicate him and grant him eternal life.

Our faith ought to mirror Job's—strong and steadfast. In the face of trials and challenges, will you be able to rest your entire life on the promises of the Savior? Can you confidently say, "I know that my Redeemer lives, and He will see me through every dark valley"? As we await the Lord's return, may we boldly say, "Jesus shall stand on the *latter* day on the earth and bring us deliverance!" This is the message of salvation; this is the blessed hope!

Day 247

*But the **Meek** shall inherit the earth; and shall delight themselves in the abundance of peace.*
Psalm 37:11

In today's semantics, meekness is associated with weakness. When I was a girl, we learned this maxim: "The humblest calf gets the most milk." However, as I matured and saw the world through a different lens, I soon learned that the humblest calf goes without milk and is usually on the brink of starvation and possible emaciation.

We live in a very competitive society where everyone is vying for the best in everything. No one wants to be at the first rung of the ladder or at an entry-level position. But to demonstrate meekness in this competitive society is an anathema—a quality to scorn at or shun completely.

However, the very wise and learned King David stated that meekness should be considered a cherished and enviable quality because it brings an abundance of peace. Jesus, many centuries later, reiterated and affirmed the same principle. He pronounced blessings and happiness on those who practice meekness. What is it about this principle that people should want to possess it and delight themselves for having it? More closely, what are the characteristics of meekness? It must be something precious and valuable. Let's find out.

Meekness is humility, calmness, and a contented, controlled spirit. This spirit is one that is not constantly enraged, contentious, or combative. Meek people have their wits about them. They think before they act and are able to make wise decisions. They listen to counsel and advice and are never bombastic or proud.

Regarding life's spiritual challenges, God's children must focus on His peace, contentment, and goodness. We must maintain a spirit of thankfulness and show appreciation to others. Meek people allow God to fight their battles, for only He can assuage the rough waters and bring calm, solace, and deliverance. The meek will sit and wait until God works out His plan for their lives. There will be reduced anxiety for God is in charge. They will have a delightful demeanor, and people will gather around them because they emanate a Christ-like radiance. Their words heal rather than smart, and they are happy, peaceful, and joyful because God directs their lives, actions, and expressions. Akin to David's utterance, Jesus promises abundant blessings and eternity: "Blessed are the meek: for they shall inherit the earth" (see Matt. 5:5).

Jesus told His disciples that the humble seekers will be recipients of this blissful abode where there will be neither quarrels nor rebellions because the inheritors will have had their natures changed. God does not need to arm the saints, for they will be holy and righteous people. While we await our Lord's return, may we be clothed with the garment of humility and wait patiently on the Lord as He directs our steps! That is true *meekness*.

Day 248

*Ye have lived in pleasure on the earth, and been wanton; ye have **Nourished** your hearts, as in the day of slaughter. James 5:5*

This is James' severe rebuke to wealthy employers who gloried in their wealth, using it to satiate their palates. In the meantime, they remained insensitive to the needs of their workers and the needy. He was not railing against the acquisition of wealth but the corrupting influence that riches had on its possessors.

The apostle saw this lifestyle as insensitive, selfish, and overtly evil. The wealthy lived lavishly, practiced self-indulgence, and were totally oblivious of their oppressive acts of demanding hard labor for little pay.

He uses the imagery of a continuous feast—food literally snowed in their house. Amidst all their effulgence and hedonism, he wanted the wealthy to be cognizant of the wants of the poor and needy.

This message is a clear warning to the rich and those with possessions. Riches are worthless if they are used only to satiate the pallet of the ones who already have everything. Wealth should be used judiciously: to bless others, provide employment, and assist the poor. It should not be used as many seemed to use their wealth to slake their thirst and craving for more of the same sumptuous, hedonistic life. They nourished their taste buds with the effulgence of their wealth at the expense of those who languished for some scraps from their tables.

Wealth is fleeting and transient, and those blessed should rather seek to nourish themselves in the Lord and the study and meditation of His Word so that they can care for the widows, fatherless, and the orphans (see Isa. 58:7–10). When the wealth is used this way, their souls will indeed be nourished with God's great graces–His goodness, love, tenderness, and compassion. But when it is used to lavish on self and like-minded cohorts, they are indeed nourishing themselves in infamy, selfishness, and greed.

God frowns upon such behaviors. He gives some people wealth, so they can use it to bless others and erase selfishness from their character. James said that using wealth oppressively was condemnatory. Thus, many people's wealth is a curse rather than being a blessing.

Everyone should heed the words of King Solomon: "If riches increase, set not your heart upon them" (Ps. 62:10). Neither should the wealthy use it to lambast the needy and the less fortunate. Used thus, it is an effrontery to Jehovah, who gives all men the power to get wealth. May the wealthy *nourish* their hearts in God's goodness, love, and compassion!

Day 249

Thou shalt neither vex a stranger, nor **Oppress** *him: for ye were strangers in the land of Egypt.*
Exodus 22:21

This text reflects the previous one that addresses oppressive, wealthy employers who ignore the needs of the poor. Here, Moses reminds the children of Israel, who are newly freed from the clutches of Pharaoh's ghoulish enslavement, to deal kindly with the aliens among them remembering their former status as aliens in Egypt.

This counsel encapsulates the principle of the golden rule: "Do to others what you would have them do to you" (Matt. 7:12, NIV), which Jesus taught many years later. This premise is still being used as a guide for living in today's hostile, insensitive society.

Many of us suffer from "selective amnesia" because we soon forget our roots and the hardships we recently faced. Once we have transcended the throes of poverty, hunger, and distress, we forget our past. Then when we see others struggling to eke out an existence, we frown and snub them. This text calls many of us to remember our former status and deal kindly with the strangers who are trying to establish a footing in a new frontier.

This is a simple human relationship principle telling how we should relate to one to another: "Let brotherly love continue" (Heb. 13:1). Brotherly love and oppression are on opposite sides of the continuum.

We who have enjoyed better days should not forsake the downtrodden. Who knows? The tables might yet be turned, and the next day you might find yourself in the same situation you rebuffed with a proud, insensitive, and uncaring eye. Help everyone who comes within your purview, and give aid to those as you have been blessed.

This counsel is most appropriate in the United States of America because it is the citadel for the alien population. From every country, people have gravitated to the shores of this northern hemisphere land mass.

The country was founded originally as a haven for the alien. It has become not just a city of refuge but a land of refuge for the huddled mass of humanity. The most beautiful fact is that there is a niche for every alien entering the USA where each can create a life fearlessly and freely. At this stage in our history, almost all ethnic groups live harmoniously.

Moses' advice, which was given some 4,000 years ago, still applies in many major US cities. In New York City, dubbed the "Big Apple," millions of aliens converge. The city boasts of its accommodation–"everyone can get a bite of that Big Apple." May all aliens continue to live peaceably and harmoniously not forgetting their roots, neither seeking to *oppress* the newcomer, for it is not God's way!

Day 250

> *I* **Press** *toward the mark for the prize of the high calling of God in Christ Jesus.*
> *Philippians 3:14*

What is the high calling of God, and what is the mark for the prize? The call of God is a heavenward lifestyle that can be achieved only through the gift of Jesus' power and His grace imputed to us. This lifestyle consists of living the life that Jesus lived, doing the things He did, and having His mind directing our minds. That goal requires a daily striving for the characteristics of Jesus, our Redeemer and Intercessor. Thus, we have to press.

Paul saw all of life as a race to be run; he drew heavily on the athletic games parlayed in the Roman Colosseum. He was totally engrossed in the athletic competitions that teemed there and having been converted, he could constantly see similarities between the runners' feat and that of the Christian's challenge. Because of this inspiration, he used much athletic imagery in his writings and discussions pointing to the Christian lifestyle of reaching out to God and living the fulfilled life.

At the end of each race, there is the prize but only one winner. Referring to his race, Paul declared, "I therefore so run, not as uncertainly; so fight I, not as one that beateth the air: But I keep under my body, and bring it into subjection ... I myself should be a castaway" (1 Cor. 9:26, 27). Based on his analysis and observation, Paul counseled Christians to run even though there was only one first prize to be given. He said athletes run and compete to receive a temporary crown- laurel, but the Christian's crown is incorruptible and permanent–it portrays the gift of eternal life.

Running, racing, and entering the track is a very worthy ambition. However, the apostle was not talking about a physical land race; he used the analogy similarly to how Jesus used parables to present profound lessons regarding the kingdom of God. He was referring to something more permanent–running the race of life and running to receive God's prize–eternal life. This is a race for victory over all impediments and obstructions that interfere with the Christian's marathon.

Paul recognized and had even experienced that the Christian track was and is beset with cobblestones of ruts, trials, steep hills, and deep, dark valleys, yet he makes it clear that he will never give up. It is so important to press forward and persevere. We must do what we can to cross the finish line and hear the Commander congratulate us and tell us we have won the prize.

Every Christian man and woman must heed the admonition to press on amidst life's challenges. We have no other choice but to continue with our eyes fixed on the prize–eternal life–which Christ shall imbue us with when we burst the tape, win the race, and receive our crown of life. May we never look back to see who is behind us, but *press* on until we reach the zenith of our aspirations: heaven at last!

Day 251

The earth shall **Quake** *before them; the heavens shall tremble: the sun and the moon shall be dark, and the stars shall withdraw their shining. Joel 2:10*

This is the warning message Jehovah gave to the prophet Joel to be delivered to His chosen people, Israel. Though it was directly theirs, it has overtones for God's people living in the end time of earth's history. The message is both present and futuristic. It is a call to repentance and humankind everywhere needs to respond.

Joel's warning portends that the forthcoming preternatural mishaps are the result of humanity's constant rebellion and disobedience. It happened to the antediluvians that were destroyed with the flood. But before that great and terrible display in the natural world, God had sent a warning to all people calling them to repentance. Faithful and righteous Noah preached for 120 years prior to the event, but they rejected his counsel. So, they all perished. What God says He will do, He does; therefore, humankind must heed the call, turn to God wholeheartedly, and acknowledge His authority over the earth before all these earth-shattering and fearsome disasters break forth upon the land. God sent out warning after warning through Noah, and humankind turned deaf ears, so God brought judgment and punishment upon the transgressors of His law. Destruction came on them, and the same will come to us unless we heed and respond to the warning.

It is marvelous how Jehovah God spoke through His prophets of things to come to the point where even hundreds of years after, Jesus, the Son of God, validated Joel's prophecy that a similar demonstration will occur in the heavens before the Lord comes. That prediction came to pass in the eighteenth and nineteenth centuries respectively, when the Great Lisbon earthquake (1755) occurred, the stars in a great meteoric shower fell (1833), and the sun refused to give her light (1780). These signs tell us that Jesus' return is imminent.

Based on the events of sacred and naturalistic history, we can concur with Paul: "Behold, now is the accepted time; behold, now is the day of salvation" (2 Cor. 6:2). We must not let anyone or anything deter us from heeding and responding to God's warning.

God's words stand fast. He does not lie or change, for He is constant. Humanity cannot and will not be allowed the pleasure of ignoring God's offer of mercy. When the Almighty stretches forth His hand of wrath, it is hoped that the obedient will find shelter under His strong and mighty-outstretched wings.

Currently, we are stricken with frequent tsunamis, fires, earthquakes, and floods, but this is not the end. These are only harbingers. While there is still time and Jesus is still interceding on our behalf, let us come to Him before the final judgment day comes! For who then shall be able to stand? May we press on and draw near to the Savior, so we can be sheltered and remain stable when the earth begins to *quake*.

Day 252

The **Righteous** *cry, and the Lord heareth, and delivereth them out of all their troubles.*
Psalm 34:17

Now is the time to serve the Lord; now is the time to seek His face. God is waiting in tender compassion for us to come to Him. Listen to David: "The righteous cry and the Lord heareth, and delivereth." Isn't that a just, caring, and concerned God? He responds when we cry; his Word is true. His spokesman said, "Seek ye the Lord while he may be found, call ye upon him while he is near" (Isa. 55:6). Our responsibility is to act.

This text assures the righteous that God is their stronghold and sure defense; He hears their cries and delivers them out of all their troubles. He also sees the actions of the wicked and revolts at their behaviors.

Under Pharaoh's 400 years of brutality and enslavement of God's chosen children in Egypt, they cried unto Yahweh for deliverance, and He sent Moses and Aaron to deliver them. God delivered them, and He will deliver us. He is a trustworthy God, and there is, has never been, nor will there ever be another like Him. He stands alone as the supreme Majesty of heaven and earth. He is the All-knowing, All-caring, All-powerful God. Consequently, humankind can trust him. He declares Himself: "I am the Lord, and there is none else" (Isa. 45:5).

When the righteous are oppressed or afflicted and they call upon God, through His compassion, mercy, and loving-kindness, He intervenes and delivers them out of all their troubles. Righteous people are obedient, pure, and unpolluted with sin; they do right things and stand blameless before the triune God.

When Jesus returns, He is coming for the righteous—the saints who are without guile or deceit. He is coming for those that have gotten the victory over every kind of addiction or sinful practice. Righteous living demands commitments to a life of purity, one in which sin and its allurements have no dominion over anyone. The righteous have no taste or desire to revisit the past, for God, through Jesus, has set them free and empowered them to live righteously and uprightly.

Let the upright cry unto God always, for this God can do everything. He frees, delivers, restrains, and retains. May we, by God's grace, strive to live *righteously* knowing that Jesus gives us the power to live victoriously!

Day 253

> *My* **Soul** *is weary of my life; I will leave my complaint upon myself; I will speak in the bitterness of my soul. Job 10:1*

At this time in Job's life, he was not as confident and upbeat as the last time we heard him speak: "Though he slay me, yet will I trust in him" (Job 13:15); "Naked came I out of my mother's womb, and naked shall I return" (Job 1:21); "Shall we receive good at the hand of God, and shall we not receive evil?" (Job 2:10). At that time Job expressed great confidence in his Redeemer, who would vindicate him in the latter day when He returned to earth. But now, Job was courting a defeatist mentality and venting his anger. His pain, discomforts, anguished spirit, and traumatic losses had taken a toll on his psyche, and his spiritual reservoir was running low. Now he even loathed his life—"my soul is weary of my life." Could Job be suicidal?

Reflecting on his condition, he engaged in self-therapy: "I will leave my complaint upon myself" or in other words, "I will speak through the bitterness of my soul." He hoped to make sense of his dilemma, but those were his realities: an emaciated body with unbearable pain, a scorned wife, and comfortless friends, who chasten rather than console. All left Job very isolated and alienated. He was not just dismayed; he was downright discouraged, despaired, and depressed. He is "right for the picking" from Satan's perspective; for on that weapon of despair, Satan places his highest bid. When he gets a person in the vale of despair, a demise by his or her own hand is nigh.

Certainly, Job knew his God and assuredly said, "I know that my redeemer liveth" (Job 19:25). He also knew that in his dissolute condition, he could reach out to God, who would hear and help him. Righteous Job was neither ashamed nor unwilling to cry out unto God for immediate help.

Even though Job was at his wits end and weary of the severe challenges, he never expressed suicidal thoughts, even though his wife encouraged him to "curse God, and die" (Job 2:9). His response was, "Thou speakest as one of the foolish women speaketh" (Job 2:10). These are not the words of a man on the brink of the grave, but of one who is prepared to fight life to the hilt.

Job's talk therapy brings about catharsis. He gains insight, wisdom, and knowledge, and he finally arrives at that moment of truth. His condition becomes real, and he can now converse intelligently with his Maker. He said, "I will say unto God, Do not condemn me; shew me wherefore thou contendest with me" (Job 10:2).

God heard his cry, came to his aid, and delivered him from all his adversities. Job endured; he won the prize. He pressed on through suffering, chastening, and rejection from his closest and dearest ones and emerged as pure gold. Through his ordeal these words buttressed and stabilized him: "I know that my redeemer liveth!" God stood at the side of his faithful servant, and He strengthened and encouraged him to endure the challenges. Through it all Job did not blame God neither did he sin, but he maintained his integrity. He knew that God was at work in his life, and God honored his faith. He avowed that though worms destroy his human body, he would one day see God. God gave him the victory! May we strengthen our *souls* to be able to stand as Job did!

Day 254

> **Trust** *ye not in a friend, put ye not confidence in a guide: keep the doors of thy mouth from her that lieth in thy bosom. Micah 7:5*

Holy Writ states, "A man that hath friends must shew himself friendly: and there is a friend that sticketh closer than a brother" (Prov. 18:24). In this text the prophet warns against trusting in friendship relations. It seems puzzling. Let us get to the essence of the text.

There was a sad time in Israel when no one could be trusted. Selfishness abounded, and there was total moral decline. The good men and women were all perished from the land, and only evil prevailed. Even those who were supposed to be the best and exemplars (leaders) were like briars. They had spines and thorns that pricked. There was none to trust. Since the land was devoid of honesty, sincerity, and trustworthiness, every man and woman was the enemy of the other. Therefore, the counsel was not to trust even your friend for he or she too might be devious. Things were so bad that the counsel extended to the closet companion or lover—one who shares your bosom and your confidence i.e. your spouse, sweetheart, or concubine. You could not even share your thoughts with your lover, for he or she might pull a Delilah number on you. What a tragedy!

Deceit, cunning, and craft pervaded government, society, families, and friends. The condition was so pervasive that not even the "good families" were left unsullied. Everything and everyone was touched and tainted. A foul miasma existed; everything was at breaking point. The family system was in disarray; there was widespread immorality and flouting of the principles and statutes of the Almighty. Social graces were rejected, and there was mass confusion in the family respect to where even daughters were against their mothers and daughters-in-law against mothers-in-law (Micah 7:6). The men seemed to have lost their capacity to manage their households. Who knows? Maybe there was also widespread incest. Why the outrage among the women and such ineptitude among the men?

When families, societies, and nations walk away from the counsels and direction of the True Witness and the Word of God and set themselves up as their own leaders, then there will be chaos in the respective areas of human activity. If trust and confidence are gone, there is nothing left but an aching void. When society reaches that point, they must come back and reconnect with the Great Giver of life. They must acknowledge their mistakes, confess their sins, repent, surrender, and seek forgiveness in order to return to the hallowed paths designed from the beginning.

Selfishness, which lies at the heart of such behaviors, must be eliminated. Each person, family member, and leader of the household must reconnect with God and pray David's prayer: "Search me, O God, and know my heart: try me, and know my thoughts" (Ps. 139:23). Trust and integrity must be restored, and goodness and genuine regard for each other must be established and maintained. It is an unhealthy situation for one to go on living in fear, doubt, uncertainty, and insecurity. We must learn to trust again. Only the love of God transmitted to our hearts can make that a possibility. May everyone claim God's power to restore loyalty so that faithfulness and *trust* will be fostered!

Day 255

What do you imagine against the Lord? he will make an **Utter** *end: affliction shall not rise up the second time. Nahum 1:9*

God shall intervene and "make an utter end of the place thereof, and darkness shall pursue his enemies" (verse 8). This is the prediction and later fulfillment of the prophetic utterances and warnings against that wicked city of Nineveh. This was a city full of all kinds of profligacy, and it stands as an example of when God says He will destroy a thing, people or place, He does it.

The prophet, Jonah came and warned the inhabitants of the city of its impending doom. His message was: "Yet forty days, and Nineveh shall be overthrown" (Jonah 3:4).

The king having heard the message did not discount the warning as idle chatter. He knew that destruction was imminent unless the people repented of their evil, so he proclaimed a fast. The king believed God's warning and called a solemn convocation in which human, beast, and all creatures to fast—to forsake their evil activities and seek forgiveness just in case God might relent. God saw their commitment and accepted their sincerity.

The second generation of Ninevites reconnected with evil and did more evil in the sight of God than their ancestors; they provoked and angered God, so the prophet pronounced their doom. God's heart of mercy had reached its zenith, and they had no reprieve. The prophet said, "He will make an utter end of sin."

God carried out His mighty act, and the city was razed; no life form existed anymore. God also destroyed Sodom and Gomorrah for their profligate behaviors as well as the antediluvians, who refused to respond to Noah's message of warning. God will ultimately do so again to this fair earth and its inhabitants. Yes, He will make an *utter* end of sin this time.

Despite humankind's rejection of God's message and his messengers, the Lord is "slow to anger, and great in power, and will not at all acquit the wicked" (Nahum 1:3). Thus, they cannot conspire to outwit God. He is the powerful Almighty, and He will make a final end of sin. The city of Nineveh was utterly destroyed at the invasion of the Babylonian captivity in 612 BC.

Nineveh like its predecessors—Sodom and Gomorrah, which are now beneath the Dead Sea—received God's curse, was never rebuilt, and remains desolate to this day (according to sacred history). This act of God also prefigures the end of this world when God will send Jesus back to this earth, and sin will be utterly eradicated. The text, though one of doom, offers hope and solace to the Christian: there will be no more tears, pain, sorrow, heartaches, or affliction of any kind. There will be no more sin, but one eternal reign of peace. May Jesus come and put an *utter* end to sin!

Day 256

And, behold, the **Veil** *of the temple was rent in twain from the top to the bottom; and the earth did quake, and the rocks rent. Matthew 27:51*

This is the most cataclysmic event the world has ever experienced. This onetime event occurred in AD 31 when Jesus, Redeemer and Savior, breathed His last. The text tells the reaction of the spiritual and natural world.

The officiating priests were offering the afternoon sacrifice, but then in an instant they observed the veil that separated the two compartments split from top to bottom and reveal their activities to everyone. The sheep over which they held their knives ready for the slaughter galloped away, and there was widespread consternation, as the priests stood there with trembling hands. Jesus, the Son of God, the real sacrificial Lamb, had been offered up to God, and there was no more need for the blood of animals to atone for humanity's sins.

The great door was open to all; sinful men and women could now speak directly to God through prayer. Everyone could confess his or her errors and seek repentance. Jesus had opened the way. Do you remember what he told Phillip? "I am the way" (John 14:6). Yes, Jesus cleared the way; He unlocked the bolt and set the door ajar, and every man, woman, and child can now enter freely. The veil having been split open symbolized the permanent opening of God's presence to humanity and their free and direct access to God through Christ's atoning death.

In Germany the impregnable Berlin wall separated the east from the west. While visiting Germany, President Ronald Regan said to the leader of the Soviet Union, "Tear down that wall, Mr. Gorbachev." A series of political events led to the citizens of East and West Germany tearing the wall down on November 9, 1989. Finally, the indomitable human-made veil was removed, opening the door to free access. There was great rejoicing over the destruction of the wall.

More than 2,000 years ago, Jesus tore down the ceremonial veil and gave humanity free access to His Father. Jesus stated that He came to set humanity free, and by offering His life, He procured freedom for humankind (see Luke 4:18, 19).

Institutions should not set up strongholds to keep people restricted, separated, or alienated. Christ has unlocked the door, and humankind is free to know God for Himself and to worship the Creator. Christ came and bore witness of the way humanity should live and relate to each other, honoring God first in all their transactions and activities. Jesus tore down all the man-made cumbersome, traditional, institutional, societal, cultural, and iniquitous walls, and now everyone has free access. Jesus' death brings freedom to the entire universe, especially earthlings, for it is for our sakes that He came, suffered, bore abuses, and died. The best news is that Jesus has removed the *veil*, and now everyone is free to accept God's invitation. May all who hear accept!

Day 257

Wherewithal *shall a young man cleanse his way? By taking heed thereto according to thy word. Psalm 119:9*

The young man is asking a very vexing and troubling question about life's direction. Engaging in self-communing, he wants an answer to a seemingly uncertain, doubtful, and enigmatic issue. The question is how?

This youth desires to live a pure, unsullied life away from the corrupting influences of a filthy social and emotional environment. The task seems almost impossible. Where on earth can he find stasis, peace, self-control, and unabashed purity? In his reverie the Spirit speaks to his inner voice saying: "By taking heed [meaning to live] … according to thy word." What does the Word say? "Do justly, … love mercy, and … walk humbly with thy God" (Micah 6:8).

This is a very tall order when one is surrounded by unhealthy influences, and all one's peers are doing it. No one can attain this on his or her own. Each must have counsel and strength more dynamic than the tempting and alluring influences. Where and how can they find the power and strength required to resist? A stronger voice repeats: "By taking heed thereto according to thy word" (Ps. 119:9). Speaking through the prophet Isaiah, God says, "Before they call, I will answer; and while they are yet speaking, I will hear" (Isa. 65:24). This is God's promise, and it is a glorious confirmation to everyone, especially the struggling youth.

The seeker learns what to do to escape the corrupting miasma of the age: "Thy word have I hid in my heart, that I might not sin against thee" (Ps. 119:11). Here is the solution for all seekers of righteousness: children, youth, and adults. We must not only hide (memorize) Scripture texts to refrain from temptation, but we must daily put God's Word to work in our lives so that it will guide us in all we do.

There is still more help from the Word of God: "Thy word is a lamp unto his feet, and a light unto his path" (verse 105). In the darkness one can stumble, but God's word provides both light and heat. God's Word is God Himself (see John 1:1–3). In the journey from Egypt to Canaan, God was with His people providing both light and warmth. God never leaves any of His children to fumble and stumble in the dark. Of Him, it is said, "In him is no darkness at all" (1 John 1:5); He is light eternally!

Because the Word operates as a lamp and a light, if a person grasps and internalizes it and hides it in his or her heart, it will direct both the young and the old to the right path and enlighten all decisions that he or she makes. May they seize the Word, trust God, and turn their lives over to His care! Therein lies the answer to the question.

Day 258

> *Righteousness* **Exalteth** *a nation: but sin is a reproach to any people. Proverbs 14:34*

National righteousness and national sin have opposite effects. This message presents both sides of the equation. The two major variables that impact humanity's existence are good versus evil. For many of us, there are always two options: one is the way that seems right, but it only seems or appears to be; the other is the right way. Humanity needs sound judgment to make the right decision. Many times the decision to follow a certain path appears attractive and appealing, but it usually produces tragic results.

Robert Frost, a great American poet, wrote in his famous poem, *Two Roads*: "Two roads divide into a narrow path and I took the one less travelled ... and that has made all the difference." Every action in life presents a choice, and the person who chooses uprightness will be exalted. On the contrary, reveling in sinful and baneful practices brings disgrace, disapproval, and debasement.

Ancient and modern history are replete with numerous examples of nations that followed their own inclinations and practiced abominable atrocities that resulted in genocide, decimation of human life, death, destruction, condemnation, annihilation, and the deprecation of human dignity. Thus, a society that practices what Micah calls justice, humility, and goodness will certainly be stronger and more successful than the one that practices evil.

Moses and Joshua, in their respective roles as commanders in chief of the Israelites en route to the Promised Land, repeatedly gave those ancients a choice: "Choose you this day whom you will serve" (Josh. 24:15). In response to the challenge, some chose God, but many chose idolatry and rejected God's commands and engaged in sinful practices. Hence, Jehovah delivered them into the hands of their oppressive enemies who punished them. They became reprobates.

The Chronicles document the actions of nations and rulers engaging in unholy competition ascertaining who could eclipse each other in prowess, evil, and villainy. Even the sons who gained ascendancy to the throne sought to outdo their fathers' evil; sacred history is replete with the consequences of their actions. Thus, a people and a nation that fear, worship, adore, and obey the living God will undoubtedly be exalted, for God is on their side directing their paths. They will always triumph. Consequently, God's name will be uplifted and men and women will be drawn to Him in adoration and praise, for they recognize that there is a God in the universe directing and rewarding the inhabitants accordingly. Obedient nations will prosper.

Let kings, rulers, presidents, and all commanding leaders lead its citizens to fear and honor the great God of the universe by being an example to their people. A nation cannot rise above the norms set by the rulers. If

God is directing the affairs of all, there will be no reproach to the nation, people, society, or individuals. May righteousness and equanimity be *exalted*!

Day 259

> *Neither* **Yield** *ye your members as instruments of unrighteousness unto sin: but* **Yield** *yourselves unto God, as those that are alive from the dead, and your members as instruments of righteousness unto God. Romans 6:13*

This text points to the stewardship of one's body. Our bodies do not belong to us; they are God's property, and He dwells in us through the vehicle of the Holy Spirit (see 1 Cor. 3:16, 17; 6:19, 20). The text tells us that whoever we serve, we are his servants, whether it is to sin unto death or of obedience unto righteousness. Humanity has to choose, and his or her choice dictates the result.

This is a precious reminder as to whom we allow access to the avenues of the soul, mind, heart, eyes, ears, lips, hands, and feet. We are children of God, and we are made in His image. Our bodies are to be His sanctuaries. "What? know ye not that your body is the temple of the Holy Ghost?" (1 Cor. 6:19). Do you know that God the Creator could choose to inhabit your body?

In a temple designed for worship, nothing that is impure or defiles enters, for God's presence is forever there. Similarly, since this body and its respective parts are God's, we do not have the freedom to engage in sinful practices or behaviors that would deter God's presence in our lives. On a daily basis, we ought to yield ourselves wholly unto God.

The apostle Paul says that yielding to God is "your reasonable service" (Rom. 12:1). So, we should stop yielding to sinful practices. God's Holy Spirit is available to attend to us and help us become in our daily experience what Christ has declared us to be—sons and daughters of God, His brother and sister. However, if we choose to continue giving in to wickedness, then we are servants (or slaves) of the evil one and have abdicated our title. God wants us to be obedient and to use our bodies as weapons of righteousness, remembering full well that both sin and righteousness produce distinctly different results and rewards.

We need a determined commitment to stay away from sinful habits. We must engage our members in practicing right doings in order to become servants of the living God and not subjects of God's rival.

A stanza from "Yield Not to Temptation" by H. R. Palmer in the *Christ in Song* hymnal will suffice:
Yield not to temptation; for yielding is sin;
Each victory will help you some other to win.
Fight manfully onward, dark passions subdue
Look ever to Jesus, he will carry you through.

Let us not forget that our God "will not suffer you to be tempted above that ye are able" (1 Cor. 10:13). Through Christ, we can be overcomers. May each of us determine not to *yield unto temptation*!

Day 260

As many as I love, I rebuke and chasten: be **Zealous** *therefore, and repent.*
Revelation 3:19

These are the direct words of Jesus to His servant, John, while in vision on the isle of Patmos situated in the Aegean Sea. This message was for the Christian church then living an indifferent lifestyle toward spiritual things. It is a potent message for us as well.

God declares His love to all and urges repentance. He warns against insincerity and indifference toward Him and the love of materialism. He is a jealous God and is also zealous for our love. He promised that He would chasten not punitively, but correctively and that the discipline would change behaviors.

Let us fast-forward to our time, evaluate the counsel, and see its relevance to our situation. To cancel our uncaring and indifferent attitude of servicing the poor and needy, we must reignite the passion (zeal) we once had for the brethren and the work. If the fire of God's love is burning in our hearts, we will be obedient and shall escape God's disciplinary measures. In love, He advises us to be earnest about Him. We need to rekindle the love that we had when we first met Him. There is need to wake out of false security, for we have settled into this frame of mind.

As the Holy Spirit reenters our lives, He will convict us of our attitude and behavior, and He will lead us to repent, forsake, and turn our hearts back to God. He is waiting and urges us to be zealous and excited about the offer, and He hopes that we turn away from the slippery path on which we travel. He wants us to establish genuine faith, spiritual understanding, and a rejuvenated passion for the pure, true, beautiful, and lovely.

What vision of God do we currently have? What virtues are we practicing? How much wealth do we have in the bank of heaven? These are serious, contemplative issues. Do we prefer God's chastening rod or will we repent? There are two roads before us, and we must choose. Will we heed Jesus' counsel to repent or will we walk away saying, "I know what is best for me"? Think on these things!

May we pray to recapture the *zeal* we once had for things of the Spirit and be reinstated in God's favor!

The Power of God's Name

Day 261

*For I am not **Ashamed** of the gospel of Christ: for it is the power of God unto salvation to every one that believeth; to the Jew first, and also to the Greek. Romans 1:16*

This is the apostle Paul's manifesto. He proudly declared his relationship with Christ and his newfound mission. He may have read Jesus' words: "Whoever acknowledges me before others, I will also acknowledge before my Father in heaven. But whoever disowns me … I will disown before my Father in heaven" (Matt. 10:32, 33, NIV). To disown and deny connote shame. Having had his encounter with the Man of Calvary on the Damascus road, Paul was not taking any chances by not doing right by Jesus. He could publicly tell the brethren that he was a proud man; he had pride in the Gospel. He was proud to be aligned with the saving message of Jesus Christ and prouder yet to proclaim it.

Paul was ashamed of his former deeds, but now, joy and gladness replaced shame. God had met him on the Damascus road, thwarted his diabolical plans, and chose him to be His special vessel to bear His message to the Gentiles. In repeating his manifesto to the congregants, he was able to show that he was living proof of God's love and power to change and transform lives.

Paul was not ashamed to be associated with the cause, for it had and still has the power to save everyone who believes. Its life-changing properties are available to everyone who wants to take this step. The gospel message is non-discriminatory. It knows no creed, clime, culture, class, or status—rich or poor. All stand in need of God's saving grace. Even though grace is freely given, one simply has to reach out, grasp it, and believe that anyone can be redeemed, no matter what their situation is in life. The red blood of Jesus has within it the cleansing power to remove every stain of sin. That is the gospel message—the very good news that Paul was called to preach.

Are you ashamed because you are a Christian and believe the good news? Are you ashamed to be associated with Christ? Remember what He said. If ever you are tempted to deny your relationship with Jesus, take a look at Peter, and remember what the good news is about. It is the message of salvation—that Jesus came, offered His life, and shed His precious blood to save you and me. You are a part of the throng. The Jews had the opportunity to be arbiters of this magnificent gift of grace and to proclaim the good news to others—the Greek, aliens, and Barbarians—but they reneged. God had to single-handedly seize Paul and make him become His chosen vessel.

The good news is for all people everywhere. Christ is not ashamed to make Himself equal with God, for He is God. Consequently, we should never be ashamed to be called a Christian or a Jesus follower. We are Christians because we bear the name of Christ, and Christ is in our teaching, preaching, and in our living. That summons pride, for we are aligned to God. May you acquaint yourself with Him and be at peace so that you may never be *ashamed* of the Crucified One!

Day 262

*In the **Beginning** God created the heaven and the earth. Genesis 1:1*

Every life form has a beginning or a starting point. No one knows when the beginning began. That is a prerogative entombed in the bosom of the Creator. In Him, with Him, and through Him all things consist. Humankind, in all their ingenuity, is unable to create something from nothing. We may have an idea, but to start the initiative, we have to use preexistent matter. This beginning is still very enigmatic and is better left unexplored.

In the procreation process, there is need for an ovum and a sperm. How the Creator fuses them is still baffling to both gynecologists and obstetricians. Holy Writ tells us that God brought the entire process into existence. How and when the beginning was is still a mystery. To trace our ancestral roots to Noah's children would be unprofitable. I recently read the Old Testament book of 2 Chronicles, Ezra chapters 7 and 8, and Nehemiah chapters 6 and 7 where people traced ancestral roots generations back and that was some four millennia past. How difficult it would be to try and trace your roots back to two millennia! Therefore, it is futile to try and identify or connect with the beginning of beginnings.

Every human being has a beginning—the day he or she was conceived. Each of us, unfortunately, has a life span. Every morning when we wake up, we begin a new day, a new life, a new moment, a new hour, and even a new course of study. Our entire life is wrapped up with beginnings and starting points. When we rebel, disconnect, and reject God's way, we miss our chance to reconnect with Jesus. However, when we strive for a relationship with the Almighty, we begin a new walk with Him in a new direction.

Who is able to answer humanity's inquiry about their beginning and the existence of other life forms? If we had answers, there would still be more questions. The patriarch and sufferer, Job, gave the most poignant response to that inquiry: "Canst thou by searching find out God? canst thou find out the Almighty unto perfection?" (Job 11:7). Job's reply is our final answer. The finite cannot question the working and operation of the infinite God. God and humans are not equals. God does not have to answer to us or reveal more than we need to know. For us to continue questioning is both presumptuous and disrespectful to the Creator.

In some scientific areas, we have tried to clone our kin, but God's illimitable ways are not found in the lab but in His eternal bosom. Science cannot imitate God, for God created science. Scientists may try to mimic His power, but it will all be convoluted. God has determined our boundaries, and we must abide in His territory.

Let us begin each day with thanksgiving and praise knowing that our Creator is in charge of all things. Every person has a beginning. At the onset of our existence is God and that beginning still remains a mystery. May we thank God for all new *beginnings*!

Day 263

A foolish son is the **Calamity** *of his father: and the contentions of a wife are a continual dropping. Proverbs 19:13*

King Solomon continues his counsel to the youth, but it is specific to the young men because it is a patriarchal society. Fathers were the head of their families and sons were being trained to emulate their father and to bring him joy. Solomon extols wisdom and inveighs heavily against folly, foolishness, idleness, and forwardness, especially among the upcoming patriarchy. Repeatedly, he calls the sons to be wise and to adhere to their father's advice. He knows that young people tend not to take the counsel of their fathers (or mothers) very well. Though inexperienced, they frown upon their elders' counsel and deride their utterances. No doubt the king might have seen the calamitous results of some who behaved foolishly.

Solomon is chiding the wayward ones. It is as if he is saying, "If you do not listen, you will bring your father to shame and ruin." The son's role is to be his father's delight. Fathers expect their sons to be the progenitors of the race, and if they are acting foolishly, they cannot make sound decisions and may misuse the gifts bequeathed them (see Luke 15). Based on the wise man's observation, he is calling the son—and all youth—to attend to wisdom.

This text further calls for sobriety and self-control in the family dynamics. Two different situations are cited: the foolish son not heeding counsel and a contentious and nagging wife. There is need for common understanding, contentment, and gratitude. If the wife and mother is quarrelsome and overbearing, she grates the husband's nerves and brings calamity to the family. The father cannot find love, peace, happiness, or support from those nearest and dearest to him. The son shows no sign of leadership or any positive direction for his life, and the wife's continual nagging saps all his psychological energy. Both son and wife are a continual irritation to him.

To avoid a family calamity, the entire family must be engaged in constant dialogue. They must communicate their plans, ideas, expectations, desires, goals, and dreams. They should seek common ground and get advice and sober counsel from the more experienced. When this is accomplished, family unity will be established or reestablished. There will be common understanding, improved communication, and the family will achieve homeostasis.

The father, as head of the household, will instruct them in the ways of the Lord, and there will be joy, direction, contentment, and much wisdom circulating among the occupants. The sons and daughters will leave that house with a strong knowledge of God's will, for their lives and the father will be joyful. All children must let their fathers find delight in their actions and behaviors; they must under all occasions shun folly and embrace wisdom. The Word of the Lord authorizes it. May the wife be a continuous source of delight to her husband and not add to his *calamity*!

Day 264

A man's heart **Deviseth** *his way: but the Lord directeth his steps. Proverbs 16:9*

This is one of King Solomon's most profound utterances. He was speaking of God's omnipotence and omniscience. We like to boast and parade our ideas and accomplishments as though they were self-made. We often forget that even though we may plan our course of action, it is God at the helm. He directs the process and determines the outcome.

When I was growing up, the local rendition of this verse was: "Man plans, but God wipes out." And literature refined it: "Man approves, but God disproves." Succinctly, God controls our lives, actions, and activities as He sees best and for our own good. Sometimes we become discouraged and even angry because the best made plans go awry, and we blame God saying we prayed and asked God's direction. Why then should things go askew? We should take cue from the text: "There is a way which seemeth right unto a man; but the end thereof are the ways of death" (Prov. 14:12).

We have no idea what lies ahead–today, tomorrow or the years ahead. God, the all-seeing, all-knowing One, knows the best path, and even though our plans seem flawless, we cannot see the pitfalls that await us. The omniscient God will steer us a right. Sometimes, the road becomes a graveled path and the seemingly best plans go awry, but God is in charge. He knows the best, and He is leading. We must submit and accept His way.

Prudence suggests that before anyone embarks on any mission, he should place his plans before God. That is, pray before you plan, pray before you act, and pray in the execution of the task. Thus guided by the Holy Spirit, you cannot go wrong. With those plans before God, He will affirm and direct them so that the expected best will be achieved. With God in charge, everything must go right.

We cannot see as God does. With Him lodges all the power of greatness, infallibility, and wisdom. God cannot err! Nothing is skewed for Him; He is always on schedule. He knows everything about everybody and what is best for each person. God is great and magnificent; may we offer continual generational praise to His name!

Lay all our plans before Him and wait. God leads and directs; trust Him with your entire life, for He is the Sovereign of heaven. Our scheming, strategizing, and planning must all be placed before God. Let us cooperate with God and yield to His direction.

Ellen White, a famous inspirational writer, paraphrases the text beautifully: "God never leads His children otherwise than they would choose to be led, if they could see the end from the beginning and discern the glory of the purpose they are fulfilling as co-workers with Him" (*Ministry of Healing*, p. 479). Surely we plan, but God executes and directs. May we allow Him to *devise* a plan for our lives!

Day 265

> **Every** *good gift and every perfect gift is from above, and cometh down from the Father of lights, with whom is no variableness, neither shadow of turning. James 1:17*

Are we to understand that there is gift selectivity and preferential giftedness? That some are good and perfect and others are bad and imperfect? This is a troubling question. If some people have bad gifts, what are they to do with them? A gift is unsolicited and unexpected. It would be very sad to be given an abominable gift!

However, I am overjoyed that all are gifted in the Christian arena. According to the apostle Paul, when Jesus returned to be with His Father, He gave gifts unto all His followers (see 1 Cor. 12). Thankfully, God gives no bad gifts.

Each person is gifted. Each person is endowed with the ability to do something to aid in the harmonious operation of all public, social, and spiritual structures. The good and perfect gift is God-given by the Holy Spirit. The gift of healing, offering consolation and hope, of prayer, of teaching, of ministering, or of administrating are all good gifts because they are used to benefit a person, organization, and society in some way. Take for example, the gift of leadership, if there was no one thus gifted, how would society operate? If there were no people with the spirit of insight and discernment, how would quarrels and disputes be discussed and settled? If there were no people with the gift of understanding commerce and trade, how would the economic life be sustained? Every gift is designed to make human existence tolerable, peaceful, and operational.

The up end is: if you use your gift to stir up evil and confusion, to spew venom and to generate mischief, then you are surely misusing it. A gift is something very precious and unique. Some people have the gift of creating and understanding music. Some have the gift of wood working and cabinetry; others have the gift of working the soil. Some have the gift of administration, and some the gift of wisdom. All these gifts are designed to edify humankind. The best news is that everyone is gifted. Take for example, the gift of patience. Anyone who possesses such is highly regarded; his or her counsel is always sought after, for this person is able to bring stability to any rough situation.

Spiritually, the gifts given to the church members are designed for the uplifting and edification of the Lord's name and to build up the church. Hence, the apostle advises that the gifted ones in the Christian congregation should not use their gifts outwardly to boast their superiority to others, but use them inwardly to glorify God.

Your gift is pragmatic if it is used to bless society and humankind as well as honor and glorify God's name. God has no favorites. All His creatures are equally endowed. Every gift is heaven sent. Paul suggests: "But covet earnestly the best gifts" (1 Cor. 12:31). May *every* single one of us covet the special gift of love!

Day 266

*Wherefore by their **Fruits** ye shall know them. Matthew 7:20*

This discussion emanated from the need to identify the characteristics of a prophet, whether he or she is true or false. Both the Old and New Testaments are replete with cues of identifying the true prophet from the false. The most outstanding Old Testament reference is that "their predictions must come to pass" (see Deut. 18:22; Amos 3:7; Isa. 8:20). In the New Testament, Jesus uttered these famous words cited above. Peter also refers to prophets' validity (see 2 Peter 1:19–21).

Whereas this discussion took place in a Christian environment and among new Christian disciples, it is not only addressed to the Christian community but humankind, in general. The illustration of the tree producing fruit is very appropriate to the simplest mind. Every tree produces some kind of fruit—edible or inedible—fruit of its own species and genus.

Jesus referenced that each tree produces its own kind and the disciples understood the analogy very well having lived in an agricultural environment. Jesus, the master communicator, always used familiar illustrations to teach the more profound and didactic lessons.

All our actions produce results that are either genuine or superficial. If we do good deeds, the result will be goodness and mercy. There is no pretence or simulation in the agricultural world. A mango tree does not bear mangoes in one season and oranges or pears in the next. Therefore, a true believer cannot but exude that which is genuine and characteristic of the Lord of his or her life. We will reveal whether our actions bear evidence of a life totally committed to God or His rival. One cannot render half-hearted service; we all have to be genuine. Thus, if a prophet's messages are directed by God, his or her predictions will come to pass. The prophet must be in conformity to the doctrine he or she espouses. But if not, they will be unproductive. Nothing will happen, and the supposed prophet will be seen as a fake and an imposter. Similarly, Christians must produce fruits of holiness, purity, and genuine Christ-like behaviors.

The lives of all expositors of the truth must attest those principles. Pray that your life is a testament of the truth you posit, for by your fruits, people will know if you are real or a hypocrite and a pretender. May the real you, the Christ-directed you, bear His *fruits*.

Day 267

***Gather** my saints together unto me; those that have made a covenant with me by sacrifice.*
Psalm 50:5

God, our judge and arbiter, has issued a call to the holy angels to bring to Him all His people who have covenanted to serve Him all the days of their lives. Whatever troubles, trials, and discomforts they have endured, it will all be worth it, for no individual sacrifice can equate with the eternal sacrifice of the triune Godhead—the Father, Son, and Holy Ghost. Jesus Christ, the incarnate God, came to this world to erase sin. In that act the Father gave, the Son yielded, and the Holy Spirit confirmed.

God accepts the genuine sacrifice of those who put self aside and make room for the Holy Spirit to direct their lives. Those who have chosen God's way and have forsaken family, earthly acquisitions, and an exceedingly rich lifestyle, God offers His rest. God gave His all. A line from "I Gave My Life for Thee" in *The Seventh-day Adventist Hymnal* concurs, "I gave, I gave My life for thee, what hast thou given for Me?"

What greater joy, hope, and expectation await the saints than to come in the presence of the Father! He wants to meet with His children and crown them with blessings, honor, and immortality. He is waiting for their arrival.

We have to give up something to follow the Master who says, "So likewise, whosoever he be of you that forsaketh not all that he hath, he cannot be my disciple" (Luke 14:33). He will gather the covenanted, obedient, and faithful ones to Himself and imbue them with life everlasting. The careless, indifferent, and whoremongers will be scattered. They will be without a shelter in that great gathering up day. Plan to be among the faithful ones who honor God with all their heart and will be gathered to His bosom. Do you not want to be with the invited? I want to be. As I close today's meditation, the refrain of "When the Saints Go Marching In" floods my mind:

Oh when the saints go marching in
When the saints go marching in
Oh Lord I want to be in that number
When the saints go marching in

The angels will respond to their Commander and go forward. Each of us must ensure that we are among the number whom the angels will garner into the fold and present to Jesus, our Redeemer. May you plan to be among the *gathered* ones!

Day 268

> *But unto you that fear my name shall the Sun of righteousness arise with* **Healing** *in his wings; and ye shall go forth, and grow up as calves in the stall. Malachi 4:2*

This text offers great promise and hope to all, but especially to the obedient. Yesterday's text revealed God's commission to the angelic host to gather to Him His obedient ones who have partnered with Him for eternal life. Today's text gives further assurance that the Sun of righteousness—Jesus—will bring healing and erase all the dysfunctions that beset the obedient. Who would not want to be healed of all humankind's maladies?

Malachi 4:1 states that turmoil, confusion, sickness, disaster, and total unrest will precede the return of our Lord. Because of unconfessed sins and ungodly lifestyle among a significant group of professed Christians, there will be massive panic, fear, and trembling. These will be fearful times for the unrepentant! But for the obedient, who heard, respected, and honored God's holy name, His coming will be a breath of fresh air to a foul environment, like the rainbow of promise after a tornado or hurricane. He is the Sun of righteousness, the Messiah, Jesus, the One slain for sinners. His first coming brought hope, deliverance, and healing to the oppressed. At His second coming, there will be no more diseases of any kind, and the redeemed will be young calves fed at the stalls with holy nutrients, so they can thrive. Isaiah 65 vividly describes the new life attendant with the coming of this Sun of righteousness. Everything and everyone will be healed.

What shall be their food and nourishment? Foods that bring healing. The Lord Himself will be in charge of the menu, and He will serve the redeemed. Jesus promises that in the new environment, the redeemed will eat from the tree of life and the leaves of the tree will bring healing to them. The Redeemer, the Sun of righteousness, brings the Son and Sun power to the saved. What a wonderful, blissful occasion that will be! Yes, His presence is the healing warmth of the sun to the obedient; however, to the disobedient, it will be a scorching flame, for they will not abide the presence of the Almighty.

This promised hope for the future is for those who trust God with their lives. Let us celebrate Jesus' second coming and be ready! He is coming to put an end to every form of disease that afflicts humanity. He will bring joy, happiness, and wellness forever. May we look to that moment and find hope in His *healing*!

Day 269

Blessed is the man to whom the Lord will not **Impute** *sin. Romans 4:8*

Amen! And amen! Here is another beautiful promise from the Word. Paul shows how a merciful God deals with sinners. Any person whose sins are forgiven and covered by the blood of Jesus is deemed righteous; he or she is safe, secure, and blessed. This references the Israelites whose doorposts had to be covered with blood so that the destroying angel would pass over them when he came to wreak destruction on Egypt.

Similarly, we need to be covered with the blood of Jesus so that sin will have no control over us. The text more so poignantly affirms that humanity is blessed, doubly blessed if God does not impute or count our sin against us. In order to forget our sins, it means God has forgiven it; He has wiped it out and merited us justice and mercy instead.

Once we confess and surrender, the Father and Son don on us a robe of righteousness–His character. He cancels our sin and writes "Forgiven" beside our name. He treats us as though we have had no prior infraction. Bow and say, "Thank You, Father!" Shout "Praise the Lord!"

Everyone can connect with the apostle's reference. When you go before a judge, even if it's for a parking ticket violation, he or she can look at you and say, "There is no charge against you; you are free! Go!" You leave the courtroom jubilant; no charge is imputed to you! Your driving record remains intact, and you praise the judge. As you think of God's great act on your behalf, you are forced to ask the inevitable question: how could God exonerate me?

If you want to have your sins blotted out and live a pure and holy life, you must come to God and yield your sinful habits and practices to Him so that He can completely remove them and impart to us His righteous character.

As Christians, we are to ask God to impart to us life-eternal; we must acknowledge His offering and not despise it as insignificant. We must seize the opportunity to have our sins cancelled and replaced with righteousness. That is the only way He can make us just. God is willing and waiting to impute His righteous life to us. We must not keep Him waiting. If you are convinced that our God is able, why not let Him impute His righteousness today? If you choose to do it, you will be truly blessed. You will truly be free. When God releases you of those sinful habits and behaviors and writes against your name Forgiven, you will be exonerated. The greatest gift anyone can receive is to hear God's voice saying to you: "I do not count your sins against you anymore; I have erased them." I cannot wait to hear those loving words from my Savior's lips. May the Lord *impute* righteousness in all our lives.

Day 270

He hath shewed thee, O man, what is good; and what doth the Lord require of thee, but to do **Justly**, *and to love mercy, and to walk humbly with thy God? Micah 6:8*

This text is my life's mantra. It is the epitaph for my tombstone. It speaks to my total existence; it is my guiding star of how I live.

We are God's firstly by creation, and secondly, by redemption. The apostle Paul reminds us: "ye are not your own" (1 Cor. 6:19). Therefore, God has a plan and a design for each of us.

Firstly, in all our dealings and interactions with others, we have to act justly i.e. fairly, not defrauding anyone in any way or at anything. Justice or just behavior is almost a bad word in certain quarters because in some perspectives, it connotes negativity and weakness. Living a just life is associated with temerity and is reserved for the fainthearted. We live in a society where people are fighting for their "lion's share" at all costs. Even though fairness is a negative word for many, it must become an integral part of the Christian's vocabulary. God requires all His children to deal fairly and justly with others.

Secondly, Christians are to love mercy. Jesus taught this principle to His disciples. He wanted others to understand that those who show kindness and compassion to others will receive His Father's rich blessings. Mercy fits one for habitation with angels and God. Mercy is neither unkind nor harsh; it does not conduct itself in an overbearing and unforgiving manner. It is sympathy and empathy through and through. If an individual extends mercy to another, someone will reciprocate the behavior. It is incumbent on Christians to show kindness to everyone, but especially to those unable to reciprocate the act. Shakespeare even said that the quality of mercy is like the gentle rain from heaven; it blesses the receiver as well as the giver. Everyone should practice that enviable quality or seek to cultivate it.

The final principle espoused is humility—"walk humbly with thy God." What does walking humbly with God connote? It does not mean showing off or being bombastic with your skill, adeptness, oratory, or talent. We should be more like the publican, who in contrition and lowliness of spirit, recognized his unworthiness and with bowed head and bated breath, he claimed God's benevolence and goodness for the mercy meted out to him. He is our model of what it means to be meek, humble, and just.

Let Christians everywhere examine their motives and actions and see if their behaviors fit into God's template. If we reject the counsel to do justly, love mercy, and to walk humbly before our God, we will be guilty of disobedience and show contempt for God's counsel, which He expects His children to obey. May those *just* virtues be yours as well!

Day 271

> *And this gospel of the* **Kingdom** *shall be preached in all the world for a witness unto all nations; and then shall the end come. Matthew 24:14*

This is Jesus' reply to His disciples who asked Him about end time events and His imminent return. Jesus gave them a litany of events that would foreshadow His return: some would be fulfilled in their day and others must be seen later in the future (see Matt. 24).

More succinctly, this verse is considered the Great Commission: the good news about Jesus' life, mission, ministry, sacrifice, and power to save humankind must be told to everyone in the entire world. All nations and peoples of the great continents and the isles of the seas must hear His name. Everywhere and in every place, humankind must hear the good news about the kingdom of God. None is to be excluded.

When this commission is fulfilled and everyone has heard and made their decision, then the church age will come to an end. It is then that Jesus will return to earth and the Second Advent will take place. The message must be preached as a witness so that none living anywhere on the face of the planet can have an excuse not to accept Christ as the Lord of their lives. Of course, not all who hear will accept and respond, but the responsibility will be on them to either reject or accept the saving graces offered. People everywhere must be held accountable for their soul's salvation. The commission is that the gospel must be preached. How God directs the affairs after the delivery is a principle known only to Him.

This good news of the kingdom has been preached for more than twenty centuries, so the end is much closer than when the Master issued the proclamation. Our commission is to lead men and women to find Jesus. Jesus said, "Of that day and hour knoweth no man ... but my Father only" (verse 36). When the fullness of time comes, God will send Jesus back to earth to gather His redeemed; every living person will have heard the good news of grace, peace, love, holiness, and a sin-free new earth (see Isa. 65, 66; Rev. 21). This is the good news that we must preach to the entire world—to every nation and tribe.

In this twenty-first century, the kingdom message has taken on wings and is being preached through cyberspace: Internet, satellite, radio, TV, and all the various technological sources and social media. People living in the hamlets and remote villages can have the opportunity to both hear and see for themselves, and thus make their decision. May we do our part in fulfilling the Great Commission by sharing it with those we meet so that the *kingdom* will come, and Jesus will be enthroned!

Day 272

Shew thy marvellous **Lovingkindness**, *O thou that savest by thy right hand them which put their trust in thee from those that rise up against them. Psalm 17:7*

Here is a prayer for God's protection and intervention. This is one of David's many prayers for protection and deliverance from his oppressors and pursuers. There were many enemies, and he was constantly assailed on all fronts. He was like a hunted dog that they wanted dead.

This prayer exudes confidence and assurance: "I have called upon thee, for thou wilt hear me" (verse 6). This is also our plea because we know that God will hear, intervene, and deliver. We may not face traumas akin to David's, but the enemy, who wants to negate Christ's power and keep us in sin, constantly assails many of us. We must claim the promise of God's eternal power to intervene in our affairs and to bring about the right operational condition necessary for our survival. God's lovingkindness is marvelous. Who can fathom it? He stops to listen to my feeble petitions and groaning because He cares. Through love for us, He offered His only Beloved to come to redeem us. Our struggles become His, and He is committed to deliver us.

David's reference to God's lovingkindness is a model for all Christians facing the daily challenges of living. With implicit trust and confidence, he calls upon God to manifest himself to the nation: "Show me the wonders of your great love, you who save by your right hand those who take refuge in you from their foes" (verse 7, NIV).

God is dependable; no one fails who trusts in Him. David assures us that God is our refuge and strength and a stronghold in the day of battle. God is our fortress (see Ps. 46:1). These strong images point to the strength and ability of our God, who alone is able to deliver and rescue. David's son, Solomon, affirms, "The name of the Lord is a strong tower: the righteous runneth into it, and is safe" (Prov. 18:10). These assuring words calm any fear and sustain any troubled heart.

God is able to save to the uttermost; His lovingkindness, compassion, and mercy are new every morning. He is constantly revealing Himself to us through nature and the Word. He guides us as we drive on the highways, when we lie down to sleep, and when we are engaged in busy work. His Spirit speaks to us and tells us what to do and where to go to find the bargains that our limited resources can utilize. His eyes are all-seeing, and He corrects us without chastising and provides all the creature comforts we need. He is our Father, friend, and companion. We cannot engage in any activity without enlisting His support. Our God is truly great, caring, and loving. There is no other like Him. He loves even when it is unrequited, and there is no reciprocity. He continues to love because that is His nature. More than all, He is our Protector.

Our God is a deliverer. May we praise His name forever for His daily *lovingkindness* and tender mercies!

Day 273

Thou hast a **Mighty** *arm: strong is thy hand, and high is thy right hand. Psalm 89:13*

What words of consolation and assurance there are in the Word–the Holy Book! Surely God's eye has guided its production. How else could everything be so synchronized! It is the mighty Spirit that breathed upon the writers as they wrote God's messages to His people. There is a continuous thread of similarity running through the respective texts. We just read about God's lovingkindness and His power to save, and now we are brought face-to-face with the strength and might of His arm and the height of His right hand. This is indeed unfathomable (see 1 Tim. 3:16, 17)!

David continually refers to the right hand of God as the place where power, love, justice, and faithfulness are found. God's right hand is strong and powerful. One of David's pleas was, "Hold up my goings in thy paths, that my footsteps slip not" (Ps. 17:5).

When Jesus ascended to heaven in AD 31, He went to the right hand of God (see Mark 14:62). It is in the right hand that authority, power, and strength reside. Jesus, quoting Psalm 110:1, declared, "Sit thou on my right hand, till I make thine enemies thy footstool?" (Matt. 22:44).

We all want to be on the right side of things. The right arm is imbued with power and might. For many, it is the strongest side of the body. It sends forth the thrust while the left hand is used as a backup. Thus, God's arm is mighty; He stretches it out, and nobody or any natural force can bend it. It is also symbolic of the power with which He rules and executes justice and judgment.

Strength resides in the right hand, which explains the very many frequent references to the right hand of God.

God's right hand is mightier than any other hand, and when He raises it, the world trembles. He holds up worlds by the power of His might. Let us sing of God's great love forever and for the strength that is in His outstretched, mighty arm. Grasp it; lay hold of it, and let God's mighty arm raise you up and sustain you. May we continue to draw sustaining strength from God's *mighty* power!

Day 274

> *For the **Needy** shall not always be forgotten: the expectation of the poor shall not perish for ever. Psalm 9:18*

Poor and needy people are civilization's nemesis. They have always been there. Whoever or whatever source is responsible for this inequity still remains an enigma. The needy cannot subsist, for they do not have the means, ability, or the wherewithal to live viably. They are destitute and have to subsist on the benevolence of the compassionate. Poverty is as old as the world. It was so in Abraham's time, in Isaiah's time, and in David and Solomon's time. It is a part of society's DNA and has been so entrenched that when Jesus came along 4,000 years later, He had to warn the disciples about their attitude toward these indigent people. He quoted the Mosaic law: "For ye have the poor always with you" (Matt. 26:11). And Moses also said that "the poor shall never cease out of the land" (Deut. 15:11).

Some may argue that their poverty is due to lack of thrift, indolence, or idleness coupled with their indifference toward work and planning for the future. This idle attitude was very prevalent in the days of the kings, so King Solomon wrote very strongly to all, especially the youth. See Proverbs 6 regarding idleness, laziness, and wickedness. Later he talks about those who refuse to listen to the cries of the poor (see Prov. 21:13), and he asks us to always be mindful of the poor and needy. "He that hath a bountiful eye shall be blessed; for he giveth of his bread to the poor" (Prov. 22:9).

David called on his affluent realm to be aware of the plight of the needy and reminded the possessors of goods of their commitment to them. He reminded them that the needy and the poor must be satisfied. Who is to respond to their need? The hope is that those who have more than they need will reach out and satisfy those who are in need.

Our world today is individualistic, but do not let those who go without remaining in that position. Don't pick up the mentality where "Oh, it is too bad for them." The needy fall into the category of those that society rejects. Thus, a significant portion of society, especially the affluent, ignores the plight of the needy by crushing any earthly hope of rebound they may have.

The Creator did not make any poor people; nevertheless, He champions their cause and promises that their socio-economic condition will not remain sordid. God has not forsaken these suffering ones; He will help them and vindicate His people. Someone will turn and help alleviate their needy condition.

The very best news comes in this psalm that bears God's assurance and intervention. He knows our needs and the tendency to despair, but He has not ignored the cries of the afflicted. He is their refuge, strength, and stronghold in times of trouble: be it poverty, illness, or death. He will take care of all the needs each individual has. Let the needy look up; thy God is still the caring, concerned God He has always been. He will never leave nor forsake anyone. May you remain confident in this one thing: even though circumstances are not what they ought to be, God is always on time supplying every need and the "*needy* shall lie down in safety" (Isa. 14:30)!

Day 275

And the Lord brought us forth out of Egypt with a mighty hand, and with an
Outstretched *arm, and with great terribleness, and with signs, and with wonders.*
Deuteronomy 26:8

This is an oration of thanksgiving for the first fruits gathered after the ancients took up residence in their new territory—Canaan, the Promised Land.

The leader always recapped the reason for the assembly at every convocation the Israelites held. As the priests collected the offering of the first fruits brought to worship, they had to tell the new generation all that had transpired between Jehovah God and their ancestors. This was indeed necessary, for no one but Caleb and Joshua of the original stock remained. All the others who started the journey and had witnessed God's mighty hand leading them all the way had all perished during the forty year journey.

Joshua wanted these younger generations to have a thorough understanding of how and why they were there and that it was Jehovah God's mighty hand and outstretched arm that had led and directed them thus far. No man or woman had any part in their success. As a result of this explanation, they should not render "lip service" to Jehovah, for He had to work wonders to release their parents from the clutches of Pharaoh and bring them to free territory.

It was, therefore, mandatory and incumbent on the offspring to fear (revere, respect, honor, and obey) the decrees of the Almighty, because their God is good, faithful, and true. Consequently, they should worship Him all the days of their lives. Had it not been for God's patience and compassion, coupled with His lovingkindness, none would be saved. They should savor the opportunity to be in the presence of the Almighty. This offering of the first fruits was their appreciation and thanksgiving to God.

Like Caleb and Joshua, we must continue to tell our children and have them tell their children's children of the mercies, grace, and benevolence we receive at God's hands. We must tell them how God's outstretched arms have saved us from untold misery, tribulations, and trials. They need to hear about how He has watched over us when we faced dangerous challenges and how He opened doors that were closed to others. We must narrate God's goodness among us and let future generations know that we worship the same God that delivered the ancients. This generation must know and acknowledge God's existence, His created works, and His mighty power, wisdom, and great love. As quoted in the Deuteronomy 6:6–9, the process must be repetitive and generational.

Every time we come in God's presence, it must be about thanksgiving and gratitude. Our God is a mighty God. He knows all about our needs, and He promises to supply them all. He says that His hand is not short.

Indeed, His arms can be stretched as wide as the ocean and encompass all His children. Have no fear, for our God will do what He promises! He has done it before, and His words stand fast! May you lean into and trust His *outstretched* arms today!

Day 276

> *The good man is* **Perished** *out of the earth: and there is none upright among men: they all lie in wait for blood; they hunt every man his brother with a net. Micah 7:2*

This text reveals the moral condition of ancient Israel and epitomizes our current age. The circle is complete. Humankind, today, has little or no recognition of God's leading and His presence in the affairs of nations, society, and families. Many people simply do what they please and are accountable to no one.

Whether in politics, social issues, or spiritual matters, no loyalty can be found. There is total moral declension. There is no uprightness, integrity, or commitment to any person or cause. There is neither sisterly nor brotherly love in tow; there is no milk of human kindness flowing from any direction. Many are stuck in a desert, and the oasis of love cannot be found. There is constant mistrust of each other; many live in ambush and seek to bring down a right moral cause. What a terrible time and place to live! Moral confusion and dissidence reign supremely.

There is no familial trust; each person is edgy. All set a net to entrap their brother and sister. How can one bypass the hidden net before he or she is entangled there in? If the fish knew that the bait was in the net, they would not have swum into it to eat the food.

Honesty, integrity, sincerity and uprightness are so rare; no one wants to help anyone else. That is the prevailing mood, and we rationalize the rightness of our actions. Even Christians compromise their principles to be popular and look hip, for everyone is doing it.

Despite the moral and social malaise, God expects to find many like Elijah's 7,000 who stood firmly for Jehovah and rejected idolatry. He is still searching for the upright with the hope that not all the loyal and upright ones are perished. He is hoping that there is still a voice of reason. He is searching for the man, woman, or youth who takes his or her cue from God and not from society. God still needs that person to stand unsullied amidst the chaos and miasma that threaten to engulf and obliterate us.

He hopes that there are still some standing in His name. Will the righteous please stand up and come forward? The innocents must be saved, the unwary must be informed, and the ignorant must acquire wisdom. May the upright stand up and save the world from *perishing*!

Day 277

> *But avoid foolish* **Questions**, *and genealogies, and contentions, and strivings about the law; for they are unprofitable and vain. Titus 3:9*

This is one of Paul's many letters to Titus to help him in the administration and organization of the Cretan church. Whenever a new church is planted, the original planters or foundation members feel that they are the final authority on how things should be administered. Because of their great sacrifice, no newcomer should dictate to them, for the structure contains their blood, sweat, tears, labor, and money. The power to control has caused much angst over time.

In Crete, there was no difference; humankind is the same in every age. Their characters, unless sanctified, will not change. We have the same aspirations and the same striving for supremacy. Even when the Lord walked among men, two of His disciples clamored for the highest position in the future political kingdom. Today, people have only become more emboldened.

Before things get out of control, church planters and congregants should heed the instruction of this learned and chosen apostle on how to deal with those inclined to heretic ideas. Many people are stuck in the origins of their status, caste, or their culture, and they feel that they are better than the other whether it is black against white or Jews against Gentiles. The dissimilarity often goes unabated. Here Paul counsels the young pastor not to engage in any disputes regarding genealogy, heritage, family roots, or their claim to the lineage of Abraham. All who accept Christ are spiritual sons and daughters of Abraham through adoption. These arguments have nothing to do with salvation, so they are irrelevant. Rather than engaging in useless and vain disputes, one should spend the time searching the Scriptures as the apostle John references Jesus' words: "Search the scriptures; for in them ye think ye have eternal life: and they are they which testify of me" (John 5:39).

Now as then, the counsel stands. It is unwise and futile for church members, planters, and administrators to get involved in foolish, legalistic, and unprofitable arguments about church management. Paul distinctly states that when Jesus went up on high, He gave gifts unto His followers. Each person has been gifted, and the purpose of the gift is to establish and edify the church, not to break it down, cast a shadow over its operation, or to hinder the Holy Spirit's guidance.

The greatest need is for truth, wisdom, knowledge, understanding, and the Holy Spirit's leading. We need to remember to "study to shew thyself approved unto God, a workman that needeth not to be ashamed, rightly dividing the word of truth" (2 Tim. 2:15). When the Word of God becomes the guiding principle of all operations, foolishness and vain babblings will disappear. Leaders will know what God's desires. May the Holy Spirit be the guide in every action and in every decision! King David's counsel on leadership is very appropriate and should be practiced: "The law of the Lord is perfect, converting the soul: the testimony of the Lord is sure, making wise the simple" (Ps. 19:7). May church leaders study the Word, avoid irrelevant *questions*, and be selective in their governance!

Day 278

*"The **Righteous** shall inherit the land, and dwell therein for ever. Psalm 37:29*

Amen and amen! What a wonderful promise! Everyone who wants eternal life should practice right living: walk uprightly with integrity, give love, show mercy, and stand in humility before God.

This text implies that there are rewards for the two classes of people: those who do wickedly and those that do righteously. The heritage of the wicked shall be cut off: "For yet a little while, and the wicked shall not be: yea, thou shalt diligently consider his place, and it shall not be" (Ps. 37:10). The advice to those inclined to indulge and practice evil acts is to stop it immediately! Leave evil alone and do good.

Evil brings with it foolishness, death, and total extinction. The Word says they shall be cut off, and no trace of them will be found. They shall burn as stubble and become impotent ash. The prophet Nahum says that their evil practices will not arise a second time, for God says He will make an utter end of sin and sinners. Thus, those who can read need to understand what is written in Holy Writ. John says, "He that hath an ear, let him hear what the Spirit saith unto the churches" (Rev. 2:29).

Solomon also expresses this concept. "In the way of righteousness is life: and in the pathway thereof there is no death" (Prov. 12:28).

Our role is to find the pathway and walk therein. The prophet Isaiah says, "And thine ears shall hear a word behind thee, saying, This is the way, walk ye in it, when ye turn to the right hand, and when ye turn to the left'" (Isa. 30:21). This is solid inspirational counsel that all should heed.

For the righteous, there is no displacement or uprooting. Their place is fixed and predetermined. Let us practice right doing and then be an inheritor of eternal life. The reward is life with God, Jesus, and the angels forever.

May we remember that the nation and people who practice righteousness will be exalted and shall inherit the new earth! Moreover, God is expecting His people to know righteousness and live righteous, holy, sanctified lives. Daniel says that the righteous shall shine in the kingdom forever (see Dan. 12:3). That was the reason why the triune God consented that Jesus should be the Propitiatory for our sins. God wants to reconnect with His created beings. Jesus paid the ultimate price—His life—so that we could live a sin-free and holy life. May we never lose sight of that precious fact but move on daily in *righteousness*!

Day 279

Salvation *belongeth unto the Lord: thy blessing is upon thy people. Psalm 3:8*

These are David's words of affirmation exalting confidence in Jehovah God. With this kind of relationship exuding vibrant assurance, David felt he could lie down and sleep even though his enemies sought his life. Is there any wonder that he wrote, "The Lord is my shepherd ... Yes, though I walk through the valley of the shadow of death, I will fear no evil: for thou art with me" (Ps. 23:1, 4). Only one who has experienced God's protection could make such bold and affirmative assertions.

In rehearsing what God has done for him, he declares, "I will not be afraid of ten thousands of people, that have set themselves against me round about" (Ps. 3:6). All Christians should emulate David's courage, and express belief and trust in the Almighty.

Spiritual maturity does not come easily; we have to develop and maintain a vibrant relationship with God through the written Word and moment-by-moment prayer. Salvation and saving grace come from and through God alone; it is not earned, but granted. God said, "Look unto me, and be ye saved" (Isa. 45:22). God gives life. He is its author, and He does not destroy whimsically. The moment you look at Him your salvation begins. There was no salvation for the twin cities of Sodom and Gomorrah and the ancient antediluvian world because God's grace, patience, and salvation had run out. Despite the warnings, they neither looked nor listened.

God does not only save but also blesses His people abundantly and continues to deliver all who call upon His name. The assurance of answered prayers brings peace and confidence; it develops faith and trust in the Almighty and stability to the faltering soul.

If we face every crisis and challenge with Christ, we can lie down and safely sleep because God is in control of our every circumstance. Deliverance comes from God alone. God responds to us when we sincerely pray to Him. He saves. May we grasp the free offer of *salvation* and thus ensure eternal life!

Day 280

The name of the Lord is a strong **Tower**: *the righteous runneth into it, and is safe.*
Proverbs 18:10

At the name of Jesus, every knee shall bow and every tongue shall confess. A stanza from "There's No Other Name Like Jesus" in the *Seventh-day Adventist Hymnal* sums up His name very well: "There's no other name like Jesus; 'tis the dearest name we know; 'tis the angel's joy in heaven, 'tis the Christian's joy below. Sweet name, dear name; there's no other name like Jesus." Jesus' name means Savior; He shall save His people from their sins. That is the reason why He came to be the Emmanuel (see Luke 1:31–33; Matt. 1:21, 23). The apostles attested to this fact: "There is none other name under heaven given among men, whereby we must be saved" (Acts 4:12).

Long before He came as a Babe of Bethlehem, inspiration empowered King Solomon to declare that Jesus' name is a strong tower. And the purpose of this tower is to provide refuge, security, and safety (those who find shelter therein are safe).

God's name provides many things to those who trust in Him. He is the Jehovah Jireh, Elohim, the El Shaddai, the Almighty, and the great I AM. He is also Jehovah Raphi, meaning the Lord our healer, and Jehovah Tsedeq, meaning the Lord our righteousness.

Besides all those, God is our Shepherd, Jehovah Shalom, Jehovah Nissi, our victor, and Jehovah Tsuri. He is our Father, the everlasting and unchangeable God, the Most High God, Lion of Judah, King of kings, Lord of lords, Holy One of Israel, Creator, and the Lord of hosts. He is the Rock—my Rock and my Helper—and He is the Lord of all the earth.

That is our God; those are only some of His names. Do you not see that His watchful eyes are on all of us everywhere and in every place? What a mighty God He is! He is strength through and through. Let all the earth "sing unto the Lord" (Isa. 12:5) for His name is great. Thus, at the name of Jesus, every knee must bow and every tongue confess that He is God and He alone!

God is indeed a very strong tower where everyone has shelter and refuge. We are all in His care and must never feel fear, trepidation, or insecurity. There is no need for anxiety. He shelters, protects, provides, sustains, guards, and saves. He is always there—a very present help in trouble. And even when there is no trouble, He is always present, for He is the Omnipresent One. Let us trust Him, for He is God. Let us run to Him and find safety from the storms that may soon burst upon the earth. May we call on His name frequently and find repose, for our strong *Tower* is always there for us!

Day 281

O the depth of the riches both of the wisdom and knowledge of God! how **Unsearchable** *are his judgments, and his ways past finding out! Romans 11:33*

Job posed a very serious question regarding humanity's quest to know the Almighty: "Canst thou by searching find out God? canst thou find out the Almighty unto perfection?" (Job 11:7). As we read God's Word and reflect on all His glory, awesomeness, and majesty, how can finite minds see and know the mind of the Creator? Paul declares that His wisdom and knowledge are unfathomable.

God is everything to all humankind and has set boundaries and limits as to our scope and reach (see Acts 17:26). As we contemplate God's existence and who He is, like the aged apostle, we must concur that God's ways are beyond our scope. If we could fathom it, we would be like Him, which was the argument the fallen Lucifer used to lead Eve into sin—to be like God. If we were like God, we would not know evil, for God is all goodness.

What and how God administrates far surpasses our ability to understand. It is not for man to know the ways of God. God is God. Moses advised, "The secret things belong unto the Lord our God: but those things which are revealed belong unto us and to our children for ever" (Deut. 29:29). Each person has his or her own territory and domain, whether it is knowledge or wisdom in physical or terrestrial things, God has set the limits. Anything beyond and humanity should not seek entrance. Many may try to find out new things, for we are all on this continuous quest to know more, but God is in charge. Humanity cannot enter into the unknown unless we get divine authenticity.

At the end of this dispensation, when God sends Jesus back to earth and gives justice, judgment, and reward to all, we will truly understand and know who the great God is. Earthlings have not been endowed with the capacity to comprehend how God works. He reveals what is sufficient for our limited range, yet He operates with all justice, wisdom, and love. All are equally endowed, and according to our allotted gifts, He requires results.

We must never run before God and try to ascertain what is hidden. Rather, we need to accept His leading and be content with our exposure to knowledge. God is the Omniscient, Omnipotent, and Omnipresent One. May we give Him the glory, praise, and honor, and follow His direction.

Day 282

To me belongeth **Vengeance** *and recompense; their foot shall slide in due time: for the day of their calamity is at hand, and the things that shall come upon them make haste.*
Deuteronomy 32:35

Having written in the book the commands of God, Moses told the Israelites that because of their rebellious and stiff-necked attitude, they would revert to their past behaviors and forget God after his death. He cited their indifference toward spiritual things. Obedience, worship, and praise were evidentiary, and He pointed out that God would avenge His name for their rebellion. He then wrote the song of God's leading them and recited it to the assembly.

It recapped God's goodness, leadings, protection, and provision for them during their wilderness years and pointed out that God's justice is in His hands. Vengeance belongs to the Lord, and each man, woman, and child will be rewarded according to his or her deeds. Hence, Christians should not take it upon themselves to fight their own battles. God alone has that prerogative to judge others. So the "eye for an eye" mentality is not God's way. His judgments are fair, just, and good. He alone will avenge the wicked.

These ancients knew of God's plan for families and their responsibility to teach God's Word diligently to the children (see Deut. 6:6–9). By so doing, there would be religious continuity through the ensuing generations. If they disobeyed and reverted to their old rebellious practices, God could raise up foreign nations to oppress the Israelites as was done aforetimes.

Today, people are sometimes oppressed by others because the oppressors have forgotten the plain paths of righteousness, integrity, honesty, and truth and they are jealous of those that commit righteous acts. They lack compassion, love, tenderness, and empathy and only delight in oppressing others. Centuries later, the apostle Paul writing to the Roman brethren, counseled them, "Abhor that which is evil; cleave to that which is good" (Rom. 12:9).

We should let God work on our hearts, for He is able and is the only wise, Omniscient One. That is why Jesus, coming later on the scene, told His hearers that they should not judge anyone because judgment is God's prerogative (Matt. 7:1). That message is for us also. Paul also admonishes his hearers, "Recompense to no man evil for evil. Provide things honest in the sight of all men" (Rom. 12:17). And that is the very last word. Since *vengeance* belongs to the Lord, may we act appropriately.

Day 283

Wisdom *is the principal thing; therefore, get wisdom: and with all thy getting get understanding. Proverbs 4:7*

According to the wise man, wisdom is the quintessential acquisition that any man, woman, youth, or child can possess. It is a property of the Almighty. God used wisdom to create this world; the Creator has and is all wisdom. He is All-knowing and omniscient. Solomon equates wisdom to the "tree of life to them that lay hold upon her" (Prov. 3:18) and advises the son to "keep sound wisdom and discretion" (Prov. 3:21). Wisdom is health and life, and throughout chapter 8, he points out that wisdom is everlasting.

King Solomon received wisdom from God in answer to his request. When God appeared to him in Gibeon and said, "Ask what I shall give thee?" (1 Kings 3:5), the fledgling king asked for wisdom to be able to rule so great a people. God was very pleased with his response and added things he did not ask for but which God knew he needed.

The writings of the Proverbs and Ecclesiastes are full of counsel urging people to seek wisdom. Centuries before, the prophet Daniel referred to the totality of wisdom. He says, "And they that be wise shall shine as the brightness of the firmament; and they that turn many to righteousness as the stars for ever and ever" (Dan. 12:3).

Wisdom teaches skill in living. There is physical, mechanical, intellectual, and moral skill, and all are required to help one live successfully. It also gives the possessor the discriminative and discerning capacity to distinguish between truth and error, good and bad, the insignificant and the significant. Many people have wisdom, but they do not possess knowledge. When one acquires wisdom, he or she needs understanding to use this knowledge effectively. Many wise people have made very serious blunders because they lacked understanding.

But how to get understanding is the question! The answer comes from the Word: seek God with all your heart, mind, and soul, and He will teach you. Young King Solomon asked God for understanding; "Give therefore thy servant an understanding heart to judge thy people" (1 Kings 3:9). The young king knew his limitations and asked God for spiritual insight and discernment, which do not come by humankind's prowess or spending many years in academia.

Wise people practice wisdom because the Holy Spirit empowers them. Each of us has access to wisdom; therefore, we can boldly ask God for it as Solomon did. James affirms that God gives to all freely and is not short in His delivery (see James 1:5). May each seeker ask and wait to receive *wisdom* from the Almighty!

Day 284

O Lord, our Lord, how **Excellent** *is thy name in all the earth! who hast set thy glory above the heavens. Psalm 8:1*

Praise waiteth for thee O God in Zion and unto thee shall all flesh come! We can do nothing but give praise and glory to our God, the Most High, who sits up high and looks down at His earthbound children. This psalm is designed to exalt God and the majesty of His name for all His wonderful works to humankind.

We are fearfully and wonderfully made says the psalmist, David. God fashions, molds, forms, and imbues us with His mind. All the wonderful things we can do is due to the mind of God implanted in us. God gave us power and dominion over every living thing that exists: "Let them have dominion over the fish of the sea ... and over all the earth" (Gen. 1:26). God put us in control of all things earthly: animals, sea creatures, and vegetation. As the psalmist reflects on the immutability of God in dealing with humanity, he could not but recount God's wondrous acts to us and ascribes to Him excellence.

God takes care of every one of His created beings: humans, birds, vultures, animals, and all sea creatures. He has also set their determined boundaries. For example, fish cannot live on dry land, and four-footed cattle cannot live in the sea. We may use adaptive measures, but we cannot spoil God's plan for all His creation.

God is majestic; He is more wonderful than words can express. His name is wonderful; He is everything to everyone. God's name is truly majestic, and the entire creation ought to worship and adore Him, for there is no other God but the Creator and Sustainer. We must find comfort in exalting His name and ascribe excellence unto Him.

At the name of Jesus, every knee shall bow. Take time to meet Him, to get acquainted with Him, to know

Him, and to develop a forever relationship with Him. Job advises, "Acquaint now thyself with him, and be at peace: thereby good shall come unto thee" (Job 22:21). God is waiting with longing and earnest desire to connect with you. Do not let Him pass by without your inviting Him to be a part of your life. Remember He says, "Behold, I stand at the door, and knock: if any man hear my voice, and open the door, I will come in to him, and will sup with him, and he with me" (Rev. 3:20). Let Him come into your apartment so that you can enjoy the wonder of the Majesty of heaven. The young people sing a chorus: "O Lord, our Lord, how excellent is thy name in all the earth!" Just think of the many excellent things that God has done for you and is consistently doing! May we join them in offering *excellent* praise to His name!

Day 285

> *For we are but of* **Yesterday**, *and know nothing, because our days upon earth are a shadow.*
> *Job 8:9*

Bildad, Job's friend and consoler, tries to convince him that in comparison to the sages' wisdom and the tradition of their fathers, they and their generation have infantile understanding about life's challenges. They know nothing. Therefore, he should not wallow in self-pity, remorse, or despair because of his condition. To do so is satanic and shows disbelief and distrust in the Almighty.

We were born *yesterday*; we are fledglings to life. Based on the knowledge continuum, we are still in swaddling clothes. The wisdom of the ages is beyond us; we cannot understand it! Therefore, do not stress yourself!

We have not lived. We have no experiences even though many of us are grown. Our time here thus far is fleeting, insubstantial, and is like a shadow that shifts with the waxing or waning sun. There is no permanence in life. If you want to know about the future, you have to go back to the past. You can learn about a former generation and find out what their parents learned, and then you can learn wisdom from them. But how can one go back? Where are the records kept, and who is the historian?

Job's friends told him not to worry about his concerns. We all have fetal exposure to history, religion, philosophy, and genealogy. There is much time to learn what is God's will for your life. Your Christian path is just beginning.

As Bildad advises, we must face our individual challenges and learn from them. There is enough angst for each day's task. Youth must learn from their elders; there is no need to hurry to solve yesterday's problems today. God is in charge of your life. We have no permanence here in this lifetime; we are all tenants and transient travelers. Let us, therefore, allow God to direct our lives and daily learn from His Word.

This text does not indicate our contentment with limited knowledge. We are to seek knowledge, wisdom, and understanding so that we can embrace the challenges of new knowledge. The *modus operandi* (method of operation) comes from the Word: "Study to shew thyself approved unto God, a workman that needeth not to be ashamed, rightly dividing the word of truth" (2 Tim. 2:15). The word of God remains a lamp unto our feet and a light to our path. May we use it and be fulfilled *yesterday*, today, and tomorrow!

Day 286

Look down from heaven, and behold from the habitation of thy holiness and thy glory: where is thy **Zeal** *and thy strength, the sounding of thy bowels and of thy mercies toward me? are they restrained? Isaiah 63:15*

In this prayer, Isaiah recalls God's former care and protection over His children. Currently, they were not experiencing God's loving care and compassion, so as their spokesperson, he offers a twofold prayer of thanks and lamentation: thanks for past blessings and lamentations for fear that God is not with them.

Isaiah recounted God's past leadings in their lives: how He brought them out of Egypt with a mighty hand and an outstretched arm! Now they feel as if God has abandoned them. How shallow their memory; how soon they forget! The general feeling among the multitude is that they are on their own; there is no God.

This is certainly a challenge for the prophet and also their leader. As spokesperson, he has to go before the Lord to plead the people's cause. Thus he inquires of God about where is the zeal, the passion, and the strength that He had shown before. He wonders if God had gone soft on the wilderness folk. The people seem intimidated by the respective challenges and need assurance, physical evidence, and verification that the God of Jacob is still with them.

As an excellent arbitrator, Isaiah assures God that His people gratefully recognizes His Fatherly care extended to them, but at this time, the nation feels slightly humbled and despair is rampant. They want to feel God's presence—a visible manifestation of His reality. They want to see their God at work again. Their fear and major question is: has God forsaken and has the glory departed from them? And are they experiencing an Ichabod moment? Yet, in their moment of despondency and uncertainty, the Spirit assures them and answers their inquiry: "Thou, O Lord, art our father, our redeemer; thy name is from everlasting" (verse 16).

Calm overshadows them; they are completely at ease. God has answered them. God's zeal was not compromised to them. He retains His zeal, compassion, passion, love, care, and commitment to them. He still does for us today. We can be happy and exalt God's name, the very strong and mighty tower. May we be consumed by God's *zeal*, which never loses its intensity or fervor!

Sent by God

Day 287

For the Lord himself shall descend from heaven with a shout, with the voice of the **Archangel**, *and the trump of God: and the dead in Christ shall rise first.*
1 Thessalonians 4:16

This text carries the great promise and hope that Jesus' second coming brings eternal life. This is the Christian's glorious hope, expectation, and long awaited event. God will send Jesus back to earth and according to Nahum 1:9: "He will make an utter end [to sin]: affliction shall not rise up the second time."

The deceiver will deceive no more! Gone are the temptations, lusts, and evil desires. Everyone will be free of the malady of sin. Jesus, our deliverer and redeemer, who ascended more than 2,000 years ago, will come with a shout and triumph because He is coming to establish His kingdom of righteousness (see Acts 1:11).

The redeemed will live in a new, pure, and holy atmosphere unmarred by sinful thoughts, habits, and behaviors. The Lord is coming in one flame of glory. He will have trumpets and fanfare and the sound of many angels. The voice of the mighty Archangel will announce His arrival. What a glorious scene that will be!

Jesus' coming will be the most stupendous event in world history. There will be trumpet blasts, horrendous earthquakes, and lightening and thundering that surpass Christ's crucifixion in AD 31. Though He experienced the death of a criminal on this earth, He will return as King of kings and Lord of lords accompanied by the mighty Gabriel and a whole retinue of angels. Then they shall shout: "Open ye the gates" (Isa. 26:2)!

Jesus will return in His own might and that of His Father's. That will evoke shouting and praise and hallelujahs. The Word says that the heavens will shake, and the earth will open, and all the righteous sleeping saints will awake so that they can behold their Savior and Lord. Never more will they be removed from their loved ones because Jesus has conquered death and the grave. Paul declares, "Death is swallowed up in victory" (1 Cor. 15:54). May we all hear the *Archangel's* trumpet flurry!

Day 288

Behold, *what manner of love the Father hath bestowed upon us, that we should be called sons of God: therefore the world knoweth us not, because it knew him not.*
1 John 3:1

What an excellent greeting! How special we are that God, through His love, has bequeathed upon us the title of sons and daughters! Can you imagine that God could engraft us into His family and given us His name? Only sheer love could make Him do that. But how could He do otherwise? After all, we are His children. All of us are His children. God has no grandchildren, nieces, or nephews. We all call Him our Father. Wonderful!

Through His love, God gave us His name as an inheritance. This is God's dowry to us. Glorious is the thought, and we should be excited. God has bequeathed to us His estate and given us His name. We are His. He has endowed us with an enduring quality of love that no one can take from us. It is ours for keeps. Can you fathom this gift and the transaction? Can you envision that the Creator is giving you an inheritance that cannot tarnish, exchange, or let be snatched away? Each should revel in delight that God's gift glorifies and dignifies us. It makes us royalties—princes and princesses of the Divine.

As residents of the royal household, we should live as Jesus did. We need to live a life wholly consecrated to God so that He will be well pleased with His children. King Solomon says that a wise and obedient son is a delight to his father. If this brings delight and happiness to the earthly father, how much more will the heavenly Father be satisfied! Our new title—children of God—should elate us because we belong to the family of God!

Our new status is an enviable one. This new relationship requires severing connections with old friends, acquaintances, and some family members who might reject us and refuse to associate with us because of a new lifestyle. While our Elder Brother was on earth and went about doing good, He was berated and dubbed devil, Beelzebub, sinner, winebibber, blasphemer, etc. , but that never deterred Him from His mission. John knew that very well, so he counsels his brothers and sisters that we should not think it strange if we are sidestepped and ridiculed for Christ's sake, for they did not accept Him, the life-giver. Therefore, we, His sisters and brothers, should not expect to be treated any better than He was treated. Despite it all, we remain special because we are all God's children and have a very loving, caring Father and a very special and caring Brother, Jesus. May we always be thankful that we are part of the heavenly family!

Day 289

*Be **Careful** for nothing; but in every thing by prayer and supplication with thanksgiving let your requests be made known unto God. Philippians 4:6*

This text is the core of Counseling 101 on how humankind and Christians should face life's daily challenges. In the recent father-and-children relationship texts, we learned complete trust, hope, and assurance that our wonderful Father has elevated us to that of royalty. Royal persons are those with special endowments: money, wealth, prestige, fame, authority, and clout. They lack nothing earthly, for they are rich, powerful, and privileged. How delightful to be a royal child in the palaces of the King of heaven! We princes and princesses should have no anxious care, for our Father is rich in houses and lands and holds the wealth of the world in His hands. Thus, we are richer than any earthly monarch or royalty.

With this background and family heritage, the counsel is to not be anxious about anything or any aspect of your life, for it is not in your possession to alter or direct its course. King Solomon pointed out that we may plan, but it is God who directs. And Jesus later told His hearers that they should take a cue from nature: the lilies grow and produce and beautify the earth in a care-free manner. The birds flitter about, yet God takes care of them. Then He asked them if they considered themselves more valuable than the sparrows, the tiniest in the bird family (see Matt. 10:31). What is your worth in your own eyes, in God's eyes? You are His royal child!

After Jesus chided them, He gave sweet and direct counsel: whatever you need (and that means everything from the smallest to the greatest), present it to the Lord; ask Him and give thanks even though you have not yet received it, but you know according to His will, it will be done (see Matt. 6:33). No good and loving father would let their children go without. Even the psalmist says, "Like as a father pitieth his children, so the Lord pitieth them that fear him" (Ps. 103:13). God is more willing to give us what we need than we are to ask of Him, says the apostle Paul. The counsel is to leave it all—everything—in His hands. He is able, and He cares.

Everyone has cares and concerns that cause anxiety, but Paul's advice is very necessary at this time. He tells us to turn our worries into prayer. We need to worry less and pray more; God is able. When you are prone to worry, stop and pray and ask God to intervene and show you the way. David says that even if no words will come out, just raise your hands to heaven and say, "Lord have mercy!"

Call upon the name of the Lord always; give thanks for what you will receive from God. Do not worry about anything and have neither anxiety nor doubt. God is God, and He delivers every time. Pray more, for prayer changes things; worry less, for worry changes nothing. May you leave every *care*, concern, and anxiety in the strong and mighty hands of our Father and then go and enjoy His wonderful peace!

Day 290

Neither is there any **Daysman** *betwixt us, that might lay his hand upon us both. Job 9:23*

Job is in deep agony of soul and is feeling despair and rejection. He is calling out to God, but there is no answer, so he laments that he cannot find a mediator—a daysman—an impartial judge, who could arbitrate the case between God and himself. He now realizes that he is dealing with powers far beyond his ken. Where was Jesus at this time of Job's predicament? According to sacred Scriptures, He was then the Dayspring—symbol of the dawn—the Messiah who would come.

Ellen G. White, the famed messenger of the Lord, tells us that Jesus is the daysman in her widely read book *The Desire of Ages*, which tells of the life of Jesus.

The I AM is the Daysman between God and humanity, laying His hand upon both [cf. Isa. 9:6; Heb. 7:26; 2:11]. ... In Christ the family of earth and the family of heaven are bound together. Christ glorified is our brother. Heaven is enshrined in humanity, and humanity is enfolded in the bosom of Infinite Love. (*The Desire of Ages*, pp. 25, 26)

We can jump for joy because we know of Jesus: His sacrifice, His atoning blood, and His intercessory role. The Mediator is also our lawyer and advocate. Our Daysman is going between the Father and us to ensure that we have access to eternal life.

He is our forever Daysman. Luke calls the Daysman the Dayspring who comes from on high (Luke 1:78). John 1:14 tells us that God came down and dwelt with humanity. In this we have the dual role of Jesus as both the Dayspring and Daysman. He was first the Dayspring ushering a new dispensation of grace, and after His crucifixion and ascension, He has become our Daysman interceding on our behalf.

Christians living at the end of the church age are very fortunate to live in a world where there is a Mediator in the heavenly courts advocating on their behalf for them to receive total forgiveness. Jesus will not be the daysman interminably, for He must return to receive the redeemed. Before He left, He assured His followers that He will return. Based on His promised word, we are awaiting that event (see John 14:1–3).

Oh, weary soul, when you get bogged down with the cares of this life, when isolation, loneliness, and frustration set in, lift up your heads and look up. There is Someone at this very moment interceding on your behalf. Jesus, our daysman, sits at the Father's right hand working for us. May we access the services of our Mediator. May Jesus Christ, while He is still at work as our daysman, have our sins erased!

Day 291

But as it is written, **Eye** *hath not seen, nor* **Ear** *heard, neither have entered into the heart of man, the things which God hath prepared for them that love him. 1 Corinthians 2:9*

Glorious is this promise! Rich in beauty and majesty are the words of Isaiah that the apostle Paul referenced to the new Corinthian believers to rev up their excitement about the new earth.

Everyone likes a surprise and God will have many surprises for us in our new home—the earth reconditioned, holy, and undefiled. Of all the glories, the establishments, palaces, cathedrals, mansions of inestimable beauty and grandeur that humanity has erected and furnished, all those majestic edifices fail in significance as compared to what God has prepared for His redeemed. It will truly be surprising, for Jesus tells us He is gone to prepare mansions for us: "In my Father's house are many mansions ... I go to prepare a place for you" (John 14:2). Isaiah prophesied hundreds of years before Jesus came about the new earth thus: "Neither hath the eye seen, O God, beside thee, what he hath prepared for him that waiteth for him" (Isa. 64:4). Those things will be of incomparable beauty, defying all human imagination. I can't wait to experience them. What about you?

We cannot imagine all that God has in store for us. We have tainted eyesight and limited vision. We cannot even conjure up images of Eden lost, never mind the recreated earth cleansed of all impurities. God will create a new heaven and a new earth (see Isa. 65:17; Rev. 21:1), and we will live with Him throughout all eternity never more to be separated.

Speak now to Elijah and Enoch (two worthies who went to heaven without tasting death), and they will tell you about living a long, long time. God has this eternal plan for the obedient, and we must take courage and press on and not be overwhelmed by the challenges of this life. We must be joyful or as James says, "Count it all joy when ye fall into divers temptations" (James 1:2).

Our Father has things far superior to any earthly establishment, however magnificent it is. Let us guard the avenues of the mind and soul and focus on those things that are pure, holy, just, and good. Trust God and be prepared to accept His beneficence for nothing that is earthbound can be compared to the riches He has prepared for us. May we not refuse the free gift He offers! God's eternity far outshines and supersedes anything that your eyes can see, or your hearts can desire, or the titillating music that wafts through the air and consumes you. All will be purity, true beauty, and harmony. Plan to be there and to enjoy and revel in the beauty that God has planned for us. Let us meet under the tree of life by the banks of the river! I can hardly wait; my prayer is "Come, Lord Jesus, come quickly." May your *eyes* and *ears* one day be overwhelmed at the perfection our Creator has waiting for us!

Day 292

Behold, I have refined thee, but not with silver; I have chosen thee in the **Furnace** *of affliction.*
Isaiah 48:10

God allows His prophet and spokesperson to share His method for developing God's perfect character in us. The furnace is the kiln into that all metals are placed to burn out the dross and leave behind pure, unadulterated metal. God is refining His chosen children in the same manner as the metallurgist processes precious metals.

Since we are more valuable and more precious than metals, God cannot use the same method or tools. Ours has to be the furnace of affliction i.e. pain, illness, sorrow, distress, heartaches, heart breaks, poverty, betrayals, deceit, loss of loved ones, unsaved children, unconsecrated spouse, etc. That is our furnace and crucible, and we have to be tested in order to know our endurance capacity. We must know our melting point in order to grow spiritually.

Jesus passed through the furnace when He was tempted in the wilderness by Satan (see Matt. 4). We have to go through our unique fire so that we can be refined and made precious. The apostle Peter warned, "Beloved, think it not strange concerning the fiery trial which is to try you, as though some strange happened unto you: But rejoice ... with exceeding joy" (1 Peter 4:12, 13).

Every Christian must go through the furnace in order to develop the character of Jesus. If we want to live with Him, we have to be like Him. We have to suffer and endure as He endured. We must face our own crucible, for we need the qualities and characteristics that He possessed. We need purity of thought and action. Paul advises, "Let this mind be in you, which was also in Christ Jesus" (Phil. 2:5).

The afflictions and feats that we face are the refiner's soap that polishes and makes us as pure gold. We need to pray for a strong and enduring faith and for the determination to stand firm in the faith and in the doctrine. Paul counsels, "Yea, and all that will live godly in Christ Jesus shall suffer persecution" (2 Tim. 3:12). Paul, Daniel, and the three worthies went through the furnace as well as Martin Luther, Huss, Jerome, and many other martyrs of the early Christian church—Stephen being the very first.

If we must go through the furnace of affliction, let us rejoice that we can suffer for Christ's sake. He bore the most inhuman and excruciating humiliation of all—death on the cross with murderers, vagabonds, and thieves. Let us count our refining as mild in comparison to Christ's. Any kind of adversity or trial you are facing, your furnace will not be as hot as Jesus' was. His heat was universal heat. You will emerge as pure untarnished gold, for Christ will be there beside you to sustain you. All must be refined to become like the Master Himself. May you meet your *furnace* experience and crisis with Christ!

Day 293

And the ransomed of the Lord shall return, and come to Zion with songs and everlasting joy upon their heads: they shall obtain joy and **Gladness***, and sorrow and sighing shall flee away. Isaiah 35:10*

Amen and amen again! This verse is brimming with hope and promise, and it was not only for ancient Israel, but for people everywhere who revere the Almighty and are anxiously anticipating the Lord's return. It has global outreach and scope.

It is also futuristic and symbolic of the new earth restored without any trace of sin, sorrow, or affliction. Aren't you excited? Just as how the Jews looked forward to being reestablished in their home, in a similar manner, Isaiah uses the metaphor to assure current day Christians that a bright, glorious, sin-free state of existence is awaiting God's obedient children. Glad thought! Eager anticipation!

The ransomed, i.e. the redeemed, come singing songs and shouting hosannas; it is the song of their experiences. Not only will they be singing, but they will be wearing jeweled crowns—symbols of the souls they have led to Jesus. They will be playing all different kinds of musical instruments and shouting hallelujahs. This is certainly going to be a joyous scene.

The redeemed will be filled with gladness because they are free! Sin will never molest anyone ever again. In Revelation 21:4 John says that there will be no more pain, death, or tears, for they will all be wiped away. There will be no more Alzheimer's, dementia, diabetes, cancer, heart disease, hypertension, childhood diseases, and other debilitating and killer diseases. They will be gone, forever extinguished. There will be untold and unmatched joy and freedom, for God has declared all things new. Gladness, come Lord Jesus!

This is the epicenter of God's design; no greater hope or promise can exist and be imparted to God's faithful children—the overcomers, the ransomed, and the redeemed—than this. This is their dreams realized, their expectancy and complete joy.

God is preparing this grand entrance for the obedient and righteous. While mercy is accorded to us, secure your place among the ransomed, the redeemed, and the saved. I desire to be there; what about you? Remember our Mediator is making sure that it happens; we cannot disappoint Him.

At Jesus' triumphant entry into Jerusalem, worshippers lined the streets with palm branches and shouted "Hosanna!" At His second return, the gates will be thrown open, and He and the redeemed will enter. We are a part of that entourage. Oh, what joy, inexplicable joy and *gladness* that will be when together at last! We will be with the Savior. May none of us miss this blissful and *glad* event!

Day 294

So then faith cometh by **Hearing**, *and hearing by the word of God. Romans 10:17*

This is a continuation of Paul's counsel to the new believers in Rome, but it references Christians worldwide. He is teaching them that to understand the gospel, one has to be attuned to the Holy Spirit, the Interpreter.

The seeker of truth must listen as the Holy Spirit impresses his or her mind. In order to hear, there must be a presenter. God inspires and gifts some people with the ability to present His Word lucidly. The apostle Paul said that when Jesus returned to His Father's side, He gave gifts unto every member of the human family. Some were gifted with oratory skills, others wisdom, some understanding, some special insight and discernment. Whatever is the gift, everyone has something that he or she can use for self and others. It is the Holy Spirit that imbues people with this special gift.

Even though the Holy Spirit gifts each person, some are less inclined to hear. The Word says that some will heap to themselves "teachers, having itching ears" (2 Tim. 4:3) and will not yield to the Holy Spirit's promptings. That is the reason for John's proclaimed warnings from the lips of Jesus: "He that hath an ear, let them hear what the Spirit saith unto the churches" (Rev. 2:29).

We are made to worship; if it is not God, then we worship ambition. The question is: do we want to hear the Word of God or His Spirit whispering in our ear? Do we want to hear what He wants to say to us? Do we want to develop a pure, honest, and truthful lifestyle? If we do, then we must of necessity turn to the Word. David says that the "entrance of thy words giveth light" (Ps. 119:130). The apostle Paul says that the Word is more powerful than any two-edged sword, cutting away the frills to the very marrow and the bones themselves. In other words, it reaches to the very core of one's existence (Heb. 4:12).

The Word of God is a cleaver and a protector. We must attune our ears to hear God's voice and differentiate it from the cacophony of other voices. It does not come with screams and shouts and lightening and thundering. It is in the calm that God speaks to us, for He alone wants our attention. When we spend time in and with the Word, we will experience what Isaiah so aptly describes: "And thine ears shall hear a word ... saying, This is the way, walk ye in it, when ye turn to the right hand, and when ye turn to the left" (Isa. 30:21).

May we begin today to practice *hearing* the Word of God and listening to the message therein! He is speaking to you; may you *hear* His voice.

Day 295

Therefore, thou art **Inexcusable**, *O man, whosoever thou art that judgest: for wherein thou judgest another, thou condemnest thyself; for thou that judgest doest the same things.*
Romans 2:1

We often tend to set ourselves up as judge and jury in secular, judicial, or sacred cases. When we assume such a posture, we forget our own foible. We are quick to pass judgment on another. This has been an age-old principle; Job's friends judged him and found him guilty of hiding secret sins, living a double life, and practicing hypocrisy. This behavior pattern is a part of our psyche; it is ingrained in our DNA.

Thus when Jesus came along, they expected Him to follow the status quo, but He would not. He introduced a new dispensation of grace and made it very plain to His hearers that judgment belonged solely to God and to do otherwise was to trample on God's threshold. He set the records straight: "Judge not, that ye be not judged" (Matt. 7:1).

Additionally, Jesus challenged them to examine their own lives, motives, and behaviors. He told them to stop being so hypocritical. They seemed to have possessed a "holier than thou mentality." He pointed to the mote and the beam in each other's respective eyes.

As the apostle Paul preached, he told his audiences that to judge another was inexcusable because each one stands guilty before God. There are no pure people living, so all people should examine their motives. Paul takes the words of Jesus and translates them for the new believers' understanding and clarification. He is scolding his listeners for being self-righteous bigots and moralists.

The message rings true for us living in this very critical age. When we judge others, we are condemning ourselves. Even the thief on the cross was not oblivious that he was worthy of his punishment. For him, justice was served, and his case was inexcusable; however, Jesus was truly innocent.

The essence of Paul's exhortation is that we are all sinners and do not have the authority to judge and condemn anyone's lifestyle. Your sin may not be like someone else's. Before the Great Judge, we are all sinners and stand before Him completely guilty. All need the sanctifying and cleansing blood of Jesus. Each of us must turn to Christ, receive His atoning blood, and then receive the assurance that we are safe from sin's consequences. There is no excuse for any not to find the way. Jesus opened the door. He said: "I am the way, the truth, and the life" (John 14:6). May all enter in and find rest, peace, and freedom from guilt, May those who are lost realize that this is certainly *inexcusable*, for the Lord has opened the way!

Day 296

I know it is so of a truth: but how should man be **Just** *with God? Job 9:2*

Job asks the age-old question: can people, in any shape or form, render justice to God? What a question! How can humankind bring God to judgment? Job recognizes that there are no forthcoming answers to these rhetorical inquiries. Doing so invites presumption. The Creator and the created are not equals.

God is supreme; by Him, all things exist and consist. He is answerable to no one. Therefore, the created cannot say to the Creator, "Do this; go here; fix this." That is out of our purview. It is the Designer who calls all the shots, not the taker. Job is very wise, and he knows that he cannot argue with an infinite God, who knows all our actions, dwelling places, thoughts, plans, and expectations.

God has made us with certain limitations. He has fixed our operational boundaries and has supplied all our earthly needs. Heaven is God's prerogative, and earth is His footstool. The created cannot contend with the Almighty as to how He deals out justice. We must be honest with God. We cannot offer God any salve, for God is all purity, justice, integrity, and righteousness. God does not need vindication, but He can show justice to His neighbors.

What must we do to accord God's righteousness? David answers: "I will take the cup of salvation, and call upon the name of the Lord" (Ps. 116:13). In this cup of salvation sits the available free gift of Jesus' sacrifice. When we take hold of it and drink its contents, we will be filled with good things and a deep desire to fulfill God's requirements. God's cup has good nutrients in them. It has life-giving and sustaining principles to nurture our spiritual life. By drinking, we tell God and show Him that we accept His offerings and will be obedient. We can be just with God because He will see that our intents are noble and our motives pure.

It is God who must render us righteous (just); we can do nothing of ourselves to make that happen. Isaiah reminds us that all our pretentions to righteousness are like filthy rags—not fit to be seen in the presence of mortals much more the Holy God. It is Jesus who must impart to us His righteousness to make us righteous. We must take David's advice: "take the cup of salvation, and call upon the ... Lord." We must see our own nakedness and filthiness and claim the offer to make us clean. May we be made *just* through the righteousness of our loving Savior!

Day 297

And they took **Knowledge** *of them, that they had been with Jesus. Acts 4:13*

Can these words be said of us? When people come into contact with us, can they see Jesus' imprimatur stamped in our actions, dealings, and expressions? The onlookers of Jesus' disciples said these things of them. They knew these men's heritage, background, lifestyle, occupation, and social status and now looking at them, they were changed, transformed. The community was amazed. These were empowered, fearless, and possessed a holy boldness. Peter stood up to his challengers and declared: "We ought to obey God rather than men" (Acts 5:29).

The transforming work of the Holy Spirit changed them from crude, self-seeking, self-serving followers to men filled with the Holy Ghost. They could not be deterred from their mission. Whenever anyone comes in contact with Jesus, He changes and transforms their lives. People with whom you associate see the difference in your attitude, behavior, expressions, and general demeanor. I have witnessed that myself. This anecdote validates Jesus' transforming power on a person's life.

There once was a man whom everyone categorized as a profligate sinner. He cursed, betrayed, and engaged in all kinds of sinful practices. Then one day he passed by as tent meetings were being conducted, and he stopped. He came every night and on Saturdays for six weeks. Close to the end of the sessions, the call was made, and he along with several others came to the altar and gave their lives to the Lord. Later on after much study, he was baptized and joined the believers' fellowship. As he went back to his home and mingled with the community, they began to wonder what had happened to him. Why the transformation? He did not frequent the bars anymore, nor did he do the things he once enjoyed. Even his dress and countenance changed. When asked what had happened? He said, "I got me Jesus."

Yes, contact with Jesus changes lives. It was a marked difference when the community recognized the change in the twelve once crude, rough, coarse, and rude Galilean fellows. According to the school of thought, none of them had ever been enrolled in or attended any of the rabbinical schools, so they were unschooled in the nuances of the philosophy and teachings. Not a single rabbi had met any of them in his classroom, so the disciples were classified as ignoramuses, pariahs, and under-dogs of that society and because they were followers of the despised Jesus. However, when the onlookers heard the disciples' delivery and exegesis, style and exposition, they marveled and concluded that a wonderful change had been wrought in their lives, and it had to result from their contact with Jesus.

Being with Jesus brings about serious, drastic, and positive changes. The major question is: since you have been with Jesus, has someone seen the difference? Is your life reflective of His character? When Christ takes over your life, it will be changed. You become a new person, equipped with wisdom, knowledge, and understanding. You will convince people of His power to change their lives, for yours is a positive witness. Let people everywhere leave your presence with the good feeling that they have been with someone who knows Jesus. May we bear good fruits, "Wherefore by their fruits ye shall know them" (Matt. 7:20), and they shall *know* Jesus also!

Day 298

> *Thus saith the Lord, thy Redeemer, the Holy One of Israel; I am the Lord thy God which teacheth thee to profit, which* **Leadeth** *thee by the way thou shouldest go. Isaiah 48:17*

Here again, our God, the El Shaddai, defines Himself: "I am the Lord, thy Redeemer, the Holy Own of Israel." God speaks, and there is none to controvert this declaration.

He speaks and the earth trembles. He teaches us to profit and how to engage in business deals. He mentors us on how to be successful. This is because He imparts wisdom. After all, He is the Omniscient One. Thus no one who takes the Lord as his or her stronghold will experience any kind of failed attempts because God knows what is best and provides leadership. The wise man says it very aptly: "A man's heart deviseth his way: but the Lord directeth his steps" (Prov. 16:9).

We are to give all our ventures to God, Father, and Leader. We must trust Him, for He is the Omnipresent, Omnipotent, and Omniscient One. Can you grasp the enormity and awesomeness that is enwrapped in these three most powerful words? Because He is everything and knows everything, we only have to take our plans to Him and place them in His hands. He will direct, but He will not coerce. We must willingly yield our lives, plans, ideas, goals, and our expectations before Him. God is operating like loving, caring, watchful, and concerned parents who teach, counsel, and advise their children. No wonder He is our Father! May we be thankful for His watchful and loving care!

Based on this knowledge, we must listen to Him because peace and righteousness come to us from His word. If we disobey, we must be prepared to accept the consequences, which can range from disconnectedness from the Source, annihilation, loss of eternal life, and the forever relationship with the Father, Son, and the holy angels. We must both choose obedience and live or disobedience and die. I suggest that we each choose God, for He is our leader. Consequently, we will never get sidetracked or lost. He will take us directly to our gate and into our house.

I am enamored with this final thought: He leadeth me! Oh, blessed thought! What more can I ask for? What more do I need than the assurance and confirmation of the very Creator Himself saying, "I am He that leadeth you!" God has the universal GPS. Let Him lead you always; He provides guidance and protection, for He knows all the danger spots, deep curves, and treacherous vales. He knows the road ahead; follow Him, and sing along with the songwriter, James Lawson:

I will follow thee my Savior

Wheresoere my lot may be;

Where Thou goest, I will follow

Yes, my Lord, I will follow Thee.

Yes, friend, He knows the way! I have committed to His leading my life. May you allow Him to *lead* in yours as well!

Day 299

> *For his anger endureth but a* **Moment**; *in his favor is life: weeping may endure for a night, but joy cometh in the morning. Psalm 30:5*

Psalm 30 is replete with echoes of praise and thanksgiving. This particular one is about deliverance and release from death's expectation. The psalmist advises the saints to sing and give thanks—be joyful because of God's holy name, who with a mighty and outstretched arm has rescued His people. Isn't our God great? I just marvel with the constancy of His love. He is always responding to the needs of His children when they call upon Him. He never says "No" or turns His back away.

Even though we may provoke God, He does not hold anger against anyone for any length of time. If He did, who could endure His fury? How many would be still standing? God's character contains patience, mercy, grace, lovingkindness, and compassion. He does not, cannot, and will not retain anger against His children. Whatever He does, He does it quickly. His anger is short-lived lasting only for a moment. There is none that could endure God's anger forever; God is all about forgiveness and life, and He favors us for an extended lifetime.

God's anger may be likened to the sting of a shot given at the doctor's office (it is short and quick). Similarly, the discomfort that God's anger brings is momentary, but the good effects are perpetual. God's anger is a sharp pain that warns us to cease from wrongdoing. Then when it is all passed, there comes the long and lasting reward of rejoicing—"It wasn't so bad after all; wasn't God tender and didn't He treat us fairly?"

Despite our silliness, God overlooks our actions and brings us to that safe place where there is happiness and joy. Our sorrows here, though they seem monumental, are short-lived. We must choose God all the time, for He has more lasting pleasures for us than our mortal eyes have seen. When we behold what is in store for us, it will be joy and happiness inexorably. In the morning (whenever that may be) and we are awake from the shades of death, pain, and sorrow, persecution, or oppression, there will be a refreshing peace and a new found fadeless and eternal joy. That will be joy indeed! May we all be there to experience the *moment* that sin is erased from our lives!

Day 300

For the Lord thy God hath blessed thee in all the works of thy hand: he knoweth thy walking through this great wilderness: these forty years the Lord thy God hath been with thee; thou hast lacked **Nothing**. *Deuteronomy 2:7*

Recounting ancient Israel's forty-year feat in the wilderness, God reminds them of His constancy. God wanted their children to know that He had been with their ancestors and continued to be with them despite their diminishing numbers.

God has been with them through the night seasons in the form of a cloud of fire—providing light, warmth, and heat. In the day He was with them in the form of a cloud of light, which protected them from the sun's intense rays. These travelers lacked nothing. They had food, clothing, shoes, water, and shelter; they were not in need of anything. God was their Sustainer, Provider, and their Protector. Are we any less provided for today than when He watched over, guided, and led His children out of Egypt? Is He less mindful of us today wandering through this earth with all its travesties, anxieties, upheavals, turmoil, and challenges? Certainly not; He is the same yesterday, today, and tomorrow.

This passage brings to mind God's dependability and stability factors. Who else could fit the bill? He is our God; He has declared, "I am the Lord, and there is none else" (Isa. 45:5). He is the Holy One of Israel, the Creator, Originator, Sustainer, and Life-Giver. The text gives the assurance that we today need not fear, tremble, or panic, for He says, "I AM the yesterday, and today, and for ever. I change not" (author paraphrase, see Heb. 13:8; Mal. 3:6).

Forty years seem but a short life span; men and women are now living to 100 years or more, and God has been their hope and Provider. Why should we worry, fret, or complain or be anxious about tomorrow, next week, next year, or the end of our life? God promises that He will supply all our needs. David reminds us that "the earth is the Lord's … and they that dwell therein" (Ps. 24:1). God placed all the silver, gold, precious stones, and all precious metals exactly where He wanted them to be. Everything that man needs to sustain life, God has provided. Therefore, we must hope and trust in God for He alone can satisfy all of our needs (see Phil. 4:9). God says it and that should be sufficient for you and me.

A line from the song "Great is Thy Faithfulness" by Thomas O. Chisholm speaks to the all sufficiency of our God: "All that I have needed, Thy hand has provided; Great is Thy faithfulness, Lord unto me (us)."

Yes, all that we need, God has already provided for us. He is ever faithful on what He has promised. We shall never be in want. We shall need *nothing* more than we already possess. May we follow the apostle Paul's injunction: "I have learned, in whatsoever state I am, therewith to be content" (Phil. 4:11). Be happy!

Day 301

Open *ye the gates, that the righteous nation which keepeth the truth may enter in.*
Isaiah 26:2

Jesus addresses His attendants as He welcomes the redeemed from the earth. They are righteous and have accepted Him, washed their robes in the blood of the Lamb, and are overcomers. They have fought the good fight, stood up for Prince Emmanuel, and have gotten the victory over sin. Let these children of God come inside the heavenly gates, for they are worthy! These redeemed ones have kept the faith, faced insurmountable challenges, and have emerged from the furnace of affliction as pure gold. Give them their place; they shall walk with me in robes of righteousness.

This invitation is still open to all who will accept the gift of Jesus' sacrifice and keep the truth. All who hear must accept Jesus' invitation–to come and be saved. This is an invitation to come and dine with Him. It entails more than a lavish set table and sumptuous food; it is an invitation to be a disciple, to suffer with Him, to drink from His cup, and to be baptized with His baptism. It is also an invitation to enjoy rest, peace, and eternal joy.

The Good News is that heaven's gate is still open; Jesus is still interceding for the world. Let's accept Him now and be among the glorious and mighty throng who will enter the City of God to live and reign with Him forever. We do not want to be on the outside when the Gates are closed like the people of Noah's generation, who when God closed the door of the ark could no longer enter. Nor do we want to be like the five foolish virgins, who not having extra oil, went out to buy some, and when they returned, the bridal party went in and the door was shut. On both occasions, all perished because the doors were forever closed.

The doors of the church are still open. Heed the invitation and open your hearts to Jesus and accept His gracious invitation. Respond to Peter's altar call: "Repent, and be baptized ... receive the gift of the Holy Ghost" (Acts 2:38). Surely we each desire to be welcomed among the righteous and enter into the banquet hall with Jesus, our Host. We should all strive to be among the worthy entrants to the City of our God where righteousness shall reign forevermore.

Won't it be grand when the gate *opens* before you and Jesus greets you at the door and says, "Welcome, my child! I have a special seat prepared for you. Come with Me"? May that be the experience of everyone who reads these meditations.

Day 302

Preserve *me, O God: for in thee do I put my trust. Psalm 16:1*

As I prepare these devotional thoughts, I am humbled at the psalmist's outreach for help from his Savior.

It profoundly warms my heart that there are many of us crying out and seeking God's help. Many, many others before have cried unto Him and He has answered their pleas. This verse carries a request and an utterance of assurance; it has also become the prayer of every struggling child of God.

Throughout the meditations found in the book of Psalms, the petitioner always expresses appreciation for God's lovingkindness, trust, worthiness, and dependability. Because of David's intimate relationship with God, he could confidently believe that He would keep Him safe and continue to hold him with His righteous right hand. David knew that God was his Rock. It was only in Him that he could find refuge.

David, that mighty young man of valor, became a man most feared and sought after because of his escapades with the Philistines and other neighboring nations. Everyone wanted him dead. He had encouraged their rage, hostility, and fury. Consequently, his prayers were constantly about seeking God's protection and affirmation—he trusted that God would keep, protect, preserve, and deliver him from the enemies. David reminded Jehovah of his total dependence on Him and that when apart from God, he was nothing (verse 2). He acknowledged his own futility and asked for protection from his many pursuers who waited to seize and slay him. David's advantage was his awareness of his enemies and their several plots to kill him, so he had time and reason to call upon Jehovah.

God can also preserve us and keep us safely out of danger, but we must trust the keeping of our lives to Him and rely on His divine power, for it is He alone who can save to the uttermost. The psalms are littered with prayers for preservation. Here are a few among many: "The Lord shall preserve thee from all evil: he shall preserve thy soul. The Lord shall preserve thy going out and thy coming in from this time forth, and even for evermore" (Ps. 121:7, 8). "The Lord preserveth all them that love him" (Ps. 145:20). "The Lord preserveth the simple" (Ps. 116:6).

Holy Writ presents God as a Caretaker, Caregiver, and a Preserver. His care is available to all who need it. I invite you to read through the book of Psalms and find the comfort and assurance imbedded in God's Word. God preserves. He keeps and watches over His brood. May you trust Him, for He is able to save and *preserve* you unto the uttermost.

Day 303

> *Many waters cannot **Quench** love, neither can the floods drown it: if a man were to give all the substance of his house for love, it would utterly be contemned.*
> Song of Solomon 8:7

This verse discusses the power of love. Love is one of the strongest emotions imbued to humankind. Its grandeur requires the imagery of the turbulent river and the raging sea to describe the insurmountable energy it exudes. No seas, oceans, or any kind of water-ways can intercept love's path. It is an inextinguishable flame.

Love emits so much passion, desire, and fury that millions have lost their lives in pursuit of it. Kings have been dethroned, nations go to war, and some commit suicide all for the sake of or the lack of this mighty emotion. But love is stronger than death and the grave, and it burns its possessors like an unquenchable and inextinguishable blazing fire.

Paul describes its force as eternal (see 1 Cor. 13). When all other acquisitions fail, love remains permanently. Love has many dimensions, but this meditation addresses the universality of love. When Solomon wrote, he was not discussing the love of God for fallen humanity. He was instead dealing with social relations—love between the sexes. He could speak to love's passion because of his many trysts. (He had 1,000 wives and concubines.)

Several kinds of love operate in society: spousal, parental, erotic, filial, and agape. All are fixed and bind people together in all kinds of relationships. Love is kind and thoughtful. It possesses all the positive virtues that keep one's life together. Life cannot exist where there is no love; it is inexhaustible and unstoppable. It does not matter how tenuous the relationship between parent, child, siblings, or spouse, one never ceases from loving those closest and dearest to them.

Genuine love, not passionate, erotic love, is a holy and noble feeling. It is an enduring virtue, and the desire to love and be loved is eternal. Read 1 Corinthian 13, which is considered the love chapter, to see love's other attributes. Love is stronger than death so that the demise of a spouse does not diminish the love one spouse had for the other. Many widows or widowers will not marry after the death of a spouse because they want to preserve the love that existed and shared in that first relationship.

Someone has described love as being pure and holy and not solely a feeling; it transcends emotion because it is God-given and noble. On the contrary romantic love could be destructive because it excites the passions and craves only physical satisfaction. Here, Solomon is referring to unbridled passion. Men and women both need to reign in self-control; we must all subdue our feelings and not let them control us. Physical love is a beautiful thing to be enjoyed. Love is an enduring quality and lasts from eternity to eternity. It is un*quench*able. May none live without experiencing love.

Day 304

Submit yourselves therefore to God. **Resist** *the devil, and he will flee from you. James 4:7*

We live in a world of complacency, ease, and commonness. Many of us lack the will, the skill, or even the desire to fight back. It is much easier to go with the flow and not ruffle any feathers. It is easiest to take the path of least resistance, and many of us just let things happen.

There is an abundance of evil waiting to sweep the unguarded one off his or her moorings. Temptations in all forms and to all ages abound. Some of them are alluring, some pleasant, and some even promise great and good things. The apostle Peter tells us that the devil is out there "as a roaring lion ... seeking whom he may devour" (1 Peter 5:8); therefore, we must be constantly on guard and be prepared to resist. We have to be ready to fight back.

James concurs and advises all Christians to resist. He tells us not to give in to the wiles of the enemy. We have to fight as if our lives depended on it. Stand up and let Satan know that you are a child of God—a child bought with the precious blood of Jesus Christ. Let him know that you know that he is a destroyer of souls and that he instituted the heavenly rebellion, stole a third of the angelic host, and persuaded Eve to respond to his wily tales in the fair, sin-free Eden. Do not be afraid to confront him with the Word. After he attempted on three unsuccessful occasions to get the Son of God to yield to him, he finally left Jesus alone. Fight with the power of Jesus and watch him run away. Resist!

Satan's acts in Eden have tainted the entire universe. Sin and its aftermath is everywhere. He is the father of lies, so one should never listen to him. The very best news is that the devil cannot make you sin; he cannot put a stain on your character unless you consent to sin. He can tempt, entice, and lure, but he cannot make you sin. It is all about your will and the power of choice. We are all free moral agents with a mind to choose. Satan with all his roars and bellows cannot force you to do wrong.

We have an advocate, the righteous Jesus Christ, who is now interceding on our behalf so we can win. We must draw near to Him and His Holy Word and follow His example of combating every temptation with what the Scriptures say. The Scriptures are our weapons of resistance. May we be covered every moment with the robe of Christ's righteousness and meet every temptation and every challenge with the Word of God. Paul says the Word is sharper than any two-edged sword. Once armed, we cannot fail. We need to follow King David's plan: "Thy word have I hid in mine heart, that I might not sin against thee" (Ps. 119:11). If we hide God's Word in our heart, we can face any of the enemy's darts; he cannot overpower us. Paul suggests that we should "fight the good fight of faith, lay hold on eternal life" (1 Tim. 6:12).

Fight the enemy with the Sword of the Spirit—the Word of God—and he will flee from you. He cannot stand up and face God or to any of God's children. May you *resist* the enemy and let God, the Alpha and the Omega, fight your battles.

Day 305

> *And the Lord said unto him, I have heard thy prayer and thy* **Supplication**, *that thou hast made before me: I have hallowed this house ... and mine heart shall be there perpetually. 1 Kings 9:3*

It is a wonderful experience to converse with God in sweet communion as Solomon did. Before sin, God had that level of communication with Adam and Eve, but sin severed that relationship. A few centuries later, King David's son, the young and inexperienced Solomon, had a similar experience with God. God saw his naivety and sincerity and covenanted with him.

Having felt God's presence in his operations, and especially in the building of the Temple, Solomon knew he needed God's approval in all that he did. With this in mind, he did not just pray once or twice, but for many days he supplicated, pled, and begged God to lead him and imbue him with a sense of direction. God heard and assured him that His presence would be in the temple perpetually.

What does it mean to supplicate? It means we need to put aside all selfishness, pride, impatience, and deceitfulness. Supplication results in seeing one's self as he or she is before God. It requires us to plead for the blood of Jesus to wash us and make us clean. It is not something to be entered into lightly. This happens when someone in deep contrition cries out for divine intervention as if his or her very life depended on it. Jacob's wrestling with the power is supplication. Jacob pled for his life, and in that moment of desperation, he exclaimed, "I will not let thee go, except thou bless me" (Gen. 32:26). That is the kind of earnestness God's children must seek and possess. We must each make time to supplicate the Triune God, so they can empower us to resist sin. Victory over sin comes only through supplication.

God is waiting for our prayer and supplication; He promises to give us strength, power, and direction akin to His covenant with Solomon. Through our supplication, He will empower us to live above sin.

Our fragile physical bodies cannot long subsist without food; similarly, our spiritual bodies (mind, heart, and soul) cannot survive without nutrients from prayer and supplication. We must feel our need of the Savior, so we must spend an inordinate amount of time in supplication confessing our sins in contrition and lowliness, seek God's forgiveness, and surrender our wills to Him. In *supplicating*, we offer thanks for His new daily mercies. May you seek His face daily and watch your life change as a result of that heavenly communion.

Day 306

> *The Lord is good, a strong hold in the day of* **Trouble**; *and he knoweth them that trust in him. Nahum 1:7*

Throughout this devotional we see God clothed in majesty and honor. We see Him exuding implicit trust, confidence, assurance, and hope, yet He is so concerned about every detail of the lives of His earthbound children.

Here again as in several places, the prophet expounds God's strength, power, and omniscience. He knows everything about every created being—He knows when things are good, when they are bad, terrible, troublesome, and distractedly overwhelming, yet He is always there with His all-seeing eyes and outstretched arms providing the care and sustenance needed. He does not waver or change His mind, and those who implicitly trust in Him will find their hopes fulfilled.

Our God and Father will stand at the side of His believing and trusting children. He is a stronghold today as He was more than 6,000 years ago. He is still the same today as He was yesterday and as He will be tomorrow. With Him, there is no past or future. Every day, minute, and hour, He is. Our God is instantaneous; He is always there and ready to help those He loves. We need not have any fear for our *Jehovah-Rophe* will be at our side the moment we call upon Him (see Isa. 65:24).

King David says it best, "Yea, though I walk through the valley of the shadow of death, I will fear no evil: for thou art with me" (Ps. 23:4). God also tests our sincerity and our reliability factor. He says, "And call upon me in the day of trouble: I will deliver thee" (Ps. 50:15). Do you believe God and think He cares? Have you taken Him at His Word? Yes, He cares. He is a kind, compassionate, and loving Father. Based on these respective factors, we have nothing to fear; let us present the heavenly Trio with our cares, anxieties, and concerns. We do not have to worry about any trouble, for our God is Manager, Supervisor, and CEO. The Holy Spirit is the Guardsman, and Jesus is our loving Advocate.

King Solomon has the last word: "Trust in the Lord with all thine heart; and lean not unto thine own understanding" (Prov. 3:5). Jesus affirmed, "Let not your heart be troubled" (John 14:1). And Jude affirms, "Now unto him [God] that is able" (verse 24). There is nothing that God cannot fix. May you call on Him at any sign of *trouble* whether it is in the morning, at noon, in the evening, and during the night season. He is always there and available for you.

Day 307

He that putteth not out his money to **Usury***, nor taketh reward against the innocent. He that doeth these things shall never be moved. Psalm 15:5*

This is a sound advice to the unwary to live a blameless life. The text points to an interpersonal integrity that all should possess. In former times and still operational today, the more richly endowed would lend money to the needy and charge huge and exorbitant interests. I know of a current case where a so-called friend loaned another a certain sum, and she had to repay the lender an interest of 200 percent. The borrower could hardly afford to repay the loan plus the inordinate interest.

Here David is reflecting on those interpersonal transactions relating to upright living and practice. He points out the requirements for such dealings, which the prophet Micah clearly enunciates, "He hath shewed thee, O man, what is good; and what doth Lord require of thee, but to do justly, and to love mercy, and to walk humbly with thy God?" (Mic. 6:8). If the usurer read and practiced the principle laid down in this text, especially "to do justly," there would not be any usuries. To charge an exorbitant lending fee on the poor, who are in a financial dilemma in the first place, does not represent compassion, mercy, or justness. In essence, usury operations are simple, downright theft and oppression. There is nothing godly or godlike in its doings. The virtues that Micah espouses are God-sanctioned behaviors of His sons and daughters.

On a human scale, if you lend without charging any interest or take a bribe, then you stand upright, steady, unmoved by circumstances, and will receive God's approval. The wise man says that there is a blessing on anyone who lends to the poor. "He that hath pity on the poor lendeth unto the Lord" (Prov. 19:17). It is the Lord who will repay the loan because He is rich; He owns everything. God will authenticate the lender: "Well done, thou good and faithful servant ... enter thou into the joy of thy Lord" (Matt. 25:21). There is no reason to take advantage of the poor and needy.

Sad to say, in today's age of graft and greed, the principle espoused does not hold good in today's cut-throat "greedonomics." Corporations and lending agencies operate in reversal to that biblical injunction. They charge exorbitant sums that put the borrower at great risk of losing the little he or she had. Usury is rampant in today's fiscal economy, and the best one can do is to beware and not borrow if there is no imminent need. I knew a man who practiced usury, and he boastfully told me that he loves doing that business because he can get rich quickly. Having heard from his own mouth, I felt sad because his delight was in getting far more than he expended. His exact words were: "If they need the money, I can give it to them, but they have to pay." I believe he either did not read Micah 6:8 and Proverbs 22:22 or he was simply an unjust, money-grabbing Scrooge.

God has entrusted some people with more means than others. Some people just fall on hard times and will always need help from those more equitably endowed. If someone comes to you for a private loan, review his or her situation. Let them have the money and repay whenever they can. Let them sign a promissory note or an IOU, but by all means, do not let their burden be heavier than when they approached you for aid. Freely you have received, freely give. Do not be false to anyone. May you stay far from *usury* and deal kindly instead; the situation could always be reversed.

Day 308

Likewise, ye husbands, dwell with them according to knowledge, giving honor unto the wife, as unto the weaker **Vessel***, as being heirs together of the grace of life; that your prayers be not hindered. 1 Peter 3:7*

This is great counsel to husbands and prospective husbands. It addresses the marital relationship inclusive of wives and all females. Peter uses Abraham and Sarah's relationship as the model behavior. Though imperfect, Sarah, the model wife, respected and honored her spouse, Abe. Sarah understood her function and role in the marriage partnership and was never high-handed or manipulative like Rebekah. Peter advises all men, but more so Christian men, to take a cue from Abraham's lifestyle.

In the life partnership, Peter described the wife as the weaker of the two. She is characterized as the vessel because she is a carrier. She has the role of childbearing and carries in her body the unborn child for ten gestational months. Because she is designed to be more delicate, men must be selective how they handle the women in their lives. To the wife and mother is committed the most beautiful experience given to human beings—that of motherhood. She nurtures, trains, and guides the mind, body, heart, and brain of the unborn, the newly born, the babe, toddler, and the youth. Hers is a magnificent yet delicate role, and she must be highly esteemed and be the recipient of her husband's love, compassion, tenderness, gentleness, and understanding.

Today's women are more vulnerable; they are open to criminal attack, family abuse, discrimination, and alienation. Humanity's treatment of women has not changed since Peter's day. In many cultures men treat women disparagingly, as if they are the handkerchiefs of the world—to be used and discarded like paper tissue. This evil practice should have no place in the church or among Christian men. Our men must rise up to their God-given responsibility as a "house band" around their women folk—the wives, mothers, and daughters—and safeguard their privacies so they do not go wandering in strange paths looking for love in all the wrong places. If the men renege on their duty, according to the Book, their prayers will not be heard or be answered.

A man must protect his wife at home and from outside influences; he must be sensitive to her needs and make provision for respite because he recognizes she is the weaker vessel. Thus, he will respect and honor her. Women must be content with their role and try not to equate themselves with or usurp the man's God-given role.

Woman being the weaker vessel does not connote inferiority in mental or moral strength; God has given her the precious gift of procreation, and she should enjoy this special gift and accept her physical limitations. The man recognizing these principles will love, respect, nurture, and stay with his wife until death separates them. May all men rise to their God-given role and protect the weaker *vessel*.

Day 309

> *As it is written in the law of the Lord, Every male that openeth the* **Womb** *shall be called holy to the Lord. Luke 2:23*

This is a sacred statement made and practiced in the Levitical and priestly systems during the covenant days. It was a special thing for the firstborn to be a male; he was to be progenitor of the race. He was meant to be the priest and take over his father's role when he became too old or died. Thus, every male that opened the womb had a special blessing from the Lord, according to their traditional customs. Strange as it may seem, I still subscribed to that principle. I have four sons, and I told the first one that he is the Lord's. As a grandmother, I still practice that principle and let first time mothers know that if their first child is a male, he is sanctified and belongs to the Lord. Mothers must not fail to communicate that fact to the infant, toddler, and youth while not negating the specialness of other sons or daughters.

The first of anything has special significance, and when it is a son, he obtains special honor and privileges in the family line. When the plagues were afflicting the Egyptian people, nothing moved the heart of Pharaoh until God rained death upon the firstborn of everything: human, beast, cattle, and fowl. The Bible says there was weeping and lamentation in every Egyptian house because of the massive slaughter.

The principle of consecrating the firstborn male was a way of life among the ancients. Isaac wanted to give the blessing to his firstborn son, Esau; Anna consecrated Samuel and placed him in the Lord's service; Sampson and John the Baptist were also consecrated and specially blessed; Mary took Jesus, who was only eight days old, to be blessed.

Women have a sacred duty regarding this special gift that opens their womb. To the father, that son is his pride and joy. The son's existence shows off the father's sexual prowess and strength. However, the parents should not forget that that son belongs to the Lord first and to them next; he is to be especially dedicated to the Lord. May God bless all those firstborn males, and may they bring honor, praise, and glory to Him and joy to their parents. Let not the firstborn sons take their role lightly; they are to be role models for their siblings and be prepared to assume leadership roles. Solomon spoke very highly about their role and relationship to their fathers. "My son, keep thy father's commandment, and forsake not the law of thy mother" (Prov. 6:20). "A foolish son is a calamity to his father" (Prov. 19:13). Another verse says, "My son, if thine heart be wise, my heart shall rejoice, even mine" (Prov. 23:15). These texts clearly show the first son's position in the line of primogeniture; he has a special blessing.

Even as recently as this spring, among our congregational mothers, three sons opened the womb. In giving the gift card, I quoted the verse cited. The *womb* is the first university in which the child is matriculated; it is there his entire learning begins. May all mothers–Jewish and non-Jewish–take a keen responsibility to nurture the child starting in the *womb*. He is God's first gift to the family and ought to be a blessing to them and to God.

Day 310

Woe unto you, scribes and Pharisees, hypocrites! for ye make clean the outside of the cup and the platter, but within they are full of **Extortion** *and* **Excess**. *Matthew 23:25*

Here is Jesus' rebuke and condemnation to the Pharisees and religious leaders, who outwardly practiced sanctimonious and holy lives but inwardly their dealings were full of corruption and greed. They obtained their living by extorting and exacting usury (Ps. 5:9). These loan sharks carried out this diabolical practice at the Temple precincts where they sold and purchased sacrificial items.

On one such occasion, Jesus saw their hypocrisy, lies, and manipulations of justice, and He threw them out of the Temple, drove them from its environs, and overturned their transaction tables. He became enraged because of their fraudulent actions under the guise of saintly acts. He said, "My house shall be called the house of prayer; but ye have made it a den of thieves" (Matt. 21:13).

Neither Jesus nor the Father, who are full of justice and fair play, will tolerate any kind of unseemly or fatuitous behavior. We should ponder: is God any different today than He was then? Does He still guard with implicit care all of His places of worship? Are we modern-day Christians extorting and oppressing the weak, needy, and marginalized? Is our Christianity a mere profession lacking substance and genuine actions? Are we real with God and ourselves? Can we be trusted? Let us never forget that "the eyes of the Lord are in every place, beholding the evil and the good" (Prov. 15:3). He cannot be fooled; He is the all-knowing, all-seeing God and knows our thoughts from far off.

Every practicing Christian must examine their behavior to ensure that he or she represents truth and obeys God's word. Be reminded that we are living epistles, so we must live what we profess so that others looking on will see uprightness, honesty, integrity, sincerity, and purity manifested in our lives and will want to emulate us because we reflect Jesus. Let us be honest in our relationship with others and represent Christ, who is truth. God is pleased when His children represent Him perfectly in their imperfect bodies, and He will help us become like Jesus. May we allow God to perform His good and mighty works of recreating us into His image and help us avoid *extortions* and *excess*.

Day 311

Now be ye not stiffnecked, as your fathers were, but **Yield** *yourselves unto the Lord, and enter into his sanctuary ... and serve the Lord your God, that the fierceness of his wrath may turn away from you. 2 Chronicles 30:8*

This is the substance of King Hezekiah's letter to Israel's faithful. Throughout the Biblical age, as recorded and preserved for us, man has constantly and consistently turned away from God. It all began in Eden when the serpent gave Adam and Eve disrelish for the truth and presented fables of self-exaltation with his subtle innuendo.

Since then, we often engage in outright rebellion against truth, verity, and righteousness. Here we see a dedicated God-fearing king's concern about the spiritual progress of Israel, so he called for reform. His words, though cutting and severe, were designed to awaken national sensitivity to their spiritual malaise. Like a nurturing father, he recounted Israel's previous behaviors and encouraged them to forget the past, submit themselves to God's grace, return to His care, and embrace His lovingkindness. He pled with them to accept God again as their Leader and Commander, but if they remained recalcitrant and stiff-necked, they would incur God's wrath and His displeasure.

The king, fully acquainted with God's wrath and His mercy, entreated his people to yield themselves to righteousness and obedience. He wanted to spare his realm the incursion of God's wrath. Many of the current population did not know of God's goodness, mercies, or watchful care over their forefathers, so they easily absorbed the neighbors' convenient and prevailing culture. Hezekiah knew his God-given responsibility to the nation and called them to return to God's original plans for them.

The antediluvians were also stiff-necked and rebellious. Consequently, they incurred God's wrath and displeasure, and the flood destroyed them. In every age those who blatantly reject God's offer of mercy, love, and compassion receive their fate, but God always sends them a warning. Humankind must be warned of imminent danger and be given the opportunity to choose. Sacred history is replete with examples of God's warnings and final destruction.

It will be no different for this generation if they do not yield to God's call of mercy. Unless we submit to the pleadings of the Holy Spirit, give it entrance to our hearts, and allow it to transform our vile nature into a more Christ-like one, we shall also incur God's wrath and displeasure, "which is poured out without mixture into the cup of his indignation" (Rev. 14:10). There is good news; the door of mercy is still open, and Jesus is still interceding on the sinner's behalf. Let all who read and hear, enter and spare themselves of eternal extinction. We must yield to the Holy Spirit's pleading and forsake every sinful practice; God will definitely have mercy and receive you into His fold and make you fit to live with Him. May you *yield* your entire life to Him today and enjoy the gift of eternal life forever.

Day 312

Of the increase of his government and peace there shall be no end, upon the throne of David, and upon his kingdom, to order it, and to establish it with judgment and with justice from henceforth even for ever. The **Zeal** *of the Lord of hosts will perform this.*
Isaiah 9:7

What a powerful affirmation! This is the prophecy bringing a message of hope regarding Jesus, the Prince of Peace. He is a wonderful Counselor; He is the King of kings! Any reader, listener, or observer hearing these words might be prone to exclaim, "Impossible! It cannot be done; no one person can be all that!" But the Holy Word declares that it will be accomplished by the zeal of the Lord of hosts, the Majesty of heaven.

This Child is the same Emmanuel, the *El Shaddai*, whose kingdom is endless. Justice, fairness, and judgment characterize His rule. The government He sets up will not come to an end. This is the prophecy concerning the recreation of the earth as promised and articulated by Isaiah: "Behold, I create new heavens and a new earth: and the former shall not be remembered, nor come into mind" (Isa. 65:17). There in a new habitation where only peace, contentment, and harmony will prevail; these things will be executed with the passion, power, righteousness, and supervision of the Lord God zeal.

God's zeal is not like our passions, which are most often temperamental; it is permanent, solid, firm, and stands fast. God's zeal is a mighty power that comes straight from the throne room, where the mighty God will be a benevolent Ruler and Executioner. God's zeal is His power, passion, and holiness. He orders, restores, keeps, and sustains; He is God and can and will do all things. He says, "I am the Lord, and there is none else" (Isa. 45:5, 22; 46:9).

Through His zeal all earth dwellers will be judged according to their actions, and the righteous will reign upon the earth. God has done it before, and He will do it again. He says, "For I am the Lord, I change not" (Mal. 3:6).

God's zeal is a mighty fury resplendent as God himself. King David declares, "For the zeal of thine house hath eaten me up" (Ps. 69:9). The idea of meeting with God in His place of worship is so majestic that one trembles at His presence. May we be empowered with God's passion, power, and zeal? He wants to transmit that zeal to us. Let us not be stiff-necked. His divine zeal has maintained this world and every human activity; it is His zeal that will bring an utter end to sin. It is also His zeal that will usher us into our new home—heaven—at last! May we share this *zeal* with all those with whom we interact.

Study to Meet God's Approval

Day 313

Till I come, give **Attendance** *to reading, to exhortation, to doctrine. 1 Timothy 4:13*

This is the apostle Paul's counsel to young Pastor Timothy, his son in the Gospel. Paul had chosen him to be his companion in ministry because he saw in him the seeds of greatness, submission, and devotion to duty. Paul often remembered and admired the faith he saw in Timothy (see 2 Tim. 1:5). Though still young in the ministry, Timothy was assigned to manage the church, so Paul wrote and gave instructions as to how he should administrate and grow the church.

Timothy's role was to read and teach the Scriptures and to exhort the new Christians to obey the truths he taught. Though a Bible student himself, he was not to neglect his own Bible study. "Study to shew thyself approved unto God, a workman that needeth not to be ashamed, rightly dividing the words of truth" (2 Tim. 2:15). Timothy had grown up a believer and was well-accustomed to studying the Word on a daily basis: "And that from a child thou hast known the holy scriptures, which are able to make thee wise unto salvation" (2 Tim. 3:15). Let this be a gentle reminder for each of us to remain steadfast in the faith.

Though written directly to the young preacher, the counsel holds good for all Christians today, especially those connected with youth ministry: pastors and leaders. Timothy was anticipating the return of his father in the faith, and we find ourselves in the same situation as he did. We are currently awaiting the return of Jesus, our Savior and Lord, so the advice is even more fitting for our situation. Sadly, humankind has not changed. Things have deteriorated exponentially, so the message is more urgent.

All Christians, young and old, need to heed this counsel and spend more time in reading the Word. There are many discordant voices claiming one's attention that the desire to read God's Word becomes secondary. We must give attendance and diligence to it, for Jesus promised some twenty centuries ago that He will come again (see John 14:1–3). Let us heed Paul's counsel to young Timothy and make it ours, too. All of us are youth in the Gospel and need to be sure we know the doctrine. We need to be firmly established in what we have read, listened to, and learned.

While we await the Lord's return, let us read, study, and memorize the Word. We need to hide the precious words in our hearts and minds that we might not sin against God. Let us settle in the truth that has been communicated to us. We need to study, dig deep, and learn all that we can learn about the Gospel, the saving grace of Jesus, and the love of God. Most important of all, we need to be ready to meet Jesus when He returns to eradicate sin from this fair universe. Study the entire Bible, the prophecies, and see God's words unfold. Fill your mind with the truth and stay ready—be on guard! Give *attendance* to the Word! May it take first place in your life.

Day 314

Let **Brotherly** *love continue. Hebrews 13:1*

The advice given then is very relevant now. We live in a society dominated by the "I" sickness, i.e. the greatest kind of "eye" trouble that one can have. People think of themselves first and last and may even negate the existence of those closest to them. Selfishness dominates.

On the contrary, Christians should think of others, especially the needy. We are called to esteem them as if they are close-knit relatives. All people are created equal; the same red blood courses through our veins, and as the apostle Paul says so judiciously, "One blood and Father of us all" (Acts 17:26, author paraphrase). He is God the Father, the Creator of male and female, all are made of one flesh. Therefore, we are all related. We are brothers and sisters because we all have the same gracious Father. It is therefore incumbent on each of us to look out for each other's safety and welfare. Can you imagine the kind of society there could be if everyone—high and low, rich and poor, educated and uneducated—took this advice and practiced it? You might say that the concept is Utopian, but no, it is pragmatic and can be practiced easily. Root out self-caring, I, and me, and replace it with thoughts of how to help others. Then we can each say, "I know where my brother and sister are; I am aware of their needs. I know what to do and where to get help for them."

Having this kind of mindset will undoubtedly root out any grouchiness, unkindness, or self-pleasing behavior. There will be place for love, care, sympathy, empathy, and loving expressions. As members of the household of faith, let us practice the "Barnabas syndrome" and not only bring consolation but also share equitably the gifts we have received from God's hands. When that is practiced, we will truly be expressing brotherly concern. Unity and love will pervade the entire atmosphere. That kind of behavior is characterized as Christ in action or Christianity on the march.

Lest we forget: Jesus, our Elder Brother, made the ultimate sacrifice. He gave His life as well as the love He possessed. He said to His first disciples, "Love as I have loved you" (John 15:12, 17, 26, author paraphrase). The command is also for us, His next wave of disciples and followers. There is need today for the same amount of love if not more than when Jesus and the first twelve walked this earth. Therefore, the command to let love among brothers thrives, whether it is your physical or spiritual brother and sister. We are all connected by that eternal thread that binds all humanity—Jesus' eternal and everlasting love.

As our Exemplar did, we must demonstrate genuine love for others: kindness to strangers, empathy for those in prison, help for the dispossessed and disenfranchised, and care for those who have been mistreated or enslaved and left as society's misfits. Our responsibility is to be hospitable to all, for except the saving grace of our Lord, it could have been you.

Let us ensure that our love runs deep and extend to everyone. Paul counsels, "Be kindly affectionate one to another with brotherly love" (Rom. 12:10). Let us, therefore, love without limitations or conditions. God's love still sustains us. May the love of Christ impel, propel, and empower us to give love to others.

Day 315

Now we exhort you, brethren, warn them that are unruly, **Comfort** *the feebleminded, support the weak, be patient toward all men. 1 Thessalonians 5:14*

Yesterday's text advised us to let love prevail at all times toward all men and women, but especially to the family of God. Today's verse brings a deeper moral obligation to the brethren.

Those strong in the faith and have an enduring relationship with our Father ought to practice the graces He has bestowed upon them. We should not think of ourselves better than others, for all have the same Fatherhood. We have the same flesh and blood, even though our physical features may be different. However, in the manner of lifestyles and behaviors, certain norms and behavioral codes exist. If an infraction is committed, then proper action in terms of corrective measures has to be enforced. If each person acted unrestrained, then chaos would stalk the land. The unruly, stiff-necked, stubborn, and recalcitrant ones must be warned that their conduct and behaviors are repulsive to God, but the corrective measures must be done in brotherly love considering that the situation could be reversed.

On the other hand, there is a nobler and more praiseworthy task to be done: to provide comfort, assurance, warmth, loving care, and tenderness to those more mentally challenged, weak in the faith, faint-hearted, timid, as well as those who are afraid to take risks. The stronger members have to nurture, teach, and show them possibilities from God's Word. We have to let them read and see for themselves the power that resides in the Word. Many times, the stronger and more richly endowed are impatient and wonder what is taking them so long to catch on, but not everyone is well-endowed, and not everyone has the same spiritual maturity. As more mature Christians, we must help them to develop spiritual muscles by sharing testimonies of what God has done in their lives. We have to teach them how to feed on the Word and develop confidence in their walk with God. Finally, pray with and for them. If we love them back to strength and wholeness, we will watch their brokenness disappear.

Above all, we must practice the virtue of patience and self-control. Do not yell at the weak in faith or physique or be critical of them, but point them to the many promises in God's word and encourage them to begin to commit some texts to memory. "Thy word have I hid in mine heart, that I might not sin against thee" (Ps. 119:11).

Finally, try to be sensitive in your ministry. Take time to understand the foibles of those to whom you are ministering, especially if a situation tries your patience. Plan ahead and give much study to the situation and people. Pray for wisdom, and by God's grace, remain calm. Seek to practice patience with everyone and under every circumstance. The Holy Spirit will assist you. Go on and be engaged for the Master! May you provide, offer, and give *comfort*.

Day 316

Keep thy heart with all **Diligence***: for out of it are the issues of life. Proverbs 4:23*

This is sound advice to all: guard your heart and mind, especially your mind, for it is the seat of intelligence and all mental activities. We are thinking and acting creatures, but we often choose to follow our heart's desires, even if our mind tells us otherwise. David, speaking of this mighty organ, says it is deceitful ... who can trust it? Yet with all its inconsistencies, it still remains the core of all our feelings: love, desire, and pain. It dictates how we live our lives. Therefore, it is imperative that we concentrate on those pure and holy desires.

The heart is a symbol of love; Jesus requested that His sons and daughters give Him their heart, and in return, He would give them His Father's kingdom. All our love, hate, desires, and wants, etc., generate in our heart

Physically speaking, the heart is an organ that pumps blood. It controls the chief arterial operation of sending blood coursing through our arteries, veins, lungs, and capillaries. But on a metaphysical level, it is the well-spring of our lives. In it we move and have our being. Every activity that we are engaged in or attempt, every behavior manifested, every thought, deed, or action has its seat of origin in the heart. Out of it issues both the good and the bad. When the heart has an accident, our life is in the balance. We are on tenterhooks—physically, emotionally, morally, mentally, and socially. Because of its indispensable characteristic, we have been advised to guard it carefully. It is delicate and that is the reason why the heavenly Designer placed it in the innermost part of our body, where it is diligently guarded by the rib cage, spinal column, and all the vertebrae.

On a spiritual level, we are advised to guard well the avenues of the soul—those organs through which information is received and dispatched. The heart is the gateway for gaining such entry. It is through our heart and mind that God speaks to us. We yield to Him through the impulses and throbbing of our heart. It is God's property. Our body is only the case that holds it. Let us yield it up to Him, and let the Holy Spirit take up residence in there so that we will be well. May this be our prayer: "Lord, take my heart for I cannot give it. It is thy property. Keep it pure, for I cannot keep it for thee."

Yield the keeping of your heart, mind, and body to the Holy Spirit, and let Him take complete control and provide the necessary oversight that is needed. We must ensure that unwanted objects do not enter in through the door of our mind or our heart. That is why we have been asked to be very cautious as to what and to whom we open its doors. "Keep thy heart with all *diligence*; for out of it are the issues of life." May that be your marching order.

Day 317

But with thee will I **Establish** *my covenant; and thou shalt come into the ark, thou, and thy sons, and thy wife, and thy sons' wives with thee. Genesis 6:18*

God established this covenant with Noah because his was the only righteous family that revered God. Even though Noah proclaimed Jehovah's saving mercies, warned the people of their sinful practices, and called them to repentance, they remained stubborn and stiff-necked and followed their own lusts. They prided in their wickedness and rejected the calling of the messenger of truth.

For 120 years Noah pounded and hammered the nails as he built the ark, and all he received was mockery, derision, ridicule, scorn, and buffoonery. There was no rain in the land so to talk of a flood that would sweep the earth into its jaws was insanity. To them, this preacher was a mad man, and his action a sheer joke and idiocy. But faithful Noah continued his daily task of hammering, driving nails, and preaching the Word.

And God looked down from His holy dwelling place, watched, and listened as Noah hammered and preached and besought the people, but they yielded neither to his counsel nor his entreaty. After 120 years of preaching to generation after generation (four in all), God's cup of mercy was full; the ark was finished, and it was time for God to act.

The ark Noah built was for the safety of all who sought shelter from the impending disaster. God said, "And, behold, I, even I, do bring a flood of waters upon the earth, to destroy all flesh ... and every thing that is in the earth shall die" (verse 17). Continuing the conversation, God told Noah that He would save him and his family (read the entire story in Gen. 6 and 7*)*.

God has also established His covenant with us. He has set His bow of promise in the sky. The rainbow is God's covenant with us. It is to remind us that He will not again destroy the earth with a flood. He has also established His covenant with us by offering Jesus as our supreme sacrifice. Two gospel writers state, "But as the days of Noah were, so shall also the coming of the Son of man be" (Matt. 24:37; see also Luke 17:26).

The good news of Jesus' soon return is being preached worldwide. Men and women are hearing God's call to forsake their sins and find shelter in the ark before it is too late. Whoever has any kind of technology from today's world can access the Good News and accept this proffered gift of love.

As these messengers of righteousness preach and the Holy Spirit impresses our hearts, we must abandon every ungodly and unwholesome trait and seek repentance. God's covenant with us is the gift of His Son, Jesus Christ, whose blood has the efficacy to save unto the uttermost all who come to Him. May you accept God's *established* covenant while the church's doors are still open and Jesus is interceding on our behalf.

Day 318

When my father and my mother **Forsake** *me, then the Lord will take me up. Psalm 27:10*

This text is brimful of confidence and certitude of the Father's loving care and watchful eyes over His children. Even if there is parental abandonment, we are certain that God, our Father, the Jehovah Jireh will not forsake or abandon you and me.

Isaiah affirms God's tender care, "Can a woman forget her suckling child, that she should not have compassion on the son of her womb? yea, they may forget, yet I will not forget thee" (Isa. 49:15). Following is the best and the most positive clincher: "Behold, I have graven thee upon the palms of my hands; thy walls are continually before me" (verse 16). What more comfort and assurance does anyone want? God Himself promises to take care of each of His children. He has your face tattooed in the palms of His hands. Whenever He opens His hands, God sees your face looking straight at Him. You cannot be forgotten or forsaken. Make sure that you are a child of God. Jesus reminds His hearers that we are more valuable than the tiniest birds that daily twitter and perch around. This is positive consolation for the downtrodden, the dispossessed, the weak, and the lonely—that God is still with them—even though circumstances may be rife.

God made us for His glory. How then can one bring glory to the Savior of all if she or he is weighed down with the cares and challenges of living? Our God will not allow any of us to languish. Our Father gives light and provides the opportunity to get work, find shelter, and build a satisfying life. He owns everything, and He has no paupers as His children. And even amid life's challenges, amidst family feuds and contradictions, He is still there not only in the shadows but also in the open, keeping watch over His own.

God declares, "I will be with him in trouble; I will deliver him, and honour him" (Ps. 91:15). That is God, the Eternal Father, speaking. You and I are never alone; we are never forsaken or abandoned. Though all earthly support may leave us, our God, the great I AM, will be with us. Isaiah says, "I will uphold thee with the right hand of my righteousness" (Isa. 41:10). No one will ever be in want who makes the God of Jacob their refuge, fortress, and hiding place. Another passage reads, "God is our refuge and strength, a very present help in trouble" (Ps. 46:1). He will be there for us. Believe and abandon your entire life—all of it—into His care. You are never alone and never will be.

May you remember that God will keep you and never *forsake* you. I hope you are as excited about this wonderful promise of assurance as I am!

Day 319

Those who **Guard** *their lips preserve their lives, but those who speak rashly will come to ruin.*
Proverbs 13:3, NIV

Earlier on in this devotional, we referred to the tongue as an untamable member in the body, and the speaker asked the rhetorical question. Who can tame it? David, recognizing the power of the tongue (in which resides life and death), prayed the universal prayer for us. "Set a watch, O Lord, before my mouth; keep the doors of my lips" (Ps. 141:3).

It is to our advantage to watch carefully what we say because the reward of cautious speech leads to a fuller life and the avoidance of trouble. When someone misspoke, the usual retort was "I never meant it to be that way; you misunderstand me." Since the spoken word like the spent arrow cannot be retrieved, the speaker must carefully weigh what they should say, how it should be said, the tonal quality accompanying the delivery, and the reception of the spoken word.

If you do not speak, you cannot be charged with heresy or folly. You can preserve your life by remaining silent, unless you are giving good advice. The wise man said, "Whoso keepeth his mouth and his tongue keepeth his soul from troubles" (Prov. 21:23). "Death and life are in the power of the tongue" (Prov. 18:21).

Hopefully, parents teach their children very early to guard what they allow to come out of their mouths so that when they become adults, they will become quite adept and skillful in how they use words. Life and death are in the tongue as well as blessings and curses. No wonder David prayed many prayers for guarding the tongue: "Let the words of my mouth ... be acceptable in thy sight, O Lord" (Ps. 19:14).

Do not forget that a wide mouth speaks evil and gushes out folly; the speaker's end is destruction. He or she will come to ruin, and there will be none to support him or her because reckless words pierce like a sword.

On the contrary the tongue of the wise brings healing and emits knowledge and soundness.

Self-control is needed to guard the tongue and its utterances. The mouth must not be an open sepulcher spewing out indiscriminately. The cure is to stop and think before you speak. Solomon says that the tongue is unruly; therefore, it must be tightly reined. Our speech should be even-tempered with words well-chosen and well-timed. Then your tongue will be a caring one that speaks truth and encourages with words of healing, peace, and hope. May we pray for the Holy Spirit to *guard* our utterances.

Day 320

And take the **Helmet** *of salvation, and the sword of the Spirit, which is the word of God.*
Ephesians 6:17

A soldier should go out to battle fully clad; if not, the soldier is vulnerable and will be shot at the weakest and most delicate part of the body. It is the brain that is the controlling mechanism, so the head must be protected with the helmet.

As Christians, we are in a spiritual combat with the enemy, and so the apostle tells us how to dress. "Take unto you the whole armour of God" (verse 13). It goes on to enumerate each article and their use in warding off the attacker.

In this spiritual battle, all believers find themselves engaged in warfare with Satan and his emissaries; everyone is under attack. The writer warns that the forces we have to contend with are not natural or physical ones, but metaphysical: principalities and powers, rulers of the darkness of this world. Thus a lonely and poorly clad believer is totally unprepared for the battle that will rage on his front. Consequently, every piece of the armor is required to ward off Satan's attacks.

Now, the helmet is that special hat used to protect the brain. Snipers like to aim at the head, for if the brain is shattered, death is instant. And snipers aim to kill—not to maim or wound. When the brain collapses, all the other vital organs shut down, so Satan wants to attack or gain control of our mind and make us doubt God's Word. The brain is where all decisions are made, and if someone can get control of that power house, he or she can easily manipulate us.

Satan used that same mind game on Eve in the Garden of Eden. He placed doubt in her mind. "Yea, hath God said?" (Gen. 3:1) and thus, he mesmerized and tranquilized her so that she could not think straight or run away.

If you doubt God's word and Jesus' act and the salvation He freely offers, there is no substance left but cold impotent ash. The helmet protects our minds from doubting God's Word, so we must fill our minds with the words and thoughts of Jesus so that when the enemy attacks us, we can lift up a standard against him with "It is written" (Matt. 4:4). That is why David says, "Thy word have I hid in my heart, that I might not sin against thee" (Ps. 119:11).

It is mandatory for every Christian to feed on God's Holy Word; eat it daily, ingest, and digest it, so it nourishes every fiber of our being, especially the mind and the soul. The Word of God is a "lamp unto my feet, and a light unto my path" (verse 105). It has the power to dispel every kind of darkness. We cannot be shot down; nothing can penetrate our minds when they are fortified with God's Word. Herein lays our strength and the victory. Put on the helmet, saints, and never take it off. There is no respite in this confrontation. Give attendance to the Word; remain fully armed and keep your eyes on Jesus. Hide God's word in your mind and envelop yourself in it. Protect your mind from the fiery darts of the wicked one. Adhere to Isaiah's recommendation: "Put on ...an helmet of salvation upon his head" (Isa. 59:17). May you guard your mind with a *helmet*—the Word of God—for the name of the Lord is a strong tower.

Day 321

For thus saith the high and lofty One that **Inhabiteth** *eternity, whose name is Holy; I dwell in the high and holy place ... to revive the spirit of the humble, and to revive the heart of the contrite ones. Isaiah 57:15*

God created the heavens and the earth and everything that dwells therein. He made every person and animal you see. God's ascription is high and lofty. Where then does He dwell? What place can accommodate Him? He inhabits eternity–every place and every time. He is everywhere. When King Solomon built the temple, the earthly king declared that it did not have the capacity to hold this magnificent God (see 1 Kings 8:27).

All space and time belong to God. He fills and occupies it all. Yet this high and lofty God has chosen to come and dwell among us, to sit at our tables, on our couches, and on our grass in the meadow. He chooses to reside wherever humankind is. Moreover, He will abide in our hearts if we will allow Him entry. Just imagine! The Creator is willing to come and stay with the humble, meek, and lowly, who feel their need of a Savior!

What an awesome and compassionate God. Surely, He is a friend of sinners and a mighty King! He knows we cannot come up to Him as we are, so He has chosen to come to us–to be God with us, Emmanuel (see Matt. 1:23)–so that He can bring us up to Him. Incomprehensible! The sinful mind can scarcely grasp its essence.

God loves and cares so much that He stimulates us to strive for godliness and perfection of character. He sees our striving for uprightness, beauty, and truth and accepts our sincerity. He is willing to stake His throne on us weak, frail human beings. He knows our hearts, intentions, struggles, and desires, yet He, the great God of the universe has chosen to come and abide with us. We are blessed and special; may you make room for Him.

God performed this miraculous task through His Beloved Son, Jesus, who came and inhabited humanity for just over thirty-three years and lived a sinless life. He became our Model Man to show us what is possible if we turn over our entire lives into God's keeping. Jesus declared, "Believe me that I am in the Father, and the Father in me" (John 14:11). God came down to the seeker of truth for one purpose: to revitalize and give hope and joy to those who feel their need of a Savior.

Is it not awesome that this high and lofty God who inhabits the entire world can look down and in love grasp the hands of the penitent and earnest seeker? God is indeed majestic, magnificent, and awesome! May all His earthborn subjects of the entire solar system give Him praise, glory, and honor. He is truly a great God; He is over everything, and He *inhabits* the entire universe.

Day 322

The Son of man came eating and drinking, and they say, Behold a man gluttonous, and a winebibber, a friend of publicans and sinners. But wisdom is **Justified** *of her children. Matthew 11:19*

Here we find a contrast between Jesus and John. In the previous verse, the Scribes and Pharisees judged Jesus and John on their social etiquette. They complained that John's moderate lifestyle invited mockery and derision, and they classified him as the devil. In the same breath, they castigated Jesus for His free mingling with sinners and called Him despicable names: a winebibber, a drunkard, and a glutton. In essence, there was no middle ground accorded these two great preachers of righteousness. Neither of them could do anything right; they were always up for scrutiny.

John, the more ascetic, often ate locust and wild honey out in the wilderness. Jesus, because He socialized with the new converts and disciples, was called all the aforementioned names plus a friend of the underdogs, the lower classes of humanity. The Pharisees saw this behavior and could not believe that He was God's Son or that He came from heaven. They totally denied His Godliness and His power all while being both obnoxious and skeptical.

Jesus assessed their thinking and recognized that foolishness, bigotry, ignorance, and an unwillingness to know what the Scriptures said about His coming and ministry characterized their assertions. Jesus told them that if they had any idea of who He was, they would be appalled at the notion of classifying Him as a low life. He told them that wisdom is justified in her children, which was a paradoxical statement. It showed their blindness and bigotry. Wise people act intelligently and utter sagacious words. On the other hand, the Pharisees showed they were fools because they did not know or recognize who was in their presence. They lacked integrity, uprightness, knowledge, and sound judgment. Solomon says it so well, "The tongue of the wise useth knowledge aright: but the mouth of fools poureth out foolishness" (Prov. 15:2). They did not want their lifestyles to be challenged, so they rejected and mocked the Son of God.

Jesus made it perfectly clear that He came to make well the sick and the lame. He did not come to call the righteous; He came to lead sin-sick souls to the Father.

Jesus ate with them, fed them, and healed them of all their sicknesses and diseases, and then bade them to follow Him. Those for whom He came are justified. Their sins are blotted out, and they have the assurance of eternal life. They have been wise in following His counsel and are deemed just. They are forgiven before God and the holy angels.

The prophet Daniel says, "And they that be wise shall shine as the brightness of the firmament; and they that turn many to righteousness as the stars for ever" (Dan. 12:3). Those who act thus are indeed wise and justified. May we each be rendered *justified* when Jesus returns!

Day 323

> *Be **Kindly** affectioned one to another with brotherly love; in honour preferring one another.*
> *Romans 12:10*

Paul is specifically addressing the brethren in Rome, but his counsel is generalized to all members of the Christian community. Thus he exhorts unselfishness, kindness, sympathy, care, and concern for each other. In a steep competitive world, corralled by the "me, myself, and I syndrome," people sidestep the weak, helpless, and those circumstantially handicapped. The crippled man, who could not get into the pool of Bethesda because the more assertive and agile ones plunged in ahead of him, shows the selfishness and unkindness —"me-first syndrome."

Society is full of many indigent, sick, and helpless people, and the apostle advises that the strong and well should help the weak and the less able. Kindness is almost a lost virtue in the secular world where selfishness dominates, but it should be a shining characteristic in any Christian environment.

Unlike Cain's response to God when asked about the whereabouts of his brother, each of us in the family of faith is indeed our "brother's keeper" and has a Christian responsibility to them (Gen. 4:9). Jesus has left humanity an example of how to treat others. From His lips emit the golden rule: "Do unto others as you would have them do to you" (Matt. 7:12, author paraphrase). Let kindness and kindly treatments radiate from you. It is the only antidote for selfishness.

On your agenda for service is J. O. Y: Jesus first, others next, and yourself last. If we all practiced this principle, then there will be joy in our lives. That is true honor and selflessness. When Jesus takes first place in our hearts and minds, self will be dethroned and the Holy Spirit will be enthroned and will teach us kindness.

The world does not operate this way, but we are a different people and are enjoined to put others before ourselves. Jesus, our Lord and Master, placed us before His suffering and so bore the humiliation and eventual death for us. We have nothing to compare with the manifestation of Christ's love. At best, prompted by His love and compassion, we can show some tenderness, care, love, sympathy, patience, kindness, and aid to those for whom He died. If we do not have it, we pray for it. We are all brothers and sisters in Christ; let us do right by Jesus for those with whom we worship and fellowship. Let love, tenderness, and affection prevail among us. Practice kindness, empathy, sympathy, and charity to everyone. Let us emulate Jesus in everything we do. May we never be ashamed to reach out to all our brothers and sisters in Christ with a *kind*, caring hand!

Day 324

As for me, I will behold thy face in righteousness: I shall be satisfied, when I awake, with thy **Likeness***. Psalm 17:15*

Here, King David expresses the Christian's ultimate hope, which is later articulated by the apostle Paul in his letters to the Corinthian and Thessalonica brethren. To the former, Paul says, "For now we see through a glass, darkly; but then face to face: now I know in part; but then shall I know even as also I am known" (1 Cor. 13:12). This text means when Jesus returns, we shall be transformed into an incorporeal body; we shall be immortalized. To the latter, he said, "We which are alive and remain shall be caught up together with them in the clouds, to meet the Lord in the air: and so shall we ever be with the Lord" (1 Thess. 4:17). We shall be like the Lord, for we shall see Him as He is.

In this psalm David prefigures the resurrection of the righteous dead, who will see Jesus face to face. His, like all the resurrected saints' bodies, will be changed. When he awakes, he will see the face of Jesus, who will greet him with outstretched arms. He will be awake from the sleep of death in the likeness of Jesus, for we shall be like Him—sinless, pure, and immortal.

We shall be satisfied, but Jesus will be even more so satisfied when He looks upon us, the travail of His soul, and present us—the redeemed ones—to His Father as the trophies of His earth bound journey. With us being there, now transformed into His image, Jesus will acknowledge the worth of His Sacrifice. Then our Father will reach out His strong and mighty arms and receive us. It will be worth it all when we see Jesus, for we shall be like Him and see Him as He is.

In order to be like Christ, we must practice being like Him in our lifestyle: attitude, mannerisms, and behaviors. The change to being like Him is a gradual process. When He returns in all the fullness of His glory, He is coming for people who have been living the Christ-centered, Christ-directed life. He is not coming to reform our lives because it should have already happened through daily commitment and conversations with Him. It is by loving others, reading the Word, and copying His life that we will become like Him in character and in wholeness. When we see Him face-to-face we will be reflecting His righteous character.

While there is time, we must learn more of Jesus, spend time studying His Word, and, as Paul says, "Let this mind be in you, which was also in Christ Jesus" (Phil. 2:5). Only as we feed upon His Words, study how He treated people, and emulate His actions can we truly become like Him. May we become engaged now so that when He returns, we shall see Him as He is and reflect His *likeness*.

Day 325

Lord, make me to know mine end, and the **Measure** *of my days, what it is: that I may know how frail I am. Psalm 39:4*

The day I found this text I was excited to know the interrelatedness of God's word. This prayer reverberates the sentiment of Psalm 90:12 because the speaker asks for knowledge and insight about the stature of his moorings. We must continually take stock of our lives, our relationship with God, our family and friends. Ed Koch, the mayor of New York City in the 1970s and 1980s, became famous for always asking, "How am I doing?" to his constituents. He wanted feedback on his weekly, monthly, and yearly performances to ensure he was doing the people's business well.

Life is very fragile and tender; it can be snatched out in a moment. We need to be spiritually, intellectually, and morally sensitive to our standing and measure according to God's standards. How does God see us? Are we true to ourselves? Are our actions pleasing and acceptable to Him? Many of us are self-willed and go about life uncaring of others and our own destiny. We have no plan or purpose and are like driftwood moving along with the tide.

The text acknowledges humanity's frailty, instability, and lack of strength, direction, and substance. As with a flash of insight, we realize the travesty of our moorings, and we stop, ponder, and offer a prayer for guidance: "Lord, help me."

We are God's creation, and He has given us a time span to be utilized profitably and honorably in blessing others. We do not have Methuselah's luxury of 969 years or any of the other worthies blessed with longevity; ours is down to 70 or 80 if God extends it. Therefore, our allotted time must be treasured and used wisely.

This psalm shows the speaker's awareness of the brevity and transience of life. Solomon advises, "Boast not thyself of to morrow" (Prov. 27:1). This is still wise counsel for today. God has established humanity's limitations and boundaries; our strength comes from and is sustained by God's mighty power. Our frailty becomes strong through Jesus Christ.

Because life is brief and time is limited, we should use the allotted time to reach out and touch others in significant ways. We do not have time to neglect what is truly important. Tell someone what Jesus has done for you and correct the fragile areas of your life. Let your prayer be: "Lord, teach me to number my days and to know how frail I am. I depend on You for everything." May we remember to *measure* our days and find our strength in the Lord.

Day 326

For thus saith the Lord, Ye have sold yourselves for **Nought**; *and ye shall be redeemed without money. Isaiah 52:3*

This message carries a rebuke and a promise. It was a clarion call to Jerusalem, God's holy city, and particularly to the people of Judah, who had experienced ruin instead of prosperity. It was a wake-up call to them to expel the sins from among them and return to their God. They had become idolatrous and had rejected God's leading, but they were still classified as God's chosen people on whom He would bestow His special blessing. God still favored them and promised them that they would be redeemed without money.

The message reminded them that they had sold out for nothing, yet despite their action, there was hope because God was going to reestablish them. This was the prophecy concerning the coming Messiah and Redeemer, who would freely offer Himself to ransom God's children. His precious sacrificial blood far surpasses any monetary value. He would gather the errant ones and gently lead them back to the fold—i.e. redeeming them without money. In other words, they would not have to pay penance. As a result the entire Christian community can sing about how the blood of the cross is their only foundation. The apostle Peter concurred, "Ye were not redeemed with corruptible things, as silver and gold ... but with the precious blood of Christ" (1 Peter 1:18, 19).

This promise was not only ascribed to Judah but to all God's children throughout the ages. As I write these devotional reflections, I am convinced of God's manifold direction in the writing of the Holy Scriptures. Every idea is so coordinated; the messages for the ancients are just as timely for us today. We can assuredly embrace Timothy's affirmation about the wholeness and reliability of God's hand in the writing of the sacred Scriptures: "All scripture is given by inspiration of God" (2 Tim. 3:16, 17).

Like the children of Judah, if we heed the call and return to the Lord our God, we shall be redeemed and enjoy the bliss of eternity. Our ticket has been bought; the only cost is obedience, acceptance, and yielding to Him. May we grasp the opportunity while there is still time! God will always come through; whatever He promised literal Israel, He gives to spiritual Israel.

Let us not be like Eve or Esau and sell ourselves for *nought*. We are very precious in God's sight; we cost Him the life of His dear Son. God suffered a loss for us; may we be His gain.

Day 327

> **One** *thing have I desired of the Lord, that will I seek after; that I may dwell in the house of the Lord all the days of my life, to behold the beauty of the Lord, and to enquire in his temple.*
> *Psalm 27:4*

Beautiful in any language! What is the primary element you want in a relationship, whether it is with God, your spouse, parents, children, friends, or coworkers? With so many options and variables calling your attention, one has a difficult time to choose.

Let us focus on the relationship with God; what is the one thing you most desire? Is it to dwell in the house of the Lord? It can be more than just moving in and take up residence in the Tabernacle or synagogue. Would you not rather experience an inseparable communion with the Father? Additionally, David stated that he would rather be a doorkeeper in the house of the Lord than to dwell in the tents of wicked men. Thus, he has always been languishing to spend time with his Father God.

The question is still unanswered: do you long for God as David did? He did not want to be separated from God just as lovers do not want to be separated from each other. David wanted to remain in close proximity to God and be engaged in continual worshipful praise, for he knew that there was a fullness of joy and pleasures forevermore when in God's presence. Who would want to be pulled away from such a cozy position?

Beholding God's beauty, His righteousness, and His delightful presence will be so wonderful after a long, hard, and tiresome life here on earth. A good analogy is when a young man visits the home of the young lady he is in love with, and he wants to spend as much time as he can with her. This young man wants to soak up the environment and get a general feel of the entire parental relationship and their affect toward him. David transfers the same feeling to his relationship with God. His only desire is to be with Him, to linger in His presence, and enjoy His sweet fellowship.

Do you feel the need to be closely connected to your Father and to spend an inordinate amount of time in His presence, talking and listening to His counsel? Is the Lord God the light of your life and do you pant after Him as young lovers do for each other? Is your desire to court or woo Him? If you do, then David's prayer is also your prayer.

Pray to live in God's presence each day. Seek Him out, then cultivate and nurture that relationship. Spend time with God in worshipful praise. If you seek for Him diligently, you will find Him, for He is also searching for you. The quest is mutual. May you pray to have sweet communion with Jesus and the Father.

Day 328

> *A **Prudent** man concealeth knowledge: but the heart of fools proclaimeth foolishness.*
> *Proverbs 12:23*

Prudent people are wise and concerted ones; they are not "blabber mouths," and they think before they speak. These are people who are well assured of their status and standing among others. They may be well schooled in the arts, sciences, logic, and philosophy and know how to conduct themselves. They know full well the power that resides in the spoken word, so caution is their watchword.

Prudent people have quiet confidence; they do not have to prove anything. Insecure people always feel the need to prove themselves and justify their actions, so they are very verbose. Prudent people know their capability and can work unhindered and unpretentiously.

Wise people are thinkers; they measure their words before they utter them. Silly and hasty people are in a hurry to show-off, and their tongue utters foolishness and vain babblings instead of bringing healing and wisdom. These do not spend time in the presence of the Master Teacher. Unlike the king in our previous meditation, they do not have any desire to seek after the Lord, to dwell in His temple, and to listen to his voice. They are too busy listening to their own voices, so they miss the opportunity of communing with God and gaining wisdom from His Holy Word.

King Solomon spoke strongly about foolish people's behavior and stated that wisdom deals with both life and health. He felt an individual should give diligence to the musings of his or her heart and mind and stated that a foolish person's lips do not express knowledge, and the prudent should avoid his or her company. Read the Proverbs 10 through 14 for more of King Solomon's counsel.

All Christians ought to make the Bible their primary study book. In it is wisdom and counsels for guiding, directing, and teaching us the way to conduct ourselves in every sphere of life. The Holy Spirit residing in the heart and mind will teach us what, when, and how to say things. Jesus promised that "the Comforter ... shall teach you all things" (John 14:26).

The prudent must show that they are connected to the higher Powers: the Trinity–Father, Son, and Holy Spirit. We will learn from Them, for They have covenanted to be with us to the end. If we are short in knowledge and choose to ask for help, They will richly supply our needs and fill our minds with words of wisdom. Isaiah said, "The Lord God hath given me the tongue of the learned, that I should know how to speak a word in season to him that is weary: ... he wakeneth mine ear to hear as the learned" (Isa. 50:4). That is the prudent person's mantra. Oh, that all will pray to be wise and seek the wisdom of Him who gives to all humankind freely! May we follow the Master Teacher and be *prudent* learners rather than foolish failures.

Day 329

> **Quicken** *me after thy lovingkindness; so shall I keep the testimony of thy mouth.*
> *Psalm 119:88*

King David's prayers established the model approach to God: TCR. He always included thanksgiving, confession, and a request. In this particular prayer, based on God's lovingkindness, compassion, and tender mercies, he requested revitalizing and renewing his former relationship with God.

This man, mighty in words and deeds and dubbed "a man after God's own heart," acknowledged God's acquaintance with his slippery paths. He contritely and humbly came back to God seeking reparation. In covenanting with God, he proposed that if God would bound him to Him then he would not forget his precepts but would obey His laws, statues, and testimonies.

David's plea is a cry for help; he was surely desperate and needed immediate heavenly intervention. This is like a child pleading with a parent for dissolution of the intended punishment. God is our true parent, and He knows when and how to chasten so that the discipline fits the infraction.

Like David, we must be sensitive to our true condition and ask for revitalization and reconnection to the source of our life—God the Father—and plead for the presence of the Holy Spirit to point out our foibles. We need to seek forgiveness through confession and repentance. It was because of David's contriteness, submission, and repentance that God dubbed him a man of His own heart. God expects when we are caught in a fault to confess, repent, and surrender in order to receive forgiveness.

God is patiently waiting to restore His image in all His errant children, but we must first acknowledge our transgression, forsake our disaffection, and seek God's mercy and forgiveness. We must confess, repent, and surrender. Ownership, confession, repentance, and surrender are the four prongs of the forgiveness fork and must be utilized for reconciliation with God. Let us begin again today.

Pray for the Holy Spirit's quickening power to sensitize our consciences so that we abandon our shortcomings and be drawn closer to our heavenly Father, as He is waiting to receive us.

Like King David with the prophet Nathan and like the prodigal son in Luke's discourse, we must come to ourselves and in contrition call out to God, "I will arise and go" (Luke 15:18), or "I have sinned against the Lord" (2 Sam. 12:13). Once we call out to Him, we can return to God. May we receive the *quickening* power of God's illimitable grace!

Day 330

> **Recompence** *to no man evil for evil. Provide things honest in the sight of all men.*
> *Romans 12:17*

Today's society has little tolerance and much intolerance. We are not willing to be the butt of another person's joke or prank. Ever since that fatal day when sin entered in the precincts of humankind's domain, people have sought retribution. Even the newly born baby and the toddler learn very quickly how to be intolerant. They scream and fuss and shuffle their bodies all while fighting back through gestures, actions, or overt retaliation. This seems to be a principle ingrained in one's psyche and may have emerged through the generational DNA.

The apostle Paul and many Christians unsubscribe to the philosophy of "an eye for an eye and a tooth for a tooth," even though the revenge principle is still operational in today's insensitive culture. However, when Jesus came on the scene, he abrogated many of the Old Testament practices. For example, Jesus repeatedly said, "It has been told … But I say" both in the book of Matthew and the book of John. Jesus' presence and teaching brought a new dynamic to human life and existence. By His pure and godly life and His sacrificial blood upon the cross, He erased that premise. It is a law of brutality. Mahatma Gandhi once commented on this principle. He said, "An eye for an eye will leave everyone blind." If that Old Testament principle persisted, there would be mayhem for no one would be able to see his or her opponent. Similarly, a "tooth for a tooth" leaves everyone toothless. To take that saying literally is foolish; both people will be left blind, toothless, and lacking integrity.

Jesus said, "This is my commandment, That ye love one another, as I have loved you" (John 15:12).

Love neither maims nor fights back; it is not retaliatory, which is why Jesus told His disciples that if they were slapped on one cheek, they should offer the other. That is a potent lesson on retribution.

People will always attack and do us harm, but if we seek to justify all the wrongs meted out to us, then there would be continuous fracas. That behavior pattern has produced wars, battles, distress, and untold amounts of deaths. We cannot thrive in a society that recompenses evil with evil. The cure for this malady is forgiveness, love, understanding, and concern for others. The Golden Rule is the operative medium—do to others what you want done to you. If taken literally, beauty, love, and common understanding would be everywhere. The formula is simple: just do the right thing.

Christian families must follow the footsteps of the Master. We must practice forgiveness and all the other virtues and principles He taught. Hard as it may be, we must repay evil with good acts and pray for those who hurt you. We will find ways to compromise if we have the love that Christ has for each of us. Forgive as you have been forgiven, shake hands, mend fences, and move on in the love of Jesus, the Model Man. The apostle John documented Jesus' words: "Greater love hath no man than this, that a man lay down his life for his friends" (John 15:13). Jesus laid down His life to save the world. Can we not follow His forgiving example? May we *recompense* evil with kindness, love, and more love.

Day 331

Thou wilt **Shew** *me the path of life: in thy presence is fulness of joy; at thy right hand there are pleasures for evermore ...* **Shew** *me thy ways, O Lord; teach me thy paths.*
Psalm 16:11; 25:4

In King David's interaction with God, he declared that their relationship was benign. He was confident that Abraham's God would guide him and take him on righteous paths that lead to eternal life. His belief was contingent on the premise that in God's presence, there is not sadness, bitterness, or turmoil. Instead, there was constant and eternal joy.

He further pointed out that at God's right hand are illimitable pleasures that will last throughout eternity. The best place to be is at God's right hand. When Jesus ascended to heaven, He went straight to sit at the Father's right hand where He became our Intercessor (see Acts 1:11). He will only leave that place when He returns to claim the righteous ones and present them to His Father.

The Holy Word says that when Jesus returns, He will place some people on His right hand and some on the left. Those on the right side are classified as sheep and will be accorded eternal life. The people on the left will be considered as goats and will be given eternal damnation. They did not accept Christ's sacrifice, did not confess their sins, and rejected His offer of mercy. There will be no place for them at His right hand because of their continued defiance and disobedience. I am sure we want to be found at Jesus' right hand where pure, unadulterated, eternal pleasures are found.

David's hankering for righteousness caused him to plead with God: "Shew me thy ways, O Lord; teach me thy paths" (Ps. 25:4). How many of us feel the need to prostrate ourselves at the feet of the Master and Intercessor and plead with Him to both show and teach us what we ought to learn and where to go? David is desperate for heavenly direction. In his first request, there is a note of certitude, as if he were saying, "I know you will do it!" However, in the second request, there is a certain kind of earnestness, expediency and expectation: "Please show me; teach me; I am willing to learn and to follow. I am in a jam and am teetering between hope and despair; I need to hear from You now." I feel these must have been similar to his innermost thoughts.

As if the request is not intense and urgent enough, he pleads, "Lead me in thy truth, and teach me: for thou art the God of my salvation; on thee do I wait all the day" (verse 5). Like Jacob with the angel, he was not about to let go until he heard from God. This is the kind of tenacity every Christian needs if he or she would walk with Jesus and learn of Him.

God is willing and able to lead us and to show us the paths, but we, like David, must wrestle with Him and surrender our wills to Him. Our plea, like David's, should be desperate. When God takes over, our eyes will be opened to see where and how He is leading us. He will give us wisdom, keen vision, and provide protection along the way. He will not leave us in the stocks or in the desert or to the caves of wild and savage beasts. May we trust Him, follow His leading, and continue to ask Him to *show* us the right direction! He is the Way; follow Him!

Day 332

*And they that know thy name will put their **Trust** in thee: for thou, Lord, hast not forsaken them that seek thee. Psalm 9:10*

Do you know the name of Jesus, of God? There is a list of many of the names of God in the back of this book. He is everything to all humankind—the creatures of His hand bear His image. He is the El Shaddai (the Almighty), Jehovah Jireh (the Lord my Provider), Jehovah Nissi (the Lord my Banner), and Jehovah-Rophe (the Lord that heals). Whatever you want Him to be, He is. Wonderful, Counselor, Everlasting Father, Prince of Peace, etc., etc., etc.!

The Lord has not and will not forsake all who put their trust in Him. We know that there is nothing impossible with our God; He can do all things. Remember what He said through the prophet Isaiah, "I have graven thee upon the palms of my hands; thy walls are continually before me" (Isa. 49:16). You are tattooed on God's hands; He will never forget you.

God sees every part of our total being: our eyes when they are watery and heavy with care, our lips when they utter prayers of distress and cry for help, our head when it throbs with pain and spasms, and our ears when they cannot distinguish between the voice of God and the enemy. Yes, He, our El Shaddai, Jehovah-Rophe, Jehovah Jireh, Jehovah Nissi, Jehovah Uzzi (the Lord my Strength), Jehovah Sali (the Lord my Rock), Jehovah Machisi (the Lord my Refuge), and my Lord God and Master—He sees and knows it all.

God will not leave or forsake any of His children to single-handedly navigate the rough waterways of life. Our Rock and sure Defense is always available; He is our one constant—the unchangeable I AM. Be encouraged that our God is everything to all humankind—rich and poor, healthy and ill, faint and strong, tired and stressed. He will uphold, guide, lead, and protect you.

We can go through the rest of our days leaning on His strong and mighty arms, for they are powerful enough to bear up all of us. Trust, believe, act; take Him at His Word. Develop your faith muscles and go forward with your hands placed in His. Remember always that faith is unutterable trust in God. Trust is what makes us know that He, our God, will stand by and come through for us. He always delivers.

Trust God with all your heart and every fiber of your being. He is God; He cannot fail. The psalmist reminds us that "they that trust in the Lord shall be as mount Zion" (Ps. 125:1). May we continue in hope, belief, faith, and *trust* so that we will never fail, for our God is faithful.

Day 333

But when ye pray, **Use** *not vain repetitions, as the heathen do: for they think that they shall be heard for their much speaking. Matthew 6:7*

In this discourse Jesus gives the prerequisite for communing with God. In the pagan culture, familiar to the disciples, people usually babbled and called God's name irreverently because they were worshipping idols. It was necessary for them to shout and scream because they needed their god's response but were unaware of their inability to reply.

Using vain repetitions was the common practice accorded in the worship of the Baals and Astoreths. They had to shout and gnash their teeth hoping these silent objects would answer, but they never did. The worshippers became utterly frustrated and even committed bodily harm, but to no avail.

Jesus cited this case so that His new followers and those that were to come along in the Gospel dispensation would understand the essence of prayer and how to approach God, the Father. It was upon the heel of that discussion that he told them to address God as "Our Father which art in heaven; Hallowed be thy name" (Matt. 6:9).

God is not far away, so there is no need to shout. We can communicate with Him just where we are. We can talk to Him anywhere and at any time. We should speak to God in a humble, reverent tone with a lowly and contrite heart, with thankfulness and confessions for sins committed and omitted, and then make our request known to Him. Remember, we need to use the TCR method we learned from David: thanksgiving, confession, and a request.

Unlike the pagans orating to lifeless objects, Christians should pray to the point: tell God what your needs are and do not repeat His name listlessly. We should come to God with sincerity and the belief that our God is capable to do unto the uttermost. Tell Him everything, for there is nothing that our God cannot do. Matthew and Mark affirm, "With God all things are possible" (Matt. 19:26; Mark 10:27).

We should be specific in our prayers. Solomon says the wise keep their words few and well chosen. God already knows what we need before we ask; therefore, pray in the Spirit, and God, who hears the Spirit, will answer you openly. Pray until something happens. God is only a prayer away. Like young Solomon, pray for an understanding heart; pray in reverential awe, for you are addressing the Majesty of heaven–the Creator of the universe.

The Lord's Prayer should be named the "Disciples' Prayer" since it was their model. God does not need to pray; we are the ones who must address Him as "our Father." May we *use* His name reverentially!

Day 334

Having your conversation honest among the Gentiles: that, whereas they speak against you as evildoers, they may by your good works, which they shall behold, glorify God in the day of **Visitation**. *1 Peter 2:12*

The apostle Peter counsels the new believers on how they should live as God's children now that they were Christians. They were not to engage in any of their former practices, but were instead to act as those who have affixed the name and stature of Christ unto themselves. They were to allow the gospel of Christ and its power to transform their lives. Even if they were accused of doing wrong, if they let the Spirit transform them, their Christ-like reaction would cause their accusers to glorify God because they represented Him and the gospel nobly. Their witness is proof of their new relationship.

He told them they are the King's ambassadors, and if they practiced what they knew, their behaviors would cause their enemies and scoffers to be forced to come and accept the Christian's way of life. Peter further exhorted them by saying that they could be classed as epistles because their lives were an open testament to the power of the gospel to transform lives.

God visits with us when the Holy Spirit knocks on the heart's door. If we choose to open the door to Him, He will enter and settle in. God is in the business of visiting each of us, and He invites us to give Him a little space in our lives. He wants to develop in us His character. He wants His portrait to be perfectly restored in us so that as we interact with non-Christians, they will behold our beauty, purity, integrity, and gracefulness and want to emulate what they see in us. God wants to recreate His image in us; we must give Him room.

When the preacher orates or when the song is sung and something touches you, it is the Holy Spirit visiting with you and inviting you to give your heart and your entire life to God. He whispers that if you choose to give Him your heart, He will give you His kingdom. ,

God calls everyone. We are His. Some, through stubbornness and rebellion, will not yield to the gentle, small voice, but He calls anyway. Eventually, God will come to take those who have yielded their heart to Him. Based on our anticipation of this final visitation, we should be in a constant state of readiness, for we do not know the day or the hour when He will come. All we know is that He will. His last words to John were "Surely I come quickly" (Rev. 22:20). May we all be ready at that final *visitation*.

Day 335

Wait *on the Lord: be of good courage, and he shall strengthen thine heart: wait, I say, on the Lord. Psalm 27:14*

David knew what it meant to wait on the Lord. Having been anointed king at the tender age of 16, he had to wait for 14 more years before he took the throne. During this time he had become a snare to Saul, the ruling monarch, who was jealous of David's youthful gifts: agility, adroitness, and confidence.

While waiting, David had to learn patience and practice self-control. He had to wait on the Lord for the fulfillment of the promise to be the reigning monarch. As a young man with such God-given gifts, He may have been anxious to start reigning, but he had learned very early in childhood to not run before the Lord. It was always best to wait on Him. He knew that God had chosen Him, and in God's time, it would come to pass. Patience and forbearance were his daily companions. It's no wonder he wrote so much on the matter of waiting on the Lord. His book teaches how to develop the virtue of patience. The psalms (chapters 3, 23-106) are strewn with advice on waiting.

Not many people are good at waiting for an event. Many of us grow impatient and wonder why our host is not more particular about the value of our time. In the New Testament, Jesus told the story about the delayed wedding party. The attendants had to wait an extraordinarily long time. They became tired of waiting and went off to sleep. At midnight the party arrived, and the ready ones went in to the wedding hall, and the door was shut.

From this anecdote we ask: how should one wait? We need to wait fully dressed, and be prepared to act at any moment (see Eph. 6:10–18). Keep the eyes of the mind and heart open, have spiritual insight and discernment, know the doctrine, know who the Trinity are, and above all, have God's word hidden in your heart.

Waiting on and for God is not easy because we want action ASAP. People are always anxious to execute their tasks, but God is never in a hurry. Everything and every part of our lives for Him is well ordered. He said that the very hairs of your head are all numbered (see Matt. 10:30). He knows the street on which you live. He is the Omniscient One who cannot err; therefore, if it seems as if God is not answering our prayers speedily enough or He does not understand the urgency of the situation, we err. God's timing is always just right. To think that God cares less is to minimize the power of the great I AM and that He is not in control of our problem. Jeremiah assures us that we should both wait and hope for the Lord because often times God is waiting to refresh, renew, and teach us some valuable lesson (see Lam. 3:24–26).

While waiting for God to act, let us discover what He is trying to teach us. We must cultivate patience, remembering that we plan, but it is God who directs (Prov. 16:9). Therefore, as David says, we need to wait patiently on the Lord. Take heart, be strong, and wait. In His own time God will bring it to pass. Be advised, we can do absolutely nothing to alter God's plans. May we learn to always *wait* on Him!

Day 336

For the needy shall not always be forgotten: the **Expectation** *of the poor shall not perish for ever. Psalm 9:18*

Here is an assurance given to the needy and the destitute. It speaks to the generosity of the wealthy and at a higher level of the Jehovah Jireh, who will always provide for them. It is a very reassuring promise; the poor will be richly supplied, "and the needy shall lie down in safety" (Isa. 14:30).

God cares for all His children—the rich and the needy alike. Those who anticipate and expect to find food will not be disappointed; someone will reach out to them. The more blessed and the affluent may ignore the plight of the needy because of their sumptuousness and effulgence. They may even ascribe the need of the poor to their lack of industry, indolence, and laziness. Consequently, those most richly endowed reject them, see them as nuisances, snob at them, and completely ignore them. Thus, they leave them without any hope of escaping the triangle of poverty, need, and helplessness. In many cases, the condition into which these needy folk find themselves is none of their own doing.

On the contrary, God is the Champion of the weak, and He promises that they will not always be in that life-threatening situation. Deliverance is coming to them. Jesus promises that the needy shall be fed. All God's creatures are precious in His sight, and David later says that he has never seen the righteous forsaken. Jesus, quoting an Old Testament law, asserts that the poor will always be a part of the fabric of our society: "For ye have the poor always with you" (Matt. 26:11; see Deut. 15:11). They cannot be eliminated and should not under any circumstances be ignored and left to starve. The needy are in our society so that those who have abundance can express their generosity and godly care toward them.

The needy can find comfort in the thought that even when others forget them and throw insults at them, God has neither forgotten nor forsaken them. Their faces are stamped and inscribed in the palms of God's hands; they are continually before Him. Therefore, let all the needy hope in God, for help is nigh. The needy do not have a choice but to expect relief when life throws them situations they cannot handle alone. May we help to satisfy their *expectation*!

Day 337

Even the **Youths** *shall faint and be weary, and the young men shall utterly fall: But they that wait upon the Lord ... they shall mount up with wings as eagles. Isaiah 40:30, 31*

Isaiah, God's spokesman, affirms God's power to protect, strengthen, and support everyone. He states that when situations and circumstances become dire even the strongest and most robust among the group can fall. This goes to show that physical strength is not the zenith. Young men and youth, in general, take pride in their strength and the ability to conquer the unconquerable, but here Isaiah is saying this is not important. Unless God is their guide, strength, and support, even those boasting of their physical stamina will fall like the hoary head and the enfeebled.

However, amidst this dilemma of strength versus weakness and wisdom versus folly, God is in the midst of it all. That is God's message. His strength never diminishes; He is never tired or too busy to help and listen. He gives strength to the weary and increases the power of the weak so they will need less care. In contrast, the strong, robust young men will stumble and fall under life's many pressures. It goes to show that physical prowess is not all. We must continually seek to draw power from the Source—our wonderful Father. The text implies further that there is a vulnerability residing in the arms, legs, and sinews of the youth.

Circumstances catch up with these brave and valiant ones; their strength soon sags, and some faint and drop out; therefore, one should not brag about their strength and physical achievements because all of that is transient and temporary. Youth is not enduring. The wise man advises us to "rejoice, O young man, in thy youth; and let thy heart cheer thee in the days of thy youth" (Eccles. 11:9).

Youth has been characterized as the "spring of life" when all the sap is flowing through the veins and the possessor is full of energy, pep, and vitality. At that stage he or she seems to be on top of Everest. Let the youth glory in their strength, prowess, and agility, for it shall soon pass away, and they will become faint, tired, and weak;. Think of the shot-lived life of the athletes, Olympic champions—only one brief moment in glory!

The good news is that perpetual youth is futuristic; when Jesus returns and clothes humanity in immortality, then all of us—the young and the old—will be renewed, revitalized, and enjoy perpetual youth. Isaiah 35 tells of the promise to be fulfilled. It will be a new earth without sin. There will be no old people; all will experience and enjoy perpetual *youth*. May you experience that robust life forever!

Day 338

Thus shall mine anger be accomplished, and I will cause my fury to rest upon them, and I will be comforted: and they shall know that I the Lord have spoken it in my **Zeal**.
Ezekiel 5:13

God's zeal is like a consuming fire ravishing everything in its path; it is merciless and unrestrained. What God has determined to do, He does. God doesn't have a indecisive mind. He is strength, truth, endurance, and stability. He spoke, and it was done. How can the created being compete with its Maker?

When God gives a command and we sidestep it, we are saying that we neither value nor respect the authority of the Creator. Generally, we are unable to grasp the concept of the Maker of everything that exists; it is too vast for our limited minds.

Though we bear the image of God, we must stop and consider who He is. We must respond to the great existential question: what am I doing here and where am I going?

God is the Creator and humanity must learn in quiet obedience to respond to God's request. If we do not, then God will treat us as we deserve. Sacred history records God's dealings with those who ignited His anger. Sodom and Gomorrah were wiped out, and the entire antediluvian world that Noah preached to for 120 years was also denudated. When God's anger is upturned, He will not relent. Judgment came upon those who slighted and refused His call to repentance. His zeal performed it.

When God speaks or acts, there is no one to intercede, quiet, or calm Him down. He has no need for a mediator; God has the first and last word. And when a nation's cup of iniquity has reached up to God, and humanity refuses to become contrite or repentant, then God will act in the fullness of His power. God must be obeyed under all circumstances; we must sooner learn our place in the universe of things.

God alone reigns supremely. When He acts, the earth and all that are in it tremble. God's zeal is like an unquenchable fire whose embers will not be quenched. Therefore, we must ensure that we do not incur God's wrath, for it can burn for a very long time. Besides, no one can tame or cool or extinguish God's passion. Only by willing obedience to His laws will God relent and alter His course of action.

God is our Maker. Let God be God; He is the Majesty of heaven and earth; let everyone obey Him! Let us do our best to stay on the right side of God by obeying all His laws, statutes, and testimonies. May we always trust and obey our *zealous* God.

We Are More Than Conquerors

Day 339

*Many are the **Afflictions** of the righteous: but the Lord delivereth him out of them all.*
Psalm 34:19

This is a victory text offering promise, hope, assurance, and solace, especially to the oppressed and abused. It tells of God's unending care and loving-kindness to all His children, and it even carries a futuristic ring.

Those who are righteous and honest will face very serious challenges, threats to their survival, and possible extinction and annihilation. There is assurance in God's Word that Jehovah will deliver them out of it all. None of His children need be afraid.

Psalm 91 offers full assurance of protection from all the attacks this world has to throw at us. Why should the righteous be afraid of outside forces when God is our Protector? None can fight with God and win.

Christians will be harassed, berated, and threatened, but the Good Shepherd will not allow any of His lambs to be snatched by the wolves of dissidence, treachery, apostasy, or debauchery. There will be nothing to defile or despoil. He is our Deliverer; therefore, the obedient need not fear when the shadows of death threaten us. Our God will deliver according to His sure promises. He is from everlasting to everlasting; He is the beginning and the end, the Alpha and the Omega. Allow God to perform His mighty acts in your life.

Pain, suffering, injury, and disease—what are they in comparison to Calvary? How many have been spat upon for the Cause? How many have been imprisoned and how many have been crucified? Jesus paid the ultimate sacrifice; He bore the affliction of every man, woman, and child who has lived and will ever live. Therefore, whatever discomforts we face on behalf of the Savior, we need to remember that our suffering will not ever come close to His. The apostle Paul calls our troubles "light afflictions."

There is cause to rejoice, for joy follows affliction. Let us celebrate our afflictions because Jesus bore our share, so we have much less to bear. Even though daily frustrations wear us down, God says that He is near the broken-hearted. Hold onto hope and bear your scar proudly! Through Jesus Christ you are a victor! In the face of our trials, may we be strong, courageous, and brave, for hope is in God, our Deliverer!

Day 340

***Be** strong and of a good courage, fear not, nor be afraid of them: for the Lord thy God, he it is that doth go with thee; he will not fail thee, nor forsake thee. Deuteronomy 31:6*

As I write, I cannot help but be excited to see the unfolding of the leading of the Holy Spirit's hand in the preparation of this meditational book. Yesterday, we ended the discussion on afflictions with the thought "Be of Good courage," and today we open the study with the same words—"Be strong and of a good courage." God surely knows that in these trying times of earth's last days, we will need courage to face each day's challenges. Thank God for His guidance in directing this study. Truly, this is His work, which is all about God, our Father.

As God's children journey from place to place and from one stage of their spiritual development to the next, there is need for counsel. Several centuries ago, Moses, before his departure, gave Joshua this charge. Both had been with the company since they left the Egyptian bondage. Joshua, like Moses and Aaron, had seen and lived through the people's rejection of God's leading and their rebellion against Him. Now, it was time for Moses to leave the scene and Joshua was now the new commander-in-chief to lead the travelling band of Israelites into the Promised Land–Canaan.

Joshua, having been Moses' co-leader, had seen how his faith was severely tested through the wilderness wanderings. He was privy to the latter not entering the Land of Promise. The crowd of more than six million had become almost unmanageable; they made several attempts to return to Egypt, hankered after the flesh-pots, onions, leeks, and garlic that they had left behind. They complained and murmured, but Jehovah remained faithful to His promise and led them on day and night.

Moses, wanting to affirm Joshua's position, charged him to stand his grounds: "Stand firm for Jehovah" (verse 7, author paraphrase). He also told him to develop and practice courage and to have no fear, for the eternal God would be his refuge and would see him carry out this special assignment.

Moses' charge to Joshua resonates today with all Christian leaders. God calls for dependable leaders. God could depend on Moses, Aaron, and now on Joshua. He wants to depend on you. Whatever leadership quality you are gifted with, can God depend on you to be a witness for Him in this fast-paced day and age? Do you have time for God in your life? Can you be strong in the might of the Lord and go forth doing His work with courage and commitment?

God is looking for today's Moses, Aaron, and Joshua among the youth and all the leaders. Will you stand up and say like Isaiah, "Here am I; send me" (Isa. 6:8)? As you respond to the call, God promises that you will never be alone in your ministry for He promises to be by your side forever. May all leaders stand firm for God and *be* courageous.

Day 341

Beloved, if our heart condemn us not, then have we **Confidence** *toward God. 1 John 3:21*

This is a great self-assessment and evaluation text. What does your heart tell you about your status toward God and humankind? A pure and consecrated heart is trustworthy, honest, serviceable, and falls into accord with the principles of Christian living.

The Word says the heart contains all life-giving forces. If your conscience is void of offence, you can come and go to God confident that your request will be heard.

We must be discriminative in what enters the mind, for it is through our minds that God speaks to us. If the mind is cluttered and filled with unholy, unlovely, and un-gracious thoughts, there is no room for the Holy Spirit. We cannot hear God's voice early in the morning, at mid-day, or in the night seasons.

We control our fate; we decide our eating, sleeping, and waking patterns. As free moral agents, we control our passions, emotions, and desires, but many people go through life carefree. The question then becomes what direction is their life taking? How will they answer to their children for their life's trajectory! What will they bequeath to the next generation? Are they satisfied with their life path? These are deep contemplative issues, and if after careful reflection, one can answer, "I have done my best; I have chosen the path that will lead to a fulfilled life," then, there is no condemnation. There is only confidence and elation.

Since the mind is the seat of our intelligence and our actions are, hopefully, Spirit directed, we can be confident that God will bless all our undertakings, for He is managing every aspect of our life. We can step out in faith saying, "I know in whom I have believed and that he will see me through to the end." That is great confidence.

May we hide God's Word in our heart having full confidence that He will lead us into peaceful paths and keep us from condemnation. Daily meditate on God's Word and keep a running conversation with our heavenly Father by praying David's prayer: "Let the words of my mouth, and the meditation of my heart, be acceptable in thy sight, O Lord, my strength, and my redeemer" (Ps. 19:14). With this spiritual mantra, we can move ahead fully *confident* that the Triune God will keep our hearts pure, holy, righteous, and undefiled.

Day 342

Through the tender mercy of our God; whereby the **Dayspring** *from on high hath visited us.*
Luke 1:78

This is Zachariah's prophecy relating directly to Jesus, the Messiah, who would come as the dawn—the Dayspring—from on High. Jesus is the Dayspring arriving in the morning of our civilization; He brings hope and a future, and He opens the way of peace. Zachariah stated that when He comes, He will usher in a new age, a new dispensation, and a new beginning.

The Messiah came from heaven and visited us six months after John the Baptist's birth. Jesus has also been called the rising Son, the dawn, and the Dayspring. It is the Sun that gives birth to a new day, so Jesus, the Rising Son/Sun, came from heaven and brought new life and hope to humanity. Before visiting us, He was crowned in majesty as Creator of the universe, but the Incarnate One took on Himself a human form and identified with all of humankind's afflictions and joys. God sent the Dayspring from above as prophesied. The angel, when visiting Mary, said, "Thou shalt conceive in thy womb ... and shalt call his name JESUS" (Luke 1:31).

The Holy Spirit is a part of the Godhead that moves and breathes and gives life. It is by coming down to humanity that He could bring men and women up to God, the Father. Job in his affliction cried out and said that there was no mediator to hear his cries (see Job 9:33). And here the priest Zachariah foretells the coming of the Dayspring in answer to Job's complaint. Yes, God came down and dwelt with humankind and remains the Dayspring to all who will accept Him.

Have you accepted the gift found in God's only Son? Have you positioned yourself so He can mediate for you? In His role as the Dayspring, we have the greatest gift ever accorded mortals. Let us access these gifts before time runs out. Seize them today!

Also, Malachi reminds us that the Son of righteousness will arise with healing in His wings and erase every illness and affliction. That is indeed glory for the entire human family. Jesus is the Dayspring and rising Son of righteousness. Even now, Jesus is still offering hope and interceding on our behalf. At the end of the age, He will appear as the Son of righteousness and heal humankind's ills. May we accept the *Dayspring* before it is too late?

Day 343

Before the mountains were brought forth, or ever thou hadst formed the earth and the world, even from **Everlasting** *to* **Everlasting**, *thou art God. Psalm 90:2*

Who is there among the living that can compare with God? Who is like Him? Who has eternity all wrapped up in His bosom, and who has neither beginning nor end? There is none! There is none who knows what was and when it will end! All of that is God's parameter.

The created cannot fathom the Engineer's uniqueness. He is the developer, so humanity cannot ask God where He came from. Most children ask where God came from because their curious minds want to get to the root of things. But because of God's grandeur, we will let the question pass; there is no answer that could be given to satisfy the inquiring mind. We cannot ask God where is His origin or when will He stop being who He is.

God has no limits, no boundaries, and no limitations. Moses knew this very well and extolled God and acknowledged His preexistent supremacy. Working with a new generation of travelers, he wanted them to know and recognize the supremacy of this mighty God. Their parents knew of Him, His wonders, and His miraculous leading in their lives. But the current children needed to know that their parents' God was still the same great, eternal One. God was before time began. He instituted time. Thus, Moses began his prayer, "Lord, thou hast been our dwelling place in all generations" (verse 1). This statement shows God's eternal concept. Before He even called the earth and world into existence, He was; no wonder God identifies himself as the "I AM" (Exod. 3:14).

Inspiration breathed on Moses as he wrote this psalm acknowledging God's preeminence and preexistence. Moses could not fathom how it all transpired; he just allowed the Spirit to speak through him as he magnified the Lord's name. God's ways are unsearchable. If we could fathom out God then we would cease to be human and would be a god.

Everlasting suggests perpetuity, but is there an end? When our grace period ends, the eternal reign of glory will begin, and the redeemed will enter into a new phase of unending living. Finite humans are unable to fathom the intricacies of God's operation. Moses also reminded the nation that "the secret things belong unto the Lord our God: but those things which are revealed belong unto us and to our children for ever" (Deut. 29:29). Therefore, we should be content with the level of divine knowledge revealed to us. Before anything was, God is. May we remember that God is still the great and glorious I AM, and He will be from *everlasting* to *everlasting*!

Day 344

I will extol thee, my God, O king; and I will bless thy name **For Ever** *and ever. Psalm 145:1*

I think David's prayer of thanksgiving ties in very nicely with Moses' adoration of God's everlastingness. The king had much to be thankful for, and he pledged that he would continually bless the name of the Lord. May we join David and ascribe praise and thanksgiving to God all the days of our lives! Here are four reasons why we should extol the Lord before family, friends, and associates:

The Lord is great and magnificent; there is no other like Him. Can you recall the last time you told Him something very personal and private, and He told it to some other person? You surely cannot; God is dependable and reliable.

He is gracious and merciful. He shows constant loving-kindness, patience, and tenderness to all who call upon Him.

He lifts up and sustains all who fall so we do not slip again.

God is righteous in His ways and kind in His deeds. He treats everyone with uprightness, dignity, honesty, and fairness. God has no favorites, biases, or partiality.

Who else could fit the bill except our wonderful, compassionate, and loving God?

In praising God, you are sharing with others who He is and what He has been to you. You can tell others how His loving compassion is new every morning; His patient endurance is continuous; His forgiveness is constant, and He is the Chief Supplier of all that we need.

The gifts of His love, forgiveness, justice, faithfulness, daily upholding, and deliverance from escapades, are more than enough for which to praise our God. Shout and sing; praise His name! Let people know what He has done for you!

Like David and Moses and the other great men of prayer, let us lift up our voices and tell all who will listen that our God is a great God, and there is none like Him in all the earth. Tell what He has done in your life, whether it is about answered prayers or His capacity to hear, help, and heal. Let our mouths continually offer praise and thanksgiving to the great God of heaven and earth. Help humanity everywhere extol the name of the Lord and exalt His mighty works. Our God is a great God—He is so merciful and kind. May we praise His name *forever* and ever as long as He gives us breath!

Day 345

*For **Godly** sorrow worketh repentance to salvation not to be repented of: but the sorrow of the world worketh death. 2 Corinthians 7:10*

Sincere and genuine sorrow for wrongs committed may lead the violator to repentance. David tells us that "he that covereth his sins shall not prosper" (Prov. 28:13). Likewise, Isaiah 55:7 says, "Let the wicked forsake his way, and the unrighteous man his thoughts: and let him return unto the Lord, and he will have mercy upon him."

When the prophet Nathan confronted King David and narrated the scenario of injustice, David condemned the transgressor. When he found out that he was the guilty one, he confessed, acknowledged his sin, and repented. As a result of his contrition and godly sorrow, we have a profound prayer found in Psalm 51.

On the other hand, when God confronted Cain about his brother's whereabouts, he became very arrogant and aggressive and sassed God. Similarly, when Jesus confronted Judas, He said, "Betrayest thou the Son of man with a kiss?" (Luke 22:48). Rather than confessing, he remained silent. Neither Cain nor Judas showed godly sorrow. Neither person received reprieve or salvation and each received his just reward.

Preaching in the respective synagogues, Peter called upon his hearers to repent of their sins so that they could receive the promised Holy Spirit. One cannot turn away and forsake their misdeeds unless they are genuinely sorry for their actions. Anything else is hypocrisy. Once they have acknowledged the infraction, they will never go back to those practices.

Many people are sorry that they are caught and their image is tarnished, but they are not rueful about their recalcitrance. Unlike Judas and Cain, Peter initially denied his Lord, and when Jesus' eyes met his, he went away and wept. His reaction showed genuine, godly sorrow. Jesus knew his heart and that is why he said, "When you are converted, strengthen the brethren" (Luke 22:32). Putting Peter to the ultimate test of godly sorrow and genuine repentance, Jesus asked three times, "Simon, son of Jonah, lovest thou me more than these?" (John 21:15). Peter answered in the affirmative every time. Jesus read Peter's mind, saw his godly sorrow, and commissioned him to take charge of the church.

If one does not genuinely own their misdemeanors and begin walking on the right path, they are sure to continue on a destructive course, for they are goaded by the Deceiver, who promulgated the first lie. In their sin, neither Eve nor Adam showed any godly sorrow. Instead, they played the "blame game" and pointed their finger at anyone but themselves. If today's miscreants do not show remorse for their wrongs, they will lose eternity. *Godly* sorrow promises and offers eternal life. May all sinners genuinely forsake their sins because Jesus is waiting to receive them!

Day 346

> **Honour** *the Lord with thy substance, and with the firstfruits of all thine increase.*
> *Proverbs 3:9*

Honor is a popular word used in Holy Writ. In the Decalogue, God directs the children of Israel to honor and respect their parents. The apostle Paul reiterates the same message in writing to the brethren in Ephesus.

People of every generation respect the elderly because they have lived long and have many experiences and wisdom that can be passed on to the youth. Strong, robust, and healthy people could easily shun the elderly and the feeble, whom they may see as getting in their way, but Holy Writ demands honor and respect for the hoary head.

The message addresses selfish and greedy people that are unmindful of who gave them the power, ingenuity, and capacity to acquire things. To combat envy and covetousness, the advice is to honor God first with all that one possesses: chattels, land, houses, money, and even their children.

We obtain because God gives. Nothing we have is ours; we are stewards of God's resources. Everything belongs to Him (see Ps. 24:1). Even though the text only references possessions and land, we should all still be aware that in all our labors and returns, God has first place in everything.

Many people live as they please and squander their time pursuing some illusory dream, then once they are in their last days, they give the leftovers to God. This behavior dishonors God, who formed us for His own glory. Solomon advises the youth to remember their Creator and to honor Him in the first years of their lives when they are young, strong, and capable of giving Him their best (see Eccles. 12:1).

We honor God with our time, talent, and means. When God takes first place in our transactions, we acknowledge Him as the Supreme Ruler of the earth. Whatever God blesses you with—children, wealth, houses, or property—the first acquisition belongs to Him. Put God first and watch how He works for you.

Besides honoring God, this message is designed to combat greed and selfishness. It acknowledges God as the rightful and established owner of all things. As we yield to Him first, we open ourselves to receive His special blessings. We should show no deference to God; He is to be honored, revered, and respected. When we honor the Lord with the first fruits of all our increase, we are telling God that we adore Him, love Him, and appreciate all the bounties He gives us for *honoring* Him.

Day 347

> *Let* **Integrity** *and uprightness preserve me; for I wait on thee. Psalm 25:21*

As we approach the end of these devotional readings, let us contemplate on the messages that came through God's Holy Word. We were reminded that God shall take first place in all our life's actions and activities. You ask why? We are His property; we belong to Him. So we honor Him because He is God. In doing so, we pray that integrity, prudence, wisdom, and righteous behaviors will be our forte. We recognize our own frailties and proneness to go in the wrong direction and follow our tastes and desires. As Christians, we must maintain an eye singly to the glory of God and look neither to the right nor to the left. We must focus on the goal ahead. We can admit no diversion. No guile or impurity shall characterize our speech. David wrote, "I will set no wicked thing before mine eyes" (Ps. 101:3). I like to add, "let no wicked thing out of my mouth."

This is a special prayer of a recognized helplessness and personal dependence on God. This ought to be the prayer of every Christian man and woman. When we pray such, we are saying, "Oh, Lord, I have faith that You will make it happen."

These two powerful virtues—integrity and uprightness—are pivotal in protecting and preserving us along life's trajectory. Step by step, our Father will guide the submissive seeker of righteousness. Uprightness makes us learn God's requirements and helps us strive to fulfill them. Micah tells us to be just, love mercy, and walk humbly with God (see Mic. 6:8). On the other hand, personal integrity, which is being what we say we are, keeps us from claiming to be upright while living as if we do not know God. Uprightness tells us what is the Shepherd's way, and integrity helps us consistently walk in His way. God will hear and answer our requests if they are upheld by integrity and uprightness. He is very pleased when His children ask for such things.

Let no wicked thing come out of your mouth; let love, purity, and holiness characterize all your interactions. One should hold on to instruction, if not, you will certainly go askew where neither integrity nor uprightness can be found. Following uprightness leads to joy and contentment. May we meditate on God's requirements and hide His words in our heart that our lives may be full of *integrity* and uprightness.

Day 348

> *Thou shalt not bow down thyself to them, nor serve them: for I the Lord thy God am a* **Jealous** *God, visiting the iniquity of the fathers upon the children unto the third and fourth generation of them that hate me. Exodus 20:5*

This is the first major principle of the Ten Commandments that God wrote with His own fingers and handed down to humankind. This is part of the prohibition and its attenuated costs for extolling and worshipping images.

This was an important command to ancient Israel journeying from Egyptian bondage to the land of freedom and promise. They had lived among heathen idol worshippers and adorers of the sun god and other Egyptian deities. Now that they were out in the wilderness, God had to remind them that He was God, the great I Am, and that it was He who wrought their deliverance. He is above all the gods they knew. Therefore, they ought to worship Him, their Deliverer. Because He was so worthy, it was only fitting how they ascribed worship to God to be very particular.

In the ancient peoples' distress and servitude, they called for help and Jehovah delivered them. Now that He had them unto Himself, He had to remake them and redirect their minds to revere, worship, and accept the true God. He wanted them to know that worship belongs to their Creator, Deliverer, and Leader.

God is jealous for all worship, and once they persisted in their idolatrous practices and rejected His leading, He punished them over a ninety-to-120-year period. A generation lifetime was 30 years, so the curse dealt with four generations of the Israelite people. The threat is conditional; God would do it if they were disobedient.

While living in Egypt and surrounded by some many deities, they thought Jehovah was just one more god they had to contend with. They had no real understanding of Yahweh, the Great God of the universe. Consequently, God had to assert His divine authority and power and let them know that He was preeminent and that none other should come before Him. They were not to bow and worship any other except Jehovah. God stated that He was jealous, and He wasn't prepared to share His glory or praise with any other object. Worship should be ascribed to Him alone.

When Jesus came, He echoed His Father's words, "If ye love me, keep my commandments" (John 14:15). And in Satan's third temptation, Jesus responded, "Thou shalt worship the Lord thy God, and him only shalt thou serve" (Matt. 4:10). God is jealous for worship, and if you comply, you will be blessed.

Like our predecessors, we are also on a journey, and we should stake out who is our Guide. What or to whom do we render our most tender affection? Is it to our Father, Creator, and Sustainer or is it to some object? God requires our total obedience. Never forget that in whatever station you find yourself, especially if you obtain money, fame, prestige, and power. Remember that worship, adoration, and praise belong to God alone. God is *jealous* for our worship. May everyone give Him His praise! Read Psalms 92, 95, 105, 107, 112, and 118 for more reasons to praise the Lord.

Day 349

> *"How great are his signs! and how mighty are his wonders! his* **Kingdom** *is an everlasting kingdom, and his dominion from generation to generation. Daniel 4:3*

This is King Nebuchadnezzar's exaltation of the divine God. This great and mighty king of Babylon, symbolized by the head of gold in his dream, had established his stronghold and fortification in that famous Assyrian city, Babylon. He ruled ruthlessly, defied God, and established idolatry in Babylon. He made that city one of the seven wonders of the ancient world. He was the greatest of thirteen kings, and since his reign, there has never been another city like Babylon. When he surveyed his territory and all his glory, he declared, "Is not this great Babylon, that I have built ... for the honour of my majesty?" (Dan. 4:30).

God saw his arrogance and had to teach the proud king humility and reverence by bringing him through many tests until he acknowledged the Master of the universe. God is the Ruler, and He is jealous. He will not allow humanity to dethrone Him or claim His praise, adoration, honor, or worship.

Jehovah had worked miraculously for the three Hebrew God-serving youth, who stood for God amidst pagan worship. He rescued them from the fiery furnace and later saved Daniel from the mighty jaws of the hungry lions. When the proud king was confronted with the presence of the awe-inspiring God, he humbled himself, acknowledged the God of the universe, and issued a decree that said if anyone spoke unkindly about the God of these four worthies, they should be chopped into pieces, for there is no other god who can deliver its people out of harm's way (see Dan. 3).

Referring to the signs and wonders that God had revealed to him in his dreams, he extolled and exalted the name of God and declared His rule was everlasting: people everywhere must acknowledge that God is powerful (Dan. 4:37).

Rulers, statesmen, and leaders should take a cue from King Nebuchadnezzar and recognize that their power and authority come from God and is time-constrained. Their administration is temporary. God's kingdom is the only one bound up with eternity; it will endure for all eternity, from generation to generation as long as humanity exists.

May we, as God's ambassadors, affirm His majesty and awe so that others will know and believe that there is still a God working and that His *kingdom* is eternal!

Day 350

> *O love the* **Lord**, *all ye his saints: for the Lord preserveth the faithful, and plentifully rewardeth the proud doer. Psalm 31:23*

After David had lamented his plight and pled with God for continued guidance, direction, and deliverance from his pursuers, he paused for a moment, reflected on God's goodness toward him, then said, "Blessed be the Lord: for he hath shewed me his marvellous kindness in a strong city" (verse 21). Then he turned to his listeners and encouraged them "O love the Lord, all ye his saints." He's talking to you and me.

God first loved us, so we must reciprocate that love. If we are faithful to the Lord, He will preserve, protect, and cover us with His strong and mighty arms. Those who love the Lord will lack nothing, for He repays them bountifully. Every person is rewarded according to the measure he or she meted out to others. If we do not care for the poor and needy or reach out in compassion to the dispossessed and disenfranchised, God will hold us accountable for derelict in duty to our fellow persons. There is a great reward for those who reach out to the needy. King Solomon says that when we reach out to the needy, the giver will not suffer any lack. "He that giveth unto the poor shall not lack: but he that hideth his eyes shall have many a curse" (Prov. 28:27). Moses also states this idea in Deuteronomy 15.

By attending to the needy, we reveal God's love in our hearts and show to the world that we are God's children manifesting His love to others. We can only give love if we have love. God first loved and then He gave. We must emulate His love, share it, and show it to others.

As we travel the Christian pathway, let us practice the godly virtues Micah espouses: justice, mercy, and humility. Let us love the Lord and all of His children—your brother, sister, and even your enemies. We need to pray for those who hurt you badly. Leave judgment to God; He pays well and even gives the obedient dividends.

May we continue loving the *Lord* and His children while boldly claiming the promise that our God will preserve the faithful until Jesus returns.

Day 351

> *He answered and said, "A* **Man** *that is called Jesus made clay, and anointed mine eyes, and said unto me, Go to the pool of Siloam, and wash: ... and I received my sight."*
> *John 9:11*

A man called Jesus. What is in a name? What is so special about the name of Jesus? Everything. Holy Writ says, "At the name of Jesus every knee should bow" (Phil. 2:10). It is Jesus who shall save His people from their sins. He came, lived, touched, healed, and restored life to all who were oppressed with some kind of malediction. Peter said, "For there is none other name under heaven ... whereby we must be saved" (Acts 4:12). That is the man called Jesus.

This man called Jesus released the demon-possessed, stopped the woman's hemorrhaging, and empowered the paralytic to take up his bed and walk home. Yes, this man called Jesus unloosened the tongue of the dumb and unplugged the ears of the deaf. Yes, a man called Jesus made clay poultice, plastered it over the blind man's eyes, and told him to go wash his face. The man could have said, "How do you expect me to get to Siloam?" But the incapacitated man did not ask any questions–he was simply glad that Jesus had noticed him. He got up, obeyed, and received his sight. Now he could see everything.

Jesus offers sight and new vision to the blind entrapped by circumstances of life, whether it is social mores, traditions, cultural habits, or sinful behaviors. Jesus wants to give you new vision. He desires to impart the Holy Spirit to remove the darkness surrounding us and give us sight. Which pool do you want to wash in? There was no mystique about Siloam's pool, but healing came when the blind man obeyed.

Jesus is that pool; He can cure every malady. He is the balm in Gilead that heals the sin-sick soul; He is the fountain filled with blood drawn from Immanuel's vein. All you need to do right now is to plunge in and be healed. Like the blind man, will you respond to the man called Jesus?

If you have yielded, reach up and say, "Lord, I accept; take my hand and lead me where You want me to go and guide me to do what You want me to do. You have taken away my darkness and have given me light; I can see. I am now ready and available for You to use me." Just watch Him take over your life and remake you into more than you ever dreamed you could be.

Jesus gives sight, insight, and discernment to the blind that cry to Him. Go to Him now. Jesus, the Light of the world, will remove the fog and darkness that envelop you and usher you into His marvelous light. Darkness or blindness will never more invade your body, mind, or muscles, for He is light, brings light, and dispenses light to all who know Him. May you find this *man* called Jesus today.

Day 352

> **Nevertheless** *we, according to his promise, look for new heavens and a new earth, wherein dwelleth righteousness. 2 Peter 3:13*

Despite the Doomsday preaching and the expectation of a grand collapse of civilization (such as another cataclysmic event like Noah's flood), Christians, need not be stirred by the baulking of so many discordant trumpet sounds heralding the end of the age. The apostle Peter penned these reassuring words more than twenty centuries ago to calm the anxiety of the early Christian believers, who expected Jesus' imminent return to earth.

Ever since that sad day in Eden when all vegetation lost its luster and humanity and animals became subjected to sin and death, there have been untold tragedies: brother versus brother, parents versus children, husbands versus wives, nations versus nations, and the rage of wars goes on unabated. Despite it all, Peter brings hope and comfort to his hearers. We Christians should be delighted and encouraged because the apostle Paul tells us that what is written are examples of what has previously transpired. Because of what we know, we are able to live with hope even if terrible things have happened or will happen to us. Every Christian in every age has had to face similar challenges. It is part of the Christian walk. But just as we all go through trials, we all have the same beautiful hope.

The world of the first century was no different from the twenty-first century. Satan, the master deceiver, is still on the warpath deconstructing the stability of families and society. He has almost six millennia of practice to perfect his craft of destabilizing our lives. Paul and Peter both offer hope because they tell us that the current happenings are transient, and righteousness will one day be established.

Jesus offered hope; He promised that He will come again. He told us that He will bring with His reign a new heaven and a new earth (see Rev. 21). Those anticipating Jesus' return must gird up the loins of their mind and be strong. Stand firm in what you believe and hide God's word in your heart. Feed on His word, digest it, and let it become an integral part of their spiritual DNA.

This sinful world will be purified through God's intense heat. Be calm; He assures us that out of the rubble of this sin-ravaged earth will emerge a new heaven and a new earth where only righteousness reigns supremely. That is our true home; there will be no trace of the miasma of sin once His breath of freshness and purity envelops the atmosphere. We will all go through many trials and tribulations. *Nevertheless*, may we experience it vicariously and live with the hope that it already exists.

Day 353

> *And he called his ten servants, and delivered them ten pounds, and said unto them,* **Occupy** *till I come. Luke 19:13*

Jesus taught primarily using parables. To His hearers, it was coded language, but it was ultimately understandable because it was based on the dialectics, exegesis, and economies of the time. This was a city scene no less materialistic and businesslike than ours. It was an entrepreneurial world: people were constantly trading, which was how they became wealthy. There was buying and selling and making investments similar to the activities on Wall Street. Solomon averred, "Whatever is has already been, and what will be has been before; and God will call the past to account" (Eccles. 3:15, NIV). Being enterprising is a basic part of the human spirit. It is part of the way we strive for success.

Jesus told this story to teach His hearers a very significant moral and spiritual truth that pointed to humanity's industry and ingenuity. In this story a business man called his ten servants, gave them a three month salary advance, and told them to invest in some profitable business venture while he went away for a little while. He was ascertaining their business savvy and work ethic. That was and still is a sound business principle, and Christians should not shrink from engaging in honest trade.

This is also an important lesson to combat indolence and sloth; no one should sit and wait for things to be given to them. Jesus wanted his listeners to know that everyone should occupy his or her time wisely and effectively. The secondary lesson points to Jesus' leaving and the events that will occur before His return. Christ is the Investor and Business Man who has commissioned us to become occupied in meaningful activities such as teaching and sharing the Great Commission of the Gospel and leading men and women to Jesus.

The story is far more than a business trip; in fact, it concerns the business of soul saving. No one who has truly come into contact with Jesus can sit around with folded hands and say, "Jesus is coming soon" without getting up and doing something for others. Jesus will come, and while we wait, we must be fully occupied in doing Christ's work by using our talents to improve our life as well as someone else's. When I was a girl growing up in the church, they never emphasized the "occupy" phrase of the engagement; it was only "Christ is coming soon." Many young people were confused and thus derailed their intellectual quest and thwarted their dreams: if Jesus was returning soon, why bother to seek higher learning? That was their thinking. Now several decades later, the same message is being preached, and Jesus has not returned, but many have left His path. It is more than just knowing He will return; we must be continually be engaged in all spheres of life. May we remember to always *occupy* ourselves with spreading His word until He comes to take us home.

Day 354

> *For* **Precept** *must be upon* **Precept** *... line upon line ... here a little, and there a little.*
> Isaiah 28:10

This statement sounds like a teacher's rule; I see this as the blueprint for conducting Bible studies and biblical research.

It has been said that the Bible is its own expositor and needs no great minds to present new truths. Inspiration guided the minds of some forty writers as they documented God's message to humankind. The Bible is interconnected and cyclical; the beginning of the story gives meaning to the end, and the end of the story gives meaning to the beginning. Consider what David said in the psalms and Jesus repeated when He was on the cross: "My God, my God, why hast thou forsaken me?" (Ps. 22:1; Matt. 27:46). Peter and John and the apostle Paul continually referenced the psalms and the Old Testament books to validate their statements. The prophet Isaiah forecasted Jesus' suffering and death in Isaiah 53. In the New Testament, we see Jesus fulfilling the predictions. These writers from different walks of life wrote as the Holy Spirit gave them direction; they did not concur with each other, for many centuries separated most of the writers (see 2 Tim. 3:16, 17).

David also prophesied in Psalm 118 about Jesus' triumphant entry into Jerusalem. This would take place prior to the Last Supper. There would be shouts of praise at that glorious entry: "Blessed be he that cometh in the name of the Lord" (Ps. 118:26). Mark 11:9 says that the throng that followed Jesus shouted in praise and acclamation, "Hosanna; Blessed is he that cometh in the name of the Lord." Thus the prophecy came through exactly as was foretold. The Bible cannot lie. We can follow it precept by precept because it is the sure Word of God.

Additionally, Jesus told us how to find truth. In John 5:39, He states, "Search the scriptures; for in them ye think ye have eternal life: and they are they which testify of me." What more evidence do we want? In the first, second, and third books of John, he bore record of Jesus' direct words. In 1 John 1:1, he says, "That which was from the beginning, which we have heard, which we have seen with our eyes, which we have looked upon, and our hands have handled, of the Word of life."

Jesus' advice is to search: "And ye shall seek me, and find me, when ye shall search for me with all your heart" (Jer. 29:13). Therefore, it is incumbent on us to take the sword, which is the Word of God, and wield it to ward off the enemy (see Eph. 6:10–18). We know it works and David says: "Thy word is a lamp unto my feet, and a light unto my path" (Ps. 119:105). And how shall a young man walk uprightly amidst all the inviting challenges of the day? Here is the answer: "By taking heed according to thy word" (verses 9, 11).

The final advice is to "Study to show thyself approved unto God, a workman that needeth not be ashamed, rightly dividing the word of truth" (2 Tim. 2:15). Jesus' words provide light so you can see a clear path, and they give guidance to the seeker and the errant's redirection. May we search the Scriptures *precept* upon *precept*, for in them is life, health, and Jesus' testimony.

Day 355

> *Happy is the man that hath his* **Quiver** *full of them: they shall not be ashamed, but they shall speak with the enemies in the gate. Psalm 127:5*

Many men use this text to free-fall into procreation and engender children. It is a sign of their virility. In some farming communities, there is a requirement for a man to have a whole army of children who grow up and become his farm hands. They do this instead of having to hire labor, and thus, they swell the economy of the family. This was a common practice in biblical times, even long before the Bible was written. During those times men often had many wives and so sired many children.

Not only were the children needed for agronomical and economical purposes, but they were important for combat, so the more sons a man sired, the more prestige and standing he had in the community. He was both feared and revered and any would-be attacker would think twice before aggressing toward him. Thus, the children also became the guards and protectors of the family.

When I was growing up, if a man had many children, he was classed as lascivious, sexually greedy, and uncontrolled. They cited this text as a pretext for their actions and gloated in their adventures saying that the Bible sanctioned their behaviors. I never quite understood their rationalization.

Previously in history, a man's greatest delight was a house full of children. Their presence not only showed his prowess and virility but also his capacity to protect and defend his and his neighbor's stronghold. Fathers were not ashamed because having many children was not seen only as a gift from God but as invaluable assets to the progenitors. Fathers needed to validate their children as God's heritage and his greatest gift to the family.

Based on this premise, the man who had not engendered an offspring bears much shame, sorrow, fear, and distress. He had no guard and was vulnerable to the enemy. He also does not have the sound of mirth or laughter in his house.

In today's busy and more challenging life style, this text is no lifeline for unwarranted procreation. A man today must control himself and have children as he is capable of nurturing. None should have children to become a burden on other family members or the state. Reason and sound judgment are required in the procreative process. Blessed is a man who has children and is able to nurture them! May we all take time to fully appreciate the kind, generous, and gentle fathers in our lives today.

Day 356

Lay not up for yourselves treasures upon earth, where moth and **Rust** *doth corrupt, and where thieves break through and steal: But lay up for yourselves treasures in heaven ... where thieves do not break through nor steal. Matthew 6:19, 20*

This is one of Jesus' counsels on the futility of focusing all one's energy in acquiring transient, materialistic, and insubstantial things that lack permanence. Jesus wants us to know today that earthly acquisitions are hindrances in our path to the kingdom and advises, "But seek ye first the kingdom of God, and his righteousness; and all these things shall be added unto you" (verse 33).

Seeking after worldly, transient things deters the development of a Christ-like character; we cannot take any of the earthly things to heaven. When a person dies, it does not matter how much prestige, fame, wealth, and chattels they possessed. They will take nothing with them. All they will get is a good sending home voyage: an expensive coffin and excellent attire. But they will have no money, land, deeds to property, or any other holdings. Besides, the individual is not even aware of all the fuss and ado.

When one dies, all that he or she had acquired goes to his or her heirs, who will use these gifts lavishly. What if during the acquisition process the deceased loved one had sidestepped the poor and the needy and trampled on others to get what he or she wanted? What if he or she had neglected time for Bible study and prayer and what if he or she had forgotten to share the love of Jesus with his or her coworkers, staff, and clientele? It is sad if all one's focus is to acquire things to become moth-eaten and rust-covered.

Our treasures are to be placed on the things that are most valuable: the price and worth of a soul, love for God, and our fellowmen. This is best done by following Isaiah's injunction in Isaiah 58:7–11 and Jesus' in Matthew 25:33–46. God expects us to feed the hungry, visit the sick, and care for the forsaken and the incarcerated. In this, we are laying up treasures in heaven and are acting as the hands and feet of Jesus.

If our focus is primarily on earthly things, our life is a joyless life. Service to others brings joy and inward happiness. Where do you want your heart to be? "For where your treasure is, there will your heart be also" (verse 21).

Time is of the essence; let us not lay up treasures that will be moth-eaten or rust-corroded, but rather let us use the treasures to relieve suffering humanity and thus hear from Jesus' lips, "Inasmuch as ye have done it unto one of the least of these my brethren, ye have done it unto me" (Matt. 25:40). May we today send on our treasures (kind deeds, acts of love, and compassion) unto judgment so that God will justify us.

Day 357

Sanctify *them through thy truth: thy word is truth. John 17:17*

Here is a prayer within a prayer. John 17 contains Jesus' last powerful prayer for Himself, His first disciples, and for all His future sets of disciples. This prayer contains the holistic measure of the Gospel, Jesus' mission and ministry. He told His Father that He had fulfilled His mission and then asked for their reunification: "Glorify thou me with thine own self with the glory which I had with thee before the world was" (verse 5).

This entire prayer is reminiscent of the Father and Son dialogical engagement after several years of separation. Jesus had been on earth for more than thirty years, so He was not physically there with the Father, and He longed for His Father's company. Read all of chapter 17 to get a more profound understanding of the exchange and level of communication between Father and Son.

After Jesus had presented His case to the Father, He turned his attention to the needs of His disciples. He asked God specifically to keep His chosen ones under the Holy Spirit's direction: "I pray not that thou shouldst take them out of the world, but that thou shouldst keep them from the evil" (verse 15); and then He said the above the verse, "Sanctify them through thy truth." Jesus wanted to seal them in the truth so that evil desires and lusts would not overpower them.

The most sublime thing about this last prayer is its total unselfishness. "Neither pray I for these alone, but for them also which shall believe on me through their word" (verse 20). This prayer includes you and me. Jesus prayed the universal prayer for us long before we came on the scene.

Whenever God answers that prayer, we are sealed in righteousness, possessing one mind, one purpose, and one goal. Commit this verse to memory and let it be your daily prayer. We are guaranteed safety and protection because Jesus has already prayed for us. He told Peter before his conversion, "I have prayed for thee, that thy faith fail not" (Luke 22:32).

Jesus is no longer praying for us; He did that some twenty centuries ago. He is now interceding on our behalf with His Father to secure us eternal life. He is focusing on our redemption, for He wants us to spend eternity with Him, the Father, and all the angelic hosts. May we not sabotage the process. Let Jesus be proud of us and His sacrifice. Let us give Him confidence that His blood was not shed in vain. Then He can take us home and present to His Father the trophies of His sacrifice: you and me.

Day 358

He is the Rock, his work is perfect ... a God of **Truth** *and without iniquity, just and right is he. Deuteronomy 32:4*

Throughout the ages, God's people had to be continually reminded that He was a great and magnificent God. When people face difficulties or challenges, they quickly forget that the omniscient God is their Leader and Provider. That is how it was with ancient Israel, and it is how it is today with us, modern Israel.

We manifest selective amnesia. Either that or we are all experiencing cognitive dissonance. God's people so easily forget that God is our Rock. We forget He is Jehovah Sali, the Unmovable, Creator, and Sustainer who holds up worlds. Why should earthlings think that they are beset with the most vicious challenges and that God has forsaken them?

Rocks are unmovable substances deeply embedded in the earth's crust. God is our Rock; He is the only constant force in the universe. He is unmovable, unshakable, and unbound by our limitations. His work is perfect. You can neither add nor subtract from any aspect of it. There is none to compare with Him. Isaiah declares of Him, "I am the Lord, and there is none else" (Isa. 45:6).

He is the God that delights in the truth, for He is truth. He is the Word, and the Word is truth, which is why He can sanctify us. He is the truth—He is the *Jehovah El Emeth*.

There can be neither sin nor iniquity because He is just and righteous. He is the *Adon Kol Ha'arets*—the Lord of all the earth. May we ascribe praise and honor unto Him, for He is worthy.

It was imperative for Moses to present God to the assembly using such vibrant and strong words: perfection, justice, truth; He is a God of Truth. Ancient Israel had experienced more than 400 years of deceit, falsehood, impersonations, and godlessness, so it was important for them to get a fresh glimpse of Jehovah God. Based on their disaffection, complaints, and murmurings, Moses had to present to them a tangible God.

God is a God of truth. They did not listen, so we must learn from their mistakes and listen and believe in Him. *Truth* always prevails because it is eternal as God is. May we always remember our God of *truth* and follow His example in our daily life.

Day 359

> *Give therefore unto thy servant an* **Understanding** *heart to judge thy people, that I may discern between good and bad: for who is able to judge this thy so great a people?*
> 1 Kings 3:9

This is King Solomon's response to God's question when He appeared to him in a dream at Gibeon. The young king was suddenly thrust into the kingship, and he had to be ready to govern and execute justice over a very expansive territory. God knew his frailty and his inability to manage the great challenge before him, so our great and magnificent God, our present help in trouble, appeared to the young king and said that He wanted to help him. God told Solomon that He wanted Solomon to be successful and that he had the special honor of building His temple. He then offered to give Solomon anything he wanted. What a conversation! What an opportunity for this young king!

Humbled and frightened at this confrontation, Solomon simply requested to have wisdom in regards to executing judgment and justice during his years of being king. .

Solomon has been dubbed the wisest man that lived because he offered the model prayer. Many of the political, social, moral, and religious misunderstandings stem from the lack of common *understanding* of one another and of human needs. Understanding is a virtue that cannot be procured in the colleges and universities and research centers of the world. It has to come from the Giver of gifts. If we need understanding, we must first fall upon the Rock, Christ Jesus. We need to take our concerns to Him, the Arbiter of all knowledge. He is the Omniscient One, and He will give us the direction, wisdom, knowledge, and understanding that He knows we need.

If there were more tolerance, patience, and common understanding, there would be fewer conflicts and wars. Even now, it is not too late to ask God for an understanding mind. Let us also teach the children and youth that in all their scholarly pursuits, they are to ask God to give them the ability to understand. James tells us that God gives wisdom and understanding to all who ask, and He is not partial. Thankfully, He gives to all of us freely (see James 1:5). Let us ask for the right thing. Each of us has much to accomplish, and we need sound judgment to carry out the task.

May our prayers be sincere like that of the young king: "Give therefore thy servant an understanding heart."

Day 360

> *Where there is no* **Vision**, *the people perish: but he that keepeth the law, happy is he.*
> Proverbs 29:18

As far back as I can recall I have heard this text being quoted when people do not act judiciously and timely. This is more so in the event of a deal that could benefit the individual or group, and they did not seize the moment or the opportunity. For example, if there was a project to be done or if there was the need for a certain course of action to be taken, and it was not done, then the onlookers would say that those in leadership positions lacked the foresight to act and so missed an opportunity. They had no vision.

Having gotten older, more informed and observant, I have a fuller understanding of the significance of the text. People in any state of life whether they be leaders, CEO's, administrators, religious leaders, etc. , they all must have a plan for executing their task. Whether it is finance, education, business, church, the mission field, attacking the war on poverty and other social issues, there has to be a plan. The leader must be acquainted with the territory and has a strategic leadership plan. Without a plan of action, the project is a fiasco. Everyone acts on a vision—an idea or a blueprint of what they want to accomplish.

Leaders without a vision are blind leaders leading a sheepfold of blind people. No one knows where he or she is going; the ditch is their resting place. We need to get our vision from God. The prophets received divine revelation from God through *vision* concerning the nation, and they transmitted God's message to the people.

In a society where none hears from God and reports God's counsel to the people, there is ultimate chaos; every person is their own law and does what is right in their own eyes. There is no moral soundness because there is no spokesman for God. His counsel is neither given nor received. Humankind needs to know and acknowledge that God controls this vast universe and reveals His will to His prophets who in turn communicate same to the people (see Amos 3:7).

Public morality draws on God's statutes and laws from which the laws of the land are based. In order for people to function well, they must keep God's laws. He has established these basic guidelines for our benefit. If God does not direct, we will have no guiding principles and there will neither be insight, foresight, nor discernment. There will be no *vision*.

All leaders should make God their mentor. They need to be able to hear his voice directing them. David says, "Happy is that people ... whose God is the Lord" (Ps. 144:15). We should also heed Proverbs 14:34, "Righteousness exalteth a nation: but sin is a reproach to any people." May His people receive His *vision*.

Day 361

> *Finally, brethren,* **Whatsoever** *things are true, whatsoever things are honest, whatsoever things are just, whatsoever things are pure, whatsoever things are lovely, whatsoever things are of a good report ... think on these things. Philippians 4:8*

This text may be classified as the Christian's mantra for daily living. It contains the inclusive requirements for practicing total conformity to the Word. We live in a world where gossip and juicy stories run rampant and everyone wants to hear the latest.

I once had a newly baptized sister in the faith who always called and told me things she had heard. I was tired of her diatribes, and I told her the next time someone called her to gossip that she should read to them this verse. She needed to help them focus on the pure, the noble, the true, the virtuous, and the lovely. If the story did not fit into the category of the "whatsoevers," she needed to cut the conversation. It must have worked because she ceased calling me. The kind of information relayed was no good to her spiritual growth. I am glad the Holy Spirit helped me use the word of God to show her what God expects of her.

Paul advises us to be discriminative users of information. If the stories do not meet the Pauline criterion cited, cut it. Our speech should be well flavored, as if it were seasoned with salt. Our words should be like apples of gold in pictures of silver, and we should not be hasty with our tongue. Whatever we put into our minds comes out in words and actions. Consequently, the apostle Paul tells us to program our minds with thoughts that are pure, holy, and good. Our words should be full of excellent praise and worthy of repetition. We need to live by Jesus' prayer for us: "Sanctify them through thy truth" (John 17:17).

Another cure for idle prattling is what David suggests. We need to hide God's Word in our hearts and mind (see Ps. 119:11). We should meditate on His Word and pray, "Let this mind be in you, which was also in Christ Jesus" (Phil. 2:5). Pray to have the mind of Jesus enthroned in your mind. The Holy Spirit will give you the victory so you will be a *conqueror* and not a victim.

Finally, let this be your guide: "I will set no wicked thing before mine eyes" (Ps. 101:3). And I think another great thing to add is telling yourself that you will let no evil thing out of your mouth. Guard well the avenues of your soul; you are bought with a price—the precious blood of Jesus. Allow the Holy Spirit to reside in your body so that you may be *conquerors* today. May you not turn him away.

Day 362

> *How **Excellent** is thy lovingkindness, O God! therefore the children of men put their trust under the shadow of thy wings. Psalm 36:7*

Here is an adoration of exultant praise to God, the Father, for His watchful care and tender mercies toward humanity. David spoke from first-hand experience about God's goodness. Certainly, today, you and I can echo a similar adulation to the most high God based on our experiences with Him.

Excellence is the highest mark obtainable on the completion of any assignment, whether it is service rating or a scholarly presentation. When someone ascribes "excellent" to a finished task, it means that person has achieved the highest point one can reach. When Sir Edmund Hillary ascended Mount Everest, there was no higher point to reach. He was at the top. His had achieved an excellent feat. Can you imagine a sinful person ascribing excellence to the Creator of all knowledge? It is bold and audacious, but David used the best words in his language repertoire to offer praise.

God's lovingkindness is precious, and everyone finds shelter, repose, and solace under His broad, outstretched wings. How excellent is God! It is only a loving, caring Father who would expend so much energy to care and protect His children. His priceless love is unfailing and encompasses all: rich and poor, high and low, free and bonded.

The meditational reflections tell the many different names of God—all of which reveal His excellence: God is good, great, majestic, and praiseworthy, but the most outstanding superscription is excellent! Our zenith is excellent, and God understands our desire to praise the Creator.

There is none other like this our God. He is majestic, glorious, and honorable. He cares for us now and will throughout eternity. God's name is excellent in all the earth. Let everything that has breath praise the Lord who is the same today, yesterday, and forever—He is the everlasting one! His *excellence* is incomparable. May we praise His name forevermore.

Day 363

> *And Joseph made haste; for his bowels did **Yearn** upon his brother: and he sought where to weep; and he entered into his chamber, and wept there. Genesis 43:30*

This is very episodic. Joseph is testing his brothers' fidelity, sincerity, and trustworthiness. On their first visit to get corn and fodder for the family and animals, he inquired about the status of his father and youngest brother,

Benjamin. He told them that they had to bring the latter with them on their return to get more supplies. They returned the second time and most assuredly, the youngest brother was with them. When Joseph saw his blood brother, son of his deceased mother, Rachel, "his bowels did yearn upon his brother." He was deeply moved; he could not believe his eyes, so he turned aside and wept. The question in his mind must have been, "What has God wrought?"

We will never unlock the secret that resides in God's bosom. Joseph's life story to this point is a saga of unmatched beauty and mystery. Upon seeing his brother in the flesh, he could have been very angry, but instead the Holy Spirit moved upon him, and he left their presence for a short moment to contemplate on the reunion that God had engineered. He marveled at God's goodness, His mercy, and His guiding hand in the affairs of the family. No wonder David was forced to express the excellence and the majesty of God. Only He could make such a thing happen.

Joseph yearned for his brother. He wanted to give him a hug, to embrace him and do what they could to make up for lost time. They were the only two blood brothers of the twelve. Their mother had died in giving birth to Benjamin, and Joseph's love for his younger brother was tender and undying.

God is our sustainer, keeper, protector, and shield. Do you yearn for Him as a brother to a brother or a sister to a sister or a husband for his absent wife? God longs to reunite us to Himself, and even now His bowels of compassion yearn for us. He longs to cradle us in His arms and draw us to Him. He wants to hug and embrace us and bring us into His special fold. May we *yearn* for God, for He is waiting to give us His fond embrace. Let us not keep His hand empty, but instead rush to His arms. They are waiting for you.

Day 364

Who gave himself for us, that he might redeem us from all iniquity, and purify unto himself a peculiar people, **Zealous** *of good works. Titus 2:14*

Brother Titus is exhorting new believers on how to live the Christian life. He recounted to them everything about Jesus of whom they had heard and accepted.

He counseled them that their lifestyle should reflect Jesus' character and reminded them that He will return one day to claim them as His own. He gave a detailed account of Jesus' sacrifice and its redeeming power to purify and preserve spotless. Jesus has reserved them unto Himself as a very special people. They were unique and needed to be zealous and passionate about doing noble, upright, honest, and praiseworthy things.

In communicating with the new believers, he urged them to become excited about the glorious hope of meeting Jesus and not to let anything deter them from seeing Him. He pointed out that they cannot serve two masters. They are Christ's purchased possession; hence, they are totally His. They were not bought with silver or gold, dollars or rupees, lira or euros. They were bought with His precious blood. As a result of this, they should obey Him in everything.

Reflecting on Titus' counsel to the new believers, his message resonates to Christians living in the twenty-first century who are awaiting the Lord's return. These are potent counsels that every practicing Christian should heed. They were relevant then and are more relevant and urgent now, for Christ's return is much closer today. We need to be zealous and carefully guard the avenues of our soul.

May we cultivate a daily passion in letting our Lord guide us. We are His by creation and redemption. As we grow in Him, He will give us the power over sinful influences. May we be *zealous* about following in the Master's footsteps and obeying His laws and statutes.

Day 365

Now when much time was spent, and when sailing was now dangerous, because the fast was already past, Paul **Admonished** *them. Acts 27:9*

As passengers and crew traversed the watery highway on Paul's fourth missionary voyage, they ran into a serious storm that their boat was ill-equipped to face. Paul told them that not only were the ship and all its moorings, tackling, and food in danger but their lives as well.

Paul's shipmates were made up of a motley crew of all class and distinction: criminals on their way to Rome, business men trading their wears, and tourists going for the ride. When the storm began to rage, the men forgot their niceties. Fear and anguish gripped them, and each man struggled on how to save his life. Even though Paul was a prisoner, he assumed leadership and calmed the disoriented, frightened crew and passengers and admonished them that everyone should remain on the ship for an angel of the Lord appeared to him in the night and guaranteed everyone's safety.

As we travel on life's sea, dangerous shoals will encompass us. Many will toss us to and fro, and we may succumb if it is not for the intervention of the good Captain, Pilot, and Admiral, Jesus Christ, who knows all the shallow, deep troughs, sandbanks, and the narrow bays of life. He knows how to navigate and take us into a safe harbor. God never leaves His people to perish. He is always there amidst the storms, tsunamis, earthquakes, and fires. Based on God's watchful care, Christians are admonished to cherish their faith and to trust God completely, for He is the Deliverer. We are to be cognizant of the enemy's respective snares, deceitful insinuations, and suggestions because he wants as many as he can entrap.

Be admonished that God is very near to us, so we must draw near to Him and reciprocate His actions. Be admonished that His Word is a lamp unto our feet and a light to our path. Be admonished that Jesus is looking out for us, and we are safe in His strong and mighty arms. Therefore, be *admonished* that we have abundant hope because our God—our Father, Brother, and Redeemer—are rooting for us. May we go forward fearlessly with our hands placed in Theirs.

Day 366

Nay, in all these things, we are more than **Conquerers** *through him that loved us.*
Romans 8:37

Despite the physical, spiritual, moral, economic, and mental challenges that beset the Christian, Paul could creditably say that Jesus has already won our victory and has endowed us with His strength, character, and charisma. He gave us absolutely everything He could.

We must always recall that we are His by creation and redemption. We who trust in Him cannot fail because His mind is directing ours. No height or depth will be able to move us. Neither things present nor anything in the future can shake us. We are grounded in Jesus. We are standing on the solid Rock; no physical, psychic, or metaphysical forces can wrest us apart from Christ, for we are anchored by His Power. We are victors because He won the victory at Calvary, so we can sing and shout "Victory is Mine" by Dorothy Norwood:

Victory is mine; victory is mine
Victory today is mine.
I tell Satan to get thee behind,
Victory today is mine.

We Are More Than Conquerors

Yes, we are more than conquerors!

Jesus paid it all; you are released and free. We must follow in His steps. He will guide us all the way.

Once you are a victor, you cannot become a victim again. You are a winner and an overcomer. Christ has broken our chains, and we are free—we are conquerors through the blood of the Lamb. May we go forward reveling in this our present joy.

Victory is mine and yours! Jesus conquered the grave and gave us eternal life. Let us claim this gift. We are able to surmount every obstacle and overcome any tragedy. Through God's help, we have gained the victory.

I found that this stanza from "Victory Through Jesus" in *Christ in Song* applied well: "Not to the strong is the battle; Not to the swift is the race, yet to the true and the faithful—Vict'ry is promised through grace." Yes, we are more than conquerors through our loving Christ. He goes forth as the conquering Lamb of the tribe of Judah. Through Him, we are all *conquerors*.

My Own ABC's of Assurance

A–nd thine ear shall hear a word behind thee, saying, 'This is the way' (Isa. 30:21)–all things are possible.

B–ehold, I stand at the door, and knock (Rev. 3:20)–be not afraid.

C–asting all your care upon him; for he careth for you (1 Peter 5:7)–come and see.

D–raw all men unto me [Christ] (John 12:32)–come, all things are now ready.

E–ven "though I walk through the valley of the shadow of death, I will fear no evil (Ps. 23:4)–hope in God.

F–ear God, and keep his commandments: for this is the whole duty of man (Eccles. 12:13)–obey and worship.

G–o ye therefore, and teach all nations (Matt. 28:19, 20)–teach the people.

H–o, every one that thirsteth, come ye to the waters (Isa. 55:1)–free food and wine.

I–will lift up mine eyes unto the hills (Ps. 121:1)–hope and trust.

J–udge not, that ye be not judged (Matt. 7:1)–do not judge anyone.

K–eep back thy servant also from presumptuous sins (Ps. 19:13)–people must know their limits.

L–et not your heart be troubled (John 14:1)–trust and hope in God.

M–y soul doth magnify the Lord (Luke 1:46)–give glory to God for all things.

N–ever man spake like this man (John 7:46)–Jesus speaks with authority.

O–ne thing thou lackest ... follow me (Mark 10:21)–Jesus requires all.

P–eace, be still (Mark 4:39)–Jesus has power over nature.

Q–uench not the Spirit (1 Thess. 5:19)–let the Holy Spirit work.

R–estore unto me the joy of thy salvation (Ps. 51:12)–keep the promise.

S–earch me, O God, and know my heart (Ps. 139:23)–God knows all about us.

T–rust in the Lord (Prov. 3:5)–depend on God always.

U–nderstandest thou what thou readest? (Acts 8:30)–Philip teaches the eunuch.

V–ex, "grieve not the holy Spirit of God" (Eph. 4:30)–do not interfere with the Holy Spirit.

W–eeping may endure for a night (Ps. 30:5)–cry if you must.

X–pect great things from God (Jude 1:24)–God is able.

Y–ours is the kingdom of God (Luke 6:20)–God's promise to all.

Z–ealous of good works (Titus 2:14)–keep the faith.

The Names of God

God's name is very precious and special; throughout this devotional, I have tried to utilize the respective names by which He is known and called. The essence of all these names is that God is everything to all creation. God is considered:

Adonai–Lord or Master
El Olam–The Everlasting God
El Rai–God Seest Me
El Shaddai–the Almighty
Elohim–God, Creator
Elohim Ozer Li–God My Helper
Jehovah–Lord, the Self-existing One
Jehovah Adon Kol Ha-arets–The Lord of All the Earth
Jehovah El Elyon–The Most High God
Jehovah El Emeth–Lord God of Truth
Jehovah Eli–The Lord My God
Jehovah Elohe Abothekem–Lord God of Your Fathers
Jehovah Jireh–The Lord Will Provide
Jehovah Machsi–The Lord My Refuge
Jehovah Metsudhathi–The Lord My High Tower
Jehovah Moshiekh–The Lord Your Savior
Jehovah Nissi–The Lord My Banner
Jehovah Ori–The Lord My Light
Jehovah-Rophe–The Lord That Heals
Jehovah Sali–The Lord My Rock
Jehovah Shammah–The Lord is there
Jehovah Tsidkenu–The Lord Our Righteousness
Jehovah Tsuri–O Lord My Strength
Jehovah Uzzi–The Lord My Strength

Additionally God is:

Our Father–Matt. 6:9
My Shepherd–Ps. 23:1
God of Glory–Ps. 29:3
Emmanuel–Isa. 7:14
Lord–Exod. 14:15
I AM–Exod. 14:4
Holy Ghost–Luke 3: 21, 22
Jesus–Matt. 1:21
My Lord, my God–John 20:28

Jesus Christ—Acts 3:6
Son of man—Matt. 8:20
Son of God—Matt. 16:16; John 11:27
Redeemer—Isa. 49:26
Everlasting God—Gen. 21:33
The most high God—Gen 14:20
Deliverer—Gen. 14:20
Almighty—Gen. 17:1
Provider—Gen. 22:13, 14
Healer—Exod. 15:26
Righteousness—Jer. 23:6
Lord of the Sabbath—James 5:4
God of Israel—Isa. 37:16
Lord of hosts—Isa. 14:24
Creator—Rom. 1:25
Prince of Peace—Isa. 9:6
Lamb of God—John 1:29
Savior—Luke 2:11
The Way, Truth, and Life—John 14:6
King of glory—Ps. 24:7
High Priest—Heb. 4:14
The Rock—Ps. 31:3; 18:2
Wonderful—Is. 9:6
First and last—Rev. 1:17
Rabbi—John 3:26
Messiah—Mark 8:29
Heavenly Father—Matt. 23:9
Comforter—John 14:18, 26
Lion of Judah—Rev. 5:5
King of kings—Rev. 19:6

Bibliography

Belden, F. E. *Christ in Song: Best Gospel Hymns, New & Old*. Mountain View, CA: Pacific Press Publishing Association, 1908.

Donne, John. *The Holy Sonnets*. Baltimore, MD: Penguin Books Inc., 1969.

The Seventh-day Adventist Hymnal. Hagerstown, MD: Review and Herald Publishing Association, 1985.

White, Ellen G. *Christ's Object Lessons*. Washington, DC: Review and Herald Publishing Association, 1900.

White, Ellen G. *The Desire of Ages*. Mountain View, CA: Pacific Press Publishing Association, 1898.

White, Ellen G. *Gospel Workers 1915*. Washington, DC: Review and Herald Publishing Association, 1915.

White, Ellen G. *The Ministry of Healing*. Mountain View, CA: Pacific Press Publishing Association, 1905.

We invite you to view the complete
selection of titles we publish at:

www.TEACHServices.com

Scan with your mobile
device to go directly
to our website.

Please write or email us your praises, reactions, or
thoughts about this or any other book we publish at:

P.O. Box 954
Ringgold, GA 30736

info@TEACHServices.com

TEACH Services, Inc., titles may be purchased in bulk for
educational, business, fund-raising, or sales promotional use.
For information, please e-mail:

BulkSales@TEACHServices.com

Finally, if you are interested in seeing
your own book in print, please contact us at

publishing@TEACHServices.com

We would be happy to review your manuscript for free.